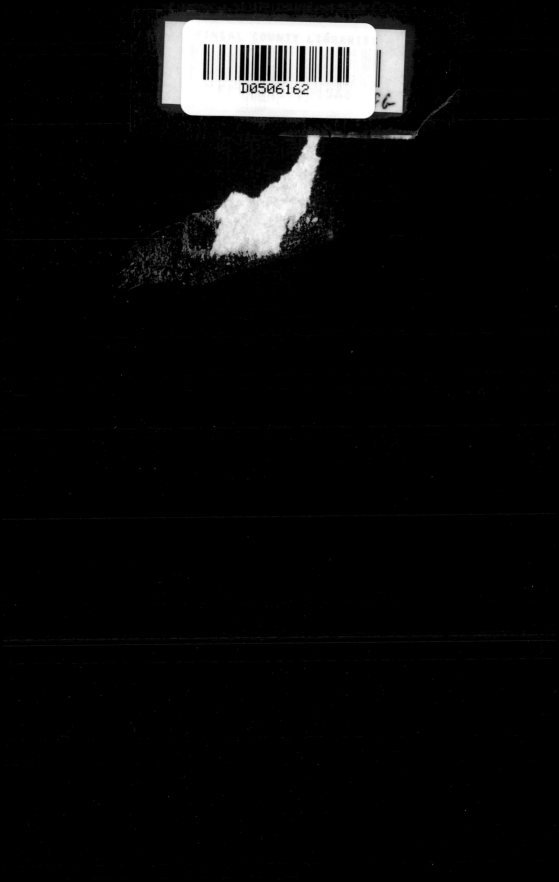

Kingstown Republican

DAVID ANDREWS

KINGSTOWN REPUBLICAN
First published 2007
by New Island in association with First Law
2 Brookside
Dundrum Road
Dublin 14
www.newisland.ie

ISBN 978-1-905494-79-8

British Library Cataloguing in Publication Data. A CIP catalogue record for this book is available from the British Library.

Book design by Inka Hagen
Printed in the UK by Mackays

10 9 8 7 6 5 4 3 2 1

Kingstown Republican

DAVID ANDREWS

To my family

ACKNOWLEDGMENTS

I owe a deep debt of gratitude to Ian McGonagle S.C. who was dogged in encouraging me to write this book. I am also grateful to Bart Daly of First Law who persuaded me to persist at it. Brian Maye was tireless in his help with research and I probably tried his patience sorely. Thanks are also due to Judge Rory McCabe for reading an early draft and righting a few wrongs.

I also very much appreciate the help of Gerry Gervin, always at the end of a telephone to jog my memory; Noel Quirke for help with photos; Seamus Haughey, Assistant Librarian in Dáil Éireann; and First Secretary Laurence Simms of the Anglo Irish section of the Department of Foreign Affairs for being so accommodating and helpful in tracking old files. The very professional help of Deirdre Nolan of New Island was much valued and vital to the completion of the book.

Finally, I am much indebted to my wife and family for their help and encouragement, and generally putting up with me over the last eighteen months.

CONTENTS

Acknowledgments   v

Preface   vii

Before Politics   1

A Novice in Leinster House   25

Mixed Fortunes   56

Backbencher Again   80

Miscarriages of Justice   107

Other Humanitarian Causes   131

Dilemma, Divorce and Departures   146

Back on the Inside   183

Defence, Marine and Endgame   218

Opposition and Return to Defence   246

Foreign Affairs Mark Two   267

Exit   306

PREFACE

When I reflect now on my almost forty years in politics, and the eleven occasions I stood successfully for election, I am struck by the huge debt I owe to all those people who came out to work for me during each campaign. They were Fianna Fáil party workers, family, friends, and indeed every election would bring some new people who would just turn up and commit themselves to helping. People even took holidays to be able to be involved full-time.

At the end of each campaign you try to thank everyone, maybe buy a few pints, but there is really no way to repay them for their work, loyalty and commitment. Without them I would never have got the votes I did. I won't dare to name names for fear of leaving someone out, but they all know who they are. I can only say again how grateful I am and always was to all those teams, some of whom are still helping Barry's campaigns.

None of these people ever stood to gain in any way from their efforts for me. In fact each election would have caused considerable disruption in their lives. But I believe that what motivated them was their wish to be involved in the democratic process as well as their trust in me. I have a lot of wonderful memories of marvellous people and will never forget them.

BEFORE POLITICS

A VILLAGE CHILDHOOD

I grew up in Dundrum, then a small village in south County Dublin, in the late 1930s and early 1940s. The middle child of five, I had three brothers, Christopher, Niall and Hugh, and one sister, Catherine, who was much younger than the rest of us. My father, C. S., or Todd, as he was generally known, liked to think that he was working-class, but we were, in fact, a comfortable middle-class family, living in a comfortable middle-class environment.

From early childhood I was aware that my parents were somehow 'different'. Both of them had been involved in the War of Independence and the Civil War, and that marked them apart from most of my friends' parents. In fact, some of our neighbours, while remaining good neighbours, had very strong views on my parents' former activities.

This was a time when every Catholic went to Sunday Mass and the churches were full. My father, having been excommunicated for his IRA activities, never attended church or chapel, and that also marked him apart. My mother, however, remained a familiar figure in the local church, making her own way to Mass and Confession, usually accompanied by some of her children. My father explained rather

1

vehemently to us children when we got to a certain age why he didn't attend Mass. He remained upset throughout his life about the decision of the bishops of the time to excommunicate him, and he was highly critical of them.

Then, at the end of his life, when he knew he was dying, a priest contemporary of his called to see him over a three-week period. I always suspected that he allowed these visits to help console his family rather than that he made a 'deathbed conversion'. In the end of course it is a matter between himself and his maker.

My mother never referred to my father's non-attendance at church. As she would typically say, 'Ah, sure leave him at it'.

My father wasn't a 'hands on' father as would be understood in today's terms. He always said that his main role was to be supportive to my mother. Nevertheless, he was a constant influence, albeit in the background. He was a great believer in the work ethic and when he was in the Turf Development Board he used to send us down to Lullymore in the midlands during the summer months to foot turf to earn a few shillings. We would have been in our teens at this stage and we stayed in hostels. It was hard work – particularly hard on the hands – but I have very good memories of those times. In the evenings we would regularly find ourselves in the local houses where talking was the relaxation of choice in those pre-TV times.

I know that my father was seen as a rather tough figure, but he had a great sense of humour. This was evident around the time of the closure of the Harcourt Street line when he was Chairman of CIE (a decision for which he got a lot of stick, but which was made by the government of the time). The then press pack (all three of them) would be outside our house wanting to get a photo or comment from him. A driver came with his job at that time, so he would sometimes put me into the back of his car with his hat on my head, and the car would drive off as a decoy to draw off the 'journos'. The combination of the hat and the Andrews nose proved a successful ploy on such occasions.

My mother was a very supportive wife to my father's high profile. By choice she always remained in the background. She was a cultured woman and a great reader and had a close circle of friends, including her sisters, Nancy, Eithne and Rosemary Coyle. Another sister, Nora, had died of TB in her late twenties.

Like all good Irish mothers, she would never believe that her boys would ever misbehave in the neighbourhood. The neighbours seldom complained, but if, in desperation, they did, she would roundly defend us, totally rejecting the possibility that we could be anything but models of good behaviour. I loved her loyalty, but I'm afraid it was occasionally slightly misplaced!

In those days, Dundrum was a real village, part of rural Ireland. While it had a cinema, a few shops and quite a few pubs, it was surrounded by fields. It was a far cry from the Dundrum of today, with all its development and its astonishing shopping centre. The Dundrum of my childhood was small and unsophisticated and a happy and safe place for a child to live and grow up. Apart from my brothers, I had plenty of young pals and we explored and roamed the village and the fields around us.

And we were no more or less prone to mischief than might be expected. Orchards were fair game and 'boxing the fox' was probably the most insidious aspect of our miscreance. To those of a later generation I should explain that 'boxing the fox' was a common expression which meant quite simply robbing orchards. I have no idea of the origin of the expression. In Dundrum today, you'd be hard put to find an orchard worth robbing. A favourite orchard then was Walshes'. The Walshes, our wonderful next-door neighbours, had a shop at the junction of Highfield Park and Dundrum Road and they supplied it with fruit, including delicious apples, from their very large back garden, just over our garden wall. On one of our forays into their fruit garden, disaster struck when my brother Niall decided to climb over the top of a greenhouse, slipped and fell through. He received quite serious injuries to his leg. It is what is known as being caught red-handed. No explanations. No excuses. Fortunately the shock of Niall's injury diluted somewhat the fury that descended upon us. This brought to an end our mischief making on the orchard front – at least for a while.

The Odeon Cinema was one of the focal points of our young lives and I remember going to see Errol Flynn in *They Died with their Boots On*, and Roy Rogers in *Red River Valley*. Even then, westerns had a mystical charm and I loved playing cowboys and Indians. The prairies were never far from Taney Road.

While the pictures were a weekly feature, another and much more exotic annual event was the circus that came to McCann's field, just on Taney Road – a really high point in the year.

My closest friend at that time was Brendan Healy, who lived up the road from us in Sydenham Road. Brendan was the best footballer among us and he later became a professional footballer with Drumcondra, which was owned by the Prole family and which played at Tolka Park. My other friends were Bernard (Bernie) Dundon and Eddie Mellon. Bernie's father was the manager of the local Leverett and Fry's at the top of Dundrum village and Eddie's people ran the local garage. They were my main companions in my 'cowboys and Indians' stage. We subsequently graduated to football in the Dublin Schoolboys' League, and we had a very good team.

The three of us got into a few scrapes in our time. There was at that time a garage on Taney Road owned by the Timmins family. Indelibly printed on my memory is the time they closed down their business. The large underground petrol tanks were being removed. As a consequence and probably by accident a small stream of petrol ran down the gutters of Taney Road into the drains and on into the village. Not about to let the opportunity pass, myself and my pals decided to set fire to the petrol, which naturally caused havoc in the community. It was of course a shockingly dangerous thing to do. We disappeared into Taney Church grounds, aware of how horrified people were by the sheets of flame coming out of the drains. Sergeant Kilmurry came to investigate. In no time fingers were pointed in our direction and we had no choice but to own up. We were very lucky that we got no more than a severe reprimand for what could have been a serious enough incident. My father's considerable wrath was also thrown into the mix. However, thankfully, there was no harm done.

At home, like all young people of the time, we had to do our share of domestic chores. I recall being sent down to Sweetman's, where the local dairy herd was, for our milk – the Jersey cows were in a field off the main street in Dundrum – and bringing it back in a tin. The tin had to be emptied and sterilised with boiling water and off we'd go again, this time down to the local butcher's for blood. This would be used to make light black pudding, a bit like the 'drisheen' you get in Cork. There was very little variety in the food available and people had to be quite resourceful. My mother was overseer of all matters domestic, but at the time we also had a maid (which sounds very politically incorrect nowadays) called Lizzie Merriman. My memory of her was of a tough lady who, apart from her normal day's work, saw to it that we would each get whatever was our entitlement in the context of the rationing of the time and not a piece of food less – or more, for that matter.

I have vague memories of the 'Emergency'. Our house shook when the North Strand, to the north of Dublin city centre, was bombed in May 1941. I remember being brought into our parents' room, which was ever a safe haven. Perhaps our parents thought it was an earthquake or even that the end of the world had come. It certainly was very frightening.

During the 'Emergency', there was severe food rationing, although inevitably the black market ensured that resourceful and sometimes unscrupulous people at both ends of the food supply chain could circumnavigate the strictures of the times. My mother had very strong views about that sort of thing: she argued that there were many who could not afford to buy on the black market and that we should all be prepared to shoulder any hardship equally. She felt so strongly about it that on one occasion she refused to socialise with a family who had treated her to bread and cake that they admitted had been made from white flour bought on the black market. As a child I took a less moral view than I might today. Cake was nice.

My overall memory of Dundrum is of a society and a community where the people got on extremely well together. We had good and close neighbours and it was a quiet and peaceful environment. Next door to us was Mr Orr, whose son subsequently became a parson. We were very friendly with that family. There were no obvious tensions between the substantial Protestant community, which was centred in the thriving Taney Church of Ireland, and their Catholic neighbours. It was a very well settled community and a good introduction – at a very young age – to different religious, social and political values.

Two of our neighbours, the Overend sisters, Letitia and Naomi, were very well known. They earned quite a reputation in Dublin and, indeed, further afield for their unapologetic eccentricities. Nowadays they are remembered mainly for their very fine herd of Jersey cattle and their spectacular motor cars, which, incredibly, they learned to maintain themselves, but my memory of them is of a predominantly charitable and generous pair of exotic and ethereal creatures. They generously left their farm, known as Airfield Farm, on the Upper Kilmacud Road, to the nation. Today it is a real national resource and it has allowed generations of visiting city children to get some insight into the farming way of life. In the Dundrum of today, Airfield is a unique reminder of a world long forgotten to all but people of my vintage.

SUMMERTIME IN THE WEST

Among the happiest memories I have from my childhood are those of the holidays our family took in the Gaeltacht in Connemara in the 1940s and 1950s. This was an annual event in our family for well over ten years. The train journey from Dublin to Galway in those days was something of a test of endurance and inevitably we arrived exhausted. The excitement built from the first sight of a stone-walled field west of Ballinasloe and continued as we passed each well-known village or familiar bend in the route. We then caught the bus for a two-hour journey out to Carraroe. Johnny Geoghegan, who subsequently became a Fianna Fáil TD for Galway West, drove the bus. His daughter, Máire Geoghegan-Quinn, succeeded him to the Dáil and in time became a successful and impressive Cabinet minister and representative in Europe.

My mother would have already made whatever arrangements were necessary for us to go straight into a rented house on our arrival in Carraroe. One particular house we often stayed in belonged to the Leonards of Bothar Buí, and one of the Leonards, Julia, still lives there. I remember the long currach-making shed in which 'the Bird' Leonard used to make his currachs, and he and his daughter Biddy lived in a sort of a side shed opposite the house during the summer, while they rented their house to us. As to the basic necessities in the house itself, there was no running water or flush toilets and the water always had to be carried from a well, by one of the children, of course. Electricity was then a thing of the future and television was not even within the contemplation of the population.

My memory of the Bird himself is that he was a very friendly, kind and decent man. It seems that he had, unfortunately, a problem with the poteen, which from time to time made him believe he could fly: hence the nickname.

Of course, the summers at that time were always sunny. We spent our time swimming in the 'Dóilín', the beautiful Coral Strand, and generally making our own amusements, which included re-running the Galway Plate on the backs of the local donkeys, who were no worse off from the experience. Barefoot, brown and bold, we spent the days outdoors and returned home, tired but happy, as the expression goes, to devour whatever was laid on the table. It was really an idyllic time and Connemara remains a special place to all the family.

My main memory of our summers in Carraroe is that my father was mostly absent because of his work, and my mother was there all the time with my three brothers, my sister and me. Occasionally aunts and cousins joined us. On two or three occasions we were in Carraroe for four months at a time, and Chris, Hugh and I attended the local national school for the end of the school year, becoming fluent in Irish and beginning to feel that we were accepted as part of the locality.

One of the few other families from outside the area who lived in Carraroe at that time was the Lamb family, the father being the painter Charles Lamb from Portadown. We were very friendly with Mary, Lallie, John and Peadar Lamb. They had built a house in Carraroe, a fine granite house. Charles's wife, Katherine, was a veterinary surgeon and she gave her services free to the local people. I remember her as a big jolly woman and a very good gardener. Like my mother, she loved the people of the area and learned to speak Irish fluently, as did her children.

I remember being struck by my mother's devotion to the area. She was a very compassionate woman and she always had great sympathy for and empathy with the local people. The poverty at the time was immense and the state did little to help. I have over my lifetime visited many developing countries and have seen dreadful deprivation and misery. The Irish people respond generously time and time again to alleviate deprivation abroad and I can't help thinking now that the people in Connemara could have done with some such help during the thirties and forties.

For many of those years, people just struggled on as best they could. Then the so-called 'dole' was introduced and it was a seismic event. For the first time, people had money on a regular basis. Not much money, but enough to change their lives. I am talking about a place and a time when, almost literally, the animals lived in the houses and the people went barefoot. Their diet consisted mainly of potatoes, salt, eggs and homemade bread, and they drank tea in copious quantities. On Sunday, Mass was the centre of their day and they dressed in their Sunday best – usually bainin clothes. These were clothes – usually trousers and jackets – made locally from 'bainin' cloth, a sort of white tweed, which was locally spun. Aran sweaters, now quite fashionable, would be part of the ensemble during the winter months. Emigration and periods working abroad were harsh facts of their lives.

When I return to Carraroe today, I see incredible change. Perhaps it has become overdeveloped in some parts, and people do talk about 'bungalow bliss', particularly perhaps people who live in the cities and view 'the country' as a place to visit and preserve for their entertainment. That is all very well, but if people could have seen what it was like fifty or sixty years ago, they might take a different view and have more understanding of what it was like for the countryfolk to live in abject poverty.

Connemara is now both vibrant and prosperous, and emigration has turned full circle, through repatriation to immigration. From a time when the west of Ireland was emptied of its young people, many have already returned, young families are growing up there and the future is bright. New faces appear regularly and, like the rest of Ireland, the sound of foreign languages being spoken on the streets is not confined to tourists.

THE HAPPIEST DAYS OF MY LIFE, PERHAPS

My first experience of school was Scoil Bríde, run by Bean McAteer. Then, in 1942, at the age of seven, I went to primary school in Coláiste Mhuire on Parnell Square. It was a school where the subjects were taught through Irish and it was run by the Christian Brothers. I don't recall my time there with a lot of affection and most of the time it was not a pleasant experience. However, I made some very good friends and continued to play football. But, to be frank, some of the Brothers – one in particular – were brutal in their teaching methods and, as a child, I found this both frightening and unjust.

Mathematics had been one of my best subjects, but I remember vividly an incident in school that stymied my progress in the subject. I had my adenoids and tonsils out and was absent for a while. When I returned to class, naturally having no maths homework to present, I explained the reason to the Brother who was my teacher. He would have none of it, accused me in front of the class of telling lies and said that I hadn't been out of school at all. He then proceeded to beat the living daylights out of me. I turned against mathematics as a subject after that bad experience. Of course, in those days, if you went back to your parents and told them the Brother or teacher had beaten you, they always took the view that you got what you deserved and that was the end of that. So I never 'reported' this and, like many others, simply took it as part of life.

In 1951, I went as a boarder to Roscrea College in County Tipperary, which was and still is run by the Cistercians, and I spent four years there. I found the first two years difficult enough. It was probably partly because I was away from home, but also I didn't get on too well with the President of the College, Fr Thomas. The last two years, however, were much happier for me. Fr Aidan Cusack had become President, and I liked him and he seemed to like me. Overall, I have good memories of Roscrea – very good teachers, good friendships, good food, with a heavy emphasis on sport. I played lots of rugby and soccer and competed in athletics.

Many of the friendships I made in Roscrea lasted for life. Dick Brannigan, who became a Fine Gael councillor and a solicitor in Drogheda, now sadly deceased, was one of them. The school had a system of house captains and Gerry Culliton, who subsequently played rugby for Ireland, was my house captain at one stage. Another schoolmate and house captain was Gus Martin, who died at the tragically early age of 59. Gerry and Gus were both good pals. Many people of the same quality and calibre were fellow inmates at Roscrea, including another good friend, Paddy O'Halloran. Other school friends drifted in their own directions and I have not been able to keep in touch with as many of them as I would have liked. Dick

Spring and Brian Cowen are also past pupils of Roscrea from a later time. Three foreign ministers from one school isn't a bad record! Brian Cowen was reckoned to be one of the brightest students ever to come out of Roscrea.

SPORTOMANIA

I am now, always have been and always will be sports mad. I played Gaelic football, soccer and rugby and spent a lot of my time and some energy – not enough, my coaches might have observed – at sport. I certainly approached it with much more devotion than schoolwork! It's hard to say which was my favourite sport, but if I had to choose, I suppose it would have to be soccer. It was the game I played most. I played schoolboy soccer for a team called St Joseph's, in Terenure, which competed in the Dublin schoolboys' leagues. The late Paddy Quigley was manager and the heart and soul of the club. Willie Norton (of the well-known fuel suppliers) was general factotum.

We finished runners-up in the under-14 league and that was the only medal I won for soccer at under-age level. Willie was generous to a fault and I recall my friends and I celebrating our minor victory with large bottles of lemonade supplied by Willie! I absolutely lived for those games.

As I was growing up, there was so little money about that we largely made our own entertainment. For us, football continued to be the great outlet – in our case the League of Ireland club, Shamrock Rovers. We would go down to Glenmalure Park in Milltown every other Sunday and, inevitably, the ground would be so full that it was bursting at the seams. Though we had no realisation at the time, it was probably very dangerous at our young age to have been at some of these matches with the crowds that they used to attract. For the youngsters of Dundrum, Milltown was our Mecca on a Sunday. The hated 'fancy dans' of Shelbourne, often our conquerors, or the 'foreigners' or culchies of Cork Celtic or Cork Hibs, often received a warm welcome and an even warmer farewell. Glenmalure Park has long ago fallen to the developers and I never pass the site without a few wistful memories.

I was very tall at quite a young age – six foot five at around 16 or 17 – and I was only thirteen and a half stone. I was like a reed in the wind, really, and took some pretty gruelling punishment as a result. I broke my nose more than once and suffered painful back injuries which I have lived with ever since.

After secondary school, I spent a year in University College Galway and played for the college soccer team. The team won the Collingwood Cup (the inter-university soccer competition) for the first time ever that year. Tony Corcoran was the manager of the team for many years. Like his counterparts in St Joseph's, he was one of those many people who sacrifice their personal time and give their energy generously and on a totally voluntary basis to sport. Without people like Tony, many sports clubs would simply not survive. Johnny Dooley was one of our outstanding players and later played international rugby for Ireland. He was a brilliant sportsman. The late Terry McCabe, who also played on that team, became a close friend of mine. As recently as February 2005, we celebrated the fiftieth anniversary of winning the Collingwood Cup and received our medals – fifty years late!

I played rugby in the Connacht League and Cup for Galwegians Rugby Club, both at lock and wing forward. We never won the Cup, but finished runners-up on two occasions. We had an outstanding team in Galwegians at that time and men like Dickie Roche, Brendan Guerin, Sean Healy, Johnny Dooly and Tony O'Sullivan became international players. All of them of course also played for Connacht. Tony O'Sullivan was one of the best ever rugby forwards to play for Ireland. Playing for Galwegians entitled me to play inter-provincial rugby for Connacht and I was honoured to have been selected for the province on a number of occasions. Another member of the Connacht team at that time was Sean Calleary, subsequently a TD. Sean had to play under a pseudonym, Sean Kelly, to avoid the dreaded GAA ban. He was a superb all-round footballer and a very likeable man.

When I returned to Dublin, I continued to play a lot of sport: rugby with Palmerston FC and soccer with UCD, where I played with the Brown brothers from Longford. Willie Brown went on to become a soccer international. Although an amateur, he was selected to play with the professional Irish international team. He was also a great tennis player. Willie was another one who died too young.

Palmerston Football Club was at that time located between Mill-town and Ranelagh. 'Palmo' was a rugby club, but, because it was founded before a certain date, it was entitled to be called a football club. The older, more serious and largely Protestant members were ever sensitive to the distinction.

I consider myself quite a good sportsman, but perhaps not always the most disciplined or dedicated. I know that I would turn up for matches without essentials like boots and togs. I didn't train very much either and depended on my general all-round fitness and skill. At that time, I didn't smoke or drink and considered myself to be in pretty good shape. Annette, now my wife, who was then my girl-friend, recalls an occasion when I brought her along to a training session at Palmerston. I was playing for one of their teams at the time and Annette remembers quite a number of players coming out of the changing rooms on to the pitch and going through their paces for a while, but there was no sign of me. Eventually, she recalls seeing me come loping out in tennis shoes, running round a few times and then going back in again. That was the extent of my training session for the day and I would say that that was fairly typical throughout my sporting life.

Palmerston, of course, changed and moved to the 'country' in Kil-ternan. It merged with De la Salle, then a junior club, and they now have an impressive premises and grounds just beside the Golden Ball, a long walk on a wet night from the usual Saturday night rugby hops!

To show what an active sporting life I had at the time, I would play as many as three games over a weekend: a soccer match on Saturday morning, a junior rugby match on Saturday afternoon and a senior rugby match on Sunday afternoon.

Long after my playing days I continued to have a great interest in soccer. I became a life member of the FAI and President of the UCD Soccer Club. Dr Tony O'Neill ran the club and in due course became Sports Director at Belfield. He was a man of outstanding vision and began the soccer scholarship scheme for young footballers at UCD, setting the standard for similar schemes in other areas of sport. One of his innovations was bringing student football teams to far-flung lands to play football – anywhere from China to the United States.

The first of these excursions was to China in September 1976, and Tony invited me to go on the trip. I was a TD at the time and I think he thought my presence might be useful. The average age of the team was about 18 and this was an immense opportunity for them. By an extraordinary coincidence Mao Tse Tung died two days after our arrival. We had known that he was on the point of death and from loudspeakers all around quite sombre music was being played. I noticed that this suddenly changed to requiem-like music and I knew what had happened. I turned to Tony and said 'Tá and Cathoirleach marbh'. I'm afraid this became a bit of a mantra ever after. We were in fact in the town where he was born on the day he died.

The match programme was abandoned but we continued with our tour. What was a little disconcerting was that anti-aircraft guns suddenly appeared on the tops of tall buildings. The Chinese people believed that they might be attacked at their weakest moment – the death of their 'great leader'. There was a nervousness about, but the young men on the team took the situation in their stride. There were genuine outpourings of grief from the people. This was just at the end of the Cultural Revolution, which had caused such universal hardship to the Chinese people. They still loved their leader, despite all the horror.

Tony continued each year to bring young teams on all sorts of fascinating trips including to India, where the famous 'Callaghan of India' (Leybourne Callaghan, Ireland's Honorary Consul, who was quite a character) put them all up in most generous fashion. I was also on that trip.

Throughout his time in UCD Tony did an enormous amount for sport there until his untimely death, and it is a great disappointment to me that the university authorities have not yet honoured him appropriately.

MORE GROWING UP

When I left school, I have to confess that I wasn't acutely conscious of the economic inertia of the country. The 1950s have the name of being a pretty grim decade and there is a lot of substance to that reputation. Not for nothing is it known as 'the decade of the vanishing Irish'. As many as 50,000 or 60,000 people a year were emigrating, and close to half a million left over the whole decade. There was rising unemployment and very little money around.

When I left school in 1954, there was a general awareness that life was no bed of roses, and one couldn't but feel that something serious was wrong with our society at the time. I saw that communities had seriously diminished in numbers in the space of a few years. I have memories of missing friends and acquaintances, only to learn that they had 'taken the boat'. They had gone to England or America, most of them to prosper, but few to return.

I gradually became aware of censorship, of the strength and power of the Church and indeed of other institutions, like the Garda and the teachers. Since that time their power and authority have gradually diminished to the point where they have little influence. Many may regret the diminution of the influence of the Church, as it was in many ways a power for good, but the shattering of the foundations upon which the authority of the Church was built by the recent and appalling revelations of abuse is a natural consequence. People have become disillusioned and the Church will have to go through a period of reflection in order to find a role in our increasingly secular society. It is my belief, as a practising Catholic, that the Church needs to go back to its roots as a servant of the people in order to rebuild confidence. An obvious analogy to the events of clerical abuse is the disregard in which politics in Ireland is now held. This is a sad thing for the country. Great institutions should be leaders for the well-being of society. But I digress.

As the country struggled into the sixties, the pall of greyness began to acquire tinges of colour. There was a palpable sense of hope in the country with the emergence of T. K. Whitaker and his Programme for Economic Recovery, and Seán Lemass's determination to put its recommendations into practice as quickly as possible. This did much to heave the country out of the economic and social morass into which it had sunk in the 1950s. The rural electrification scheme was pushed forward with great vigour, and by the early 1960s, as much as 95% of the areas designated for modernisation had electricity available. This made such a difference to the quality of life for so many people all over the country.

Television in Ireland in the fifties was confined to that part of the country north of a line drawn roughly from Bray to Sligo. Even then, coverage was limited to the BBC and UTV and, difficult as it may be for young people to comprehend, the coverage was black and white and operated for a few hours in the afternoon and evening, finishing at about 11pm. The opening of our own national televison station, RTÉ, in 1961, without doubt contributed enormously to people's exposure to new and exciting ideas and to a greater awareness of the outside world. My late brother Niall was one of the first people to work (as a presentation officer) in the new Irish television service or Telefis Éireann, as it was known at the time.

After leaving school I moved to Galway for three years to work for my uncle, Donny Coyle, in his manufacturing chemical business. Donny decided that a chemistry course might be of assistance to me in understanding the manufacturing process and he sent me to do a one-year course in UCG. I enjoyed living in Galway and both Donny and his wife Roisín were very good to me. Roisín was a wonderful lady. She often fed me and I think generally kept an eye on me. It was during my time in Galway that I met Eugene O'Connor, who was then a medical student. We had some good times in Galway together. He subsequently became a doctor and a lifelong friend.

I began working for my uncle as a travelling salesman, but soon discovered that I wasn't cut out for that kind of work. Part of my job entailed going around the country visiting chemist's shops selling Hygeia products. I was a woefully bad salesman. My shyness forced me to stand at the back of a shop for ages, hoping the chemist would spot me. Not exactly aggressive marketing! So, with a lot of encouragement from Donny, I decided to go back to Dublin to study law in University College Dublin. He was enormously generous, in both his moral and financial support. He gave me £3 a week, which was a lot of money at the time, for the duration of my time in UCD. My father of course paid my fees. Donny, in his wisdom and generosity, realised that, having been earning money for the previous three years, I would have found it very difficult to go back to the student's pittance that my father would have been able to manage.

I took a Bachelor of Civil Law degree (BCL) in UCD. I was among the first, if not part of the very first class, to sit that degree in Earlsfort Terrace. At the same time I studied for the degree of Barrister at Law (BL) at the King's Inns. I qualified as a BCL in the summer and the following autumn as a BL. I was always proud of the fact that I succeeded in achieving both qualifications within three years.

I had a very pleasant social life in UCD and at the King's Inns. I recall with fondness some of my King's Inns teachers, especially Professors Fanny Moran and James O'Reilly. The latter very kindly on occasion gave me credits for attendance, even though absent, on the basis that I had played a good game of soccer that weekend. He followed the UCD soccer team avidly. Rules were more amenable to interpretation at that time.

I made good friends at university and I was particularly close to David Montgomery. David became one of the best friends anyone could have and he was one of my closest confidantes. As time went on and we both married, David and his wife Gertie became close friends of Annette and myself. David and I fished Lough Mask every summer together for over thirty years. He died, too young, in 1991 and I still miss him.

Garret Cooney, who became a prominent senior defamation lawyer, was and still is a very close friend. Garret comes from a very strong Fine Gael background. He had a famous uncle, Seán Mac Eoin, who was known as the 'blacksmith of Ballinalee' during the War of Independence. Our different political persuasions never interfered in any way with our friendship, although we would probably avoid each other at election times.

EARLY WORK

During my summers at university I did what most people did at that time – I went to London to work and make a little money. I spent a short period of time working at Wall's, the ice cream manufacturers (I became an expert at putting the ripple in ripple ice cream) and then I graduated to Hudson's Bay Fur Company in Great Thames Street. I prepared furs and hauled them up to the floor to show the buyers. The foreman of this company was Tommy Bryan and he would only employ Catholics. One of my companions happened to be non-Catholic, so he saw the light and converted briefly during his employment. I returned there to work on a number of occasions. Another place of employment was the Mayfair Hotel where I worked as a porter. It was quite a lucrative job as the tips were good. I discovered that courtesy was the key to the clients' generosity. I was recently in London and stayed there as a paying guest, but everything had changed utterly. Some of these jobs were hard work, although sometimes good fun. However, they laid down experience in dealing with people and understanding the difficulties of life in lower-paid employment.

After I qualified in 1961 I decided to take a year out and went back to London where I got a job teaching English in the Secondary Modern School in Dagenham in Essex. The children we taught were the offspring of the Ford workers, who had a large factory there. The principal of the school was a Mr McDermott from Galway and the students were a tough lot. I felt I got on quite well as a teacher. One of the essentials of teaching is maintaining discipline in the class and I had no problems with this. I also coached one of the football teams and this I think helped me in my ability to control the students. The standards in class were low, as were expectations, but it was an immensely rewarding experience. In the evenings I worked in a pub called the Dick Turpin to top up my teacher's salary. It was a well-run pub and I quite enjoyed working there. However, after a year I decided enough was enough and I returned to Dublin.

I was called to the Bar in 1962. Knowing that it would be a good while before I could hope for any income from law I took a job with the *Irish Press*. My job was that of sub-editor, basically trying to fit reporters' pieces into the pages of the newspaper. One of the first jobs I was given was editing the knitting column! I became an expert in the language of 'plain and purl', or at least managed somehow. From this time I remember Maurice Hearne, son of an Irish ambassador, Hugh O'Flaherty, who was very helpful to me, and also Michael Hand. Hearne became a barrister and O'Flaherty eventually became a Supreme Court judge. We worked from five p.m. until one a.m. three or four days a week and the pay wasn't bad. In the *Irish Press* at that time there was a very strong sense of brotherhood and there was a palpable pride in the place. I continued working there until I got married in 1964, the *Irish Press* being the source of funding for Annette's engagement ring!

A year later I became a TD and that influenced the way my career at the Bar developed. It was not easy to marry life as a young barrister with the requirements of all-hours public representation. There was a tradition of political involvement at the Irish Bar, probably originating in the type of people who aspired to political office, the absence, until relatively recent times, of any remuneration for members of parliament and the need to earn a living to keep body and soul together. In the best traditions of Fine Gael, a number of people (such as members of the O'Higgins and Costello families, and Patrick Lindsay) had been following both careers for some time. What really permitted this 'dual mandate' was that the Dáil hours in those days were set to the convenience of lawyers. They could practise during the day and attend the Dáil in the evening and late into the night. Things have changed a lot since then.

Building up a practice was the first problem. I didn't have many connections – essential to an aspiring barrister – despite the fact that my father was well known. Also, as time went on, I concentrated much more on the political than the legal side of my career. Gradually I built a practice, mainly in the area of personal injuries. Later on I managed to develop a decent practice, particularly during my 'Haughey wilderness' years, of which more anon.

My colleagues in the Law Library were always very supportive – both when I was starting out and at the various times I had to return to pick up a practice after government service. There is a great collegiality in the Law Library and a strong tradition of support for any colleagues who fall on hard times. When I came to the Law Library there were only 250 barristers, but now there are 1,700 to 1,800 practising. Over the years, I lost touch with the place from time to time, because I was to a large extent away from it for many years working as a minister at junior and senior level. I was in and out of there four or five times during my political life, so my legal career lacked continuity. Politics always dominated my life and took up most of my focus, but I still enjoy life at the Bar and the brilliance of many members who ply their daily trade in and out of the courts.

I became a Senior Counsel in 1992 and was honoured to be elected as a Bencher of the King's Inns. The Benchers' Society is the ruling body of the King's Inns.

POLITICS – THE HEART OF THE MATTER

Politics was in the blood and bones, the pith and marrow of my family. My father, C. S. – or Todd as he was more generally known – had fought in the War of Independence. He was a member of Michael Collins's 'squad' and on Bloody Sunday went out with the other members to deal with a particular target. It turned out that the person was not at home and my father expressed himself to have been relieved not to have to do the deed.

He opposed the Treaty and fought in the Civil War, during part of which he was with Cathal Brugha in the Hammam Hotel on O'Connell Street, then Sackville Street. Brugha was severely wounded and died two days later after refusing to surrender when the hotel was overrun. My father fought on and was wounded. I remember as children we were always asking him to show us his 'wound'. Eventually he was captured and interned for a year after the war ended. He didn't talk to us very much about his Civil War experiences, but I know that he had a lot of bad memories of that dreadful conflict. At the same time, he was a great admirer of Collins and was very saddened by his death. But the deaths of certain other people didn't distress him. He told us that some of the things that were done during that conflict were horrendous.

My mother, then Mary Coyle, was in Cumann na mBan, and acted as a despatch carrier during the War of Independence. She also strongly opposed the Treaty and spent a year in Kilmainham Gaol for her activities during the Civil War, much to the chagrin of the very respectable Coyle family. They disapproved not only of her activities but also of her burgeoning relationship with an IRA man. However, despite this their relationship survived and they married.

When the anti-Treaty party, which retained the name Sinn Féin, split in 1926, my father went with Eamon de Valera and was present in the La Scala Theatre in Dublin when Fianna Fáil was founded that same year. He always had profound respect and admiration for de Valera, which can be seen clearly in his two volumes of autobiography, *Dublin Made Me* and *Man of No Property*.

During the Second World War, my mother joined the local Fianna Fáil cumann in Dundrum, and at election time there were fierce verbal battles at various community gatherings between herself and Mrs Mary Mulvey, whose family had a hardware business in the village and who was, as my father described her in his second book, 'the local chieftainess of Fine Gael'. Between election times, though, our families were friendly.

My first personal memory of political involvement was during the 1945 presidential election, when Seán T. O'Kelly of Fianna Fáil was elected President for the first time. I remember our mother sending us out to put fliers in through doors and to distribute other election material. I also remember being perplexed as to why some of our neighbours were less than receptive towards us. I didn't fully realise at that young age that not everyone would vote for our candidate. The other two candidates were Sean Mac Eoin for Fine Gael and the Independent Republican, Patrick McCartan. Dundrum was a particularly strong Protestant/Fine Gael area at that time.

That was my first real sense of the reality of politics. It was then too that I became aware that my mother – and my father too – was very insistent on making us realise that there were people other than Roman Catholics in the community, and also that we must take account of the fact that there were people with different points of view. In that regard our upbringing was a liberal one.

I later became a member of the Dundrum Fianna Fáil cumann. The first spin-off from my political involvement was that, at the age of 17, I learned how to drive a car. O'Byrne and Fitzbibbon were well-known tailors in O'Connell Street in Dublin, and Mr Fitzgibbon, who was a particularly strong supporter of Fianna Fáil and who lived in Churchtown, had a car that he lent out to the cumann during elections, and I was one of the lucky young lads asked to drive it. I'm afraid the car was used outside political hours as well and Mr Fitzgibbon, at the end of an election, was always glad and probably lucky to get his car back in one piece.

Prominent politicians were regular visitors to our house when I was growing up, especially Frank Aiken, Erskine Childers and, to a lesser extent, Seán Lemass. What was striking in retrospect was the intensity of the conversations that went on. Matters of state and politics were discussed at length and everything hinged on what was good for the country.

My father had enormous respect for de Valera and he was personally close to him. When Annette was still my fiancée, such people fascinated her, as she came from a completely apolitical background. She recalls my father being invited to tea with de Valera in Áras an Uachtaráin and she couldn't wait to find out what they had for tea. She was very disappointed to discover that it was nothing more elaborate than tea and scones.

Frank Aiken was probably one of my father's closest friends. They went back a long way and had a lot in common, especially their involvement in the Civil War, though I never heard them speak on the subject. I have very clear memories of Mr Aiken calling to the house. He was quite an austere man and I never got to know him very well. This was mainly because he always wanted to get down to the business of the day – whatever it was he wanted to talk to my father about – and scarcely seemed to notice our existence. We children wouldn't be allowed to stay to listen to the conversation. In his *Man of No Property*, my father says that he afterwards regretted his attitude of the time that children should be seen and not heard, but it was hardly exceptional or unusual in those days. So we were sent out of the room when, for want of a better expression, 'important people' came to the house. Perhaps arising from this, it has always been my belief that children would and should benefit from the knowledge, whatever about wisdom, of their parents. Perhaps my own children might be better judges of how this worked out in practice.

The friendship between my father and Mr Aiken cooled over a certain incident. Maudie Aiken, Frank's wife, was very much involved in the Royal Irish Academy of Music at the time and she wanted my father, then chairman of the RTÉ Authority, to intervene in the retention of the conductor Tibor Paul as head of the RTÉ Symphony Orchestra. My father, straight as an arrow, refused and this sadly led to a cooling of his lifelong friendship with Frank Aiken, not because of any direct falling out between the two men, but clearly because Maudie, a pretty formidable lady, had put the arm on Frank.

I also have very clear memories of Erskine Childers. His English, or Anglo-Irish, accent always amused us. As children, we were again given the order of the boot when he called to the house. I always thought Erskine quite eccentric. He wasn't at all what one might term a glad-hander and politically tended to be somewhat distant. I think my father sometimes liked to pull his leg. I remember on one occasion while Annette and I were engaged she had come over to the house with two of her very glamorous friends, Vera Sturze and Mary Hayes (who later married, respectively, the hotelier Colin O'Sullivan – son of Toddy – and my good friend Eugene O'Connor). The trio were about to leave, but my father, who was holding court up in his bedroom – something he rather enjoyed – insisted they stay just another ten minutes. We realised why five minutes later, when who should arrive, obviously by arrangement, but Erskine? My father had the three glamorous ladies sitting on his bed and was quite delighted at the look of shock on poor Erskine's face.

Mr Lemass was an occasional visitor, who I knew least at that time, although of course I got to know him quite well subsequently. He was a man for whom I developed great respect and affection in later years.

My mother was very democratic in her outlook. The local messenger boys were made as welcome as anyone else. I remember Tom Turner, who was messenger 'boy' (he was a man in his forties) for the Leverett and Fry grocery store. She was a particular friend of Tom's and they would chat for hours when he came to deliver the groceries.

My father was unreconstructed IRA. My mother had her own record, of course, but she was a liberated woman for the times. She could forgive. I'm not certain whether she could forget what happened during the Civil War, but my father could neither forgive nor forget. That was the difference between them. My mother was not prepared to inflict on us the bitterness of the Civil War. While my father didn't inflict it on us either, he did nothing to dissuade us from the belief that his side in the Civil War was all right and that the other side was all wrong.

He did attend the funerals of some of the people who had been on the opposite side during the Civil War. At times he would joke afterwards that he went to make sure they were really dead. I vividly recall him having a very genial two hours one Saturday afternoon with Lieutenant-General Michael Joe Costello, who had successfully run the Irish Sugar Company – obviously they had made things up between them, because they had been on opposite sides during the Civil War.

My father was a very tough but hard-working man. He was loyal to old comrades from the War of Independence and the Civil War – even those from the opposite side. He would always do his best for anybody who came to him looking for help – always having due regard to his integrity as a public servant, on which he was unshakeable.

During the late fifties and early sixties, my parents would invite various prominent people to lunch on Sundays. These lunches went on for hours. There were fierce arguments, mainly about politics, and occasionally people would walk out in high dudgeon, eventually to be coaxed back again. An American ambassador whom my father had invited one Sunday was listening to my mother talking about how she had got up on the Abbey Theatre stage to protest at Seán O'Casey's play, *The Plough and the Stars*. She described how something of a mini-riot developed and how Yeats jumped on the stage and shouted: 'You have disgraced yourselves again!' The ambassador turned to my father and said: 'Gee, Todd, it's like going back in history and talking to Joan of Arc!'

Those lunches were very important in my political development. My father very much held the republican line – we were all republicans of one sort or another, but he was, as I mentioned earlier, unreconstructed. He was of the view that the border should not be there *simpliciter* and that the British presence was the beginning and end of all our troubles. In present-day terms, it wasn't what would be called a sophisticated appraisal of the problem. But with the counterbalance of my mother's moderation, it made me start to think for myself on the subject.

My father, however, would not have condoned what the Provisional IRA did in Northern Ireland in the name of Irish nationalism during the last three decades of the twentieth century. Some of the atrocities of that period shocked and horrified him, and brought back to him the tragic and terrible things that were done during the Civil War.

Another family friend I recall well was F. H. or Freddie Boland. He was very close to both my parents. A man of great brilliance, his diplomatic skills brought great credit to Ireland. One of his great achievements was being elected President of the UN General Assembly. This is another example of Ireland, a small country, earning international recognition through the ability of its public servants.

He was an excellent public speaker, and to me he exuded charisma. Freddie's wife was the painter Frances Kelly and I have a number of her paintings. She was a most charming woman who greatly contributed to the success of her husband's career.

As time went on and I came to the end of my studies I became more interested in politics again and I decided to rejoin Dundrum Fianna Fáil cumann. By the late fifties and early sixties, my mother had become gradually less involved. The cumann had been taken over by younger people. A new generation of politicians was emerging in Ireland and the Civil War generation was beginning to depart the stage.

A NOVICE IN LEINSTER HOUSE

THE FIRST STEP – GET ELECTED

When I look back on my return to Dublin and my re-involvement with the local cumann, I realise that, although I had been brought up in a political household, I was really something of a political innocent, totally unaware of the stresses and strains that existed between political parties.

Annette and I got married on 19 December 1964. She was an air hostess and a daughter of Paddy and Peggy Cusack of Ballyjamesduff, County Cavan. They were enormously hospitable people and I became very fond of them and they, I believe, of me. Paddy, a local solicitor, did a huge amount to promote his village, involving himself in everything from bringing new industries to the area to running the local Tidy Towns committee. They won that competition twice, on one occasion beating neighbouring village Virginia into second place, much to Paddy's delight. I always enjoyed my visits to Ballyjamesduff.

I particularly remember the day Ballyjamesduff received their first Tidy Towns award. This was of course a big event in the village with the then Minister for Health Erskine Childers making the presentation. Paddy was a superb organiser and he was absolutely determined that everything would run with precision. He had timed everything exactly and was anxious that there would be no evidence of the easy-going attitude that visiting VIPs might expect to find in a small village. The proceedings started with an excellent lunch in Shaffreys, the local hotel, and then the party of bigwigs (and I certainly wasn't included in this at that stage of my career) paraded up the main street to the village square while a band played. They then mounted the platform, which had been specially erected in front of the market house. There were the usual speeches (everyone having been warned by Paddy exactly how much time they had). The occasion was then to have ended with more rousing music from the band as the VIPs came down from the platform and made their way back to the hotel. Despite his best efforts, and I suppose inevitably, things were running very slightly late. It wouldn't have mattered at all except for Norbert.

Norbert Reilly was a local man who was a senior civil servant in Dublin. One of his hobbies was aeroplanes, both building them and flying them. I once went up with him from his runway (two fields with the ditch between them removed) and I have to say my heart was in my mouth. However on this occasion Norbert had persuaded Paddy that while the band was playing and the VIPs were returning to the hotel it would add to the event if he did a sort of 'fly-past'. This he did, swooping very low over the square. Unfortunately, however, due to events running a bit behind time, Erskine was midway through his speech. All the locals waved up at Norbert, vainly trying to stop him. Norbert of course took all the waving as encouragement and did another swoop. Paddy was disconsolate, but really apart from Erskine himself I think everyone enjoyed it immensely.

Our first home was a fairly run-down flat in 22 Belgrave Square, Monkstown. At the time we were driving an old Fiat 500. You can imagine someone of my height (six foot five) getting into a car that small. Not only was it small, but it was not the most reliable vehicle. At least it was not too hard to push and I remember many times pushing it up and down the length of Belgrave Square in the mornings in order to get it started.

We didn't have very much money between us. As an air hostess, Annette had to give up her job when she married, but we did get cheap flights for our honeymoon: in fact, we got ninety per cent off the cost. We went to Beirut first, then to Cairo and Alexandria and finally on to friends of Annette, the Billards, in Paris. From this somewhat heady start to our married life, we returned to a fairly frugal existence, which my move to politics was unlikely to improve very much. My father always had a very definite point of view in relation to standards of living and politics. He believed that if you entered into political life not particularly well off, you should come out of it not one whit better off.

Why, then, did I decide to become actively involved in politics? I had joined the local Blackrock cumann when we moved to Monkstown. Seán Butler, then a Senior Counsel, was constituency organiser for the Dún Laoghaire-Rathdown constituency at the time. He was the father of the present High Court Judge Paul Butler. He apparently saw me as a promising young candidate, who presented well and carried a little bit of ideological currency, given both my parents' records and my mother's long-term input into the Dundrum cumann. I certainly had strong views about the need for major improvements in Irish society of the time. Ireland in the early to mid-1960s was still significantly lacking in development, despite the economic and social improvements that are associated with the decade.

Having witnessed the work that my mother had done in the Dundrum cumann, I felt that when my turn came, I would have the opportunity to do some good as well. She did a lot of decent work on behalf of the people of the area. She was very dedicated and devoted and did a lot of good in the community. My ambition at that time did not extend beyond politics at a local level. My parents, especially my mother, welcomed my intention to become more actively involved politically. I'm not too sure that my father, who was well known for his very forceful views, would ever have been elected as a Dáil deputy himself. At times it is necessary to temper the expression of strong views in politics, certainly in party politics – there are more subtle ways of getting opinions across – but that wouldn't have been in my father's nature. He was more concerned with expressions of his conviction than considering the personal hurt such expression might, and often did, cause. Witnessing this over a period of years no doubt influenced my style of expression.

Local elections were due in 1965, and it was my hope to take part in them as a candidate. Events, however, intervened, as they often do in politics. In this case, the event was a snap general election. Seán

Lemass had been operating very successfully with a minority government, which was dependent on the support of Independents, since the 1961 general election. He had had by-election successes in 1964 and was so confident of winning a general election that he threatened to go to the country if Fianna Fáil lost a by-election in Cork in early 1965. It did and the general election was duly called.

I was asked by Seán Butler to stand in that election and, somewhat recklessly, I suppose, I agreed to do so. I know now that I didn't have the remotest clue what would lie in store for me were I to be elected. I put my name forward as a prospective candidate and had to go through the selection convention in the constituency, together with five if not six others. Scán gave me a list of names of people to canvass. New in the area, Annette and I knew very few people. Some of the people I remember approaching for their support were the postman in Killiney, Fay Redmond; a housekeeper in Deansgrange named Mary Byrne; Henry Harkin, the film operator in the Ormond Cinema in Stillorgan; and Martin Kennedy, a well-known barrister from Dalkey. Martin was a polite and courtly gentleman, whose demeanour belied his steely reputation as a prosecutor and his penchant for fast cars. He drove in the Monte Carlo Rally more than once and still drove a Porsche at the age of sixty-five. It was impressive how broad the range of social backgrounds was among the members of the Fianna Fáil constituency organisation in Dún Laoghaire-Rathdown at the time. These were people who had power because they ran the various cumainn in the constituency.

I went round to visit some twenty or twenty-five people asking for their support. The reception was good in places and bad in others. I felt that the older the delegate was, the worse were my chances, and, as it turned out, that was a fairly accurate perception. However, two or three of the older delegates felt it was time for Seán Brady, first elected in 1927, to move on.

Two of the other people seeking nominations were Bruce St John Blake and John Rochford, both solicitors. Another candidate competing against me was a Senior Counsel, Aidan Browne, who subsequently became very successful at the Bar. Interestingly, all three were, like myself, making a living from practising law. Unlike me, they had all been in the constituency for some time and I thought I had little chance against them.

The selection convention was held on the second floor of a rather dingy hall on St Patrick's Road in Dalkey, which was packed to the rafters. Nothing attracts Irish people more than an election of any sort. Remarkably, I got through the convention, albeit by only one or two votes. I was lucky in that Fay Redmond favoured me, and he was very influential in the local party. He was quite a character. It was said that he was so Fianna Fáil that when he was delivering the post, he always knew when there was Fine Gael or Labour literature to deliver and that these letters didn't always reach their destination. How he knew there was Fine Gael or Labour material in the post always remained a mystery to me. There were a lot of stories about Fay and most of them were probably apocryphal.

I realised that I had made a serious mistake after the convention in that, having succeeded in getting selected, I made my speech and then went straight home without even buying my supporters at the convention a drink. This was unheard-of behaviour and shows how unaware I was at the time of how the social side of politics worked. Annette and I didn't even celebrate the event at home – we had boiled eggs for tea and carried on as if it were just any other evening.

Our marriage was just a matter of a few months old by the time the election was called (polling day was 7 May), so it was a lot to land on Annette's plate, but she threw herself into the campaign with enthusiasm. The Fianna Fáil ticket in Dún Laoghaire-Rathdown was Andrews, Booth and Brady. My running mates were well-established Dáil veterans. Seán Brady had been a TD for almost forty years; Lionel Booth's first general election had been in 1954 and he was elected to the Dáil three years later. I was really meant to be an also-ran, the third candidate who would provide transfers to get the other two elected. My main aim was to save my deposit; actually getting elected didn't enter my mind at all.

The election campaign itself was run by Seán Butler, from the constituency headquarters on George's Street, the main street in Dún Laoghaire. He was a first-class director of elections whose authority was never questioned by the local organisation. An essential member of his team was his wife, Ada. She was in the Dún Laoghaire headquarters day after day and gave both Annette and myself good advice and great moral support. Seán's instructions to me were to spend my time, day in and day out, morning, noon and night, knocking on doors, getting myself known. At the time, because of my youth and general appearance and demeanour, it was thought that I would appeal to a sector of the electorate who might not have been particularly Fianna Fáil voters.

The door-to-door canvass that my team carried out was novel for its time. Up until then, election campaigns tended to consist mainly of large rallies, and church-gate addresses after Sunday Masses were seen as all important. People were initially surprised to see Annette out canvassing with me. Then and now, she was my greatest supporter and wisest counsellor. At that time, the role of wives in politics was mainly to make the tea, and a woman's place was still seen as in the home. There were even a few cumainn (Booterstown, for example) that still did not allow women to join.

A great source of support to me in that first election was the number of friends and family who just turned up to help – canvassing, writing envelopes, putting up posters – whatever was required. They were led by my brother Niall, who really worked indefatigably for me. He had such a cheerful and positive attitude, which was a constant source of encouragement to me. His wife Bernadette was also hugely helpful, although because of the recent arrival of their baby son, Christopher, she was 'confined to base'. (Christopher was recently elected TD in Dublin South East.) She did, however, act as quartermaster and in that capacity performed the most important job of feeding us every day. In those days when there was in reality no money splashing around during elections, we didn't even think of feeding our canvassers. It was as much as we could do to feed ourselves!

This election campaign was the first time I went from door to door asking people to vote for me. I have to admit that I didn't find that easy and, indeed, up to the very end of my political career, I found this part of the job difficult. It has never been my nature to ask anybody for anything for myself. I have always found it much easier to ask on behalf of others.

The way elections were organised in those days was very different from today. The cumann directors had a lot of power. To canvass in an area, you had to go and see the cumann director and say that you would like to cover that particular area on a particular day. You would be told what parts of the cumann area you could go to and be given an appropriate electoral register. When you had done the canvass, the register had to be returned duly marked with the result of your call to each house. There was no scope for trespass outside the designated areas and we had to canvass the party ticket – and the party ticket only – on pain of death. We would never have the temerity to ask for 'number ones'. There was also far less money involved in campaigning in those days. All the election literature was party literature and one could not, under any circumstances, produce a piece of personal literature. We put up our own posters. Annette and I spent the weekends during the hours of darkness putting posters on poles, she up the ladder and me bravely holding it steady. At no time did we ever countenance the removal or defacement of any other candidate's posters.

I had the rather unnerving experience of making my first television appearance during that 1965 campaign. I went on with Michael O'Leary, who was running in Dublin North Central, and Tom Fitzpatrick, who was running in Cavan. All three of us were elected to the Dáil for the first time that year. I made a total botch of it. Never having been on TV before, I had no idea what was required on the medium. I was inarticulate, nervous, fidgeted a lot and interrupted other speakers. Annette's abiding memory of first seeing me on television was the whiteness of my knuckles! My abiding memory is the redness of my ears when she gave her views of my performance.

The general view afterwards was that my performance was a disaster, so much so that Mr Lemass said to me that the next time I went on television, would I please present myself properly – in other words, go off and do a course. That was, I believe, my first, but also my last, completely inept appearance on TV. There may have been times thereafter when I felt less than satisfied, but at least I learned how to achieve a reasonably presentable performance. After a few years, I began to feel more comfortable on radio and television.

There was a pretty formidable line-up against us in the constituency. There were the long-established Fine Gael TDs Liam Cosgrave, who always topped the poll and was on the point of becoming his party's leader, and Percy Dockrell. Labour always fielded strong candidates in Dún Laoghaire as well. The day of the count in my first general election is one that I will never forget. I assumed that I wasn't going to be elected and, money being scarce, all I wanted to do was to ensure the return of my deposit. I was at the time, for no reason that I can now understand, fairly confident of doing that. On the morning of the count, for the first time in a while, Annette and I were able to have a lie-in. At about ten-thirty the phone rang and Annette got up to answer it: there were no phones by the bed then. It was Lionel Booth and he said to get me down to the count centre straight away because I was going to be elected. When Annette came back into the room to tell me the news, I didn't believe her and was sure Lionel had got it wrong. She tried to persuade me otherwise but I remained unconvinced and unimpressed and determined to remain in the pit. She then decided to go and see for herself, so up she got and off she went to the town hall. She had never been to a count before and had no entry ticket, but, after some explanation, she managed to get in.

The first person she met was Senator Michael Yeats and he said to her, 'What do you think about being a TD's wife?' She was nonplussed and expressed disbelief, so he brought her over to the tables where the votes were still only being sorted. The pile of 'Andrews' votes certainly looked bigger than those of some of the other candidates. He then showed her the tally figures. Michael was a seriously expert tallyman and eventually it dawned on her that this was it – I was going to be elected.

Annette rang me, but I was still sceptical, so she rushed home and said to me that I had to get down to the count centre. We both went to the town hall and hung around as one has to do at election counts. We were told the first count would be announced at about five-twenty in the evening. After a bit of lunch we somehow got separated. As it was getting nearer the time, people noticed that I wasn't there and began to ask Annette where I was. She thought I was around the centre somewhere but I was not to be found. She really could not work out what had become of me. I had actually gone for a walk down Dún Laoghaire pier, as the atmosphere at the count had become a bit much for me. It was a fraught and emotional time and I just needed to be on my own for a bit. I walked back into the count centre at about ten past five, by which time the nerves of those waiting for me had become a little frayed as well. I had made it back in time for the announcement of my election on the first count, much to my amazement and probably to the shock and disbelief of our families and friends.

As it turned out, I topped the Fianna Fáil poll and was the first Fianna Fáil candidate elected, winning nearly eight thousand first preferences. Lionel Booth, who was also elected, was nearly three thousand votes behind me. I was sorry to have won at Seán Brady's expense, as he had served the constituency ably for a very long time and was a very pleasant man. I wasn't to know at the time that my political career would last a year longer than his. Between us, Brady and Andrews spanned seventy-five years as public representatives, an eternity in political terms.

For a new candidate to poll as well as I did was something of a surprise and a great achievement. But it was the time of young politicians and not long after the Kennedy era. He had visited Ireland two years before and had been received rapturously everywhere he went. Perhaps some of that glamour rubbed off on us younger candidates! I presented well and people must have liked what they saw and heard when they opened their doors. More important, I had a young team working with me. My family were very supportive. My sister Catherine and her husband Pat worked tirelessly. All my friends turned out and if we lacked experience, we made up for it in enthusiasm.

One of the first realities to strike me now that I was elected to the Dáil was that I would be drawing a salary, which at that time was £1,500 a year. To us then that was a fortune. Before then we couldn't afford to buy a house but now we were able to get a mortgage. The house we found was in Oakley Grove off Carysfort Avenue in Blackrock. It cost £5,250 – an enormous amount of money from our point of view. It was as much as we could do to service the repayments and it would be ten years or more before we could afford to go on our first holiday. However, £1,500 a year was at least a regular income.

It took me quite some time to settle down to the rhythm and routine of attending the Law Library during the day and the Dáil at night and I soon discovered the commitment that a life in politics was going to require. I don't ever recall – particularly in my early political life – being at home very much. All my time was spent out and about the constituency, building up a very strong base, which I did over the years. I developed a very good reputation as a constituency worker but it was a reputation built upon a massive commitment of time and energy.

LEINSTER HOUSE

My first day in Dáil Éireann was full of new experiences, among them meeting both famous people and men and women who, like myself, were there for the first time. None of us neophytes was too sure of protocol and one rural deputy's mother had to be removed from the members' bar where she had accidentally strayed. I was aware of total confusion and the necessity to find out everything for myself with no official assistance. I took my place in the chamber on the back benches where, after the usual conventional speeches, Seán Lemass was elected Taoiseach.

The 1965 election had been a success from Fianna Fáil's point of view: although the party's number of seats increased by only two, from seventy to seventy-two, it was enough for an overall majority. It was also the first time since 1933 that any government had increased its popular vote on an improved turnout. Commentators have also said that through this election Lemass had rejuvenated an ageing party. His economic policy of opening up Ireland to free trade and foreign investment had won the approval of the voters, as had his Northern Ireland policy of establishing closer relations with that part of the country (he had had meetings with Terence O'Neill, Prime Minister of Northern Ireland, in January and February of 1965).

Shortly before his resignation as Taoiseach and leader of Fianna Fáil in 1966, Lemass established an all-party Committee on the Constitution with a view to introducing changes that would improve the chances of better relations with the North. I was appointed to the committee. Other members of the party I recall being on the committee were George Colley, Bobby Molloy and Michael O'Kennedy, then a senator. Lemass had deliberately appointed younger men to the committee and he himself became a member after he had stepped down from the leadership. It was a privilege for me to be associated with him on the committee. I got to know him quite well then and could see how kind and encouraging he was to young people. He also had a good sense of humour. We were sitting next to him at a dinner at one of the Texaco Award ceremonies and when we asked if he was going anywhere on holidays that year (this was after he had retired as Taoiseach and Fianna Fáil leader), he replied: 'No. I'm a director of a few companies and I'd be afraid if I went away that they'd find out they didn't need me.'

I have no doubt that Seán Lemass had a considered view of some members of the party, his own son-in-law included, and I think he worried very much about that. I feel he was ill at ease about the direction in which the Haughey-Lenihan-Blaney-Donogh O'Malley group was taking the party.

During meetings of the constitutional committee, I expressed my serious concerns about the special position the Catholic Church enjoyed in our Constitution. I felt that no church should be given such a position, and many of the other members of the committee took the same view. The question of divorce was also discussed and the view was put forward that provision had to be made for it in the Constitution. Unfortunately there was no rush to implement the recommendations of the committee and it took many years for the people to be consulted and to remove the provision banning divorce.

My maiden speech was on the theme of industrial relations. I began by saying I wished to keep my contribution short, which must have pleased most deputies present! In summary, I expressed my belief in the need to continue to improve the machinery of industrial relations. Among other things I said that the apparatus of the Labour Court had become outdated and that its authority and prestige needed to be enhanced by conferring on it the same status as the High Court. The main point I put forward about the Labour Court in that first Dáil speech of mine was that it should be the final court of appeal in labour disputes. I'm glad to say that much of this has come to pass.

When I thanked the House for listening to me and resumed my seat, I was relieved that the ordeal was over. I cannot recall exactly if it was this speech, but it was certainly one of my earlier speeches that evoked a reaction from James Dillon, one of the grand old men of the House and a wonderful orator. He had just stepped down as leader of Fine Gael at the time. James had been very friendly with my mother. He was always very courteous, which my mother had always liked about him. In any event, I had stood up, unsmiling and rather nervous, to deliver my speech. When I finished, Mr Dillon's response was, 'Not bad, but the deputy should smile more often.' It was sound advice from a good man. (Interestingly, James Dillon had been my father's election agent when he ran for office in the students' union in UCD.)

Becoming a member of the Dáil is an unusual job, in that there is absolutely no training of any sort before or after one's arrival in the Dáil. It is still the case to this day. This is nothing short of extraordinary when one considers how vital the role of a public representative is in the life of the country.

Apart from the obvious people like Seán Lemass and James Dillon, the people who stood out for me from my first term in Dáil Éireann were Donogh O'Malley, Brian Lenihan, Charles Haughey – the Young Turks of Fianna Fáil. I also have a very strong memory of Neil Blaney. He was a seasoned politician by that time, having been first elected to the Dáil in 1948 and having served in a number of ministries. Another who made an impression on me was Michael Hilliard, who was a TD even longer than Blaney, having been first elected during the war. Paddy Smith from Cavan also remains in my mind; he had been in the Dáil since 1923 and had resigned as Minister for Agriculture in 1964 because he felt Lemass was too soft on the trade unions. He was a very fine speaker. Those deputies were a mixture of the Civil War generation and the following generations.

The conditions in Leinster House in those days were very different from today. Not to put too fine a point on it, they were pretty appalling. The current interview room, which is off the main hall, was our main party room, not only for parliamentary party meetings, but also where Fianna Fáil TDs would try to get secretarial work done. There was one secretary to every three TDs and – in contrast to today – there were no researchers. Annette had an old portable typewriter at home and she did a lot of work for me typing letters and speeches. There was only one phone for a large group of TDs and you would have to queue up to make a call. The restaurant and bar facilities were also primitive in the extreme.

The Dáil at that time may well have been a primitive place but it was also a fascinating place and the people in it were hugely interesting. Many of them came to dominate politics in later years.

One Fianna Fáil TD of the time I remember very well was Kevin Boland. He had a very austere, almost forbidding, public image. He gave the impression of being a very gruff, abrupt and unpleasant man. In fact, in my experience, he was anything but. I found him to be enormously kind to young and new politicians. I could not say the same for Neil Blaney at the time, though he subsequently became mellower and friendlier as the years went on.

I never got to know Donogh O'Malley very well – he died too soon. He had entered the Dáil four years before me but died suddenly and tragically young in 1968.

I got to know and like Brian Lenihan very well. It would be hard to meet a person one could like as much as Brian. I will always cherish his memory. It is probably fair to say that he never really reached his potential; I believe he was used politically. Unfortunately he either did not see this or, if he did, allowed it to happen. Regrettably, he let himself be abused as well as used. His presidential ambitions were thwarted in 1990 in the most terrible circumstances by an individual to whom he gave huge loyalty. That loyalty certainly was not returned, but I will have more to say on that score later.

A number of other members of the parliamentary party became friends of mine during that first period in the Dáil. Bobby Molloy, elected for Galway West for the first time also in 1965, became quite a close friend. Lionel Booth, my constituency colleague, who knew his way around the Dáil by this stage, was hugely decent and helpful to me. After he died it was a great honour for me, and I considered it a privilege, to be asked by his family to read the eulogy at his commemoration, and I am very grateful to the Booth family for that honour. Lionel was 'shafted' at the 1969 general election in favour of another candidate, not by me but by Neil Blaney. The beneficiary of Blaney's interference at the constituency selection convention was Mrs Carmel Gleeson, who, though a decent lady, was not at all a good choice of candidate. Blaney was not blamed for that; it was all loaded on me. By that time I had begun to realise that politics wasn't all sweetness and light. I also came to understand what a friend describes as 'The First

Law of Thermodynamics', which states that when the heat is on someone else, it can't be on you.

I was also close to Jim Gibbons from the Carlow-Kilkenny constituency, who had been a TD since 1957. He was Parliamentary Secretary, as ministers of state were called in those days, to the Minister for Finance during my first period in the Dáil and was afterwards Minister for Defence and then Minister for Agriculture. I used to have my tea with him in the Dáil most evenings. (Dinner was really in the middle of the day then.)

Jim was a very witty, sardonic speaker, with an enormous breadth of interests, and a voracious reader on a remarkably diverse range of topics. A skilled observer of people, and especially of their foibles, he was also blessed with a wonderful sense of humour. He had a great fund of stories about parliamentary trips abroad and his comments about some TDs and their attitude to foreign travel were priceless. He was also a skilled caricaturist. On dull days in the Dáil he would while away the time drawing caricatures of speakers droning their way through forgettable speeches. On one occasion he did a caricature of Barry Desmond, then a fellow constituency TD of mine and a good colleague, which he presented to me with the caption: 'Now I know why you got 10,000 votes!' Jim suffered terribly as a result of the arms crisis in 1970 and his reputation was most unfairly damaged by the events of that time. He incurred the enmity of Haughey who dropped him as a minister when he became leader of Fianna Fáil. It was harrowing to see how much he changed as a result of these bad experiences. The flame of humour, which had once burned so brightly in the man, was reduced to a flicker and his health deteriorated seriously.

Michael Carty from Loughrea in Galway, who was Chief Whip at the time, was another TD I became friendly with – Michael was an easy man to get to know and to get on with. Des O'Malley won the by-election caused by his uncle Donogh's sudden death in 1968 and I subsequently got to know him well. My wife Annette became friendly with Des's wife Pat and they have remained firm friends ever since.

A major event in our lives was the birth of our first son, David, on 5 February 1966. I was absolutely overjoyed and on the morning of his birth, having left Annette and the baby in hospital, I went first to tell the good news to the two ladies who had lived in the flat above ours in Belgrave Square in Monkstown. They were the Behan sisters, two delightful older ladies, and they were very happy for us. We had lived in that flat for most of Annette's pregnancy and they were always kind to us. I knew they would want to hear our good news. David was the first of our five children and, though I didn't realise it then, getting the balance right between family and political life was to prove a constant challenge over the coming years.

Seán Lemass's decision to retire as Taoiseach and leader of Fianna Fáil in October 1966 took many in the party by surprise, but I think it could be said that his writ had run and that he was tired. His health had not been good for some time. I recall from the meetings of the Constitutional Committee that he seemed at times to have difficulty catching his breath. I will always remember – I was genuinely shocked by this – Seán MacEntee standing up at the parliamentary party meeting on 9 November, which was to elect Lemass's successor, and saying, straight up to the former leader's face, that he was behaving like a traitor to his country, that he should not stand down, and that he owed it to his country to stay on as its leader. He also accused Lemass of deviousness and of sowing confusion in the party. What he said had no visible effect on Lemass one way or the other and the outburst was most likely the result of the tension that had existed between the two men over the years.

The main contenders for the succession were George Colley and Charles Haughey. Donogh O'Malley emerged as the latter's campaign manager, while Jim Gibbons performed the role for George. Neil Blaney also threw his hat into the ring and Kevin Boland canvassed support for him, but I don't think he had much backing or that he was a serious contender. Jack Lynch then emerged as a candidate and it soon became obvious that most support within the party was for him. I remember Professor Joe Lee using the image of a horse race to sum up the development of the first ever leadership contest in the history of Fianna Fáil. He described Lynch as coming through quietly on the rails, giving the impression that he was just out for a canter, while his more thrusting rivals churned up the ground in the centre of the course. Haughey decided to withdraw from the contest for reasons that are unknown to me. I was never close to him.

George Colley remained in the race against Jack Lynch. I got involved in his campaign to try to win the leadership and I voted for him, but he was defeated. It was my first experience of a leadership contest, but not the last time I failed to back a winner.

As well as the Fianna Fáil leadership contest, there was also a presidential election in 1966. Once again, as in 1959, Eamon de Valera was the party's candidate. He had managed to win the election seven years before by a comfortable majority of 120,000 and there was little doubt within the party but that he would emerge comfortably victorious again. He won, all right, but his victory was far from comfortable. We worked extremely hard for Mr de Valera in our constituency but we were pushing uphill because Tom O'Higgins, who lived in Sandycove in the constituency, and Fine Gael were very much in the ascendant there. So while our effort in Dún Laoghaire was dedicated, this was not reflected in the ballot box, and O'Higgins won well there.

I have some very vivid personal recollections of de Valera. One memory from a later time is of taking my young family – our first four children, David, Barry, Mary and Sinéad, who was just a babe in arms – to visit him at Áras an Uachtaráin and of how very kind he and his wife, Sinead, were to us on that occasion. I also visited him towards the end of his life at the Linden Convalescent Home in Blackrock where he went to live after retiring from the Áras, and I recall him saying something like, 'You're making a right mess of things'. I hasten to explain that I believe he was referring to the party and not exclusively to myself. It was obvious that he was keeping a close eye on the party he had created and was well aware of what was going on, even into his nineties.

My father, of course, admired him enormously and was utterly devoted to him. He wasn't so close to de Valera's sons. One of them, the late Terry de Valera, who was Master of the High Court, attacked my father for closing down the Harcourt Street line in Dublin. I think my father was dead by the time Terry de Valera criticised him in print. He seemed to have forgotten that my father was a public servant who was acting on the instructions of the government of the day.

The fundraising organisation for the party, called Taca, which was set up in the 1960s, has come in for much comment over the years. One deputy who was head, neck and toes into Taca was Neil Blaney.

Others who were well known for attending the monthly Taca dinners in the Gresham Hotel were Haughey, Lenihan, Donogh O'Malley and Boland. In the public mind, Haughey was the man most strongly associated with Taca because he had organised the first dinner, a very lavish affair attended by the whole Cabinet. This unhealthy closeness between government ministers and business was grist to the Opposition mill. Members of the Opposition were not the only ones to express unease. At an Ógra Fianna Fáil conference in Galway in May 1967, George Colley made his famous reference to 'low standards in high places'. I shared his views.

Taca was an organisation that may have led people to believe that by giving donations to politicians or political parties they could purchase political influence and goodwill. While many of those involved in Taca saw it as a legitimate means of fundraising, and while it should be remembered that Taca was open in its fundraising operations, it was the aura around it that was significant. Taca was to my mind a political disaster and a time bomb set to explode for Fianna Fáil and for politics generally, and time has sadly shown me to be correct. We could have done without it.

There was a definite element in the party that did not approve of Taca or what it came to stand for. It seemed to develop a life of its own and there were many, myself included, who wanted it stopped. Eventually Jack Lynch set about bringing it to an end, but it left a bad odour. It was the first time such an organisation intruded on the integrity of the party and it damaged Fianna Fáil.

By this time, we had two children, a second son, Barry, having been born in May 1967. Sadly, my mother died suddenly some months after Barry's birth, and this was a great blow. Throughout my life I was very close to my mother and relied on her judgement to a great degree. She was an immensely generous woman and if at any time I had any worries or concerns, it was easy to share them with her. She was very bright and extremely well-read and understood history and the political nuances of the day very well. I felt her loss very badly.

After my mother's death my father was a lonely man. We were all married and he was living alone. Joyce Duffy, who had been his private secretary in CIE, was a great source of strength to him throughout this time and he subsequently married her. It turned out to be wonderful for him and probably added many happy years to his life. I believe that my mother would have been pleased that he remarried.

Back in the Dáil I was making a bit of a name for myself but, in the eyes of the party hierarchy, for all the wrong reasons, concerning one piece of legislation during this Dáil term. The measure I am referring to was the Criminal Justice Act 1967. I felt very strongly about some sections of the Bill, because of their implications for individual liberty. I was concerned that the balance between public good and individual rights was being skewed unnecessarily. Having expressed my reservations in the Dáil, I remember appearing on television in late 1968, or early 1969, with Jim Tully of the Labour Party and detailing my reservations and my inability to support those particular sections of the Bill. The Minister for Justice at the time, Micheál Ó Móráin, certainly went some way towards meeting my concerns.

Afterwards, in the Dáil, in the debate on the second stage of the Bill, I thanked the Minister for his willingness to amend sections 30 and 31, but I also urged him to amend section 45, which dealt with the transfer of civilians to military custody. I was particularly anxious that the conditions that applied in civilian prisons be replicated in the case of military custody and I suggested that a currently serving prison officer be appointed to look after the custody of people transferred from civilian to military detention. Indeed, I felt uneasy about this section of the Bill and I said that to me it was not appropriate for soldiers to look after civilians held on what might be minor criminal offences.

At that time, it was unusual for backbenchers, especially in Fianna Fáil, to make statements criticising government proposals outside the party rooms. I felt strongly enough about the issue to do so. While my stance caused some people to think of me as somewhat of an independent within Fianna Fáil, this didn't seem to do me any harm in my constituency. Dún Laoghaire was – and still is – a constituency where liberal views predominated. My son, Barry, now a TD in the constituency, reminds me of this almost daily.

The next general election, which was called in June 1969, returned Fianna Fáil to power with a gain of two seats and an overall majority (seventy-five in a 144-seat Dáil). This result strengthened Jack Lynch's position as leader of the party. I was selected automatically to run in the election for Dún Laoghaire and succeeded in getting re-elected comfortably. Unfortunately, our number of seats in the constituency fell from two to one. My running mates were Carmel Gleeson, who polled a little over a thousand first preferences, and Neville Keery, who did better at over two thousand. My own first-preference vote increased by some two thousand to over ten thousand (just a few hundred votes behind Liam Cosgrave, leader of Fine Gael), but my running mates were much too far behind for my transfers to be any good to them. I took no part in the process of selecting the candidates in the constituency.

Neil Blaney became involved in the process in 1969 and this unwelcome and unsolicited intervention led the other sitting TD, Lionel Booth, to withdraw. It gives me no pleasure to reflect that the choice of running mates was a bad one. Neville Keery was a very courteous man and a very clever, erudite person. He drove a Morris Minor and, by his own choice, used to go around canvassing on his own. I don't think it sends out a good message when people see a candidate working alone. It gives the impression that he lacks support. I tried in my own way to advise him on this score, but he seemed to be happy that his way was the right way and he proceeded accordingly, with sadly inevitable results. Another thing he did that was less than wise was to go into the pub where cumann members were relaxing in the evening and suggest to them that it wasn't a good idea to be taking a drink during an election campaign, while they stood around with pints in their hands!

While the failure to retain two seats in Dún Laoghaire inevitably reflected on me in the eyes of the party hierarchy, the reality was that it was something over which I had little or no control. I did not expect promotion to government office once Haughey became leader, but I confess that I was more than a little disappointed that I failed to progress further than I did under Jack Lynch, and I'm sure the situation in my constituency didn't help me.

Nothing in particular stands out for me from that 1969 campaign. It was very much like its predecessor of 1965, one obvious difference being that I knew a little more about the right and wrong things to do and I suppose my political eyes were a little more open this time. During a campaign, a candidate is pushed quickly from door to door by his team, with the local party members directing affairs, telling you where to go, what to do and what to say, and the days pass in a bit of a daze. Sore feet and sore hands are part of the deal. Annette again was fully involved in this campaign, and my mother-in-law Peggy Cusack heroically took care of the children for the three weeks of the campaign.

In his book on Fianna Fáil, Dick Walsh said that, after the 1966 leadership contest, the party came to be seen publicly as a party of many factions. That wasn't my experience in my first period in the Dáil. Looking back now, I must say that they were a peaceful four years, those years between 1965 and 1969, in the light of what was to come afterwards. There was a terrific sense of unity in the party. Sean Lemass had unwavering support. When Jack Lynch took over, there was initially the same unity and the Colley side of that particular equation was very strongly behind Lynch.

This unity began to unravel towards the end of 1969 and what happened in the North was to act as the catalyst in that process of unravelling.

THE ARMS CRISIS

When the Northern Ireland crisis broke in August 1969, there is no doubt that the violence provoked an upsurge of traditional anti-partitionist, anti-Unionist and anti-British feelings among many people in the Republic. There was widespread sympathy for the Catholic victims of what was seen as a state-sponsored pogrom and the Irish Government was expected to act strongly to defend Northern Catholics. I recall a widespread feeling in late 1969 that we should have given more assistance to our Northern brethren.

After the August violence, barricades were set up to defend Catholic areas and Citizen Defence Committees were established. People from these committees, among them prominent nationalist politicians and IRA men, came to Dublin demanding aid. In Cabinet Blaney and Haughey in particular called for more far-reaching action than the majority Cabinet position, which was one of criticism of the Northern and British governments, and a demand that UN rather than British troops be sent in to defend Catholic areas.

Like many people around the country, Annette and myself were part of a group that ran various fundraising events in the constituency, in order to raise much-needed money to help Northern nationalists. Violent sectarianism was rife at the time and some nationalists were forced to flee from their homes. Many of these unfortunate people – ordinary families who in the main had nothing whatever to do with the events of the time – made their way south and were accommodated in Gormanston Military Camp in County Meath. As part of the fundraising effort we approached Pat Quinn of the Quinnsworth supermarket chain. He was very generous, giving us huge supplies of baby food, and also offered to double whatever amount of money we managed to raise. We went out to visit Gormanston on one occasion. The purpose of the visit was to bring supplies, but also to hear the accounts of what had happened. We encountered people who were very upset and very frightened by their experiences.

Serious disorder had developed in Derry and Belfast in August 1969, involving the deaths of Catholics and general mayhem, including street violence and widespread destruction of property. This posed questions for the government and for Fianna Fáil as a whole. Lemass had redirected our approach to Northern Ireland by stressing the need to create the economic and social conditions in our part of the country that would make the prospect of unity more attractive to Northern Unionists. Lynch was of one mind with Lemass on this and continued his policy. What they wanted to see in the North itself was internal reform which would improve the situation for Catholics and bring about the conditions for better cross-community and cross-border relations. Simple solutions to partition, like British withdrawal, were no longer put forward as a priority. However, Jack Lynch retained his opposition to partition, as he made clear at the 1970 Fianna Fáil Ardfheis.

It was said at that time that Haughey was a politician who would use anything and anyone to further his own position. If militant republicanism was the tool as in the context of late 1969 – he would use it. On 16 August, the 'hawks' (mainly Boland and Blaney) succeeded in pushing through a Cabinet decision to give Haughey, as Minister for Finance, control over a fund to provide aid to victims of violence in the North. The Cabinet established a sub-committee, consisting of Blaney and Haughey and two ministers for border constituencies, Padraig Faulkner of Louth and Joe Brennan of Donegal, to liaise with nationalist entities in the North. This sub-committee did not function and Blaney and Haughey went their own way. Over the next six months their actions (although there is much dispute and much that is opaque about those actions) went far beyond where the majority of the Cabinet intended.

It has often puzzled me how anyone could be in any doubt about the official government position at that time. When the IRA announced on 18 August that it was resuming its military campaign, the Taoiseach issued a statement making it clear that any IRA action would not be tolerated. The statement said that only the lawful Government of Ireland, freely elected by the people, had authority to speak and act on behalf of the Irish people and that the government would not tolerate any attempt to usurp the power legitimately conferred upon it by the people.

In Tralee on 20 September, the Taoiseach made a major speech on Northern policy in which he emphasised that the government had no intention of using force to end partition. Instead, he stressed, we wanted unity by consent, by creating conditions of mutual respect and tolerance, and that such an approach was clearly going to take a long time.

A detailed memorandum from the Department of External Affairs followed, which the rest of the Cabinet endorsed, stressing the need for co-operation with the British Government, in order to bring about reform in Northern Ireland. This memo also put forward a federal Ireland as a long-term objective, but argued that fundamental changes on such issues as divorce and contraception would be necessary in the Republic. The establishment of an Anglo-Irish division in External Affairs, which would work closely with the Department of the Taoiseach, was also proposed. This division was to liaise with nationalist political and community leaders in the North.

By November 1969, the government's Northern policy was laid down clearly and unambiguously, but Blaney and Haughey continued their work behind the scenes. In early December, at a function in Letterkenny to mark his twenty-one years in the Dáil, Blaney took the opportunity to declare that Fianna Fáil had not ruled out the use of force, if circumstances north of the border demanded it. This was a naked contradiction of the line Lynch had been laying down. It made newspaper headlines and gave the Opposition the chance to declare that Fianna Fáil was split.

At the party's ardfheis in mid-January 1970, Boland made a hardline speech echoing Blancy's comments. Lynch's enemies in Cabinet lost no opportunity to embarrass their leader publicly. He, on the other hand, continued to declare in public that there was no disunity in Fianna Fáil on the issue. From the imbroglio of that period between mid-August 1969 and April–May 1970, there emerged a number of protagonists, whose paths were eventually to cross in the courts of the land. As well as Blaney and Haughey, the other members of this cast were: Jim Gibbons, Minister for Defence; Micheál Ó Móráin, Minister for Justice, who was in poor health at this time; Peter Berry, Secretary of the Department of Justice; Captain James Kelly, an army intelligence officer, and his superior, Colonel Michael Hefferon; John Kelly, a Belfast republican, and Albert Luykx, a Belgian-born businessman.

The attempt to import arms secretly, the failure of the attempt, the dismissal of Blaney and Haughey and their arrest and trial are normally referred to as the arms crisis and culminated in the famous arms trial, so accurately and atmospherically narrated by Tom Mac Intyre in his book *Through the Bridewell Gate*. There has been much controversy about who did what and who knew what and the truth is not easy to find. My state of knowledge was limited by my absence from the Cabinet table. I had not yet been asked to serve. Not being a member of the Cabinet, I was very much on the outside and it was very difficult to know what was happening on the inside. When so many Cabinet members themselves did not know what was going on during that time, it will hardly surprise anyone that I, a mere backbencher, was in the dark.

By the time I became Chief Whip, people had taken up positions and, when that happens, the truth is usually the victim. I do know, however, that Jack Lynch was under extreme pressure, and that he was not getting any support from Blaney, Boland and Haughey or a number of junior ministers who also took anti-Lynch positions. It is important to recall that Seán MacEntee, himself a Belfast man, was strongly of the view that if we had attempted to go in and cross the border, there would have been mayhem and many of the people we were trying to rescue would have lost their lives before we had any chance of getting near them. People like Frank Aiken, Erskine Childers and others were also totally against any attempt at intervention. These were men with flawless republican pedigrees and their position was the very opposite to that of Blaney, Boland and Haughey.

The only good news for me in this period was the birth of our first daughter, Mary, in March 1970, although I'm afraid I was at home very little during this period and missed out on her infancy.

THE ASCENT TO OFFICE

In early May 1970, the Taoiseach asked Ó Móráin to resign as Minister for Justice and he agreed to do so. Des O'Malley, who was government Chief Whip, called around to my house at about eleven o'clock at night to tell me of Ó Móráin's resignation. He told me that he himself was going to be made Minister for Justice and that I was to become Chief Whip. O'Malley was very young at the time and Lynch relied on him to a huge extent. I think O'Malley was an extremely brave Minister for Justice, whose sheer bottle certainly belied his youth and inexperience.

Jack Lynch confirmed what O'Malley had already told me the next day. I was both elated and relieved, but, because of the anxieties of the times, there were no celebrations of my promotion.

The first I knew of the sackings of Blaney and Haughey was when I heard it on the early morning Radio Éireann news bulletin. A state car pulled up to take me to the Dáil that morning and I went in, feeling happy but apprehensive. Chief Whip! A seat at the Cabinet table and a pivotal role in the party and the parliamentary process! What do I do now that I have got the job?

I was certainly thrown in at the deep end at the start of my career in government. The whole country was shocked at the sackings and so was I. No one could have anticipated such an occurrence. The atmosphere of those few days is etched indelibly on my memory. One meeting followed another; wild rumours swept Leinster House and we wondered whether the government or the party – or even the basic institutions of the State itself, like the army and the Garda – would survive. It was a very harrowing time for the country. People must have been utterly bewildered at what was happening. It won't come as news to anyone when I say that the arms crisis divided Fianna Fáil deeply and it took a long time for the poison of the crisis to be extracted from the party. I don't believe the party was united again until Bertie Ahern became leader

On this particular occasion, as on many others, Fianna Fáil had the party organisation to thank for its survival. It stood fast and steady and the members trusted us to do the right thing. Had they known that we hardly knew what was happening ourselves, their support may have been more qualified.

To his eternal credit, Jack Lynch also played a blinder. He held things together and displayed a skill and steeliness that he had not up to that time revealed. His government survived, he held the parliamentary party together and proved a fearless captain of the ship. The initial, and emotional, Dáil debate, which took place from ten p.m. until three a.m. on 6–7 May, was confined to the appointment of Des O'Malley as Minister for Justice. Next day, the motion before the House was the appointment of three new ministers, and this debate lasted for over thiry-six hours, an extraordinary occasion in the history of Leinster House.

Sixty-nine TDs spoke in the course of this debate, only sixteen of whom were Fianna Fáil. Boland took a hard line and declared that he did not think the importation of arms into Northern Ireland was illegal. In his speech, Blaney swore his allegiance to Fianna Fáil as long as the party was standing by its constitution. The Opposition had their say, but the motion appointing the new ministers was carried and Lynch had extracted the government from a potentially catastrophic position.

Like all upheavals, that fateful time had its funny side as well. Garret FitzGerald of Fine Gael had his notes purloined by Joe Dowling of Dublin South West during that long debate. I don't know how Joe managed to snaffle Garret's notes, but Garret had planned to make a long speech and came to me in some distress. The word on the grapevine was that Joe was responsible. I confronted Joe and he admitted to having the notes. I persuaded him to return them, and then rang Garrret to tell him that he would find his notes where he left them and not to ask any questions.

During the same debate, there were instances of deputies drinking too much, and at two or three o'clock in the morning the odd deputy could be seen staggering into the chamber and falling down the steps onto the floor. They would have to be lifted back up and dusted down and put sitting in their seats. I remember a Fine Gael backbencher, somewhat the worse for drink, who would wake up every now and then and shout 'hear, hear' at inappropriate moments. One deputy forgot himself sufficiently to attempt to light a cigarette in the chamber until promptly jumped on by one of the ushers. Imagine the mileage the teetotal, non-smoking political correspondents would extract from such occurrences today!

At another stage in the marathon debate, the veteran Fine Gael deputy, Oliver J. Flanagan, who was a Knight of Columbanus and well known for his Catholic views, claimed he had been called a Communist. This seemed to be as much as Joe Leneghan, the sometimes outspoken Fianna Fáil TD for Mayo, could take. He stood up, muttering 'Jaysus, I could stand anything but that' and left.

It was also, of course, a time of great tension, of people not being able to sleep, or sleeping in the very uncomfortable conditions of parliamentary party rooms. I had the task of going to our parliamentary party room to find out who was there and trying to discover who was sleeping under a particular coat without waking them up. Such was one of the less glamorous but no less important roles of the Chief Whip at such an unusual and disturbed time in the history of our country.

The main consequence of the changes for me was that I was now Chief Whip, Parliamentary Secretary to the Taoiseach and Parliamentary Secretary to the Minister for Defence and, of course, had immediately to leave the Law Library and abandon my career at the Bar. My career as Chief Whip could not have had a more traumatic beginning. I can freely admit that it was a rollercoaster period in my life. My task was to balance the vote and I was trying to do that in a situation in which you could not be sure who was for or against you. You had to go to people within the party, who were perceived as your enemies, and ask them if they were going to vote. Given the personalities involved, at times that was very difficult. I was often met with hostility or dismissiveness. Their attitude could be quite aggressive. I have a very clear recollection of Blaney telling me to run away with myself back to Dún Laoghaire and not to be bothering him, that he would decide himself in his own good time whether he would vote or not. At the same time, it has to be said that whatever influence Fianna Fáil had on them, in the end they all came into the voting lobbies, despite their views on the Taoiseach, or whatever views they may have had generally.

Another fly in the ointment of office was the disposition of my private secretary, the late Hettie Behan. She was a Kildare woman and she had been private secretary to various government Chief Whips over the years. Like other permanent civil servants, she perceived herself as the 'real' Chief Whip, while the politicians occupying the position came and went. Unlike many others in her position, she did not hesitate to make this known to me regularly. Most private secretaries I have known at least had the decency not to parade their job security so openly. She had a serious problem with asthma and any time she got upset she used to almost convulse, so the whole idea was not to upset her. She wasn't reluctant to express her views and always wished to have those views implemented.

So not only had I to deal with mavericks outside the office but also with a very strong-willed maverick within. Hettie and I were in such strong disagreement on one occasion that I moved the Whip's Office to another part of the Dáil and operated from there. This caused me to be dubbed 'the Whip in exile'. At one time, Hettie had been secretary to de Valera and also to Lemass and she considered me a whippersnapper who wasn't to be treated too seriously.

I can't say I had a pleasant initiation into the role but, remarkably, we survived the crisis and stayed in government until 1973. It is something of a mystery how we managed to pull through. We depended on Independents like Joe Sheridan from Westmeath. He had been an unsuccessful Fine Gael candidate in the three general elections in the 1950s, entered the Dáil as an Independent in 1961 and proved a stalwart supporter of the Fianna Fáil governments thereafter. I used to send the state car to bring him to the Dáil for crucial votes. I would ring him in advance to see whether he would be available or not. If his wife answered, invariably he wouldn't be available, but if he answered himself, usually he would be willing to travel. So the Chief Whip's state car knew the side roads and by-roads of the midlands well in those days. Joe was a genuinely decent man.

My position as Chief Whip also saw me dealing with some of the Dáil 'characters' of the time. Joe Leneghan from Mayo was one of them. He was unpredictable and you never knew what he was going to come out with, so much so that the Ceann Comhairle had to intervene at times to tell him not to use unparliamentary language. Joe had to be handled with kid gloves. If you annoyed him, you couldn't be sure of getting him to vote with Fianna Fáil, because he had started political life as an Independent TD before joining the party.

Another occasional thorn in my side was Dickie Gogan from Dublin North West, a veteran of the 1916 Rising and the War of Independence. He was fond of a drink and at the time of votes in the House he would go up the division-lobby steps and, just to annoy me, he would go in the direction of the Opposition lobby, so that one of us would have to turn him around and push him into our own division lobby. His was a crime of mischief rather than malice and everyone knew and enjoyed this.

Another character of the time, Liam Ahern from Cork North East, had the nickname 'Bags a' Guns'. This came from an occasion during a debate in which certain Fianna Fáil TDs were accused of gun-running, at which he piped up: 'There should be bags a' guns.'

Fianna Fáil didn't have a monopoly on colourful characters. Frank Cluskey of Labour came into the Dáil on the same day as myself, and he definitely made an impact. He was a very decent man and a real 'Dub'. In the cut and thrust of debate, he could be sharp-witted and incisive. Probably no one who ever became a TD had as much compassion for the less well-off as Frank. He was to die at the relatively young age of 59 after a long battle with cancer, although he achieved high office and enjoyed the perks that came with the office, in particular foreign travel. It was said of him that proximity to Dublin Airport made his nose twitch.

I think it is true to say that there were far more 'characters' around in those days than there are now. When speaking in the chamber then, the most you could have in front of you was notes. You weren't allowed to read full speeches as you are now. So you had to be able to think on your feet and a witty riposte or put-down in response to interruptions was a great weapon to have in your armoury. I believe one of the greatest exponents of this art was John Kelly of Fine Gael.

I remember Muhammad Ali, arguably one of the greatest sportsmen of all time, visited the Dáil during my tenure as Chief Whip. It was on 12 July 1972, the day our fourth child, Sinéad, was born. He was most pleasant and courteous to everyone. There was a good photograph of the two of us published in the *Evening Press* – I had my fist up to his chin and Ali had a wide-eyed, alarmed look on his face. After Sinéad was born, a nurse brought Annette some tea and toast and propped up on the tray was the paper, with the photo showing. The nurse said to Annette: 'Oh, look at that good-looking husband of yours. You'll probably be in here next year again!' Not true!

In my role as Parliamentary Secretary to the Minister for Defence, I was sometimes given the task of visiting barracks, reviewing military parades and having lunch with the officers. The tradition was for the Minister (or Parly Sec) to wear a hat while reviewing parades, and there was a particular moment when the hat was taken off. Now, obviously, to take off a hat one has to have one on but I refused point blank to wear a hat – I felt that I was tall enough and would feel foolish wearing one.

I'm afraid I could and can be a bit careless about reading invitations at times. As a result, on more than one occasion I have brought Annette along to events to which she was not invited. Once we, as I thought, were invited to a Mass in Collins Barracks followed by lunch. We duly showed up and were escorted up to the top of the church, and we didn't notice that there were no wives present. Afterwards, as we were coming out of the church, Annette overheard someone saying, in an urgent tone: 'Get on to some of the wives and get them here!' It then dawned on her that she shouldn't be there – the whole thing was my fault, of course. So, some unfortunate women were taken away from their Sunday lunches or games of golf or whatever other pleasurable way they planned to pass their Sunday afternoon, because this wife had turned up uninvited. I tried to be more careful about reading invitations afterwards but have to admit that there were a few repeat performances.

During the period while I was Chief Whip, the violence north of the border gathered pace and there was a garda stationed permanently outside our house. I felt sorry for the person assigned to such an excruciatingly boring task, who had the additional discomfort of having no cover whatsoever from the elements. Under no circumstances were we allowed to bring the garda assigned to us into our house. The kitchen was the nearest point to where they stood so we used to leave the kitchen door open (without remarking on the fact) and occasionally on the darkest, dreariest nights of the year they would avail of the cover provided.

The gardaí on duty outside our house tried to get their station to give them a garda car so that they could sit in out of the elements, but they were told that the station couldn't spare a car. Annette came up with the idea of leaving her car out on the road so that they could sit in that but they turned down the offer because they realised that if they accepted her offer they would never succeed in getting their station to provide them with a car. Our assigned gardaí were invariably very young – probably the most junior ranked in the station was given the tedious task. The whole scenario actually struck me as a bit daft. We lived in a quiet cul-de-sac and if anyone wanted to find our house to do us harm, it was the easiest house to spot because it was the only one with a garda outside. I'm not sure how the poor officer would protect us, as he was equipped with no more than a walkie-talkie. The local children loved the garda presence and, whenever he walked up and down, they would form a line behind him and walk up and down as well in a mini-parade. They would also want to play with his walkie-talkie and wear his peaked cap and the job generally required great patience on his part.

One of our garda's roles was to inspect the post that came to the house. One day a package arrived and, when asked if we were expecting it, we said no. Could we think what it might be? No. The garda on duty didn't like the look of it, so the package was put on the garden wall. The bomb disposal squad was called out and there was great activity and excitement – at last something was happening. I think they were glad to have the opportunity to carry out a relatively safe exercise. Annette began to wonder to herself if she had left a bit of underwear or something behind in some hotel and was this going to be embarrassing. The potential bomb turned out to be one of those calendars with detachable leaves. They were new at that time and we were being sent a sample.

The role of Chief Whip took over my life completely at this time, to the detriment of my family life. We now had four very young children. I recall returning home one evening at the end of another gruelling day and seeing Sinéad, who was then about thirteen months, playing on the floor. I bent down to pick her up, but she recoiled from me and started to cry. She simply didn't recognise me, because she had seen so little of me around the house. It was a very upsetting experience.

In November 1972, the Minister for Justice, Des O'Malley, introduced the Offences Against the State (Amendment) Bill into the Dáil. The purpose was to set up non-jury courts for people accused of terrorist offences. It also made provision for a person to be convicted of IRA membership on the evidence of a garda chief superintendent that he had grounds to believe that person was a member. This Bill deeply divided the Opposition. The Labour Party and most liberal Fine Gael deputies were opposed to the Bill, but Liam Cosgrave and a few of his colleagues supported it, and Cosgrave indicated he was prepared to vote with the government on the measure. It caused a deep rift in Fine Gael and Cosgrave might well have been replaced as leader; but when loyalist bombs killed two people in Dublin it brought about a change of heart in Fine Gael. The controversial Bill was then passed with the support of Fianna Fáil and Fine Gael.

With the Opposition then in disarray, Jack Lynch decided the time was right to call an election, which he did on 5 February 1973, the day before the Dáil was due to reassemble after the Christmas recess.

MIXED FORTUNES

BACKBENCHER IN OPPOSITION

Fine Gael and Labour were certainly taken by surprise by the timing of the election but they responded quickly and put a fourteen-point plan for the formation of a Fine Gael–Labour coalition before the electorate. This was the first general election Fianna Fáil had faced since the arms crisis and arms trial and we were uncertain how the public would react.

As it turned out, our national vote held up extremely well and was up on what it had been in 1969. It was the vote-transfer pact between the two main Opposition parties that swung it for them and helped them to emerge with a narrow majority. Considering all that had happened since 1969, it was a more than creditable performance by Fianna Fáil.

My own first-preference vote increased by over six hundred and I was comfortably re-elected. My running mates on this occasion were Neville Keery (again) and Eric Leonard. Neville increased his first preferences by about fifteen hundred. He polled the best of the losing candidates but was again too far behind for my surplus to get him elected. The other Fianna Fáil candidate, Eric Leonard, a bus driver, didn't do too well, receiving about twelve hundred first preferences. He was a good councillor and local government was then and remained his forte.

They were both very good people but, like the candidates in the previous election, badly chosen and doomed to failure. Inevitably, some blame came my way for not regaining the second Fianna Fáil seat that had been lost in 1969. As on the previous occasion, it was never my practice to interfere with the constituency convention that selected the candidates. Perhaps, in retrospect, I should have done so, but hindsight is of little value. When candidates fail, the finger of blame has to point somewhere and candidates rarely blame themselves for their poor performance.

In the interregnum between the departure of the Lynch government and the assumption of power by the Fine Gael–Labour coalition, Jack Lynch called me in and asked me if I would like to go to an Inter-Parliamentary Union conference in the Ivory Coast. At that time the Ivory Coast head of state was President Houphouët-Boigny, a former French parliamentarian and a poet among other things; indeed, he was ruler from independence in 1960 right up to 1993. Lynch felt I had had three hard years as Chief Whip and that I could do with a break. I told him I would be delighted to go, but he told me there was a sting in the tail, in that the Opposition Chief Whip, Gerry L'Estrange, a Fine Gael TD for Longford-Westmeath, was also going. I felt very uncertain about wanting to go if Gerry was going because during the previous three years, he had given me a pretty torrid time. His behaviour in the House, often outrageous and always pointed, frequently resulted in his suspension and I can recall him being literally tackled, rugby fashion, by Dáil ushers as he tried to get back into the House, having been ordered out by the Ceann Comhairle. He was certainly a very energetic individual. But my desire for a break overcame my apprehension and I decided to go.

While away I became ill – I think it was a reaction to the inoculation I had had before departing. My arm swelled up quite badly and I had a high temperature and was confined to bed for a couple of days. It's funny how your relationship with people can change so radically and so quickly but, without a doubt, Gerry looked after me like a long-lost brother. I cannot stress enough how very kind he was to me during that period. We became firm friends after that. During the rest of the week-long trip after I had recovered, we went out to dinner together on a number of occasions and did a lot of philosophising, talking about politics in general and our various experiences and discovering that we had a lot in common. On our return to the Dáil we kept up our new-found friendship over regular cups of coffee until sadly Gerry died. This is further evidence that friendships can and do develop across political divides.

During the period in Opposition from 1973 to 1977, I returned to the Law Library, where I resumed my Bar practice. I concentrated on rebuilding my personal injuries junior practice, while at the same time performing my parliamentary and constituency duties. The parliamentary duties were naturally far less onerous than they had been for the previous three years. I was shadow spokesman on Justice for a time (my opposite number being Paddy Cooney) and Social Welfare (when Labour leader Brendan Corish was minister). Constituency work, however, absorbed a substantial portion of my time, as it always had.

There was a presidential election in May 1973, when de Valera retired after 56 years as a public representative. The Fianna Fáil candidate was Erskine Childers and his opponent was Tom O'Higgins of Fine Gael. O'Higgins had done very well against de Valera in 1966 and was expected to win but Childers confounded the punters and won by 48,000 votes. In fact, he took a leaf out of his opponent's campaign notebook of 1966 by promising a more relevant and accessible presidency. He drove around the country in a 'Childers bus', which the Opposition dubbed 'Wanderly Wagon' after a children's television programme of the time. Erskine couldn't be said to be a natural when it came to electioneering. As part of his campaign he spent a day in each constituency. The day he came to Dún Laoghaire a group of us went walking down Marine Road with him. There was quite a good crowd of people out to see him and the famous bus. As he got off the bus he spotted a newspaper seller and bought an evening paper. He then proceeded to walk down the road reading it and completely ignoring the welcoming party, which went down rather badly. I snatched the paper out of his hand and told him to wave. However, it didn't damage his vote in the constituency – in fact he polled very well. His upper-class English accent, the product of a public-school education, seemed to have had an irresistible appeal for the people. A curious paradox, really.

As it so happened the day that Erskine spent with us in Dún Laoghaire was the day of our eldest child David's First Communion.

I was able to attend the church part of the day but then I had to go to assist in guiding Mr Childers around the constituency while David and his mother went off to celebrate the occasion with some friends. It is one of the drawbacks of a public representative's life that precious family moments and occasions sometimes have to be sacrificed.

Sometimes I wonder how the Childers family survived in Irish politics at all. Maybe it owed something to our fondness for eccentrics. Erskine chaired the selection convention for the Dublin South County by-election in early December caused by the resignation of Kevin Boland from the Dáil. Rita Childers, Erskine's wife, called for him in the car, before the end of the convention. As she chatted to party workers, she noticed some people were wearing little stickers with the slogan 'Jack Leads' on them. 'Tell me about this chap Jack Leads,' she said to one of these rather bemused people.

I recall another incident involving Erskine, which shows he wasn't too clued in when it came to knowing his colleagues in the parliamentary party. It was at the time of a vote in the Dáil and he went up to Mark Killilea, who was a Fianna Fáil senator at the time and was standing around waiting for someone. He asked him if he would pair with him as he had a function to attend. Just for the ruse, Killilea agreed readily to do so but being neither a member of the Dáil at the time nor a member of a different party, he could not be of much use to Erskine.

As Minister for Health, Erskine Childers campaigned very strongly against the round system that is such a feature in Irish drinking circles. Quite rightly he argued that people were impoverishing themselves by getting into rounds and, of course, damaging their health by drinking more than they may have wanted or than was good for them. In this he was certainly before his time. Another way he was well before his time was in his desire to put an end to smoking in public places. He also favoured contraception and felt that contraceptives should be available to the public. I recall him once addressing the Fianna Fáil National Executive on the subject, but I'm afraid he was speaking to an unreceptive and unsympathic audience.

Erskine Childers died suddenly in November 1974 after only a few months in office. Unusually, his wife, Rita was anxious to succeed her husband and carry on the work he had begun. Jack Lynch gave Michael O'Kennedy and me the rather unpleasant task of telling her that she was not going to be the Fianna Fáil presidential candidate. We called to Áras an Uachtaráin, where we met her son, also called Erskine. We asked to see his mother, who was upstairs, and he duly delivered the message to her. She sent him back with the instruction that he was to ask us what we wished to say to her. We told him that we were there to convey to her that Fianna Fáil would not be backing her for the Presidency. After Erskine junior carried this news to her, he returned to tell us that his mother had no wish to see us. In the event Cearbhall Ó Dálaigh was chosen as Childer's successor and was returned unopposed – without an election.

Following his sacking and demotion to the back benches, Charles Haughey had not been inactive in the party. He had toured the country, addressing the 'grassroots' and building up support among them, and had visited most of the constituencies up and down the country. This made him very popular with the party organisation. He didn't pay much attention to Dún Laoghaire; he always disliked this area and, of course, he knew how I felt about him. Neville Keery wouldn't have been a supporter either. But he had substantial support within the constituency organisation and quite a number of his supporters held key positions. In fact, I had very little to do with Mr Haughey at any time, and vice versa. In addition to my doubts about his integrity, we didn't get on well. I would have been seen as 'southside urban man', tall and relatively good looking, while he would have been seen as 'northside urban man', small and not conventionally attractive. We had a dislike for one another from the beginning, but it wasn't hatred. That came later. There was nothing we could do about the fact that we just didn't like each other. Nor did we try to do anything about it, which was, perhaps, unfortunate because my father – and indeed my brother Niall – had great time for Haughey. My father looked on him as a kind of saviour of the party in republican terms.

When Haughey was Minister for Health, I recall him attending a Fianna Fáil cumann dinner in Dún Laoghaire. He came dressed in black tie, although it wasn't a dress function. This was obviously just a breakdown in communication, but his comment was: 'In Kingstown, I presumed you always dressed for dinner.' He invariably referred to me as 'the long fellow' or 'the big fellow' – the height thing always came into it. I also understand that he sometimes used less flattering terms to describe me.

Tensions did emerge at times at comhairle ceantair meetings in my constituency because of my well-known attitude to Haughey. I think there were many in the Fianna Fáil constituency organisation in Dún Laoghaire who never understood why I got such a good vote at election time. At least one of the reasons was that I worked very hard in the constituency. I became deeply involved in the Ballybrack Housing Co-op, for example, and other similar organisations. I did what I could to help people to secure their own homes in places like Shankhill and Ballybrack, which were beginning to be developed when I became a TD. Although I didn't come from a working-class background, those areas, and Sallynoggin too, were hugely loyal to me right throughout my political career.

At the 1972 Ardfheis, Haughey was re-elected one of the five honorary vice-presidents of the party. In January 1975, in a reshuffle, Jack Lynch brought him back onto the front bench as spokesman on Health, and Haughey made the best possible use of his return to further his own popularity within the parliamentary party. Some commentators have expressed bewilderment as to why Lynch rehabilitated his old enemy in this way. Indeed one commentator has described the decision to recall him as the biggest political mistake Lynch ever made. But I think he was concerned that the party was in danger of a terminal fracture and he hoped that, by bringing him back, those who supported Haughey would be more confirmed and committed Fianna Fáil supporters and activists. There can be no doubt that from the moment he was reinstated on the front bench, his whole purpose, drive and ambition was to secure the leadership for himself.

Jack Lynch was a man without malice. Other politicians might never forgive someone they felt had done them wrong, but Lynch wasn't like that. It may well be that he did make a terrible mistake about Haughey, but it is open to question whether he had much choice in the matter. Even if Haughey had been forced to run from the back benches he would have done very well. It cannot be disputed that he had a very big following and he played the extreme republican card with great skill, particularly at times when events in the North provoked a visceral and atavistic reaction in the Republic.

Kevin Boland had resigned from Fianna Fáil in June 1970 after losing the whip, and he went on to form his own party called

Aontacht Éireann, wittily dubbed Uaigneas Éireann by some. The party contested the 1973 election, but won no seats. Some Fianna Fáil members from the Dún Laoghaire constituency had joined the new party, but gradually began to return to our organisation. I was very happy to welcome them back and there was no question of doing anything else. Indeed, Nóirín Butler, then Nóirin Ní Scoláin, daughter-in-law of Seán Butler (who first asked me to run for the Dáil in 1965), had become secretary of the Boland party but she, too, returned to us. She subsequently proved very supportive of both Fianna Fáil and myself.

The first year went well for the Cosgrave coalition, but then it encountered major obstacles. The violence in the North intensified and inevitably had repercussions for this part of the country, most notoriously with the shocking murder of the British ambassador, Christopher Ewart Bigggs, in July 1976. Then the oil crisis led to massive inflation and serious employment problems. Subsequently Liam Cosgrave shocked his colleagues, and indeed us in Opposition, by voting against his own government's Contraceptive Bill. Fianna Fáil opposed the measure, but I wasn't happy with the position of the party on the issue. As a younger member of the party, I thought there was a need for the sort of social advances this Bill proposed and I believe that other younger members of the party felt likewise.

The Fine Gael–Labour coalition had a further problem with the resignation from the Presidency of Cearbhall Ó Dálaigh, caused by the insult of Paddy Donegan, who was Minister for Defence. The incident that led to President Ó Dálaigh resigning in October 1976 caused me much distress, as I know it did many others. The late Dermot Kinlen SC (subsequently a judge of the High Court and Inspector of Prisons) was a very close friend of Cearbhall and used to invite him to a house he had in Sneem, County Kerry. Cearbhall used to go to Sneem fairly regularly and I got to know him and his delightful wife Máirín there. They had no children and looked on myself and others as part of their family. Cearbhall was also an outstanding jurist with many fine qualities. In addition, he was a very sensitive person.

So when the Donegan incident happened, in a sense I took it personally. I know I made quite an angry contribution to the Dáil debate on the President's resignation, even going so far as to refer to a 'fascist' element emerging in the government. I also accused the

Taoiseach of treating the House with contempt, because of how little he had to say on the debacle.

It is understandable that, when Cearbhall was accused by Donegan of being 'a thundering disgrace' for exercising his constitutional functions by referring a Bill to the Supreme Court, that he would take it very badly. Perhaps he resigned too quickly and should have given Donegan as good as he got – which Donegan would have understood – but Cearbhall wasn't that sort of person. He was quiet and reserved and a man of integrity. Like his brother Aengus, who was a librarian in the *Irish Press* for years, he was a saintly person. He was always very generous and was especially kind to our children. Cearbhall deserved better.

Cearbhall and Máirín had a holiday home, a schoolhouse in Cahirciveen, and we were often invited there. They subsequently moved to live in Sneem. After his death we continued to be quite close to Máirín and often visited her in. Dermot Kinlen deserves great credit for his devotion to the Ó Dálaighs. His holiday home in Sneem had an extra tiny house – actually a boathouse, which he converted into two rooms and a bathroom – on a small promontory jutting out into the sea. Cearbhall, before he bought a house in Kerry himself, loved this little house and when he and Máirín stayed there during the time that he was President, Dermot used to refer to it as the 'áraisín'. In fact he continued to refer to it by this name.

Paddy Donegan was a Drogheda man. My old school friend, Dick Brannigan, was a very good friend of his. Paddy's wife Mary was a really lovely lady. He was a rough and tough character who was inclined to go a bit far at times when he had drink taken (which seems to have been the case when he insulted the President at an army function). I don't think there was malice in the man and it was a tragic event for all concerned. It still amazes me that Liam Cosgrave didn't accept Donegan's offers to resign because this obviously made a bad situation worse.

It wasn't all bad news for the Cosgrave government. The Sunningdale Agreement was definitely a triumph. It certainly gave hope of peace in Northern Ireland and a new era in North–South and Anglo-Irish relations. But the hope was quickly dashed when the Ulster Workers Council strike brought the North to a standstill and forced the collapse of the power-sharing executive. The collapse was an undoubted tragedy and led to another two decades of suffering and loss of life.

A bright feature of Irish life during this 1973–77 term of the Fine Gael–Labour coalition was a television programme, *Hall's Pictorial Weekly*, which had become extremely popular all over the country. It was one of Ireland's most successful TV shows and was a skilful mixture of social and political satire. Its constant satirising of government ministers was so sharp that it is generally accepted – and some political analysts support this view – that it played an important part in bringing down the Cosgrave government. On the programme, the Taoiseach himself was portrayed as the 'Minister for Hardship' and the Minister for Finance, Richie Ryan, was depicted as 'Richie Ruin'. By contrast, Jack Lynch was presented as a benign, pipe-smoking, homely character who used to indulge in fireside chats with his wife Maureen.

Dermot Morgan's subsequent radio programme, *Scrap Saturday*, wasn't as damaging to governments as was *Hall's Pictorial Weekly*. *Scrap Saturday* had a different impact on the psyche of the people and they were more inclined to treat it as comedy rather than satire. *Hall's Pictorial Weekly* was both extremely funny and enormously popular. Of course, it was something very new in the Ireland of the time: and in those days, the vast majority of people could only receive RTÉ, not the range of channels that are available nowadays.

The life of a backbench TD was not exactly exciting whether in opposition or in government, but at least if your party was in government, you had some sense of achievement and felt that you were contributing to the running of the country, even if only as lobby fodder in the Dáil. Every backbencher was expected to go anywhere in the country to canvass for the local party candidate when there was a by-election. In 1975 there was a by-election in Galway following the death of the Fianna Fáil TD Johnny Geoghegan, our bus driver to Carraroe for childhood holidays all those years ago. I was assigned to the Moycullen area to canvass with the new candidate, Johnny's daughter Máire Geoghegan-Quinn. As outsiders we were well received by the people of Galway. Máire was a natural candidate and even then came across as being very bright. She succeeded in winning her late father's seat.

Naturally, I undertook a lot of work in my own constituency. There were meetings to be attended every night – meetings of residents' associations, sports clubs and other voluntary organisations. A big issue for me at that time was to get some development going in Dún Laoghaire. One of the enterprises I tried to get under way was a small fishing industry, but I have to confess that I met with little enough success. A marina was another idea I thought would be of benefit to the town, but we made little progress. Unfortunately, the prevalent attitude was that we could do without what we didn't have; there was a great reluctance to 'disturb' Dún Laoghaire at all. A marina, for instance, would be seen as an intrusion, disturbing the birdwatchers and dog walkers. There was a general view that the place was to be left as it was. It was an old Victorian town and the fabric was to be left intact, even if it was grubby and down at heel. A sad old lady, with moth-eaten furs and a posh accent.

The prevailing attitude was largely the province of the so-called chattering classes. These were people who passed in and out of the area, or who lived in Dún Laoghaire but didn't have to work there. The average person from Dún Laoghaire, particularly from places like Sallynoggin and Ballybrack, wanted jobs for their children. It was only years later that as Minister for the Marine I could find £20 million to begin the redevelopment of the harbour by building a new state-of-the-art car ferry terminal. It was a start, to be followed by a fabulous marina and soon, I hope, by the complete removal of the eyesore that is called the Carlisle Pier, a relic of hard times and often the place where sad Irishmen and women left their native soil. And then the old baths must go. I am almost ashamed at the inability of the council to take a real step to rid the seafront of this rat-infested blight. The protests at the plans some years ago seem to have frozen the local councillors into a state of fear. I wondered at the time of the protests at the ambitious plans the council put forward, how many of those who came to protest had ever used those baths, or how many of them lived in the area, or how many of them were the 'usual suspects', who see it as their role in life to protest at anything new, anywhere, as a matter of principle. Certainly, the baths in Dún Laoghaire did not close because they were overused.

The problem with Dún Laoghaire that I saw as a young, and as a not-so-young, TD was that there was a disconnection between the town and the harbour and there are not enough people living near the sea, except in the area around Sandycove. People came to Dún Laoghaire by car ferry and got straight into their cars or onto trains or buses and went off anywhere but into the town of Dún Laoghaire itself. There were so many hard-working people in the town trying to make some sort of living, from bed-and-breakfasts and small guesthouses to small shops and restaurants, who found it extremely hard to eke out any sort of reasonable existence. The 'passing-through' phenomenon is still there but, since the work on the harbour, the two shopping centres and the new Pavilion Centre, more people are now inclined to look at Dún Laoghaire in developmental terms.

I was working hard in the constituency and at the Bar during that period of opposition between 1973 and 1977. TDs were not very well paid at the time; the legal practice was ticking over but was far from lucrative; the children were being reared and it wasn't an easy time. Some indication of how tight things were might be that our first holiday since we married ten years earlier was a week in a studio apartment with a view of the bus shelter in Albufeira in Portugal. It was, nonetheless, a week we were delighted to have.

My father took a great interest in the political lives of both myself and my brother Niall, who was first elected a TD in 1977. When we were in government, he would ring me up every morning and always begin with the words 'Two things'. He was invariably critical of our performance in government and used to name two things in the state of the country that he was unhappy about, having read the newspapers on that particular day. 'What are you going to do about it?' was what he was clearly asking. It got to the stage that I sometimes had to ask Annette to tell my father that I was out whenever he rang. Annette rang him at one time to tell him that there were mornings that I woke up in the best of form but, when I received his phone call with his two gripes, my mood invariably darkened. She begged him to stop as it was making her life a misery. To his credit, he was very contrite, and for at least a week there were no complaints from him, but it didn't last!

My father also had a tendency to ring me up after elections, when I would have polled very well and say, in his best put-down tone: 'My friends tell me it was all the "aul wans" of Dún Laoghaire who voted for you.' I used to reply that I didn't care who gave me their support and that 'aul wans' number ones were as valid as anyone else's. What he wanted to know was whether the 'intelligentsia' of Killiney, Carrickmines and Foxrock supported me.

BACK IN POWER BUT NOT AT THE TABLE

One of my running mates in the 1977 general election was Martin O'Donoghue. He had been a professor of economics in Trinity College Dublin until 1970, when Jack Lynch employed him as his economic adviser. The two men were very close and, just before the election, Lynch called me into his office and asked me to pull out all the stops to get O'Donoghue elected in Dún Laoghaire. This meant asking a portion of 'my' electorate – the voters I expected to give me their number ones – to give them to the new candidate instead. It is always a risky business sharing your vote like this, but I felt I had to do my utmost to win that elusive second seat and, after all, Jack Lynch had appointed me to the position of Chief Whip and Parliamentary Secretary to the Taoiseach last time around. My other running mate was John O'Connor, who died so tragically in the Buttevant train disaster in 1980.

As well as writing to the voters in certain areas of the constituency asking for their first preferences for O'Donoghue, I asked Annette to go out canvassing with him some of the time, because she was very well known in the constituency by now and he was not. That again sent out the obvious signal that I was asking for support for Martin O'Donoghue. In the event, my first-count vote was down some two thousand five hundred, but he polled creditably, getting just over four thousand first preferences. That proved good enough to get him elected.

This election was a bit of a triumph for the family, as my brother Niall was also elected in South County Dublin for the first time. Niall had found it very difficult to get nominated. He was clearly a very electable candidate, and this can prove more of a hindrance than a help at election conventions. He went on to carve out a very successful career in politics, both at home and abroad. He retired at the last

European election. Sadly he didn't get to enjoy his retirement as he died after a relatively short illness in October 2006. I still feel his loss very badly.

The 1977 general election proved a huge success for Fianna Fáil. We secured 50.6 per cent of the vote and returned with eighty-four Dáil seats out of 148. Our manifesto has often been attacked in hindsight, especially the abolition of motor tax and rates. My Dún Laoghaire running mate was largely responsible for the economic side of the manifesto, the aim of which was to create jobs and stem mounting unemployment. There is also no doubt that the wealth and farm taxes introduced by the Cosgrave coalition had been unpopular. The voting age had been reduced to 18 for the first time and a quarter of the electorate was under the age of 26. Our emphasis on youth employment certainly had an appeal to this sector of the voters.

Of course, Liam Cosgrave, my colleague in Dún Laoghaire, was now no longer Taoiseach. I can't say that I was sorry about this, but I always had a very good relationship with him during the years we both served the people of the constituency. Annette and I got on very well with both Liam and his wife Vera. They were always very kind to us in our younger days.

O'Donoghue's understanding of the economic challenge facing the country was basically sound. There was a recovery under way following the crisis of the mid-1970s, but he believed that it would not be enough to lead to major employment. What he was advocating was a gamble, as he admitted at the time, but it was soon shown to be failing. And the second oil crisis in 1979 destroyed whatever slim chance of success there might have been.

The large number of seats Fianna Fáil won in the general election caused the party leader some foreboding. As the results were being analysed on the night of the count, he remarked that it was often better if the majority was not quite so big. He was right to be apprehensive. The bigger the majority, the harder it is to maintain discipline. Another important point was that many new TDs had been elected. Few had ever been heard of outside their constituencies. But Charles Haughey was familiar with many of them, as a direct result of his full-scale tours of the constituencies in the early and mid-1970s.

When the time came for him to launch his bid for the leadership, he knew he could depend on their support. He knew them and, as time was to show, it's a pity that they did not know him.

Charlie Haughey was Minister for Health in the new Cabinet. George Colley was in Finance and Des O'Malley in Industry and Commerce. Martin O'Donoghue joined the elite band of TDs to be made full ministers on their first day in the Dáil. Not only that, but a completely new department was created for him: Economic Planning and Development. Martin genuinely believed that a TD should not involve himself in constituency work. To his way of thinking the role of TDs, and especially ministers, was to act as legislators, and their focus should be on the national, not the local. As a result of these views, he didn't last very long in the Dáil. I don't think he understood why he lost his seat, nor do I think anyone ever enlightened him.

When Jack Lynch had called me in to impress on me the urgency of getting Martin O'Donoghue elected in Dún Laoghaire, I understood there was a subliminal message there that if I succeeded, I would be given my first full ministry. After the election I was sitting in a room on the top floor of Leinster House with Padraig Faulkner, a TD for Louth since 1957 and twice a minister by 1977. The door opened and in came Jack Lynch. His words to the two of us were, 'Will you serve?' Again, I understood that to mean that we would both be in his Cabinet. When he left the room, Faulkner urged caution, but he agreed that it sounded promising for both of us.

Subsequently it did turn out well for him but not for me. I had been very hopeful because on the following Saturday, a few days before the Cabinet would be announced, Martin O'Donoghue told me that I was going to get one of the security ministries, either Justice or Defence.. Because of my lack of ministerial experience, I thought it more likely that Defence would be my portfolio.

We were at home on the Sunday evening when the phone went. It was Jack Lynch, and Annette, who had taken the call, presumed he was ringing to tell me what my new ministry was to be. But his news was far less heartening than that. He told me that he didn't have room for me on this occasion. The disappointment I felt was enormous. What I came to believe subsequently was that there was a big lobby for Bobby Molloy. He was not going to be included in the new Cabinet and I probably was, but George Colley and, I suspect, Des O'Malley lobbied for Molloy. I have no direct evidence to support this theory of mine but it is what I and others believe happened. Bobby became Minister for Defence.

The position I got was as a junior to Michael O'Kennedy at Foreign Affairs. His was something of a surprise appointment because, two years before, while shadowing the same portfolio, he had launched a policy initiative on Northern Ireland that reverted to old-style nationalist terms in that it called for 'an ordered withdrawal' by the British. The parliamentary party, for the most part, endorsed the policy, but it was less than helpful to Jack Lynch. O'Kennedy certainly had not been sure beforehand that he would be getting anything because I remember meeting him and his asking me if I had heard anything. It was to accommodate my disappointment that the title Minister of State was introduced; in other words, I would be known as 'Minister' rather than 'Parliamentary Secretary', the existing title for junior ministers at the time. In fact, when I was told that this would be my title, I understood that there would be only a small number of such positions in the new government and that there would be three ministerial levels: full ministers, ministers of state and parliamentary secretaries. But, as it turned out, all parliamentary secretaries were now to be called ministers of state.

I wasn't very happy in my time as the junior in Foreign Affairs. I was given very little to do and my role was rather a vague one. My work was mainly concerned with the European Community, which we had joined five years before. There hadn't been a parliamentary secretary in Foreign Affairs before; I was occupying a completely new position. I was left mostly with things O'Kennedy was too busy to do. So it often happened that I would get a phone call at the last minute telling me to attend a meeting in Brussels or some such place, and I would not have nearly enough time to brief myself on the subject to be considered at the meeting. All in all, it was a very difficult and unsatisfactory situation.

My main responsibility was for our involvement in the Council of Europe. It was founded as far back as 1949 and is thus a year or two older than what eventually became the European Union. But it is true to say that as the Common Market and then the European Economic

Community developed, the Council of Europe became less relevant. It would be for the most part a human rights forum, which is of course important in itself, but the EU probably should have subsumed it as time went on. It might seem harsh to describe it as such, but in reality it was mainly a talking shop.

The job I was given in relation to the Council of Europe involved quite an amount of travelling. During the last six months of 1979, Ireland had the European Community presidency, and this increased my workload to some extent. I was busy, but not engaged.

However, it wasn't all bad news for Annette and myself. August 1978 saw the birth, in the Rotunda, of our fifth and last child, Claire. She weighed in at 12lb 11oz, and the event was described in a small and incorrect headline in a Sunday newspaper – 'Monster boy born to Minister'. Now an elegant young lady and a newly qualified doctor, she still gets a lot of teasing about this and her brothers and sisters are particularly adept at picking their time. Another result of the incorrect note in the newspaper was that a party worker came in to visit Annette in hospital with the request to call the new baby Matt Talbot, to whom she had great devotion. Annette assured her that she would have been more than willing but that unfortunately the baby was a girl!

As well as being junior minister at Foreign Affairs, for a short time I was also Minister of State at the Department of Justice, where Gerry Collins was minister. My experience as the junior minister at this department was a happier one than at Foreign Affairs. Gerry was more inclined to be inclusive and to be specific about aspects of the work of the department that I might cover.

This contrast was all the more strange when one considers that O'Kennedy and I were contemporaries and had been through the Bar together. We had been at each other's weddings and when he and Breda got engaged we had given a party for them. I think someone said 'there are no friends in politics', and my experience as junior in Foreign Affairs might seem to bear that out: but I wouldn't agree with the statement as a principle, because I made some great friends in politics. The falling-out between us is indicative of the attitude and the atmosphere that existed at the time.

I remember saying jokingly to somebody who asked me about my role as understudy in Foreign Affairs that it was mainly a case of feeding the ducks in St Stephen's Green. My secretary, Declan Kelly, now the Irish ambassador in Ottawa, did his utmost to provide me with a full diary, even if he was making things up. He knew how frustrated I was having so little to do. So Declan would invent tasks for me in order to give me some sense of belonging and for that alone, I owe him a great debt of gratitude.

JACK GETS LYNCHED

I mentioned earlier that Jack Lynch had forebodings about the size of the Fianna Fáil majority that was returned at the 1977 general election. As subsequent events were to prove, he was right to have had those misgivings, especially as he had one particular opponent within the party who was determined not only to displace him as leader but also to humiliate him as much as possible in the process.

Charles Haughey was Minister for Health in the new government. One piece of legislation he had to introduce created a situation unique in the history of the Fianna Fáil party up to that time. He had to legislate for contraception, and in what he famously described as 'an Irish solution to an Irish problem' confined the availability of contraceptives to married couples who, if they wished to acquire contraceptives, had to do so by means of a prescription. It was a pretty conservative measure, all in all, but one which Jim Gibbons's conscience wouldn't allow him to support. He was then Minister for Agriculture and a very conservative Catholic and what he decided to do, in order to avoid voting against his own government and party, was simply not to turn up for the vote. Lynch did not discipline him for this action and it was the first time in the party's history that a TD, let alone a minister, was allowed to ignore the party whip.

Although we were close, Jim Gibbons hadn't discussed with me what he was going to do on this matter, nor did he refer to his action afterwards. It was not the sort of issue he was likely to discuss with me because he knew my view on the subject was very different from his own. Apart from his conservative Catholic stance and the fact that I was a younger man, we served very different constituencies: his was largely rural and conservative, mine urban and mainly liberal.

In 1978, as Minister for Finance, George Colley tried to introduce a two per cent income levy on farmers. This caused something of a backbench revolt in the party. There were, and to some extent still are, different strands of influence in the parliamentary party. One was the teacher strand, another the publican, and a third the farmer strand – not the big farmer element, which was more a part of the Fine Gael tradition, but the small farmer. Rural deputies saw Colley's proposal as an attack on the small farmer and he had to withdraw it in the face of their strong opposition.

Colley's retreat from imposing some form of limited taxation on farmers provoked massive protests from angry PAYE workers who felt – quite rightly, I believe – that they were carrying much too great a burden of the total amount of taxation being paid in the country. They took to the streets of Dublin in their tens of thousands to express their anger. These events served to weaken Jack Lynch's authority as leader.

Then, in June 1979, came the first direct elections to the European Parliament. Since October 1977, I had been responsible from time to time for piloting the European Assembly Elections Bill through the Oireachtas. It wasn't a contentious piece of legislation, because it had all-party support. There was a good electoral turnout (64 per cent) at those first Euro elections and Fianna Fáil did succeed in winning five of the fifteen seats, but its percentage of the vote was down by fifteen points on the 1977 general election. Neil Blaney, something of a Lynch nemesis, topped the poll as an Independent in the Connacht-Ulster constituency and Fianna Fáil finished behind Fine Gael there. The party also came in behind both Fine Gael and Labour in Dublin.

Haughey exploited the nervousness of Fianna Fáil TDs who knew the party couldn't possibly do as well in the next general election as we had in 1977. Things continued to go badly for the government, with a long-drawn-out postal strike and the second oil crisis in 1979, which led to long queues at petrol stations. The popularity of the government continued to wane. A combination of these events clearly influenced Jack Lynch's decision to retire. Although still popular with the electorate generally, he seemed to feel that he was losing control of the parliamentary party.

A number of people, both inside and outside the party, were working on Haughey's behalf. One of these was his special adviser, Brendan O'Donnell, who campaigned to persuade TDs to support his boss to be next leader of Fianna Fáil. I would consider O'Donnell to be in the same mould as a later faithful servant of Haughey, P. J. Mara. He was a pleasant fellow, who was sent by Haughey around the TDs to keep them happy and to keep them informed. I remember both O'Donnell and Mara with affection. They weren't triumphalist about their association with the 'great man', nor did they try to make capital out of it. Both men, in their attitude to Haughey, met those of us with different views with a sense of humour. We said frightful things to them about him – which I'm sure went back to him – but in the meantime it was taken in very good spirit.

Then there were the many TDs who were working either openly or discreetly for Haughey. One group was the so-called 'gang of five', which comprised Albert Reynolds, Seán Doherty, Mark Killilea, Jackie Fahey and Tom McEllistrim. Pádraig Flynn and Charlie McCreevy were also strongly pro-Haughey in those days, but one of his most effective supporters was Ray MacSharry, who was junior to George Colley at Finance. As such, he might have been expected to support his minister for the leadership. In fact, MacSharry was the first prominent member of the party to come out publicly in support of Haughey and, at the leadership election in December 1979, he proposed Haughey for the job.

One of the things that distinguished Flynn, Reynolds and MacSharry was that they were non-drinkers. Those of us who were fighting the cause for Colley (and later O'Malley) often stayed up late into the evening, having a drink and planning strategy, and sometimes the atmosphere would become less focused than it might have been. But the other camp were plotting hard and sharp over cups of tea and doing it extremely well.

George Colley believed that people knew his background and what he stood for. It would never have occurred to him to phone people personally and he would get others to do it on his behalf. He did not want to compromise himself in any way and he felt that if he contacted people personally and asked for their vote that that in some way implied that a quid pro quo would be expected from him in return. He wanted to stay at one remove from everybody, so that if successful, he would be in a totally independent position when it came to appointing a Cabinet. Lofty and laudable, perhaps, but no contest for the opposition, who had no such scruples.

Haughey would go into the Dáil restaurant and sit among the TDs, something that Colley seldom did. Bonhomie and backslapping were foreign to George. He was a man of the utmost integrity, and his approach to politics was totally different from his opponent's. It was certainly a very honourable attitude but it was not always very practical. His wife Mary, a highly intelligent woman, was an endless source of support to him.

Some of the views I have expressed on what motivated the Haughey supporters are purely speculative. Various suggestions have been made by commentators about their motivation. It has been said that they were all outsiders to one extent or another because the party establishment was firmly behind Colley. The comment has been made that they were self-serving, in the sense that they saw Haughey as their route to the inside track of party power. A third motive that has been ascribed to them is that they felt Fianna Fáil had moved too far away from its true republican roots and that Haughey was the man to bring the party back.

Whatever the truth of these interpretations, there is no doubt in my mind that they had total belief in their champion. They had the utmost faith in his ability and he certainly was an able man. They firmly believed in his greatness and were so loyal to him that they would have died in a ditch for him. I am, however, completely satisfied that they had no idea what was really going on at the time – things that have since come to light. I think it is too unfair to describe them as solely self-serving: it is very likely that some were influenced by his republican rhetoric and remained disappointed at the perceived inertia of the party under Lynch in supplying aid to the nationalists in the North.

In the actual leadership contest, George Colley got little support from TDs from west of the Shannon or the border counties. Haughey's arms crisis record did him no harm with western and border deputies and it cannot be denied that he did engage in his fair share of republican mumbo-jumbo. He hardly practised what he preached, particularly when he was in power. I do think that Charles Haughey would only associate with people whom he could control.

There are people who supported him at the time, who now say that he never influenced them and that they would speak up in Cabinet. The truth is that many of them were absolutely terrified of him and his apparent personal charm could turn crude and nasty if he felt the need to censure or bully.

While people like Síle de Valera, Billy Loughnane and Tommy McEllistrim had already applied some pressure by making anti-British speeches and statements, what really put the pressure on Jack Lynch was the loss of two by-elections in his native Cork in early November 1979. He had made up his mind to resign in 1980, but Colley and his closest advisers favoured an early contest, so that Haughey would not have time to organise. They little knew that Haughey was already well organised and had been for some time.

The two people who ran Colley's campaign were Des O'Malley and Martin O'Donoghue. Colley had the support of nine-tenths of the Cabinet, but it was among the backbenchers that he needed to win some backing. Neither O'Malley nor O'Donoghue had a close rapport with the backbenchers, because O'Malley had been on the front bench from a very early stage and O'Donoghue had become a minister on entering the Dáil and, besides, had been elected only two years before.

It was expected that Michael O'Kennedy would support George Colley and, when it became known that he had switched to Haughey, it came as an enormous blow to the Colley camp. It has been said that one reason for O'Kennedy voting for Haughey was that there had been a rumour doing the rounds the night before the vote that O'Malley and O'Donoghue had promised Foreign Affairs to me. I can categorically state that no such promise was made to me, but I was indeed aware of the rumour at the time. I do believe that something definitely happened to change O'Kennedy's mind. He himself contended that it had been his intention all along to vote for Haughey. However, there was some scepticism about this contention. In some ways, I believe O'Kenndy's action on this occasion was something that dogged him for the rest of his political days.

On a personal basis, after he switched his support unexpectedly to Charles Haughey I fell out with him. I lost touch with him for four or five years after that. I didn't speak to him – it was a bit silly really. Then I met him unexpectedly in the environs of Lenister House –

literally bumped into him – and we spoke. We have communicated with each other ever since but we are certainly not as close as we used to be. I used to visit his constituency a lot and thought his mother, who ran a small pub in Nenagh, a wonderful person. All that stopped and our relationship changed, like a lot of things that happened during the Haughey era. People fell out and members of the party simply were not at peace with each other. That was one of the many unfortunate Haughey legacies to Fianna Fáil.

Whereas Haughey had been campaigning for the leadership for at least two years, Colley campaigned hardly at all. His side greatly overestimated their level of support. They had probably been too long in power or in the upper echelons of the party and they had lost touch with the ordinary parliamentary-party members. There were some very decent people who supported Haughey. There were also some very mean-minded people who supported him – people who wouldn't speak to you in the corridor, who didn't want to have anything to do with you and who would be glad to see your political demise.

When the vote was over, George Colley and his supporters were both shocked and devastated. Mary Colley invited us all to lunch in their home in Palmerston Gardens in Rathmines. Annette and I got there early and we watched as George's supporters trooped into the house lugubriously, looking as if they were coming from a funeral. They were mostly members of the Cabinet and looked extremely downhearted. It would not be an exaggeration to say that the whole thing was something of a gloomfest. Included in the company was Ben Briscoe, who had been part of the Colley team. We had the meal and perhaps a glass of wine but it certainly was not an occasion for celebration.

Ben Briscoe left early and I subsequently heard from very good friends of ours who were at Haughey's celebrations that Briscoe turned up there and congratulated Haughey, trying to imply, presumably, that he had voted for him. Haughey does not seem to have been impressed and gave his visitor short shrift.

These same friends could tell me that Eamon Moore, nephew of Joe Moore, who owned the Private Motorists Protection Association (PMPA) insurance company, for which I had done legal work, was also at the Haughey bash. Eamon, who was the claims superintendent in the company and who had had a few drinks, said, within these friends' hearing, that I would never see another brief from the PMPA. However, nothing came of his veiled threat on this occasion, but during one of the 1982 challenges to the Haughey leadership, by which time I was doing a lot more work for PMPA, the issue arose again in a much more serious way.

CAST INTO THE OUTER DARKNESS

I knew perfectly well that my junior ministerial career was over once Charles Haughey became leader. I believe it is normal courtesy to contact ministers to inform them when they are being dropped, but I received no such courtesy. The three full ministers who were being axed – Jim Gibbons, Bobby Molloy and Martin O'Donoghue – also heard nothing about their fate, but in truth couldn't have been surprised. On the first day in the Dáil of the new leadership, I made it a point to sit up in the back benches, thus making it abundantly clear that I expected to be dropped.

There is one incident from the occasion that I will always remember and that is of a – for want of a better word – creepy Cork Fianna Fáil TD, coming into the Dáil bar and not having noticed me (which was, given my size, something of an achievement) and remarking to his colleague, 'There was one great thing that happened there tonight and it was that that bollocks Andrews wasn't made a minister.' I tipped him on the shoulder and said: 'That bollocks Andrews is right behind you!' The look on his face was priceless, and I was able to dine out on the story – with plenty of embroidery, of course – for a couple of weeks afterwards.

That was part of the atmosphere of the time. I went on to make a reasonable living at the Bar, but in the political world I was certainly out on a limb and felt that, to all intents and purposes, my career in politics had come to a sudden end. The atmosphere was different. Annette recalls coming into Leinster House to meet me. She often came in for a drink in the bar on Wednesday nights and, on this occasion, after the change of leadership, she saw people literally crossing the corridor to avoid her. Before this, people would greet her with a friendly question, such as 'Are you looking for himself?' Now it was as if people were afraid to be seen chatting with her. It was a curious combination of Kafka and Myles Na gCopaleen.

There was one particular occasion around this time when Annette and I went for a weekend to the Nuremore Hotel in Carrickmacross, County Monaghan. By coincidence, Ray Burke and his wife and family were staying there the same weekend. We arrived on the Friday evening and we saw them in the restaurant and went over to speak to them, and they were fairly friendly. The following evening, Annette suggested we invite them to meet us for a drink before dinner and she duly phoned their room. Ray's wife Anne answered and then went to consult Ray. She returned to say that they were going to eat in their bedroom and they seemed to stay out of sight for the rest of the weekend. It may be that they just did not want to be seen in our company. It may also be that they feared that word might get back.

It was a new experience for me in Fianna Fáil and it was not one I would describe as pleasant. One got used to being ostracised and to the feeling of being on the outside looking in. There was a definite feeling of 'them and us' around in the parliamentary party and I was saddened to see this happening to what had been such a united, cohesive and friendly family when I first joined.

BACKBENCHER AGAIN

With the change in leadership in Fianna Fáil, my return to the back benches and the loss of my ministerial salary, earning a living became even more pressing. I recall going into the Law Library just before Christmas 1979 and meeting Colm Condon SC, who had been Attorney General to Jack Lynch (I have a very vivid recollection of this occasion). At the time I hadn't got two halfpennies to rub together. I owed a large sum of money to the bank. We had overdrawn to the tune of some £10,000 during the period while I was a junior minister – a substantial sum in the late seventies.

I may have been talking to someone in the Library about my position. Anyway, it seems to have become known that I was broke. Colm Condon was concerned for me. He got me a brief from Good and Murray, from Noel Smith who was principal in that firm. Colm knew Noel Smith, who is since deceased, very well and the brief fee was £500. As it turned out, the case was settled.

I remember that Christmas well. Colm Condon's kindness put the turkey on the table, if that doesn't sound too Dickensian. I mention this event in some detail to show that politics was not terribly well paid at that time. One might have been a Minister for State but that didn't mean that one kept one's bank manager happy. Mr Haughey wasn't getting paid any more than any other minister at the time but was still, mysteriously, maintaining an amazingly extravagant lifestyle. We now know, of course, that by 1979 he owed Allied Irish Bank over £1 million, which makes my overdraft look rather insignificant. The very amenable bank agreed to write off £400,000 of the debt he owed them. And then he had extremely generous friends.

In any event, I went back into legal practice, having more time to devote to it now that I was a backbencher. From early 1980 onwards I managed to work up a fairly decent junior practice. An uneasy truce followed Haughey's victory in the leadership contest. Colley was given a veto over appointments to the departments of Justice and Defence. After his victory, Haughey had declared that Colley had pledged him support and loyalty. I'm pretty certain that this did not happen and, in a public speech in Baldoyle a short time afterwards, Colley made it clear that such a pledge had not been made by him at all.

Haughey's first ardfheis as leader, in February 1980, set the tone for the subsequent ardfheiseanna of his period of leadership. The ITGWU brass band piped him into the RDS, playing the classic patriotic ballad 'A Nation Once Again' and some 5,000 delegates gave him an ecstatic welcome. It was customary to display photographs of past party leaders around the ardfheis building and it struck me that during the Haughey years Jack Lynch's photo was consigned to the most obscure spot possible. I recall at some of those ardfheiseanna that Lynch's photo was relegated to the cloakroom corridors. It was as if he was being airbrushed out of Fianna Fáil history in the best traditions of the Soviet Union. As for the ardfheiseanna themselves, they were not about policy issues or motions or organisational questions, but adoration of the leader, as in the North Korea of today or Communist China at its worst. Of course, Haughey had quite a regard for Chinese leaders, stating at one stage that some of them ruled on into ripe old age, the implicit message of course being that he would like to emulate them.

I have to say that I found those ardfheiseanna quite upsetting. Brian Lenihan played the role of warming up the crowd before the leader's address. Indeed, some of the delegates didn't need too much warming up: if alcohol hadn't done the job, they were drunk with admiration for their hero anyway. The scene after he finished his leader's address was quite extraordinary. The song 'Rise and Follow Charlie' would be struck up and the cameras would focus on him, and some of the

TDs and senators would rush to get in behind him so that they would be in the shot. There would be terrible pushing and jostling to get into a prime position as near to him as possible. No, the ardfheiseanna weren't pleasant places to be in those days if you were in the anti-Haughey camp. I didn't experience any personal unpleasantness, because I stayed away until the leader's speech and, the moment it was over, I left again as unobtrusively as I had arrived. I made this late arrival and early departure because I didn't want to be the subject of any hostile attention from over-enthusiastic delegates.

Another extraordinary manifestation of Haughey's conception of himself was the collection of his speeches that Martin Mansergh assembled, edited and published in 1986. The book is entitled *The Spirit of the Nation* and it is quite a tome; indeed, something of a doorstop. I don't know who conceived of the title but it is an extraordinarily egotistical thing to imagine that your speeches constitute the spirit of the nation.

It is probably true to say that Haughey interfered a great deal in the running of departments other than his own, and this would be especially true in the case of the Department of Finance. His first act in office as Taoiseach was to abolish the department that had been created for Martin O'Donoghue and he did this on the morning O'Donoghue arrived in his department in Government Buildings. The staff of the department, many of whom had been hand-picked for their skills in the field of economics, were dislocated and many were relocated throughout the civil service. Some were subsumed into Haughey's own department, where he established an economics division to police the operation of all other departments in his government, because it was his government and he wanted there to be no doubt about it.

Michael O'Kennedy was his first Minister for Finance and he was soon rewarded with a promotion to Brussels as European Commissioner. His successor was Gene Fitzgerald, a person not previously noted for financial acumen. I don't think that Haughey held Fitzgerald in very high esteem and I would say that he felt free to interfere in the running of his department. The same would be true in relation to Foreign Affairs (where Brian Lenihan was minister), especially where matters relating to Northern Ireland were concerned. Power became centralised in the Department of the Taoiseach and this presidential style of government was both novel and arguably unconstitutional. It certainly did not appeal to me.

At the beginning of 1980, Ireland's national debt was seriously damaging the economy and, in January, the new Taoiseach gave a special television broadcast telling everyone in the country that they were all living beyond their means and would have to tighten their belts for the period of hardship ahead. He stated that the government would have to severely cut back its spending. In fact, his government did the very opposite, increasing public pay by thirty-four per cent in 1980 alone. Nowhere was this more evident than in the case of the pay award to teachers.

The government at first rejected as too high the pay rise recommended by a special arbitration board and talks followed at the Labour Court. The teachers adopted an entrenched position in these talks, which dragged on until Haughey instructed John Wilson, the Minister for Education, to give the teachers a rise higher than the recommended arbitration award. This led the arbitration board members to resign – understandable given that their position was rendered pretty ridiculous by the Taoiseach's action. The spending spree was financed by huge increases in taxation and borrowing, which had serious implications for the economy in the following years. This was the first real sign that the emperor truly had no clothes.

Haughey had a promising Anglo-Irish summit with Mrs Thatcher in December 1980: the joint communiqué afterwards announced that the 'totality of relationships' between Ireland and Britain would be considered in a number of joint studies. Unfortunately, he rather squandered the achievement shortly afterwards by declaring that the constitutional position of Northern Ireland within the United Kingdom was up for discussion. Brian Lenihan got even more carried away when he said that the issue of partition was about to be resolved and that a united Ireland was within sight in the decade ahead. This bombast only served to annoy Thatcher, who responded by saying her government had no intention of tampering with Northern Ireland's constitutional position. Such goodwill as had been hard won was squandered for a soundbite and in the belief that, as in many of his ventures, nobody would dare to stop the cheque, once it had been written.

Haughey had intended to call a general election in the spring of 1981, after the Fianna Fáil Ardfheis of that year, but the tragic fire in the Stardust ballroom in his own constituency, in which so many young people died, frustrated that plan. The ardfheis was postponed until April, but by that time the H-Block hunger strike was under way in the North and the election was put off again. The Dáil was finally dissolved at the end of May and the election held on 11 June. It was to be the first of three elections in eighteen months.

ELECTIONS AND HEAVES

Campaigning in Dún Laoghaire-Rathdown during the June 1981 election as a candidate of a party with this Taoiseach as leader was not easy. There was hostility towards Haughey in the constituency and this made the job of canvassing more difficult. However, some members of the constituency organisation were pro-Haughey and they had no problem about knocking on doors and defending his record. But some of our canvassers frequently met the response: 'Get another leader.' If you brought this message back to headquarters, you were told: 'Ah, I bet you those are just Fine Gael people saying that.' The Haughey supporters did not want to believe there was such a thing as the 'Haughey factor' out there operating against the possible success of Fianna Fáil candidates.

During the election, the Taoiseach came to the constituency one day to campaign in a shopping centre. We had to get cumainn members to be there to play the role of 'the public', as it were, and to meet and shake hands with him, because we were afraid that he would try to shake hands with people who would refuse to take his hand. So we made sure to have people strategically positioned so that the photographers would get their pictures. He simply wasn't liked in the constituency and he in turn didn't like Dún Laoghaire, always referring to it as Kingstown. At the odd social function that he attended in the constituency, he would loudly express the view that the north side of Dublin was much nicer than the south side and the people much friendlier. He didn't get the adulation in Dún Laoghaire that he was used to and that he felt was his due.

I am inclined to think that at least some of the support I got at this and other general elections was personal. Annette told me people said to her when she was canvassing, 'Well, I will vote for your husband but I won't be doing any more', meaning they would not be giving their next preferences to the other Fianna Fáil candidates on the ticket. To my embarrassment, I was sometimes referred to as 'the acceptable face of Fianna Fáil', and this description was applied to me especially in some parts of Dún Laoghaire-Rathdown.

The constituency was now an enlarged five-seater one, comprising the borough of Dún Laoghaire and, from County Dublin, the areas of Ballybrack, Shankill, Foxrock, Cornelscourt and part of Stillorgan. During the course of this election campaign, I got myself into some trouble with a very argumentative lady in Shankill. She was so annoyed that I didn't accept her point of view that she phoned the *Evening Herald* and a headline duly appeared to the effect that I had left the women of Shankill in tears. My director of elections was concerned about this and said we should do something to soften my image. So it was decided to take my ten-year-old daughter Mary out of school one morning. The two of us got into tracksuits and, accompanied by a photographer, went down to Dún Laoghaire pier where we jogged up and down for a few minutes. A nice photograph of father and daughter out jogging on the pier duly appeared in the paper. The following Sunday, we were at some official Mass where we met Liam Cosgrave. He jokingly commented that Andrews would stop at nothing to get a vote and that it was a disgrace to involve that poor child in this way! In fact, Mary enjoyed the whole thing immensely, especially having her photograph in the paper, although I did take his point.

My vote held up well in the election. I got around nine thousand five hundred first preferences and was elected on the first count, along with Seán Barrett of Fine Gael. Martin O'Donoghue also retained his seat but our two running mates, Hazel Boland and William Harvey, polled just around twelve hundred first preferences each and had no chance of being elected. Hazel Boland was a medical doctor who, for some reason or another, found it very difficult to get support from our constituency organisation. There was some resentment towards her, the source of which I am uncertain, because I got on well with her. This attitude towards her meant she had some difficulty getting canvassers to work with her. Apart from getting little or no support from the organisation, she didn't seem to have a personal election team working with her either. Anybody seeking election needs family and friends to row in behind them. She didn't seem to realise that she would need this rather than relying on party support.

Bill Harvey was an auctioneer and an excellent councillor: he is quite a character. His wife Mary, a lovely woman, was a nurse and a very good businesswoman. She owned a number of successful nursing homes in the constituency. She adored her husband and provided him with anything he might want. One of her presents to him was a Rolls Royce, in which he used to go round the constituency. The car's boot was well furnished with alcohol and Bill would open the boot from time to time and help canvassers to a drop of something to sustain them during the canvassing. A very generous man, he would offer a drink to whoever was around when the boot-opening ceremony occurred. Bill is also a great raconteur and may have spent as much time storytelling as canvassing.

The June 1981 election was lacking in zest and never really caught fire. The tragedy of the H-Block hunger strike overshadowed it, two of the participants, Patsy O'Hara and Raymond McCreesh, dying on the day the election was called. Despite this, the issue that dominated on the doorstep was the economy. It was unarguable that inflation, unemployment and borrowing had increased substantially since the last election and there was much dispute about how to tackle these problems. The result of this election was so close that, in the fifteen days between the announcement of the final figures and the reassembly of the Dáil, it was uncertain who would form the next administration. As it turned out, Garret FitzGerald was elected Taoiseach of a Fine Gael–Labour coalition, which depended on the support of Independents like Jim Kemmy from Limerick East and Seán Dublin Bay-Rockall Loftus from Dublin North East.

My father, although much older than Garrett FitzGerald, always had a soft spot for him. He held the view – which I shared – that FitzGerald was a man of complete integrity. He was and is extremely bright. One of his endearing features is that he speaks too fast – it's as if his brain runs ahead of his speech – something from which

Bertie Ahern also suffers. As well as being a successful politician he is a writer and commentator of considerable note.

Fine Gael owe him much and they have never come near to returning to the heady days they enjoyed under Garrett's leadership and the seventy seats. However, in a way his leadership was doomed to failure. He had the weakness of many intellectuals in that he was not good at practical politics and his political judgement was quite often off kilter.

On a personal level he is a very likeable man. His devotion to his late wife Joan, who was an invalid for much of her life, was remarkable. On one occasion we had personal experience of his kindness. We were travelling on the ferry from Le Havre to Rosslare with our children at the end of a summer holiday. By coincidence Garrett and Joan were on the same trip, as was the late Brian Lenihan.

We had a terrible crossing in appalling weather – gale force winds – and the boat felt as though it was being tossed about like a cork all night. We all felt miserable – most of us quite sick.

Next morning, things weren't much better, but my daughter Mary, never one to miss a meal, insisted on having breakfast. Everyone else, including myself, was lying miserably in their bunks so Annette bravely got up to take her to the restaurant. The only other people there were Garrett and Joan. They asked Annette and Mary to join them. They already had their food so Annette struggled over to the buffet to get something to eat. When they sat down Mary immediately spotted something Joan had – I think it was fruit – and decided she wanted it. Annette was past moving again so Garrett hopped up and got Mary whatever she wanted. Mary immediately knew that she was on to a good thing and had Garrett running back and forth giving in to her demands for the next ten minutes or so. Annette was too sick to do anything about it.

When they finally left the restaurant, who should they run into but Brian Lenihan, who was in great form. He had just been enjoying the air while doing two laps of the upper deck. Before that he had had a hearty Irish breakfast. What a wonderful man!

After the election it was a return to the back benches for me, this time on the Opposition side of the Dáil. While the new government tried to tackle the national debt, Haughey attacked their approach as deflationary and monetarist, which earned him some criticism from within Fianna Fáil itself, most notably from an erstwhile supporter, the Kildare TD Charlie McCreevy. The latter made his disillusionment with his leader's views on the economy public in an interview in the *Sunday Tribune*. As a result, he lost the Fianna Fáil whip in the Dáil and became an Independent for a time.

The first FitzGerald coalition fell suddenly after just six months in office. Its approach on economic issues had been to increase taxes in order to reduce the runaway national debt. This meant Fine Gael had to abandon most of its 1981 election promises to cut taxes. The government fell in late January 1982 over its budgetary proposals to impose VAT on clothes and footwear and to abolish some of the food subsidies. The Independent TDs Kemmy and Loftus, who hitherto had supported the FitzGerald government, refused to support that budget.

The February 1982 election could not have come at a worse time for me personally. We had needed to move house because we now had five children, and there simply wasn't enough space in the bungalow we lived in in Oakley Grove in Blackrock. After the election of the previous June, we had put our house on the market and we bought an old house on Glenart Avenue in Blackrock. It had been divided into flats, and needed a lot of work done to turn it into a family home. So there was a period when we had no place to live and Annette's brother, Pete Briquette – real name Paddy Cusack – of the Boomtown Rats, had a small apartment, which he lent us. It had no phone. Three of the children stayed with three different friends of ours, so they had to be collected and taken to and from school every day.

In the midst of all this bedlam, the election was called. Annette and I were less than grateful to Jim Kemmy and Seán Dublin Bay-Rockall Loftus. It wouldn't be easy campaigning without a proper home and especially without our own phone in those pre-mobile phone days. Trying to deal with builders, and with children scattered all over the place, were less than ideal circumstances in which to run a campaign to get re-elected. I couldn't involve myself in the house situation once the election was called and Annette couldn't involve herself in my election campaign because she was so busy with the house, the builders and children. Despite the lack of organisation – and we really had little resembling what could be called an organisa-

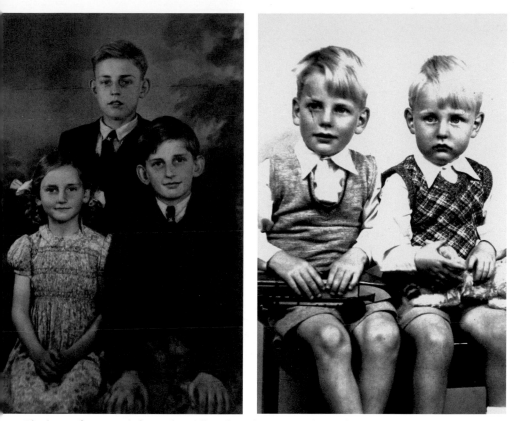

Clockwise from top left: With Niall and Catherine; With Hugh; With my mother outside Dublin Zoo. I'm on her right and Niall is on her left. Christopher is far left.

COLLINGWOOD CUP WINNERS. 1955.

BACK ROW: TERRY McCABE. JOHNNY DOOLEY. DAVE ANDREWS. DERMOT ROONEY. JOE KINNERN. VINY COYNE.
FRONT: LARRY CONNEELY. KEVIN O'BYRNE. DON McQUILLAN. WILLIE BURKE. MICHAEL MURRAY.

Winners of Collingwood Cup in 1955. I'm third from left, back row.

With my parents the day I was called to the Bar.

My father imparting advice to Annette on our wedding day
at Castlerahen Church, Ballyjamesduff.

The day I was first elected with Lionel Booth, T.D. – 8th April 1965.

Niall congratulating me on the day of the
first sitting of the 17th Dail, 1965.

New Fianna Fáil TDs of the 17th Dáil with Taoiseach Seán Lemass, April 1965.

With President de Valera in Áras an Uachtaráin.

Taking a break from the 1977
campaign with Mary.
Below: Electioneering in
Dún Laoghaire Market.

With election worker Mickey Byrne at the count.

With Niall in Moore Street during my first European election campaign.

With President Hillery and Annette in Áras an Uachtaráin.
Below: Fianna Fáil/Labour Cabinet in 1993.

tion for this election – things worked out all right. My first-preference vote was down by around fifteen hundred, the lowest I had secured since my first election to the Dáil, but given both my personal and the party circumstances, with Haughey as leader, that wasn't too bad.

In truth, the leadership of the Fianna Fáil election campaign had been less than distinguished. On the night of the dissolution of the Dáil and in his first press conference the following day, Haughey had dismissed the 'obsession' with foreign borrowing and had rejected both the central strategy and the main details of the budget of John Bruton, Minister for Finance in the short-lived coalition. But he was forced to back down from this position by senior colleagues such as Colley and O'Malley and especially Martin O'Donoghue, his newly appointed spokesman on Finance. Within a few days, Haughey had committed Fianna Fáil to the same levels of borrowing and the same budget deficit as the outgoing government.

Credibility was a major factor in this election and Fine Gael and Labour stressed, with some success, that the main question regarding credibility was the Fianna Fáil leader's own capacity and character. The 'Haughey factor' was no longer just a Dún Laoghaire thing – it was widespread. Some senior party candidates as well as party workers expressed the opinion that they would undoubtedly win the election but for the public perception of their leader. Indeed, some polls showed a strong contrast between the appeal of Haughey and FitzGerald to their own party supporters: one remarkable poll showed that a quarter of Fianna Fáil respondents preferred the Fine Gael leader as Taoiseach to their own leader. So, with the disarray in my personal circumstances militating against running an efficient, well-organised campaign, and with such deep hostility in my own constituency to the leader of my party (in Dún Laoghaire there was a swing of around five per cent away from Fianna Fáil to Fine Gael–Labour), a decrease of some fifteen hundred in my first preferences wasn't such a disaster. Martin O'Donoghue's first-preference vote also held up and he was re-elected, but our other running mate, Claire Ó Méalóid, secured only about nine hundred and fifty votes on the first count and had no hope of reaching the quota. Claire, married to the RTÉ Irish-language broadcaster Padraig Ó Méalóid, was a very good Fianna Fáil activist, but there is a difference between party activism and electability.

The overall result of the February 1982 election was that Fianna Fáil won eighty-one seats, three short of an overall majority, but three ahead of the combined Fine Gael–Labour total. This meant that Independents and smaller parties would again decide who formed a government. The result was a disappointment for Fianna Fáil, given the circumstances in which the short-lived Fine Gael–Labour coalition had collapsed, and led to the first of the challenges to Haughey's leadership. There were to be two more before the year was out.

Well-known anti-Haughey candidates, such as Jim Gibbons in Kilkenny and Joe Walsh in Cork, who had both lost their seats in June 1981, had now been returned to the Dáil, and in a television interview on the night of the count, Gibbons said that he expected the parliamentary party would discuss the issue of the leadership before the House reassembled. Haughey moved quickly to see off any threat to his position by bringing forward the parliamentary party meeting to which Gibbons was referring. This meant that his opponents within the party had to move quickly. Des O'Malley was to be the candidate nominated to take on Haughey. Seamus Brennan and Martin O'Donoghue organised O'Malley's campaign. Soundings that they took among a wide range of the party's TDs made them optimistic and the media began to forecast a close-run thing and even victory for O'Malley.

I did not share their optimism, knowing as I did how Mr Haughey operated. Some of the TDs listed in the print media as O'Malley supporters were certainly not his supporters at all and were obviously acting as stalking horses. Others, when they were named publicly, began to feel the pressure brought to bear on them by the Haughey side and their own constituency organisations. In fact, some of the media speculation, especially that in the *Irish Independent*, was completely wide of the mark, although there is no doubt either that some TDs had been subjected to threats and intimidation. Ray MacSharry, a key figure in the leader's camp, warned during a radio interview that the Fianna Fáil organisation would never forgive any elected member who voted against the incumbent.

Pádraig Faulkner, an honourable man, was one of the first to speak at the much-anticipated parliamentary party meeting and, to my surprise, he urged O'Malley not to go ahead with the challenge, because of the damage it would do to the party. Others spoke in a similar vein, but it was Martin O'Donoghue's intervention that proved decisive. Once he, too, said there should be no contest, it was obvious that the O'Malley group knew there was no chance of success.

One possible explanation for O'Donoghue's crucial intervention is that he was inclined to take an awful lot on himself without being able to see what he proposed through to a finish. I was very disappointed with his intervention on this occasion. I wondered where it was coming from, but never discovered the answer to that question. I suspect that it was just his own personal assessment of the situation. Martin was a very fine man in many ways – upright, kind, intellectually brilliant – but his political judgement sometimes concerned me. We had gone into that meeting, the adrenaline was pumping, and I was looking forward to making it clear where I stood and to voting. Then the whole thing collapsed.

Fianna Fáil went back into government, thanks to the deals Haughey did with the three Workers' Party deputies but most of all with the Dublin Central Independent TD, Tony Gregory. This so-called 'Gregory deal' committed huge sums of taxpayers' money to schemes for what was admittedly a disadvantaged part of inner city Dublin. Doing deals of this nature has, in fairness, become part of the political landscape, but I always felt as a backbench government TD that deals of this nature placed us at a distinct disadvantage in terms of constituency delivery, particularly for TDs in the same constituency as one of these Independents. Understandably the government TD feels that he is merely lobby fodder in this context.

The nine-month 1982 Haughey-led government is referred to as the GUBU government, from the acronym coined by Conor Cruise O'Brien: grotesque, unbelievable, bizarre and unprecedented, words that Haughey was inordinately fond of using. The term captures well the series of mishaps, some self-inflicted, through which his government seemed to stagger.

The first occurred on the very day of the February election, when Haughey's election agent, the likeable Pat O'Connor, was arrested on a charge of double voting. Although he was subsequently acquitted of the charge, he was often referred to thereafter as Pat Pat O'Connor. Because he was also Haughey's solicitor and close friend, the affair was damaging to the Taoiseach's reputation.

Next up was the 'stroke' of offering the vacant European Commissionership to Richard Burke of Fine Gael, thus reducing the number of Opposition seats by one. Burke accepted the position, and a Dublin West by-election followed, which Haughey was confident of winning. The by-election was held in the midst of the Falklands or Malvinas War and Haughey's manoeuvrings on that issue, by opposing the British invasion of the Falklands, were interpreted by many as playing the green card in order to gain an advantage in the by-election. I'm not sure how much weight this interpretation should be given in light of our traditional neutrality on such questions but, if Haughey thought that what happened far away in the South Atlantic would have any impact on Dublin West, he was sadly mistaken. Fine Gael won the by-election and his 'stroke' was seen to backfire badly.

Ray MacSharry had blithely forecast, when he took over as Minister for Finance in the new government, that the former administration's 'doom and gloom' would be replaced by 'boom and bloom'. His officials soon convinced him of the harsh realities of the economic situation and, after the Dublin West debacle, the rest of the Cabinet took note of this advice, spending was reined in, and *The Way Forward* was published as a strategy for coping with the spiralling public debt. But GUBU had not yet run its course.

What actually gave rise to the term GUBU – and, despite Haughey's penchant for overstatement, he was probably not exaggerating unduly when he used the adjectives 'grotesque, unbelievable, bizarre and unprecedented' to describe it – was the discovery of the murderer Malcolm MacArthur in the Dalkey apartment of the Attorney General Paddy Connolly. The latter happened to be very friendly with Brenda Little, who was MacArthur's girlfriend at the time. Connolly allowed him to stay in his apartment as he was told he was going through a bad time just then – in other words, it was a kind and totally innocent gesture. Nevertheless, he had to resign from his position as Attorney General.

I have always thought what happened to Paddy Connolly was most unfair. In the normal course of events, Attorneys General would go on to the Bench, and I have always felt that he should have been given a *laissez-passer* and should have received a judicial appointment from a subsequent Fianna Fáil government. But that didn't happen. He was left aside, which was wrong because he was completely blameless for that extraordinary event which happened in August 1982. Paddy Connolly was a decent man who suffered badly for making a kind gesture. He was then and remains one of the sharpest legal minds in the Law Library and would have been a real asset to the Bench.

Seán Doherty, Minister for Justice during the GUBU period, also made the news the following month, for all the wrong reasons. When his state car crashed in Kerry, efforts were made to hush up the incident, and this gave rise to all sorts of lurid rumours. The hullabaloo that followed certainly didn't do the government's reputation any good. Then there was the so-called 'Dowra affair', when a case against Doherty's brother-in-law, Garda Nangle, at Dowra District Court in County Cavan was dismissed because a vital witness didn't turn up. The charge against Nangle was assault against a man called McGovern and he (McGovern) was the vital witness who didn't or, as it happened, couldn't turn up. The reason was that he was detained by the RUC on the other side of the border. There was a suggestion at the time that this witness was detained to prevent him giving evidence.

There is one memory I have in relation to Doherty that has always stayed with me as something of an anomaly. Although he was Minister for Justice, he said that because he was also a TD he was perfectly entitled, in his capacity as TD, to make representations to the Department of Justice – in other words, to himself. So he was entitled to lobby himself on behalf of his constituents; otherwise they would be disadvantaged because they would not have a public representative to act on their behalf. It was an interesting point of view. How this worked in practice remains a mystery to me.

However, I always found Seán Doherty a very personable individual. He obviously fell under the Haughey spell and there is little doubt that he was doing his master's bidding. He was possessed of a bright, lively disposition. Like so many others, he died too young.

These events of August and September led to a second challenge to Haughey's leadership when on 1 October 1982 Charlie McCreevy put down a motion of no confidence for the parliamentary party meeting due on 6 October. Des O'Malley was away on holiday in Spain at the time and he rushed home to take part in the anti-Haughey campaign, although he wasn't happy with the timing. Both he, as Minister for Trade, Commerce and Tourism, and Martin

O'Donoghue, as Minister for Education, decided to resign from the Cabinet, as they would be supporting the McCreevy motion.

Haughey went on radio to say that he would be demanding a roll-call vote on the motion, so that the dissidents could be identified and, it is to be presumed, dealt with accordingly in the aftermath. He declared that Fianna Fáil wanted to get back to the situation where we had 'the strength that derives from discipline' and he said that he would ensure that discipline would be enforced. It was during this interview that he quoted the Seán MacEntee saying, 'Go dance on somebody else's grave.' The crux of this leadership vote was whether the ballot would be secret or open: the anti-Haughey lobby wanted it secret but his supporters were determined on an open, roll-call vote.

At seven o'clock on the morning of the leadership contest, I got a call from Mr Joe Moore, chief executive of the Private Motorists Protection Association (PMPA). This was the insurance company for which I acted as a junior barrister. The bulk of its business was given over to insuring personal injuries. My role was as a defence counsel for the company. I did very well out of my association with PMPA in my practice. I admired Joe Moore for what he was trying to do to provide cheaper car insurance for the Irish motorist at the time. He failed in his efforts and his company subsequently lost its way.

The seven-o'clock call was very much to the point:

'Is that you, David?'

'Yes, you have the right number.'

'I'm calling you in connection with today's vote. You know, David, of my support for Fianna Fáil and my belief in Mr Haughey?'

'Yes, Mr Moore, I am aware of your devotion to the leader.'

'I know that you are not Charlie's strongest supporter, but I would be expecting you to be doing the right thing today. Will you be doing the right thing, David?'

'Yes, Mr Moore, I will be doing the right thing.'

The conversation ended with a number of pleasantries. I was rather shocked at the tone of this call. There were rumours of much intimidation going on at the time to bring people into line, insofar as voting for the leader was concerned. My experience provides at least some evidence that this was indeed the case.

Going into the parliamentary party meeting that morning, I happened to meet Mr Haughey, and he turned to me with the words:

'You will be doing the right thing, David?' I put his words down to a coincidence of language between himself and Joe Moore.

The atmosphere on the day itself was tense, but the proceedings were conducted in an orderly manner. McCreevy explained he had put down the motion because of the lowering of political standards that had taken place, because of the mismanagement of the economy and because the party had failed to win an overall majority in two elections in a row. He said it was time to get decency back into the party. Haughey, when he spoke, defended his record but he did so somewhat nervously. There were frequent pauses as he sought the right words or consulted his notes. He referred to the enormous problems that the serious economic recession had thrown up. A lot of hard work had gone into *The Way Forward*, he said, and his government should be given the chance to put it into practice. McCreevy's motion he described as divisive, with the potential to inflict serious damage on Fianna Fáil.

Many of the TDs, senators and MEPs present spoke, so the meeting dragged on throughout the day and into the night. In the course of my own contribution, I pointed out that I thought the then leader wasn't doing the party any good. I said that he was a man of great ability but that he was basically giving the party a bad name and losing it support. Deputies like Faulkner and O'Kennedy called for a secret vote. I too favoured a secret vote but have to say that it didn't matter to me whether the vote was secret or open. I had made it clear how I was going to vote and would do so whether in secret or openly. But perhaps other TDs, for various reasons, didn't look at the situation in the way I did. When this question of the voting procedure was put to a roll-call vote, twenty-seven were in favour while fifty-three were against. When the McCreevy motion was then openly voted on, the margin was fifty-eight to twenty-two in favour of Haughey. This gave birth to the famous 'Club of Twenty-Two'. Of course there was no such club; this was merely the name given by the journalists to those of us who voted against Haughey. However, we were clearly identified and, as I had done the right thing and voted for the motion of no confidence in the leadership, I was immediately removed from the panel of junior barristers of the PMPA and lost a major source of my income overnight.

Having just bought a new house, this was quite a blow. My legal practice was somewhat 'all eggs in one basket' by now, the basket being the PMPA. This was not a good idea at the Bar. We had an extremely worrying six months or so, but then news of my predicament became known and the situation was brought to Charlie Haughey's attention. In fairness, he did show surprise and very shortly thereafter I was restored to the PMPA panel. However, it was a worrying time.

The scenes that followed the end of the long meeting did little credit for Fianna Fáil's reputation. The mood among some Haughey supporters waiting outside was ugly . Some of them had been drinking for most of the day, so much so that gardaí tried to persuade Charlie McCreevy to leave Leinster House by a side entrance. He bravely told them that he was going out the same way he had come in. For his pains, he was followed across the car park, kicked and jostled and called a 'bastard' and a 'blueshirt'. When gardaí finally managed to get him into his car, the crowd surrounded it and banged on the roof, continuing to hurl insults at him as he drove out of the front gates of Leinster House. The papers were right to describe the scene as 'disgraceful'.

Jim Gibbons was also subjected to appalling treatment. He was jostled and shouted at and one heckler actually struck him a glancing blow, so that he almost fell to the ground. He was justified in referring afterwards to a 'Nazi fascist element' in the party. Such people had little interest in free speech or freedom of assembly or expression. Jim suffered a severe heart attack shortly after that disgusting attack on him in Leinster House. In fact for the rest of his life he suffered from ill health and had a number of heart attacks and strokes and, at the time of his death in 1997, his son said that he had never recovered from the cowardly assault on him that night.

In the aftermath of this dreadful incident, new swivel doors were fitted to the Dáil to prevent mobs pushing their way into the parliament building. The television cameras captured the shameful scenes of that night, scenes that probably did a lot more damage to the government than anything that had occurred during the day. Opinion polls taken shortly afterwards showed deep public disenchantment with the Haughey administration. The sudden death of Billy Loughnane, a Fianna Fáil deputy from Clare, on 18 October, and the hospitalisation of Jim Gibbons the following day, left the government totally dependent on the support of Gregory and the Workers' Party. When *The Way Forward*, which contained proposals for substantial cuts in public spending, was published, they withdrew their support and we faced into our third election in eighteen months.

The election was held on 24 November and the electorate was less than grateful to Fianna Fáil for the second election to be held in a winter month within the same year. The people clearly blamed the government for this election, so the party candidates were in something of a no-win situation from the outset. The economy, which clearly was the major concern for most people at the time, didn't figure as an issue in the election because both Fianna Fáil and Fine Gael were offering essentially the same diagnosis and treatment. So the early part of the election was dominated by the baneful demand for a referendum on abortion, a demand to which both the big parties acceded far too quickly, a response that was to return to haunt them in the future. In Dún Laoghaire, interest in the proposed referendum was pretty limited and I did nothing to try to encourage a different approach.

Abortion was a divisive and contentious issue right across the country. Despite the general perception of Dún Laoghaire as a liberal constituency – and by and large it probably is – it had its conservative areas as well. It was put about that Andrews was a liberal and was 'soft' on abortion, and I'm sure this talk did me some damage and contributed to some extent to the drop in my vote. It was an extraordinary issue to figure so prominently in a general election and one that was really a matter for the individual conscience of each elector and each elected representative but, regrettably, that wasn't the way it turned out. I would be against abortion as a general practice, but I believe that it should be available in exceptional circumstances – particularly where the mother's life is at risk, and also in clearly established cases of rape.

Anglo-Irish relations and Northern affairs arose as a surprising – and contorted – issue in the second half of the campaign. Fianna Fáil tried to undermine Garret FitzGerald's credibility by suggesting collusion with British intelligence via the Duke of Norfolk, and that his call for an all-Ireland police force would lead to the RUC policing our streets. This playing of the green card may have had some effect in the border constituencies, where we already had probably as many seats as we were going to get, but elsewhere, and especially in Dún Laoghaire, such arrant nonsense did us serious harm. In my own campaign, I concentrated on what really mattered to the people in my constituency at the time: securing some halfway decent living for themselves and their families in extremely difficult economic circumstances.

Despite the less than propitious circumstances, I succeeded in getting re-elected reasonably comfortably. My first-preference performance was down, admittedly, but by fewer than three hundred votes, which showed that my support base was pretty solid. It also showed, I believe, that I was right to have voted against the Haughey leadership once again. Martin O'Donoghue's first preferences fell by nearly three thousand and he lost his seat. I've already mentioned that Martin didn't believe in constituency work, so he didn't have that base to fall back on in the unfavourable circumstances that pertained for the party nationally. Our constituency director of elections for this particular contest was the late Ray Burke (not the minister and TD from Dublin North of the same name). On the day of the count he and O'Donoghue were sitting chatting – at that stage it must have looked as if there was a possibility that the seat might still be held – and Ray said to him that if things went his way in the various counts and he retained the seat, he would simply have to do constituency work. But O'Donoghue responded that he hadn't the slightest intention of changing his attitude. There was nothing lazy about him; he just genuinely believed that it was not part of the role of a TD to carry out constituency work – that was the job of the local councillor. It's a point of view, of course, but one that has little validity. Deputies like Conor Cruise O'Brien, David Thornley and Justin Keating didn't think much of constituency work either, and all three lost their seats.

To disregard constituency work is a rather lofty and precious attitude and one that doesn't work in Ireland. If you sit in a somewhat rundown little room, no matter who you are, minister or whoever, eyeball to eyeball with people, and listen to the difficulties they are having with their medical card or their differential rents or whatever, you understand the realities a lot better than if you just read reports. I don't believe it is any harm at all for ministers to have to do clinics. The number of votes one gets from clinics is probably grossly exaggerated, because not that many people turn up to them and it is usually the same people who keep coming back. What matters is the availability factor and that is something that is very important to your constituency organisation. Organisation members want their TD to be visible.

To return to the November 1982 election, the other two candidates for Fianna Fáil in Dún Laoghaire-Rathdown were Lady Valerie Goulding and Owen Hammond. Lady Goulding, who died a few years ago, is probably best known as a co-founder of the Central Remedial Clinic in Dublin and a campaigner for the rights of disabled people. She was appointed to the Senate by Jack Lynch in 1977 and Haughey, a close friend of hers, reappointed her in 1979. It was his idea to have her contest the general election in Dún Laoghaire and she was added to the ticket. In the difficult circumstances in which the election was called, and given her lack of experience, she polled a respectable two thousand five hundred first preferences, twice as many as the well-known John de Courcy Ireland and as Eamon Gilmore, who was then of the Workers' Party. Lady Valerie was a delightful person but she had no hope of getting elected. Owen Hammond, who sadly died recently while still in his 50s, was a Fianna Fáil councillor in the constituency. Despite a good campaign he got less than nine hundred first preferences. Owen, like Bill Harvey, was an excellent councillor and both were good pals of mine.

Nationally, this election was something of a high-water mark for Fine Gael. That party won seventy seats over all, only five short of the Fianna Fáil total, and in Dún Laoghaire they succeeded in taking three of the five seats. In Dublin, there was a drop of four per cent in the Fianna Fáil vote and the party found itself outvoted by Fine Gael here for the first time ever. That we took just one in five seats in my Dún Laoghaire constituency reflected the general trend, but of course I, as the senior incumbent of my party in the area, had to bear the brunt of the blame for failing to win a second seat. It also has to be said that Fine Gael engaged in a skilful vote-splitting exercise to get three out of the five seats.

A coalition was formed with Garrett FitzGerald as Taoiseach and Dick Spring as Tánaiste. I returned to the back benches, resumed my role as a constituency deputy and continued with my humanitarian interests, such as campaigning on behalf of the Birmingham Six and the Maguires. Not surprisingly Mr. Haughey once more failed to make me an offer to come on to his front bench. I hadn't held my breath!

THE LAST ATTEMPT TO FAIL

The dismal election performance was quickly followed by another blow to Fianna Fáil prestige. In late January 1983 the new Minister for Justice, Michael Noonan, revealed that his predecessor, Seán Doherty, had authorised the tapping of the phones of political correspondents Geraldine Kennedy and Bruce Arnold. He also disclosed that the previous October, when they had both been government ministers, Ray MacSharry had borrowed Garda equipment to bug a conversation he had with Martin O'Donoghue. During that conversation, O'Donoghue had suggested that money would be available for any member of the parliamentary party who was supporting Haughey because they were in financial difficulties.

Mr Haughey was, of course, quick out of the blocks to deny any involvement in the phone tapping. He stated that neither he as Taoiseach nor the government as a whole knew anything at all about such activities. He particularly dismissed the suggestion that the taps might have had anything to do with his leadership problems. But in a front-page article in the *Sunday Press*, Geraldine Kennedy pointed out that the previous July, he had asked the publisher of the *Sunday Tribune*, where she had then worked, about her sources, and her phone began to be tapped shortly after that.

A special party meeting was held on that Sunday to discuss the extraordinary revelations, at which Haughey was very much on the defensive. He had already said in public that there was no justification for the taps but now he argued that Doherty had acted because 'national security' was being threatened by 'Cabinet leaks'. When Pearse Wyse asked what leaks, he replied that, for example, the party's farm plan had appeared in the *Farmers' Journal*. This provoked a chorus of laughter and Wyse pointed to the inconsistency of tapping the phones of journalists in the *Sunday Tribune* and *Irish Independent*.

When the Dáil reconvened a few days later, there was widespread speculation that Haughey would step down. The *Irish Press* had the banner headline: 'Haughey on brink of resignation'. There was extensive coverage of his career on the inside pages; his political obituary was being written. Michael O'Kennedy had begun to canvass openly to succeed him and Des O'Malley soon joined him. There were rumours that Haughey had written his letter of resignation and would formally announce his going at the parliamentary party meeting of 27 January. All the national dailies were predicting that he was finished. At the parliamentary party meeting, Ben Briscoe proposed that standing orders be suspended so that the leadership could be discussed. Haughey objected but was unable to prevent debate. He declared, however, that 'a vindictive press' was not going to drive him out of office and that he would take his own decision in his own time. I think most of us present understood this to mean that he intended to step down within a few days. Ray Burke argued strongly that Haughey should not suffer the humiliation of being told to go straight away and should be allowed the dignity of choosing his own time. His opponents allowed him this breathing space – a charitable but naive reaction.

This meeting was not without its moments of high drama – or farce, as some people might have considered it. An emotional Ben Briscoe told Haughey it was time for him to go and blurted out, 'I love you, Charlie.' Haughey replied, 'I love you too, Ben.' At the back of the room, I groaned 'I hope the papers don't hear about this.' Of course, it appeared in the *Irish Press* next day. I recall another prominent TD, who had been a minister for a long time, getting to his feet and almost breaking down in tears. I referred to him – perhaps uncharitably – as a 'cry-baby', and that found its way into the newspapers as well, though my name wasn't actually given in connection with the remark. These extraordinary incidents are indicative of the terrible tension people felt under at the time.

An internal committee of inquiry was set up to look into the phone-tapping and bugging incidents. It was chaired by the party chairman, Jim Tunney, and the party Chief Whip, Bertie Ahern, was a member. O'Kennedy and I were also appointed because we were barristers. From the very outset, Tunney showed where he stood by declaring that all the evidence pointed to the leader knowing absolutely nothing about any tapping or bugging – and this was before evidence was even considered. Seamus Brennan, a member of the anti-Haughey camp, contacted me after the meeting and advised me not to have anything to do with this committee. He felt that my presence was only lending the committee a credibility it did not deserve. I did not see the situation in that way at all and felt I had my own role to play.

Haughey had no intention whatsoever of relinquishing the leadership; he was simply playing for time and gathering his forces. One of his techniques was to muddy the waters as regards his challengers by encouraging as many as possible to enter the contest. So Gerry Collins, Brian Lenihan and John Wilson also put their names forward. With this confused succession contest under way, and the incumbent leader still *in situ*, another parliamentary party meeting was scheduled. Fate took a hand when Clem Coughlan, a Donegal TD who had called publicly for Haughey's resignation, was killed in a car accident the day before the meeting.

At the meeting, after tributes were paid to the late deputy, Tunney, as chairman, announced in Irish that the gathering was adjourned, and literally ran out of the room. Jim Tunney was utterly and absolutely enthralled by Haughey. He was a decent man, known far and wide as 'The Yellow Rose of Finglas' (he had a penchant for wearing a yellow rosebud in his buttonhole) and did Haughey's bidding with extraordinary alacrity. I don't know why – probably a combination of respect and terror – and I don't know if one was greater than the other.

A petition demanding a proper meeting to discuss the leadership was signed by forty-one TDs and seven senators, and that special meeting was then set for 7 February. On the *This Week* programme on RTÉ Radio 1 the day before, Haughey declared he wasn't thinking about defeat and that most members and supporters of Fianna Fáil wanted him to stay on. He said he was staying on because a small party rump, along with their media friends and others outside the party, should not be allowed to dictate who the leader of Fianna Fáil should be. He circulated a statement to all members of cumainn throughout the country along similar lines, saying it was his duty to stay on and lead the party out of its difficulties. As well as referring again to the media and 'alien influences', he also dragged in 'business interests'.

A big demonstration of grassroots members was organised outside Fianna Fáil headquarters in Mount Street to support him and put pressure on TDs to do likewise. My brother Niall addressed this demonstration in terms bordering on hyperbole. He accused the media of seeking to execute Haughey in the way the 1916 leaders had been executed. This was again a reflection of the emotion of the time. Niall was – and continued to be – very pro-Haughey. However, we agreed from the very beginning that I would take my position and he would take his position on Haughey and we would never fall out over it. We were determined not to let it affect us as brothers and this was terribly important to us both. I'm glad to say that the Haughey factor didn't succeed in coming between us in any way – if anything, it strengthened our relationship.

This demonstration contributed to the pressure that was being exerted on members of the parliamentary party. In fact, so great was that pressure that three of them collapsed and two were hospitalised during the two weeks this whole sorry saga dragged on. Liam Hyland from Laois-Offaly had a heart attack. Paddy Power from Kildare, a strong Haughey supporter, also became ill.

An aspect of the challenges to Haughey's leadership that is worth drawing attention to is the suggestion some of his supporters put forward at the time that it was *ultra vires* of the parliamentary party to remove him. Back in February, on a *Today Tonight* programme just before the relevant meeting, Brian Lenihan had said that the challenge was not for the leadership, because Haughey was already the leader. The challenge applied only to the party's nomination for the position of Taoiseach. No matter what the result was, Haughey would remain leader of the party because, although he was initially chosen by the parliamentary party, the ardfheis, the supreme body of the organisation, had subsequently confirmed his selection. So, *de jure*, he could only be replaced by an ardfheis. It sounded good but was based on false reasoning.

When McCreevy put down his motion of no confidence in October 1982, the argument was put forward that Haughey would still be Taoiseach, no matter what the result of a vote on that motion. The Dáil had elected him to the Taoiseach's office, so even if he lost the backing of the majority of his party, he would still be Taoiseach until the House ousted him. So his latest statement, that he felt it his duty to stay on because he had the support of the vast majority of Fianna Fáil members, seemed to imply that the parliamentary party didn't have the authority to remove him, given those earlier arguments. Ben Briscoe rightly condemned this statement in forthright terms in an RTÉ interview, saying the only conclusion one could come to from examining it was that Haughey no longer recognised the right of the parliamentary party that had chosen him to remove him. Briscoe decided to force the moment to its crisis by formally proposing a motion for the upcoming parliamentary party meeting that Haughey resign as party leader forthwith.

The fateful meeting finally took place on 7 February. It was another marathon, dragging on for more than twelve hours. It began with a wrangle about whether the leadership issue or the report of the Tunney Committee into the telephone tapping should be dicussed first. Haughey's opponents wanted the leadership question taken first but lost on a vote. On the phone-tapping report, I dissented from the conclusions of the other three people on the committee and entered my own 'minority report'. The others held that there was no evidence to link Haughey to the phone tapping and placed greater blame on Martin O'Donoghue than on either Doherty or MacSharry. Although they accepted that MacSharry's action was contrary to the normally expected standards of behaviour between colleagues, they argued that he found himself in an unenviable position. They found the discussion or proposals raised by O'Donoghue more serious, despite his claim to be playing the role of an honest broker. Bertie Ahern read the report to the meeting and when he had finished, Haughey announced that he would ask the meeting to remove the party whip from Doherty and O'Donoghue. I then read my dissenting conclusions. I expressed my belief that Doherty had initiated the taps on the two journalists' telephones and said that the motivation behind the taps was 'internal party considerations' rather than considerations of national security. I also stated my belief that, as leader, Haughey should take ultimate responsibility for the whole affair. I also wanted to put into my dissenting reservations my belief that he had directed that the taps be put on the phones but, as I had no evidence of this, I thought it would be defamatory. However, I had no doubt that he had a part in what Doherty had done, something which was publicly confirmed by Doherty ten years later.

I knew that something was rotten in the State of Ireland but could not pinpoint it exactly. All I could do was produce the rather mild rebuke that was embodied in the two reservations I had entered into the report. It did not get very much attention or coverage. Naturally enough, the Fianna Fáil press office wasn't going to promote it and it was buried without ceremony. In fact, the so-called Tunney Committee report I regard as an utter whitewash. Listening to it being read, I wondered if I had been in the same room as the others who had signed the report. I hold Jim Tunney responsible for the whitewash that the report turned into. He was an upright, decent man and could not have been more unlike Haughey in his lifestyle but, as I have already said, he was utterly in thrall to his leader.

Several hours of discussion followed, during which Haughey's supporters harped on about O'Donoghue and bribes being available from mysterious sources to influence the party. They also lambasted the media, which, they said, should not be allowed to dictate its course to Fianna Fáil. Finally, Ben Briscoe got his chance to put his motion. Speaking against it, the pro-Haugheyites returned to the same media bashing and references to mysterious forces trying to take over the party. Supporters of the motion referred to the catalogue of scandals that had so damaged the party. We also referred to how bad Haughey was for the party electorally and to our unhappy experiences over the three recent elections.

The decision this time was for a secret vote and Haughey raised no objection. It has been suggested that the secret ballot was probably to his advantage because those whose leadership ambitions had been thwarted for the moment would vote for him because he would be easier to take out in the near future than a newly chosen leader. Those who had expressed their doubts about him in public, but were really for him, could also now vote for him under the cloak of secrecy. There will always be the sort of people who like to run with the hare and hunt with the hounds. Haughey knew human nature well and was astute enough to know when and how to exploit its weaknesses.

In any event, whatever the reasons, the result was 44 for and 33 against Haughey. It was closer than it had been in October but the arch-survivor had come through again and confounded all his critics, especially the media, who had universally killed him off and buried him. It wasn't that some TDs were anti-Haughey as such; it was more a case that they were worried for the party. I have already referred to how some TDs collapsed and were hospitalised during this stressful time. My concern too was with what was happening to Fianna Fáil and that was why I stood up at the various meetings and spoke in the way I did, although I'm sure some people groaned inwardly, 'It's that fellow Andrews, going to cause us more suffering.' I'm not claiming that I was all right and Haughey all wrong, but I could only behave according to my beliefs. Some people took grave umbrage at my role in the whole Haughey affair.

During the course of one of the votes – I cannot say for certain which one – Peter Barry of Fine Gael came up to me in the Dáil and said: 'You're a great man to be anti-Haughey and you're making a real profession of it.' It was a curious remark and one that I thought about afterwards. Perhaps it meant that it paid me to be anti-Haughey – paid me electorally, of course. It did help me electorally, perhaps, but if so, it's an electoral advantage I would gladly have done without. And I did succeed in getting elected long before he became leader. That wasn't the reason I opposed Charles Haughey as leader of Fianna Fáil. Rather it was concern for the good of Fianna Fáil that was always my motivation.

MISCARRIAGES OF JUSTICE

THE BIRMINGHAM SIX

Over the many years of Charles Haughey's leadership of Fianna Fáil, I knew that I was 'on my own' and would not be appointed to any government ministry, so I gradually developed a different independent niche in public life, responding to miscarriages of justice or injustice generally. This led me to a long dedication to the case known as the Birmingham Six.

On 21 November 1974, the IRA set off bombs in two Birmingham pubs at around 8.20 p.m. The one in the Tavern in the Town killed eleven people; the other, in the Mulberry Bush, took ten innocent lives. In addition, a hundred and sixty-one people were seriously injured. The victims were mostly young people. It was a horrific event and everybody at home and abroad was deeply shocked and upset by the random nature of the act and the number of dead. Irish people living in Britain were given a tough time in their workplaces and elsewhere, as they were seen as sharing the blame for what had happened.

Within a week, the British Government passed the draconian Prevention of Terrorism Act (PTA). In early May 1975, when I was Opposition spokesman on Justice, I said at a meeting in London that I doubted that the provision of a terrorism act, rushed through the British parliament at a time of great anxiety and strain after these bombings, would help to promote understanding. While I could understand the anger of the people at what had happened, the same sort of conduct had by then become commonplace in Northern Ireland, then effectively a police state, and the legal regime that existed there had not helped to dampen the fires of terrorism or, as some would have it, the war against occupation.

Six men went on trial at Lancaster Castle for the bombings. Five of them were originally from Belfast and one from Derry, but all of them had lived in Birmingham for some years. Their names were Hugh Callaghan, Paddy Hill, Gerard Hunter, Richard McIlkenny, William Power and John Walker and they were to go down in history as the Birmingham Six. They, like the Guildford Four and the Maguire Seven, were victims of monstrous miscarriages of justice. British legal history has shown that the system of justice in that country, ancient and noble as it may be in principle, has sometimes been found wanting in practice when fundamental rights become swamped in populist crackdowns by governments under pressure.

The Birmingham Six had lived in Birmingham for between twelve and twenty-eight years. They drank and occasionally worked together in the city. They also all knew James McDade, an IRA bomber from the Ardoyne, who had blown himself up outside a Coventry telephone exchange a week before the Birmingham atrocities. In fact, they were on their way to Belfast for his funeral when they were arrested.

And who were these six men, who, along with their families, were to have their lives shattered forever?

William, or Billy, Power was a shy, nervous young man, who had emigrated to England in 1963. No work at home – not an unusual tale. He was 29 at the time of his arrest and had four children. During the trial, he gave his evidence while heavily medicated on tranquilisers. He had spent most of his adult life drifting in and out of various labouring jobs and was an obsessive gambler. He was apolitical.

Patrick (Paddy) Hill, 31 at the time of his arrest, was a tough petty criminal who had seventeen convictions for brawling and burglary. He had lived in Birmingham since 1960 and had been in and out of work as an industrial painter. He had six very young children, aged between two and nine. His wife divorced him in 1983.

Robert Gerard (Gerry) Hunter, like Billy Power, was 29 at the time of his arrest. Like Paddy Hill, he was an industrial painter. After a wild youth, he had married a Birmingham girl and they had three young children, aged four, seven and eight. The Northern priest, Fr Denis Faul, who did so much good work on behalf of the Six, said that the men's relation he admired most was Sandra Hunter. She was from Birmingham, had no Irish connection, was Church of England and, conventionally, had every incentive to walk out on her husband. She stood by him, however, and raised their three children in hard circumstances.

John Walker, aged 40 at the time of his arrest, was the only one of the six not from Belfast. He came from Derry and had lived in England since he was 17. He had been back to Ireland only two or three times in more than 20 years. He had done his national service with the Royal Irish Fusiliers. He had a steady job as a crane driver and had a family of seven, aged between two and 17. His wife moved back to Derry with the family after his imprisonment.

Richard (Dick) McIlkenny, aged 41 when he was arrested, worked as a millwright in the same place as John Walker. He also had a family of six, aged from six to 17, and had lived in Birmingham since 1956. Both he and Walker were strong republicans: they attended Sinn Féin social events and ran raffles for the internees and IRA prisoners.

Hugh Callaghan, 45 at the time of his arrest, was an unemployed labourer who had lived in Birmingham since 1947. He had one daughter, who was aged 16 at the time of her father's arrest. He was a quiet and apolitical man and the oldest of the six. He aged visibly in prison.

In August 1975, the six men were given life sentences. Doubt about their conviction was expressed almost immediately. The day after the sentences, *The Times* wrote that one of the most disturbing features of the case was evidence that the men had been beaten up at some stage after their arrest and before their trial. In March 1976, the Court of Appeal, Lord Widgery presiding, refused the men leave to appeal. In June 1976, the men took a case against fourteen warders from Winson Green Prison for assaulting them. During the five-week trial, Dr David Paul, a specialist in forensic medicine, using photos taken of the six before they had been delivered to Winson Green Prison, testified that serious injuries had been inflicted on the six men while in custody.

The case was dismissed, but serious questions had been raised and the *Guardian* was now asking them in public. That paper pointed out that it was clear that the men had been beaten up, but that those responsible had yet to be found and charged.

A civil action against the police, initiated in November 1977, finally came up for hearing in January 1980. Lord Denning, the Master of the Rolls and a famous and eminent lawyer and judge, although then quite old, presided. He stated that the whole British legal and political establishment would be undermined if the case against the police were proved and, in dismissing the case, reasoned that to contemplate that the conduct complained of actually took place, and that there was, by inference, a conspiracy at all levels of the justice system to conceal it, would be an 'appalling vista' and that he was not prepared to entertain the possibility that there was truth in the allegations. This infamous phrase was a blot on his otherwise illustrious career and remains in common use today. His judgment was upheld by the House of Lords in November 1981 and the men's legal campaign ground to a halt.

THE CAMPAIGN TO HAVE THE SIX RELEASED

In July 1977, Fr Raymond Murray and Fr Denis Faul published a pamphlet called 'The Birmingham Framework', comprising statements from the men and their wives and excerpts from the trial transcripts. The pamphlet expressed the two priests' belief that the men were innocent and called for the case to be reopened. In truth, not much more happened during the first ten years of the men's captivity. Shock and horror at the carnage the Birmingham bombs caused prevented much of a campaign being waged on the men's behalf. There was no public sympathy for the men and their families in the United Kingdom and little in Ireland.

My interest in the case was seriously aroused by an article that appeared in the *Irish Press* in late November 1984. The article discussed the reasons for disquiet about the men's convictions. The article pointed out that the convictions of four of the men were based on their confessions and there was almost overpowering evidence that they had been obtained under duress. Another was that the forensic evidence used to show that two of the six had explosive substances on their hands was based on a nineteenth-century method. The tests were never confirmed and had been challenged by experts. It was shown that residue from cigarettes and paint can produce the same results: and the men were painters and heavy smokers. And then, no trace of explosives had ever been found on the men's clothing or luggage. Finally, none of the six had been identified by witnesses as having been seen in or near the bombed pubs.

My instinct, having read the article, was that the British Government still had a case to answer for the continuing imprisonment of these six men and that the battle to have this wrong righted was not over. Many people in Ireland seemed to believe that the men must be guilty, possibly on the basis that there was 'no smoke without fire'. I realised that taking up this case was not likely to increase my popularity, especially among the staunchly middle-class sections of my constituency, but a very strong instinct was telling me that the men were 'set up' and deserved a better hearing than they had received. I did not know, at least at this stage, that they were innocent. I was uncomfortable with how their arrest and trials had been dealt with and, even if they were not innocent, they were no less entitled to proper legal process in the manner of their conviction than any other citizen of the United Kingdom of Great Britain and Northern Ireland.

The Irish in Britain Representation Group (IBRG) became active in the case in 1984 and, on the tenth anniversary of the bombings, several newspaper articles appeared, generally arguing the men's innocence. A number of British MPs began to take up their cause, such as the Conservatives Sir John Farr and Sir John Biggs-Davison and, on the other side of the political divide, Tony Benn. Chris Mullin, who was elected Labour MP for Sunderland in 1987, was a tireless campaigner on behalf of the six.

Granada Television's *World in Action* programme on 28 October 1985 cast extreme doubt on the forensic evidence used to convict the men. Two days later, at a meeting in Dún Laoghaire, I referred publicly to that TV programme and said that there were serious doubts not only about the Birmingham Six but also about the Annie Maguire case.

The Maguires had been convicted in March 1976 of unlawfully handling explosives and had been given sentences of varying lengths. The seven people involved were Annie, her husband Patrick, her teenage sons Vincent and Patrick junior, her brother Seán Smyth, her brother-in-law Patrick 'Giuseppe' Conlon, who died in prison in January, 1980 and Patrick O'Neill, a family friend. They had been refused leave to appeal in July 1977. Annie was the last of the seven to be released, in February 1985.

At that Dún Laoghaire meeting I called on the Taoiseach of the day, Garret FitzGerald, to make representations to the British Government to open an inquiry into the Birmingham Six and Maguire cases. I spoke in the Dáil on the same date, urging that the cases be immediately taken up with the British Home Secretary at ministerial level. I said that intervention at any lower level would be meaningless and that it was imperative to make these cases a priority.

I asked questions in the Dáil in early 1986. On 12 March, I expressed my concern to the Minister for Foreign Affairs, Peter Barry, about the delay in reopening the Birmingham Six case. In his response he was positive, helpful and clearly concerned. In June that year, I organised and led an all-party group of TDs to London. The purpose of the trip was to meet a group of British MPs, through the British-Irish Parliamentary Association. We were given funding and secretarial assistance for this trip through the good offices of Peter Barry. A few days before our visit, Chris Mullin's important book *Error of Judgement* had been published, so the Birmingham Six case was very much in the public's mind. The book argued cogently that the men were the victims of a gross miscarriage of justice. Our embassy in London fully facilitated our visit. Noel Dorr was our ambassador there at the time. He was later to be Secretary-General of the Department of Foreign Affairs during my first time as minister. He held a dinner at the embassy, to which British MPs and others concerned about the case were invited, and he arranged for officials from the Home Office to meet the delegation. He had hoped for Douglas Hurd, the Home Secretary, or at least his Minister of State, David Mellor, to meet us but the British were not keen on this.

During this visit, Senator Flor O'Mahony, who was a member of our group, and I spent two hours at Wormwood Scrubs talking to Richard McIlkenny and Billy Power. Wormwood Scrubs is an intimidating place, with the constant clanging of the opening and shutting of prison doors and the two hours we spent there was more than enough for me. This was the first of many prison meetings I was to have with members of the Birmingham Six. Little did I know then how many British prisons I would visit over the following years.

We met the two men in the visitors' area, with a guard present. The visit was made easy for us by the governor, who gave us the impression that he thought the men were innocent. The two men were very glad to see us and we discussed their case at length. We promised them we would be back. The demeanour of the men during this visit suggested that they were sincere and gave me enough faith to be convinced of their innocence.

On 16 October 1986, I led an all-party group, arranged by Peter Barry, to meet with the British Home Secretary Douglas Hurd to discuss the Birmingham Six, Maguire and Guildford Four cases. The Guildford and Woolwich bombings had occurred in October and November 1974 and Patrick Armstrong, Gerard Conlon (son of Giuseppe Conlon of the Maguire Seven), Paul Hill and Carole Richardson had been convicted of the bombings in October 1975. They were refused leave to appeal in October 1977. Robert Kee's book, *Trial and Error*, had cast doubt on the convictions in the Maguire case and had helped persuade the British to agree to reconsider it. Annie Maguire was free by this time but naturally wanted to prove her own and her family's innocence. A few days later in the Dáil I asked Peter Barry what more could now be done for all three cases and suggested an all-party motion of the Dáil to coincide with the motion in the House of Commons in the names of 210 MPs, calling for the reopening of the three cases.

A police witness, PC Tom Clarke, appeared on another Granada *World in Action* programme in early December 1986. He stated that he saw the Birmingham Six men being beaten and tortured. When asked about the programme by an *Irish Press* journalist, I said that it had given great impetus to the campaign to free the men, then beginning their thirteenth year in prison. An all-party motion in the Dáil in the middle of December, requesting the government to call again on the British Home Secretary to take early and positive action on the three cases, was signed by Pat the Cope Gallagher and myself on behalf of Fianna Fáil; Bernard Durkan and Liam Skelly on behalf of Fine Gael; Frank Cluskey for Labour; and Mary Harney for the PDs.

In late January 1987, Douglas Hurd decided to refer the Birmingham Six case to the Court of Appeal, but not, to my disappointment, the Maguire or Guildford Four cases. I was appointed by Fianna Fáil as their official observer at the hearing. In an interview with the *Irish Press*, I said I didn't expect the hearing to get under way for another three or four months but, in the meantime, we would be pressing to have the six released on bail, although this never happened. In the event, they had to wait until November, another nine months, for the appeal hearing. I urged at that time that attempts to reopen the Maguire and Guildford cases would be renewed.

In April 1987, an all-party Dáil delegation visited London under the auspices of the Anglo-Irish Inter-Parliamentary Union. There were thirteen on the delegation: five Fianna Fáil, four Fine Gael, one Labour, one Workers' Party and one PD. A week before our trip, I decided that we should meet with the six in Long Lartin Prison, where all of them were then awaiting the hearing of their appeals, and our embassy in London made the arrangements. The delegation met the Foreign Secretary, Sir Geoffrey Howe, and the Northern Ireland Secretary, Tom King, on 8 April, and a delegation of Westminster MPs on that and the following days. Five of our delegation, Peter Barry (Brian Lenihan was now Minister for Foreign Affairs), Ruairi Quinn, Pat McCartan, Geraldine Kennedy and I visited Long Lartin on 9 April and met the six men. We also met Gerard Conlon of the Guildford Four, who was incarcerated with the others there.

At our meeting with the six, they requested that the Irish government stand bail for them, but I explained that every Irish citizen who got into trouble abroad would demand similar treatment if their request was granted and they understood and accepted this. They were anxious that observers should attend their appeal and I reassured them in this regard on behalf of the delegation. About a month later in the Dáil, I asked the Minister for Foreign Affairs to urge the Home Secretary to send the cases of the Guildford Four and Maguire Seven for review to the Court of Appeal, in light of a recent ITV television programme, *First Tuesday*. Brian Lenihan replied that he had already written to Douglas Hurd in this regard. I asked him to make a personal representation to Mr Hurd at the earliest opportunity.

On 7 July 1987, I attended a meeting at the Department of Foreign Affairs, in Iveagh House, involving Brian Lenihan, Annie Maguire, Teresa Smalley (aunt of Paul Hill of the Guildford Four), Errol Smalley (secretary of the Guildford Four Relatives' Committee) and Mrs

Mary McCaffrey (sister of Annie Maguire). The relatives wanted the Irish Government to delay the implementation of the Extradition Act until all innocent Irish prisoners were released. Brian Lenihan was not prepared to give any such commitment about the Act. I said it was important not to prejudge the issue publicly because this might be counterproductive and might also have a negative effect on the Birmingham Six appeal. I added that it might not be a good idea to put pressure publicly on the British appeal system. Later in the meeting, I said that an all-party Oireachtas delegation could be put together again – perhaps in September – to press for justice in the Guildford and Maguire cases. I said that the previous Minister of State at the Home Office, David Mellor, had been most unsympathetic when the delegation had met him the previous year and that I hoped his successor would be more amenable.

On 25 September, accompanied by Breifne O'Reilly from our embassy in London, I had a one-and-a-half-hour meeting with the Birmingham Six at Wormwood Scrubs. Dick McIlkenny had originally asked me to visit him, but since all six had been brought together at the Scrubs on 22 September, I sought permission to see all of them. They said they felt that Irish people could not get a fair trial in Britain and so urged that the Extradition Act not be ratified on 1 December. In reference to their own case, they said that the Devon and Cornwall Constabulary had withheld certain records from the solicitors acting on their behalf. Hugh Callaghan said he was convinced that the Crown would try to discredit ex-PC Tom Clarke as a witness. Billy Power referred to the missing testimony of a Special Branch officer, who had been in one of the pubs ten minutes before the bomb exploded and who had not identified any of them. Gerry Hunter also mentioned a Mrs Linus, a cleaner, who was willing to testify that they had been abused at Queen's Road police station.

The men were very keyed up at this stage about their case and requested that the Taoiseach or Tánaiste be present at their appeal. I replied that this was unrealistic because such a high-level presence would be seen as overt pressure on an independent court and might prove counterproductive. I was prepared to recommend that the Irish ambassador in London should attend on behalf of the government and that a politician, or senior criminal lawyer, might also attend to demonstrate the widespread public concern in Ireland about the case.

The prisoners accepted this, but urged that a simple statement be issued on behalf of the government before the appeal, declaring that the six were innocent.

Gerry Hunter in particular had claimed that, for many years, the Irish government had ignored the Birmingham Six and had only recently begun to act for them. I understood the sense of frustration and anger that he and the other five and their families must have been feeling, despite the efforts of many Irish politicians, myself included, on their behalf for many years. In fairness, they always expressed their personal appreciation for the work we were doing, and always said their remarks about the government's lack of action were in no way intended personally. I told them that an all-party delegation was to meet the Home Secretary on 19 October and that, while the purpose of that meeting was to highlight the Guildford Four case, I would personally urge on the Home Secretary the innocence of the Birmingham Six.

It seemed to me that the six were both hopeful and apprehensive about their appeals and that they had put great faith in their legal teams. They were also encouraged by the expressions of public support that they had received. They didn't want any demonstrations outside the Court of Appeal and stressed that left-wing militants and Provisional Sinn Féin in particular would not be welcome. They wanted to be careful not to let sections of the British media dub the appeal 'IRA bombers' trial'.

On 18 October 1987, I led another all-party delegation to London for a series of meetings. We met representatives Seamus McGarry and Bernadette Masterson of the Federation of Irish Societies in Britain, and Errol and Teresa Smalley of the Guildford Four campaign. McGarry wondered if the tactics were wrong to have put so much emphasis on the Birmingham Six, because the Guildford Four case seemed a surer thing. I said that I had pointed out to the six that they had only a fifty-fifty chance of having their convictions quashed.

On the following day, our delegation met Home Secretary Hurd and his Minister of State, John Patten. I introduced the TDs to Douglas Hurd. I said I realised that there could be only a peripheral discussion of the Birmingham Six case, as it was *sub judice*, but that I wanted to express the delegation's appreciation to Hurd for referring the case to the Court of Appeal. As for the Guildford Four case,

I said that the delegation wanted the re-examination of the evidence to be given priority and that I hoped referral to the Court of Appeal would follow. I also raised their high-security prisoner status, saying that I thought it unnecessary and I referred to Paul Hill's forty-six prison moves and 1,441 solitary-confinement days as evidence that he had apparently been singled out for particularly harsh treatment.

Hurd accepted the possibility that new evidence had emerged in the case of the Guildford Four and said that none of what I had outlined should affect the good functioning of the Anglo-Irish Agreement. He said the basis of the Maguire convictions was very narrow – forensic evidence only – which was why the Maguires had been released from prison, but that no new substantial evidence had emerged to undermine that forensic evidence. I went on to say that the Guildford and Maguire cases were inextricably linked. If Paul Hill's alibi was found to stand up – a woman had emerged who said that Hill was with her at the time of the Guildford and Woolwich bombings – that must have implications for the Maguires, because they were implicated by Hill's evidence. All Hurd would say was that he understood what I was saying. When Peter Barry and Pat McCartan questioned the forensic evidence that convicted the Maguires, Hurd replied, 'Come and challenge it', and said the defence had failed to do that at the time of the trial and that no body of scientific opinion had successfully undermined it.

I reminded Hurd of the hysteria drummed up by the gutter media who branded the Maguire home a bomb factory before the jury returned a verdict, but he replied that he couldn't reopen the case on the basis that the atmosphere had been heated at the time of the trial.

I felt that the tone of this meeting was much more cordial than it had been at the meeting of the previous year. Hurd took on board the points about the Guildford Four case and was at least going to review it in full in the New Year. His junior minister, John Patten, hardly intervened in the debate at all but seemed to follow it with interest. This was in stark contrast to the hostile attitude of his predecessor, David Mellor, who tried strongly to refute the delegation's arguments the previous year. If there was to be any hope for the Guildford Four gleaned from the meeting, it lay in the absence of Mellor and the investigation being carried out by the Avon and Somerset Constabulary. The outlook for the Maguires, however, appeared bleak; the only slight chance was that if the Guildford Four case was referred, the link between it and the Maguire case might be implicitly accepted by the Court of Appeal.

I attended the Birmingham Six appeal in early November 1987, as an observer (as did Peter Barry). On 4 November in the Dáil, I asked the Minister for Foreign Affairs if there would be a government representative at the appeal and he replied that the Irish ambassador in London and his staff were representing the government. As the appeal was under way, he said that it would not be appropriate for him to make a statement. The appeal lasted seven weeks. I was at Court No. 2 of the Old Bailey for the announcement of the verdict on the appeal on 28 January 1988, with other Oireachtas members, Senator Paschal Mooney, Deputies Peter Barry, Mervyn Taylor, Pat McCartan and Geraldine Kennedy. To my great disappointment, the appeal was rejected and widespread dismay followed. I told *The Irish Times* afterwards that the campaign hadn't ended, and that the verdict would be viewed as 'an impetus to see six innocent men freed'. It was a bleak and bitter day.

In mid-April 1988, the House of Lords Appeal Committee refused the six leave to appeal to the House of Lords. The Irish government then said that there were compelling humanitarian reasons for the Home Secretary to consider using his powers of clemency in relation to the case.

THE STRUGGLE CONTINUES

On 26 April 1988, I wrote to the Minister for Foreign Affairs, Brian Lenihan, seeking for him to arrange a meeting of an all-party Oireachtas delegation to see Douglas Hurd in connection with the ongoing plight of the Birmingham Six and the refusal of the British justice system to release them. My intention was to seek clemency for them through Hurd. In a Dáil debate in the middle of the following June, I accused Dr Frank Skuse, the forensic scientist who swabbed the men for explosives after their arrest and who maintained that the tests proved positive, of being less than honest in his approach to the forensic evidence. I said that he 'twisted and turned' during the course of his evidence at the appeal hearing. I said that I had sat beside a prominent British legal luminary, who expressed to me his embarrassment at the evidence Skuse gave under oath. I found it difficult at the time to comprehend how the judges could have accepted his evidence. They professed themselves not in the slightest doubt about it. I was horrified, as were many others. It was well known that even the warders in the prisons where these men were locked up knew that they could not have committed these crimes. In one of the prisons, I noted that a very senior and decent governor was quite satisfied that the men couldn't be guilty. This was after having been in charge of them for a lengthy period of time and having regard to their general conduct and co-operative attitude.

Near the end of August, 1988, I visited Billy Power and Dick McIlkenny in Wormwood Scrubs, accompanied by Eamon Gildea of the London embassy. I raised the question of clemency with them and they said they would accept it but only if it was unconditional. They felt that they could do more for their cause on the outside. Power referred to their solicitor, Gareth Pierce, who was then considering an appeal to the European Court of Human Rights, but I had my doubts about the value of such a course of action. I told them about the upcoming ad-hoc committee meeting in the Dáil on 15 September, to which Ms Pierce and Chris Mullin were invited, and I told them that we would do what we could to keep their case in the public eye.

Billy Power told me that Gerry Hunter wasn't too well since the appeal verdict setback and asked me to write to him. He said that Hunter felt a bit left out and even a bit paranoid at times. I said I hoped other TDs would visit them and the other men and that I would see them again before Christmas. They thanked me again for my visit. I thought they both seemed in good shape and that their morale was not bad, considering the massive disappointment of the appeal failure, but McIlkenny seemed a little more nervous than before and tried to disguise it by talking and joking.

In October 1988, lawyers for the Birmingham Six decided to petition the European Court of Human Rights. In early 1989, the Home Secretary referred the case of the Guildford Four to the Court of Appeal. In July that year, there were media reports of the disciplining of three officers of the West Midlands Serious Crimes Squad (WMSCS) for fabricating evidence. The squad had been involved in the Birmingham Six case but the reports referred only to more recent cases. A trial judge had acknowledged at one point during the trial of the six that the credibility of the police was central to the case.

Subsequently the Home Office informed our London embassy that the terms of reference of the inquiry into the squad did *not* limit its scope to the 1986–88 period.

The European Court of Human Rights turned down the men's petition in May 1989 but this news did not become public until several months later.

In early October 1989, one of our London embassy officials, J. J. Hennessy, visited Paddy Hill of the Birmingham Six and Gerard Conlon and Patrick Armstrong of the Guildford Four in prison. He found Hill very aggressive throughout the visit. Hill said that only a handful of politicians sustained an interest in their case, naming Neil Blaney, Paschal Mooney, Tony Gregory, Dick Roche, my brother Niall, who was an MEP at the time, and myself.

Finally we had some good news. On 19 October 1989, the Court of Appeal quashed the convictions of the Guildford Four. I was both delighted and surprised about this and the clear implications it had for the Maguire case, because the seven had been arrested as the result of the confessions of Paul Hill and Gerard Conlon. Now those confessions had been found to be unsafe.

The British Government set up a judicial inquiry into the Guildford Four case, to be conducted by the eminent lawyer and former appeals judge, Sir John May, which was to include the Maguire case in its terms of reference. About a week later, one of the fourteen prison officers who had been acquitted in 1976 of beating up the Birmingham Six admitted his guilt publicly for the first time. He also said that the men bore the marks of earlier injuries sustained in police custody. This was a bombshell.

Around that time, I attended the inquest held on Gibraltar into the killing of three IRA members by the SAS there the previous March. Afterwards, I criticised the inquest for lacking breadth and depth. A few days later, Amnesty International published its annual report and highlighted the Gibraltar killings and the Birmingham Six case as areas for concern. I agreed with Amnesty's conclusion on the inadequacy of the inquest and had said so publicly. I also expressed the belief that the British authorities would not permit any further inquiry into the killings.

By the end of October, the powerful US Kennedy dynasty threw its weight behind the Birmingham Six campaign and promised to use its influence to exert American pressure on the British Government for their release. Mrs Dorothy (Dot) Tubridy, a long-time friend of the Kennedys, had assembled a comprehensive dossier on the case, which she presented to Senator Joe Kennedy (son of the late Robert). He had asked her to help prepare his case for the Senate. I supplied her with the documentation needed. Things began to gain pace.

On 23 November 1989, I accompanied Paul Hill of the Guildford Four on a visit to the European Parliament, which voted overwhelmingly in favour of a motion that my brother Niall had initiated calling for a review of the Birmingham Six case. On 12 December, 1989, the British Government finally announced the re-categorisation of the Birmingham Six from A to B status, meaning that they were recognised to pose less of a security threat. This should, of course, have occurred long before that time, but was still welcome when it at last came. On the following day, I was quoted in the *Irish News* as saying that the West Midlands Serious Crimes Squad should have been called the 'Wild West Midlands Serious Crimes Squad' because they operated by standards more appropriate to the Wild West than to contemporary police ethics. I also felt that the reduced security classification of the six amounted to official acknowledgement that they were not IRA members and, was by implication, an expression of the unsafeness of their convictions. I said that the fact that officers now suspended were involved in the Birmingham Six case gave enough grounds for extending the May inquiry and I urged the government to keep up the pressure to have the case included in the WMSCS investigation.

I visited five of the six again on 15 and 16 December 1989. On these visits, I was accompanied by John Stafford TD. At the time, Callaghan, Walker and Hunter were in Long Lartin, forty miles from Birmingham; Hill was in Gartree, forty-five miles away from the city; Power was in Wormwood Scrubs in London, and McIlkenny was in Full Sutton, near York, to which the authorities were unable to facilitate a visit at the time. Jim Hennessy of our London embassy collected John Stafford and myself at Luton Airport to take us to the various prisons.

He took us first to Gartree in Leicestershire to visit Hill for an hour and a half. I told Hill that we had been asked by the Taoiseach to visit the six. I welcomed their recategorisation as a very positive step. I said that Mr Haughey, as incoming President of the Council of the European Communities, would be able to keep their case at a high profile and attract international support to their cause. I referred to the justified insistence by the six on having their innocence established and asked if they were prepared to accept some formula for release that would leave the question of their innocence to be fought for by them from outside prison.

Hill was vehemently against any type of release that did not completely exonerate the six. He used strong language to stress that they had been fighting for fifteen years for justice, not mercy. However, he said he thought that Hunter, Power and McIlkenny would accept release without exoneration, for personal reasons. We then went on to Long Lartin. Our meeting with Callaghan, Hunter and Walker lasted about an hour. They were in very good spirits and Hunter, now fully recovered from his post-appeal depression, took a full part in the talks. I repeated what I had said to Hill and the three men expressed their appreciation. Hunter and Callaghan were emphatic about not wanting parole or pardon. They said it was vital to them to clear their names before any release for their own and their families' sake. To be even considered for parole you had to show by your attitude and behaviour that you were full of remorse for the crimes you had committed. This was unthinkable, they said, even if they had to spend the rest of their days in prison. Walker was of exactly the same view. I never raised the question of parole again.

The following day, we met with Power in Wormwood Scrubs. I outlined the purpose of our visit and said how the men's recent recategorisation had aroused intense interest internationally. I also said that after our visits to Gartree and Long Lartin the day before, John Stafford and I had already given many interviews. Power said he was greatly encouraged by recent developments and referred to some of the practical advantages of the change in their status as prisoners. He said that it was easier for him to go to Mass now. He wasn't able to go before if there were not sufficient staff to take him to the chapel.

Our visits had gone uniformly well. The five we saw were in good spirits and appreciated that their campaign was being pursued at the level of the Taoiseach and the Minister for Foreign Affairs. They were aware that they still had a bit to go before their case would be resolved. I had referred at various stages to periods of twelve and twenty-four months and none of them had demurred. I suppose time had taken on a new dimension for them by then.

Hughie Callaghan was the man with whom I probably formed the closest bond. In his book *Cruel Fate*, published in May 1993, he thanks many people for helping the six's cause, including my brother Niall and me. He describes me as a 'regular' visitor, as friendly, easy to talk to and asking lots of questions. He also says about me that I had 'a terrific sense of humour'. I hope that whatever laughter I was able to bring into his life lightened a little the dark horror of what he was forced to endure. He recalls me as knowing that he was fond of a little bet on the horses and, indeed, I used to put bets on for him. He appreciated the fact that I used to ring his solicitor's office if he won. I had also got a friend of mine to send him what he describes as 'a fabulous book about horses and the art of betting'. He says that on one visit he sensed that I wanted to talk officially and that I brought up the subject of parole. This was the visit on 15 December 1989 described above.

Gareth Pierce, the men's solicitor, was appalled at an article that appeared in the *Sunday Tribune* shortly afterwards and that was severely critical of the involvement of the Irish Government in the campaign to date, quoting Paddy Hill in particular. There was no reaction to this article from the politicians. It had been greeted with silence. She felt that the journalist had shamelessly taken advantage of Hill's serious depression and had asked leading questions and used the resulting material without any regard for the truth or the welfare of the six. I agreed with her completely. She appreciated the response or lack of response of the politicians to the criticism of them in the article. Hill, who had no family support, was the most alone of the six. He cut a pathetic figure at the 1987 appeal, looking up at the public gallery in the forlorn hope of seeing a friend or relation. He had no one to buy him clothes for his appeal appearance and Pierce did this for him.

When embassy officials visited Callaghan, Walker and Hunter on 22 February 1990, the three men expressed their fury with Hill and the *Sunday Tribune* journalist about what had happened. They were relieved to hear about the politicians' response.

I travelled to the Birmingham Six hearings in Washington on 12 March 1990, held by the Congressional Human Rights Caucus. This is a 162-member body that had held countless hearings on alleged human rights abuses in the USSR, South Africa, Cuba, Iran and Libya. This was one of the first times it had investigated allegations involving a Western democracy. My trip was approved by the Taoiseach. Gareth Pierce and Seamus Mallon also attended the hearings, which were co-chaired by Congressman Tom Lantos, one of the most respected human rights advocates in US politics, and Joe Kennedy. About seventeen Congressmen, both Democrats and Republicans, also attended.

There were two panels of witnesses at the caucus. Panel 1 comprised Lord Gifford (counsel for the six at their appeal), Seamus Mallon and me; panel 2 had Professor Robert McKay of New York University Law School, David Assen of Amnesty International and Gerard Conlon of the Guildford Four. As well as casting doubt on the conviction of the six, Seamus Mallon and I took the opportunity to denounce the IRA campaign of violence both in Northern Ireland and Britain. Gerard Conlon made a moving and measured statement that clearly impressed those present. His evidence dealt mostly with his own arrest and detention.

At the same time Senator Joseph Biden, one of the most influential Democrat politicians, introduced a motion before the Senate calling on the British government to reopen the case. He had no Irish lobby in his constituency, but he had developed a personal interest in the cause. Congressman Brian Donnelly (Democrat, Massachusetts) also introduced a resolution before the House of Congress, calling on President Bush Senior to raise with Prime Minister Thatcher his concern about basic human rights violations and for the case to be quashed. I urged Congress to campaign for the men's ultimate release, together with a declaration of their innocence and compensation.

THE ROAD HOME AT LAST

On the opening day of the May inquiry into the scientific/forensic evidence in the Maguire case, the leading counsel for the inquiry, David Clarke QC, concluded that the convictions were unsafe. This was followed on 14 June by the DPP's decision not to seek to uphold the convictions. The Home Secretary then made a statement to the House of Commons that the convictions couldn't be allowed to stand and he referred the case to the Court of Appeal. The campaign was euphoric and clearly it was the beginning of the end.

Two days earlier, in the Dáil, I asked Gerry Collins, now the Minister for Foreign Affairs, if he would raise the case of the Birmingham Six before the end of the Irish Presidency of the European Community with the EC Council of Foreign Ministers. I also asked him if his attention had been drawn to the need to raise the issue of the six at every opportunity and, in that regard, if he would send representatives to the forthcoming Commission on Security Co-operation in Europe (CSCE) meeting in Copenhagen. I also asked the minister if he would ensure that the case would be raised by the Irish Government at the CSCE meeting. He replied that the government's view was that the most effective course to follow was to raise the case directly with the British Government and that the Irish Government would not be raising it at the CSCE meeting. On the same day, I asked Gerry Collins if he knew that the Home Secretary had indicated that the report of the Devon and Cornwall police into the WMSCS was not to be made available to the six men's solicitors. The minister assured me that the government was closely monitoring progress.

Campaigners on behalf of the six went ahead and organised a presentation to the CSCE at the Parallel Activities Conference on Non-Governmental Organisations of the CSCE on 25 June.

On 8 August 1990, Dick Roche and I, accompanied by the Dublin solicitor Tony Taaffe, who had observed the Court of Appeal hearing, visited Billy Power and Dick McIlkenny at Gartree. Paul Murray, of the London embassy, was with us. (Hill and Hunter refused visits.) Power gave us a message from Hill to the effect that the Irish Government wasn't doing enough for them. McIlkenny and Power agreed with him and raised some old grievances, including the missed opportunity at the CSCE meeting. They reiterated that they wanted their sentences quashed but intimated that they would accept bail, if offered, pending a final settlement of their case. McIlkenny was fairly aggressive throughout the meeting, although at times his aggression was heavily laced with irony. Power was more despondent than anyone had ever seen him before. He mentioned going on hunger strike and this was ominous, because only Hill ever threatened this (he actually did it for a time back in the early eighties). This was obviously a very frustrating time for the men. Roche and I explained that the government had asked us to make the visits to inquire what further actions the men thought we could take on their behalf and to point out the dangers of an over-aggressive or too public approach by the Irish Government. I said I would report back that I had met two very angry men and that a third, Hill, was so angry that he refused to meet us. I said, however, that the London embassy had done all it could and that criticism of public servants who were bound by instructions was unfair. Power raised the question of the Irish Government holding its own inquiry. Roche replied that there would be obvious difficulties about this but promised to bring the request to the attention of the government.

It was agreed that Roche and I would issue a six-point statement after our visit: (i) the six were upset by the lack of progress in their case; (ii) the Devon and Cornwall police needed to bring their inquiry to a speedy conclusion; (iii) new conditions of substance already existed, so new evidence was not necessarily needed; (iv) the Irish Government should take more public action in support of the six at international gatherings (the EC, European Parliament and UN were mentioned); (v) the men believed the British Government was playing for time; and (vi) it was wrong that the onus should be on the men to prove they were innocent.

Later that evening, we went to a meeting of the Birmingham campaign directors and Paul Murray accompanied us at our request. We met Sue Milner, secretary of the national campaign, Fr Taaffe, head of the Birmingham end of it, and Kate and Maggie McIlkenny. They all wanted a more public profile from the Irish government, although they noted how Anglo-Irish meetings often coincided with developments in the case. We pointed out that any sort of public bickering (attacking embassy officials, for example) benefited no one in the campaign. On the following day, we visited Hughie Callaghan and Johnny Walker at Long Lartin. We again explained that we were on a direct mission from the government to emphasise its continuing support and to bring back the men's views. The talk was mainly about the need for a more co-ordinated campaign. They told us that John Hume had made the same point to them on his recent visit and that

Gerard Conlon had told them there were too many campaigns. Callaghan said that they wanted to leave the prison exonerated. He reminded me that I had raised the question of parole with him during my visit of the previous December. Walker and he were afraid that there might be a 'plot' to make them accept parole. Paul Murray said that the embassy's concern was the damage some media stories could do to the six's own cause. The men agreed on the need to keep united.

There was a good deal of discussion during both visits about the health of Gerry Hunter and Paddy Hill. Hunter was again not seeing anyone and was displaying signs of paranoia. Hill simply couldn't handle the strain of waiting and who could blame him? The visit ended cordially with the men relaxed and joking with us. They were glad of the chance to clear up misunderstandings. This was a warmer visit than we had had to Gartree.

Almost three weeks later, the Home Secretary at last decided to refer the case of the Birmingham Six to the Court of Appeal. It was now up to the DPP to decide whether to contest the case, which would mean it would take at least six months for the case to come to hearing. The Devon and Cornwall Constabulary investigation had discovered discrepancies in the McIlkenny interview record, which could undermine the credibility of the police evidence in the case. The case was now *sub judice*.

On 19 September 1990, Paul Murray visited Hill, Power and McIlkenny at Gartree, and Walker and Callaghan at Long Lartin on the following day. Power asked him to express the six's appreciation to Peter Barry and myself for our long-term commitment to their case.

In November 1990, it emerged that an independent report, commissioned by the Crown Prosecution Service, concluded that the forensic evidence against the six would no longer stand up in court. Skuse was discredited. At the end of November, the British DPP told the men's legal representatives that he would await the grounds of appeal before making any final decision about the stance the Crown would adopt, but said he intended to invite the Court of Appeal to review all the evidence and to decide whether the convictions were 'safe and satisfactory'. At this stage we knew that, as far as the British authorities were concerned, the game was up while, at the same time, the wheels of justice were moving at a snail's pace. This was a cause of great frustration to everyone, most particularly to the six men still languishing in prison.

The British-Irish Parliamentary Body met in Dublin in early December 1990. At the plenary session, I said I hoped that the Birmingham Six would get bail. I also said that I hoped that the British members present would bring their influence to bear to ensure the men's early release.

I attended the preliminary appeal hearing with Dick Roche and Tony Taaffe. The court fixed 25 February 1991 as the date for the full hearing of the case – based on the presumption that the Devon and Cornwall police inquiry would conclude by the end of January and that there would be another preliminary hearing in early February. No application for bail was made.

The report of the Devon and Cornwall police was given to the DPP on 4 February 1991. Another preliminary hearing on 18 February put back the main hearing to 4 March. On 25 February, Peter Barry, Tom Kitt and I attended the Court of Appeal hearing of the Birmingham Six, when to our great relief and delight, the DPP announced that he no longer regarded the convictions as safe and satisfactory. The court set 4 March as the date for the main hearing of the appeal to begin. The Crown was no longer relying on the evidence of the police who interrogated the six in 1974 and had already conceded the unreliability of the forensic evidence. Our London embassy reserved places for Barry, Kitt, Roche, Senator Paschal Mooney and me at the hearing.

Paul Murray, who deserves much credit for his tireless role in securing the release of the men, visited five of the six in their respective prisons at the end of February and beginning of March. (Dick McIlkenny could not be there, because Bishop Crowley of London was visiting him at the time.) He found Gerry Hunter, who had suffered from severe depression, better than he had ever seen him. Hunter, Callaghan and Walker told Paul that Hill was the most likely person to make a post-release outburst and that they were deeply critical of his attack on me some months before.

On 4 March, Barry, Kitt, Roche and I attended the full Court of Appeal hearing. The following day, Kitt and I saw the six before that day's proceedings and found them in excellent spirits. Two days later

I was in the court for the appeal of the Birmingham Six. I was fairly certain that this was the day when the men would be freed, but inevitably there was tension in the air. Could something still go wrong? When I actually heard the words that the convictions were quashed the feeling of elation was immense. The overjoyed men were freed there and then. They quietly walked out of the Court to face the world media in a very dignified fashion that impressed everyone. It took them a while to realise they were actually free and it was only then that the celebrations really began. I was in the crowd when they came out but didn't approach them. I felt it was their day, but I had an enormous sense of achievement and relief that it was all over.

The response of the British Government was to set up a Royal Commission to inquire into the whole system of justice in England and Wales. As expected, Paddy Hill made some critical remarks about the Irish Government at the six's press conference that night. He was the most volatile of the group. In his defence, it must be pointed out that he had been an inveterate letter writer on behalf of the six down all the years and was perhaps the most ardent campaigner for their release. Gareth Pierce is quoted in the *Guardian* of 9 June 2002 as saying about him: 'The reopening of the case and the final successful appeal were in large part due to his fight from within prison.'

In Seanad Éireann, on the day after the six were released, Maurice Manning, Leader of Fine Gael in the House, said it was 'individual English people who, more than any other, secured their release'. He referred by name to Chris Mullin, Gareth Pierce and Cardinal Hume. He also praised Peter Barry and me for having been persuaded of the men's innocence from an early stage.

Senator Shane Ross, on behalf of the Independent group of senators, paid particular tribute to those who were involved from an early stage, 'at no great political benefit to themselves. There was no percentage; there was no political kudos in championing the case of the Birmingham Six in the early and mid-80s. It should be recognised that people like David Andrews and Peter Barry took up this cause when it was not in any way popular and they persisted with it when it was not popular and indeed when others were not willing to get involved. It showed great political courage to take up the cause of those whom most people believed at the time did not have a particularly strong case for being released.'

So the seventeen-year nightmare of the men known as the Birmingham Six was over – or was it? Could anyone ever wake up from so prolonged and intense a nightmare? Could they ever recover from the unimaginably horrendous ordeal that they had endured?

OTHER HUMANITARIAN CAUSES

THE GUILDFORD FOUR AND THE MAGUIRES

The Birmingham Six were free at last, but I can't say they all lived happily ever after. Despite the quashing of their convictions, a smear campaign was conducted against them that cast doubt on their innocence, emphasised the 'technicality' of their success and hinted that, well, they had done it and a faulty system had secured their release. It was believed that members of various police authorities were responsible for this campaign, members whose colleagues were facing criminal charges. The results of the trials of these policemen were very disappointing. The shadow of the 'appalling vista' school of thought remained alive. It was well summed up by Rachel Borill, London correspondent of *The Irish Times*: 'For the Guildford Four, the Birmingham Six, Miss (Judith) Ward and other victims of the British judicial system, freedom has not brought them peace of mind. The quashing of all their convictions coincided with a whispering campaign, fuelled by off-the-record conversations with Cabinet ministers and police sources, questioning their innocence and insisting they were merely freed on a technicality. Both sides view the prosecution of the police officers involved in both the Guildford and Birmingham cases as the acid test of whether British justice could face up to what has been done in its name.'

Round One had been won by the police, she remarked, because the Guildford Four officers had been cleared of fabricating interview notes. And the police won Round Two as well. In early October, three officers of the WMSCS went on trial charged with conspiring to pervert the course of justice in the Birmingham Six case. Four days into the trial, the judge decided to drop the case against them, ruling that they had no chance of obtaining a fair trial because of adverse publicity. Ironically, it might be said that it was they who had escaped justice on grounds of a 'technicality'.

The collapse of their trial was quite amazing, given that the Court of Appeal, in quashing the convictions of the six in March 1991 had stated that the police had deceived the court. The Birmingham Six, the Guildford Four and the Maguires had spent tragically long periods in prison, yet nobody had been brought to book for such appalling miscarriages of justice.

Meantime, in their various ways, the men had great difficulty re-adjusting to life on the outside after so many years of suffering and deprivation. Added to this was the appalling attitude of the British authorities. They offered no assistance whatever to the men and were extraordinarily mean-minded and, as Billy Power said, mean-spirited in their attitude to compensation.

I stayed in touch with the six over the years through Pat McAndrew of the Derby Justice for All Campaign and some of the men themselves. Our embassy in London continued to battle on their behalf. Five years after their release, when not a penny had yet been paid, a meeting took place between the Birmingham Six and the Department of Foreign Affairs to discuss the difficulties with compensation. I wrote to Dick Spring, by now the Minister, on behalf of Hughie Callaghan, who had been offered the derisory sum of £260,000. Paddy Hill wrote to me at this time telling me that they were still being 'mucked about'.

During my own two terms in Foreign Affairs I pursued this whenever I could and finally in 2001, a full ten years after their release, the men were awarded compensation – amounts ranging from £800,000 to £1.2 million sterling. Small comfort for lives destroyed. How could anything compensate them for what they had gone through – their own personal suffering and also that of their families? Gerry Hunter's wife, Sandra, put it so well when she said, 'The police destroyed the lives of twelve adults and twenty-seven kids.' These men went to prison as fairly young people and came out so much older, especially in terms of human suffering. Their children grew to maturity without their fathers and the fathers missed all that that entails. No amount of money could restore the lost years and lives. The poignant title of Paddy Hill's book (published in 1995) *Forever Lost, Forever Gone*, captures more eloquently than I ever could the awful deprivation I am talking about.

The miserable attitude of the British authorities in regard to compensating the men for what had been inflicted on them defied belief and remains a source of real anger and disappointment to all those who were involved.

Life goes on; and while I continued with my usual constituency work, I became deeply involved in a number of cases where there had been, to my mind and to the minds of others, serious and blatant miscarriages of justice. Regarding the British system of justice I realised that, while our domestic justice system, based on a written constitution with an express bill of rights, policed by an active and independent judiciary, is not without its faults, the system that exists across the water was proven time and time again to be deficient, both in its content and its administration. Justice was at that time blind, but blind to the truth. In personal terms and especially with regard to the Birmingham Six, it is not easy to forget the effort that it took to convince an entire nation that the 'appalling vista', which their judges were so reluctant to countenance, was a fact. No search for wrongdoers should ever prevail over fairness and due process.

Being involved in humanitarian work not only reaps benefits for the recipients, it can also be a source of immense personal satisfaction – especially because of some of the incredible people that you meet on the way. Two people I met during the cases I outlined in the previous chapter made a very big impression on me. They were Sister Sarah Clarke and Annie Maguire.

Sister Sarah Clarke was a Galway-born nun of the Sainte Union Order. Her name is a byword for persistent hard work on behalf of Irish prisoners and their families in Britain, and she tirelessly carried out her great work for more than thirty years. She fought courageously to clear the names of all those she perceived to be victims of injustice. She was a constant visitor to the growing numbers of Irish prisoners held under the Prevention of Terrorism Acts. Paddy Hill referred to her as 'the Joan of Arc of the prisons'.

No case outraged Sarah more than the imprisonment of Giuseppe Conlon. He was arrested in 1974 after he came to London to visit his son Gerry, then under interrogation for the Guildford bombings. A much-respected Belfast working-class family man, he was seriously ill, but was tried, convicted and sentenced to twelve years and was later to die in prison. In a 1996 interview with *The Irish Times*, Sister Sarah recounted her reaction on first seeing him in prison: 'The old man's name was Giuseppe Conlon, a man that meant little to me then, but was to haunt me for the rest of my life. I had been asked to visit this man but nothing could have prepared me for the sight of him as he came in – an emaciated old man, gasping for air. "I am an innocent man," he said to me. I was very worried; I had never seen a prisoner so ill. He was almost crushed and broken. With every breath he said "I am an innocent man."'

Annie Maguire remains one of the most extraordinary people I have ever met. She was born on the Falls Road in Belfast in 1935. Her husband, Paddy, had served in the British Army but was demobilised before they were married in 1957. He had been living in England, so they moved there when they married. They have four children, three sons and a daughter. In her autobiography entitled *Miscarriage of Justice*, published in 1994, she wrote: 'Paddy was unashamedly proud to have been a British soldier, and thought England the best place in the world to live and bring up a family.' At weekends, he went for a drink to the local British Legion club or the local Conservative Club. They had a bust of Winston Churchill in their house. Their son Vincent wanted to be a policeman and was waiting until he was old enough to join. Another son, Patrick, hoped to join the army when he was old enough. The youngest child, Anne-Marie, was only eight when her mother was arrested.

Despite her horrendous brutalisation, she was at pains to recall some people who displayed 'decent humanity' to her during her prolonged ordeal: among those people are policemen, prison officers, workers in the social services, neighbours and friends. Many others who knew her, some of whom she had helped, turned away, didn't speak to her, presumed her guilty. But she didn't blame them because of the climate of the time.

She particularly remembered a young Scottish prison officer who was very kind to her young son Patrick. Patrick was then only 13 years old when he was arrested under the draconian provisions of the Prevention of Terrorism Act and beaten savagely. When her family was convicted, this young prison officer was overheard to say that he would never believe in British justice again.

Annie was sent to Durham jail, where Sr Sarah Clarke visited her during her first week in prison. The Gillespie sisters, Judith Ward and Carole Richardson were also there and they looked after her and helped her over the initial shock, grief and turmoil of separation from her children. She said about Sr Sarah that she was 'tirelessly determined ... to remind the outside world that we were still alive'.

The night she heard of Giuseppe Conlon's death was vivid in her mind. She said to herself, 'Giuseppe, you were a gentle, peace-loving man. You didn't deserve to die in these circumstances.' She vowed that night that she would be strong and would do everything in her power to clear all their names.

Her brother Seán's son, also named Seán, died from cancer on 11 June 1981, but the father was refused permission to go to his dying son's bedside or to his funeral. I have described Annie Maguire as a remarkable person and the following passage from her *Miscarriage of Justice* is an example of what I mean:

'I never bore hatred to those responsible for our situation. That would be pointless. From day one, I forgave. I believe unforgiveness is like a sickness, a cancer that eats away inside you. If I had not forgiven, I would be a sick woman today. People continually ask me how I could remain without bitterness after all we have been through. I have to say it is because of my faith. Faith does not mean that everything becomes easy, but it does mean that you have hope.'

She never ceased praying or believing that one day their innocence would be proved. Another heartbreak for her was that when her son Vincent married in 1982, she was not allowed out for the wedding.

Annie Maguire was released in 1985 after spending nine years in jail for a crime she did not commit. Her father died two weeks after her release. It was so sad that they had so little time together, yet she consoled herself with the thought that he had lived to see her free.

The Maguire Seven convictions were finally quashed in 1992. Annie went to see her local MP, John Wheeler, shortly after her release and he promised her that he would do all in his power to clear her family's name. Other public figures that campaigned for her and the Guildford Four were Sir John Biggs-Davison MP, Christopher Rice MP, Lord Fitt, former Home Secretaries Roy Jenkins and Merlyn Rees, and Law Lords Devlin and Scarman. She believes that the involvement of Cardinal Basil Hume, Archbishop of Westminster, was a turning point in swaying the perception of both the public and officialdom, and she feels great respect, love and affection for him.

Annie was unhappy with the reasoning of the Court of Appeal in quashing their conviction – the possibility of 'innocent contamination' of their hands and her gloves with nitroglycerine – because this allowed a whispering campaign against them. Sir John May himself was dismayed at this conclusion of the court. She wrote about the terrible consequences of their ordeal for her family, in particular her sons' broken relationships. Patrick junior suffered further police brutality, even after his release. He was unable to work due to health problems, suffered breakdowns and is on constant medication. Annie's husband died in 2003. And, like the Birmingham Six, she waited years for compensation. I can only add that as a lawyer involved for years in personal injury litigation, it is an axiom that although money may be the only way that the law can seek to right a wrong that results in injury, the injury remains and cannot be erased.

Anyone who meets Annie Maguire cannot but be impressed by her quiet dignity. She has been widely recognised for her ready willingness to forgive. She proved herself able to rise above the injustice visited on her by society. She was prepared to accept the fruits of a flawed system of justice, until such time as the chasm between truth and falsehood became so wide that even the most hardened advocates of the status quo could stomach it no longer. In May 2005, Annie received a papal honour from the Archbishop of Westminster. Pope John Paul II made the award three days before he died.

On 9 February 2005, the British Prime Minister Tony Blair apologised on behalf of the British Government to the Maguires and the Guildford Four for both their wrongful imprisonment and the stigma that still attached to them even after they were released. He said that they deserved to be fully exonerated.

The British Government still has not apologised to the Birmingham Six.

BRIAN KEENAN

My involvement over so many years in these cases of British miscarriages of justice was an important and deeply affecting personal experience for me. And as time went on I found myself getting involved in other human rights issues both at home and abroad.

One of these was the case of Brian Keenan. In 1986, Brian had left his native Belfast and gone to Beirut in the Lebanon to teach at the American University there. After a few months in Beirut he was kidnapped by Hezbollah and held hostage. In his book *An Evil Cradling* he describes how, a few months after being taken captive, and while striving to come to terms with the enormity of what had happened to him, he suddenly recalled an image on the entrance to the American University. Carved in stone there above the gate are Homer's words 'To strive, to seek, to find, and not to yield.' He said he knew this was a motto he must permanently stamp on his being for however long a time he would be held captive. His captivity continued for four and a half years and anyone who read *An Evil Cradling* will see that he did indeed take Homer's words as his motto throughout that prolonged nightmare.

What he was anxious to do from the outset of his ordeal was to stress to his captors that he was Irish and carried an Irish passport. A few days after his kidnapping, one of his captors told him that the Irish government had placed a large advertisement in the local Arabic newspaper, with his photo and a copy of his passport, appealing to the kidnappers for his release. His captor laughed at this because he found it somehow funny. Brian laughed too, but out of relief that finally his insistence that he was Irish had been confirmed and that our government was on his case.

At an early stage of his confinement he went on hunger strike. He was being told nothing and took this drastic course to demand why he had been kidnapped, how long he was going to be held and whether there was any communication with representatives of the

Irish government. When his captors eventually told him that he had been kidnapped because of the US Air Force attack on Libya and the death of some of Colonel Gadaffi's family he was amazed and responded, half laughing and half angry: 'What the hell has this got to do with me? I am not American. I am not British. I am Irish.'

When John McCarthy joined him in his imprisonment for the first time and the latter told him that he had come to Beirut to make a film about Brian's kidnapping, Brian says his first concern was that whatever had been reported by John or by anyone else should have established that he was Irish. When John assured him that it was known that he was Irish and that he himself had interviewed a senior Irish embassy official Brian had known during his short teaching spell at the American University, Brian says he drew great relief from this.

In his first in-depth interrogation as a hostage, Brian tells us he argued with his interrogator, asking what value was he, an Irishman, to the cause of Islam or the freedom of the Arab peoples. At every opportunity, he emphasised his Irishness to point out how ridiculous it was to have kidnapped him as a hostage to American or British imperialism.

Along with my brother Niall and Eoin Ryan TD, I became interested in Brian Keenan's plight and we did what we could to bring about his release. After protracted discussions with the Iranian Embassy in Dublin, Niall, Eoin and I went to Iran. We knew that this country had enormous influence with Hezbollah (the Iranians always denied this, of course), the organisation responsible for taking many of the hostages in the Lebanon. Hezbollah was a Lebanese Islamist group formed in 1982 to fight the Israeli occupation of southern Lebanon. We went to Tehran to urge the Iranians to intervene with the kidnappers and get them to release Brian.

We met with officials from the Iranian Foreign Ministry, including the Foreign Minister Ali Akbar Velayati. We succeeded in establishing a very good rapport with them, partly by showing respect for their culture and traditions. The Iranians treated us very well and were very genuine with us. I found them very straightforward and I'm pretty certain that our visits were partly responsible for getting Brian Keenan released. I met him after his release. I was very glad to have contributed to ending his nightmare captivity and have great admiration for the extraordinary fortitude he showed in the way he dealt with it.

THE DEVELOPING WORLD

Throughout this period I was involved in various 'causes' and problems in the developing world. I joined forces with that great humanitarian, Michael D. Higgins of Labour, on many – always memorable – occasions.

We went to Palestine during the first Intifada in the early 1980s. This was just after the first local elections in the area. Quite a number of Palestinian mayors had been elected and we visited them in various towns including Bethlehem and Bethsahur. We also visited Ramallah. It was basically a listening exercise to hear about violations of human rights and how democracy was developing. It was a very useful visit. Subsequently, during the same trip we met with some smooth-talking Israelis in Jerusalem. They were very anxious to know whom we had met, whom we had talked to and what they had to say. I don't believe they believed us to be sufficiently co-operative. At the airport, as we were trying to leave, there was more questioning. I have to admit I got quite angry, because they held us up so long that we missed our flight. However, we caught the next one without any harm done.

Michael and I visited Uganda in 2001 as members of the Development sub-committee of the Foreign Affairs Committee. Uganda is a priority country for Irish aid and we mainly wanted to see how Irish aid was being spent. We were in fact quite impressed. The development of the political process was also encouraging. In one village we visited we had the great honour of 'opening' a well and there was great celebration. We did actually unveil a sort of plaque on the side of the well with our names duly inscribed, although it didn't look like a plaque that would stand the test of time. However, there was a great atmosphere and a lot of ululating. We visited a number of schools and found the people warm, charming and friendly. At one stage we were given a present of a turkey, but as we had no way of bringing it home we 'recycled' it at the next village.

At that time there was a civil war continuing in the north of the country. A brutal organisation known as the Lord's Resistance Army was carrying out a campaign of violence against the local people and the government. We had talks about this with some very concerned local officials. One issue causing great anxiety was the question of children being stolen, which, wherever it happens in the world, is always a source of terrible grief. On our return to Ireland we reported our findings in detail to the committee.

I will touch on my work in Somalia in Chapter 8, but there is one incident I particularly remember on my second visit with President Robinson and her husband, Nick. We had just landed at Mogadishu, but the President couldn't immediately leave the aircraft as she was awaiting the arrival of a representative of the United Nations. I got off the aircraft for a few minutes to stretch my legs at the bottom of the steps. Who should I see standing around quite nearby, wearing scruffy shorts and covered in mud, but Michael D. He had just come from the refugee camp in Mandera, just inside the Kenyan border. He had a terrible tale to tell of the conditions in which the Somalian refugees found themselves there. I invited him on board the aircraft to meet the President, as I was sure she would want to hear what he had to say. Michael had been in the area for two weeks doing a documentary for Trócaire, so was quite well versed in what was happening. In fairness to the Robinsons, they weren't fazed by Michael's appearance and we all chatted for a while. Michael D. just happened to be at the airport because he was trying to hitch a lift back to Nairobi. That was one of the many problems of life in Somalia: there were no regular or commercial flights in or out of Mogadishu at that time.

Another venture that Michael and I undertook was just before the Gulf War in 1990 when we went to Baghdad. We were joined by Paul Bradford of Fine Gael, at that time a very young and newly elected TD. Our concern and reason for travelling was that quite a large number of Irish medical personnel, mainly nurses, were being held in Iraq against their will and were in danger of being used as human shields by Saddam Hussein. War was imminent and the nurses' families were naturally very concerned for their safety. These medical people were under contract to Parc, the company who supplied medical personnel worldwide. The Iraqis liked to refer to them as 'messengers of peace', but in fact they were of course hostages.

When the word went around in Leinster House that Michael, Paul and I were about to go to Baghdad, I was told not to do so by both the Taoiseach and the Minister for Foreign Affairs, Gerry Collins. I decided to go anyway. I was an out-of-favour backbencher with nothing to lose. A few days before we left Michael and I were chatting in the Dáil voting lobby when Charlie Haughey came over to us. 'I can understand why you two eccentrics are going off to Baghdad but why are you dragging along that poor innocent young man from Fine Gael?' was his comment. The day before we left he drawled to me, 'If you get yourselves into trouble over there we won't see you stuck.' I think he meant it.

We flew first to Amman in Jordan, where we were met by the Irish Honorary Consul, Salim Said. He arranged a meeting for us with the Jordanian Foreign Affairs Committee, who seemed most anxious to help us. They offered to put Jordanian medical personnel into the places that would be vacated by the Irish if they were let go. We discovered later that their interest wasn't altogether altruistic. It seems that Parc had won the contract to provide medical personnel in Baghdad ahead of a Jordanian company.

From Amman we travelled by jeep to Baghdad. We managed to arrange meetings with the Minister for Health and the Minister for Foreign Affairs, Tariq Aziz. I suppose we plamásed them a bit. We talked at length about the history of Ireland. We also told them that we were not in favour of sanctions, which affected children and old people. We got on very well with them and in fact did better than the Italians, who had met with them just before us. The Italians made the big mistake of referring to the hostages as hostages, but the Iraqis would only hear of them as 'messengers of peace'. It seems that one of the Italians said, 'But they could get killed.' The reply was that wouldn't it be a wonderful to die as a messenger of peace! Of course the Italians were absolutely correct, but sometimes one has to zip the lip in the interests of diplomacy. The ends do occasionally justify the means.

Before we left we knew that all the medical personnel would be released. There was some difficulty about a haematologist, because of the difficulty of replacing him, but in the end, he too was released. They wouldn't announce immediately that the release would happen because that would have to be done through Parc. However, we were very happy with the outcome.

Although what we were about was always serious, there were inevitably funny moments. At the beginning of the trip, when we were still in Amman, the three of us were having a few beers when the question of who was the leader of this 'very important' delegation came up. Both Michael D. and I put forward very excellent reasons why each of us should be leader. In the end we decided to put it to a vote. Michael D. voted for himself and I voted for myself. The crucial deciding vote was down to Paul. He spoiled his vote!

Another cause I was brought into was that of the Saharaoui people. Their territory in the Western Sahara desert had been disputed for many years between Spain, Morocco and Mauritania, and was known as Spanish Sahara, although the Saharaoui people would always refer to it as Western Sahara. It is a territory, about half the size of Spain, wedged between Morocco and Mauritania. The area is mainly desert and it is said to have a population of about a quarter of a million. The people are of Arab ancestry.

Spain first occupied the Western Sahara in 1884, possibly because the soil was rich in phosphates, and more or less since that time the Saharans or Saharaoui have been looking for independence. As time went on Morocco and Mauritania also laid claims to the territory. The UN has been taking an interest since the 1960s and since then a referendum has been seen as the solution. However, there have been many difficulties, caused, it appears, by Moroccan intransigence. In 1974 Spain, Morocco and Mauritania agreed a tripartite transitional administration, which would conclude in 1976. At some stage Spain withdrew, leaving Morocco and Mauritania. They basically halved the territory between them, causing the Polisario (the military wing of the Saharaoui) to declare war immediately. They defeated Mauritania, who withdrew their claim, and then continued the war against Morocco. The issue still has not been settled. The Saharaoui people in the meantime fled into the desert and have been living there ever since in camps on land loaned to them by Algeria.

Michael D. had already been to the Sahara on a number of occasions when I was asked to become involved, and I flew out with him via Algiers to Tindouf, a tiny airfield in the extreme south of Algeria. We were driven in a jeep through very barren desert to the camps. The Saharaoui, who are financed mainly by the UN, are very organised and orderly. Many of the men were away fighting and women largely ran the camps. There were schools and hospitals, primitive but clean. We were brought around to a number of different camps where we met the senior people, who always included women. This was unusual enough at that time for an Arab people. Alcohol did not figure at all in their lives, but we were told that they had no objection at all if we wanted to bring a bottle or two with us to sustain us. Somehow it wouldn't have seemed right to do so.

We slept in tents at night on thin mattresses on the ground and I must say I had no difficulty sleeping. Washing arrangements were meagre but adequate. Meetings were held in one of the bigger tents, where we sat around in a circle on mats on the floor. They usually took place late in the evening when people would come in from the desert. They were very colourfully dressed, in long robes – really like characters from the *Arabian Nights*. Many of the men wore rings, both on their fingers and on their toes. They all wanted one thing – independence. They owned a lot of camels and goats and the fare each evening was either one or the other, often, surprisingly, with chips.

A year later I was invited to visit the Saharaoui again, and this time they suggested I bring Annette. They also asked me to invite Gerry Collins and his wife Hillary. Gerry was at that time Fianna Fáil spokesman on Foreign Affairs. Both Gerry and I were struck by the rightness of the cause of the Saharaoui.

Both sides of the conflict had taken prisoners of war and, having once more visited the camps, we were brought to see the Moroccan captives in a sort of stockade in the middle of the desert. We talked to the prisoners, who seemed to be well enough treated. However, many of them had been there for many years and were sad and depressed, above all because they had no contact with their families. At that time the Moroccan government would never acknowledge that they were prisoners of war, simply because they denied that there was a war at all.

The big issue through many years of conflict has been the question of holding a referendum to settle the question of self-determination. However, there is endless difficulty about who will have the right to vote, and every time the problem looks like being solved, a new objection is raised. One happy note, however, is that in August 2005 the Polisario released all their 404 prisoners of war as an act of goodwill. Sadly quite a large number of the Saharaoui have 'disappeared' without trace. Agreement still hasn't been reached on the referendum.

We found the Saharaoui a very warm, reasonable and generous people. One day we visited the chief of a village in his tent. His wife was there with her baby girl of two weeks old. He told us that they already had a number of names for her, but they would like to add an Irish name. Gerry suggested Aisling, explaining its meaning, and it was duly decided upon. So presumably there is now a young teenager in the Sahara who perhaps wonders where she got this funny extra name.

Michael D. and myself have over the years done what we could to promote the case of the Saharaoui and indeed many Irish politicians, including my son Barry, have taken up the cause. I was glad to note that in August 2006 Foreign Minister Dermot Ahern stated, 'Ireland has consistently supported the principles of self-determination for the Saharoui people.' I feel a lot of sympathy for these intelligent and cultured people. They deserve a better way of life.

Senator Michael Lannigan had for many years been involved in a number of issues in various Arab countries, and in 1987 he asked me to accompany him to Libya. We were invited there to examine the damage caused by the US bombing of that country. The most important aspect of the trip was our meeting with Colonel Gadaffi in his tent. The main subject of the conversation, however, was Libya's connection with the IRA. There was some discomfort when we said that their support for the IRA was not acceptable to the Irish Government. Gadaffi's reaction was to gaze into the far distance and make no response. Most of the interview was taken up with Gadaffi checking with his interpreter. He had perfect English, of course, but would only conduct the interview through Arabic. It was altogether an uncomfortable meeting but I feel that we made our position clear vis-à-vis the IRA. We left feeling very much personae non grata and that we would be lucky to get away with our lives! Nevertheless, that afternoon we were brought on a sightseeing tour of some well-preserved Roman ruins which were absolutely magnificent. Our final visit was to where the Americans had bombed a residential area. We were shown bomb casings – 'Made in America' – and were given long lectures on the evils of that country. Since then Libya has renounced support for terrorist organisations.

Over the years I had developed a name for being interested in humanitarian problems. One of the downsides of this was that I became well known to the Indian, Pakistani and Bangladeshi people who lived in Dublin, many of whom had problems with work permits and visas.

I did try to help when I could, but one of the slight disadvantages for me was that when Annette and I went out for an Indian meal – we are both very fond of Indian food – we would invariably be spotted and in no time there would be a waiter standing within a few yards of us waiting to get my attention. The owner of one particular restaurant was quite aggressive about his various problems and began to berate me every time we came in. The last straw was when he was trying to get a visa for his daughter. He went on at length about how beautiful she was, as if this would make her automatically entitled to a visa or work permit. When I didn't respond as he expected he told me that I was useless and made some other uncomplimentary remarks. We had had enough of him by then and never went back to that restaurant. However, he was the exception and most of them, even if they were a little intrusive at times, were decent, polite and hardworking.

These miscarriage of justice cases and my various involvements in humanitarian causes happened throughout out my political life. Despite the various difficulties we face in this country from time to time, I am always keenly aware of how lucky we are in comparison to so many peoples around the world and I think a lot of my fellow countrymen and women are of the same mind.

DILEMMA, DIVORCE AND
DEPARTURES

THE NEW IRELAND FORUM

In May 1983, the New Ireland Forum had its first meeting and I was part of the Fianna Fáil delegation. It might seem surprising that the leader of the party should have chosen me to be a member. All I can offer by way of explanation is that from time to time, during the course of my long stay on the back benches, Mr Haughey used to call on me to go on radio or television when matters relating to the North were being discussed. Perhaps he felt I was a safe pair of hands, or perhaps he also saw me as an acceptable face for the Fianna Fáil that he led.

It was unfortunate that the elected representatives of the Unionist tradition on the island chose not to take up the invitation to participate in the Forum. Nevertheless, its establishment and operation were historic because it brought together, for the first time since the partition of Ireland in 1920, the elected nationalist representatives North and South. The purpose was to discuss the shape of a new Ireland in which the people of different identities on the island could live together in peace and harmony, and in which those different identities would be equally valued.

The Forum sessions were held in Dublin Castle. Over the course of nine months, there were twenty-eight private and thirteen public sessions, and the steering group, comprising the leaders of Fianna Fáil, Fine Gael, Labour and the SDLP, held fifty to sixty meetings. Also, subgroups of the Forum carried out detailed examinations of economic issues and the options of unitary state, federalism and joint authority.

Submissions were invited by means of newspaper advertisements in both parts of the country. No fewer than 317 written submissions were received, from both the Republic and Northern Ireland, but also from the UK, US, Belgium, France and Canada. These reflected both nationalist and Unionist views and covered a wide range of topics. Thirty individuals and groups were invited by the Forum to make oral submissions to elaborate on what they had put forward in their written submissions.

A Forum delegation of the four parties involved visited Northern Ireland in late September 1983 and met a wide spectrum of opinion there. Then, in late January 1984, a similar delegation went to London and met with groups from the Conservative, Labour, Liberal and Social Democratic parties.

John Hume and Seamus Mallon of the SDLP had a very deep input into the proceedings. I was close to Seamus Mallon. He and I always got on very well and spent a lot of time together during the Forum. We became much closer thereafter.

I intervened to make my own contributions to the Forum sessions from time to time, but it was essentially Mr Haughey's gig. He was the leader, as far as Fianna Fáil was concerned, and it was his line that was to be followed by the delegation. It is certainly true that there was tension between Fianna Fáil delegates to the Forum and the other party delegations over how the traditional aspiration to a united Ireland could be presented in the final report. Eventually, the following formula (to quote from *The New Ireland Forum Report*) was agreed: 'The particular structure of political unity which the Forum would wish to see established is a unitary state, achieved by agreement and consent, embracing the whole island of Ireland and providing irrevocable guarantees for the protection and preservation of both the Unionist and nationalist identities.' However, federalism and joint authority were also put forward as other possible solutions worthy of consideration.

When the report was published in 1984, Charlie Haughey discarded the last two options mentioned and declared that only unity could bring peace to the North. Garret FitzGerald, Dick Spring and John Hume were taken aback by Haughey's stance, which received almost more attention than the actual report itself. There was some unhappiness within Fianna Fáil at the way the leader was unilaterally deciding party policy without consulting the parliamentary party. The late Senator Eoin Ryan demanded that a full parliamentary party meeting be called to discuss and enunciate Fianna Fáil's position on the report. When that meeting was held, I spoke and agreed with Senator Ryan that discussion must precede pronouncement. I recall that Deputy John Wilson from Cavan-Monaghan, who had also been on the party's Forum delegation, intervened and stated clearly that Mr Haughey's position was not in any way contrary to party policy, which favoured a united Ireland. He also said that that was what the party founder wanted. In that way he linked Haughey with Eamon de Valera and that certainly contributed to the Haughey line receiving overwhelming support at the meeting.

Des O'Malley was not happy with what happened at the meeting and afterwards publicly criticised what he said was the stifling of any sort of debate within Fianna Fáil. This stance provoked the leader's displeasure and he immediately demanded that the party whip be withdrawn from O'Malley. At the subsequent parliamentary party meeting, and on a roll-call vote, the need for which I could not understand, but which was becoming something of a fundamental plank in the Haughey modus operandi, the motion to withdraw the whip from O'Malley was passed by fifty-six votes to sixteen.

I was one of the sixteen who voted against the motion. I felt that O'Malley was entitled to make the points he had made and I certainly felt that the penalty of withdrawal of the whip was excessive. That was the core of my contribution at the meeting in question: that the punishment being sought far outweighed any possible wrong that had been done.

What was becoming worryingly clear was that not only would no form of dissent be tolerated within the party from then on, but any sort of healthy debate would be stifled. It was after this meeting that the party press officer, P. J. Mara, made his famous 'Uno duce, una voce' remark; in other words, any disagreement with the leader was not going to be tolerated. P. J. was given to that sort of thing. He is a very decent fellow with whom I always got on extremely well. He knew where I stood and I knew where he stood and there was never anything by way of doubt between the two of us. I always felt that, like Brian Lenihan, P. J. was underestimated, used and abused at Haughey's whim. In addition, he was Tunney-like in his utter and unquestioning devotion to his master.

TO STAY OR TO GO?

George Colley passed away suddenly in September 1983, just one month short of his fifty-eighth birthday; far too young. He had gone to Guy's Hospital in London for exploratory tests for a heart condition. It was supposed to be a simple procedure, which is why his sudden death came as a terrible shock. To this day I can remember very clearly the sadness I felt at his funeral in Rathgar church.

George was an honourable, decent, upright man of enormous integrity. He had been a pillar of the party for more than twenty years and it was hard to think of Fianna Fáil without his presence. His republican credentials were impeccable and he was an Irish speaker. He had always been highly critical of big business's connection with and its investment in political parties. I would like to think that his ideology was not too different from my own. I think he might have been a little stronger in my support at the time when my ministerial hopes were dashed, particularly in the aftermath of the 1977 election. At that time, he may well have been one of the people mainly responsible for the appointment of Bobby Molloy to the Defence portfolio in preference to me. Time, I suppose, heals all such disappointments and his role at the time didn't in any way dilute my affection for him. I always thought that George Colley represented the best qualities in Fianna Fáil.

The return of Seán Doherty to the Fianna Fáil party fold in late 1984 was further evidence of Haughey's tightening control. Doherty had taken the rap for Haughey the year before for the phone-tapping scandal and had been trying for some time to have the whip restored to him. Haughey felt sufficiently confident in his position to call for the whip to be restored to Doherty and the parliamentary party did so with barely a whimper. I did not express any opinion one way or another on the restoration – in fact I cannot recall whether I was present at the relevant meeting or not. (My practice at the Bar caused me to miss some meetings from time to time.) I had made it quite clear that I believed Doherty had done wrong in the phone-tapping scandal but equally I had no doubt that the ultimate responsibility was not his.

What caused Des O'Malley's ultimate break with Fianna Fáil was the Bill to liberalise the country's family planning laws, which was introduced by the coalition government in February 1985. He refused to vote with his party against the Bill and made a strong speech in the Dáil setting out his reasons. In particular he drew attention to how a defeat for the Bill would affect opinion in Northern Ireland and condemned those who opposed it as displaying a partitionist mentality. He favoured a pluralist state, which is what all republics should be, he said, and he finished with the memorable phrase: 'I stand by the Republic.'

I tried to speak on the Bill, but my name was not put on the list of Fianna Fáil speakers. Anyone whose views might not coincide closely with the leadership's often had difficulty getting the opportunity to speak. I voted with my party on this issue, not because I agreed with the stance being adopted but because there was in reality little other choice for me. With the whip being applied, to abstain, as O'Malley did, or to vote with the opposition meant immediate removal of the whip and possible expulsion from the parliamentary party. Having been chief whip for three years, I understood and respected the necessity of the procedure, as a means of ensuring order in the Dáil. But an issue like contraception is one of personal conscience, and whips should not be applied on any such issues.

At the end of February 1985, the party's National Executive was called to headquarters in Mount Street, at Haughey's behest, to 'debate' a motion calling for O'Malley to be expelled from the Fianna Fáil organisation for 'conduct unbecoming'. There were 82 people present on the occasion. O'Malley was permitted to address the meeting and called for a secret ballot on the motion. According to the party's own rules and constitution, such a vote should indeed have been secret. The parliamentary party is free to decide its own procedure as regards open and secret votes – the latter being extremely unusual, of course – but not so the ard comhairle, which is supposed to be bound by the party's constitution.

Haughey made it clear at the meeting that he wanted a public and unanimous decision to expel O'Malley. When it was finally made clear to him that he would not be able to secure a unanimous vote, he demanded an open, roll-call vote. This was blatantly contrary to party rules, but, as on so many other sorry occasions, he succeeded in getting his way. The result was overwhelming. On a vote of seventy-three to nine, Des O'Malley was expelled from Fianna Fáil for 'conduct unbecoming'. When O'Malley left the meeting, he came out to a large group of his supporters who had gathered outside, including his wife, Pat. Of course they knew what had just happened and they cheered him. He gave Pat a kiss and questioned whether this might be seen as 'conduct unbecoming'!

With O'Malley's departure, the Haughey takeover of the party was complete. One of his strongest opponents, George Colley, was gone to his eternal reward and the other was just gone. For the rest of us, it now became a matter of putting our heads down and getting on with the work. In some ways, I suppose we had become weary of the battle. We had tried very hard to give the party a different leader but had got nowhere and it had cost us.

I had come into the parliamentary party at a time of peace, which endured from 1965 to 1969. From then onwards, it was attrition of one sort or another. There were so many points of conflict that we could have done without. Instead, we should have been able to direct our energies to the much more important matter of running the country. On a personal level, friendships suffered, but on a national level it was the country that suffered. Had the talent and energy that resided in the Fianna Fáil organisation been channelled into running the country, rather than into shafting each other, politics might not now be held in such low esteem.

It had been a long, hard struggle that lasted almost fifteen years. The worst occasions were the arms crisis, the three elections in eighteen months, and the three leadership challenges. For those of us opposed to Haughey, and who wished to remain in Fianna Fáil, there was really nowhere else to turn at that stage. In my case, I was not prepared to abandon the party to which I had devoted so much of my time and energy just because a bully had the ball. Bullies don't always win and nobody survives forever, either in politics or in life.

We were not to know then that the expulsion of O'Malley would have such fateful consequences for his old party. One of those who were deeply moved by what happened to him was a young barrister from a Fine Gael background named Michael McDowell. He was a member of the Law Library and I knew him there. In addition, I am related to him in that my maternal uncle was married to his maternal aunt. He is a grandson of the Irish scholar and revolutionary Eoin MacNeill, one of whose daughters, Róisín, married my mother's brother Donny Coyle, with whom I spent a few years in Galway before going to UCD. Róisín was extremely kind to me during my time in Galway – a surrogate mother, really. I always got on well with Mc-Dowell. He is a very bright man and was a very successful barrister, Attorney General, Tánaiste and Minister for Justice until he lost his seat in the 2007 election. At that time, though, I didn't know him that well. His group of friends in the Law Library comprised barristers like Gerry Danagher, Adrian Hardiman, Hugh Hartnett and Paul O'Higgins. They were a closely knit group of people. He wrote to Des O'Malley shortly after he had been expelled from Fianna Fáil and suggested the formation of a new political party, offering whatever assistance he could. He had some political experience, having been chairman of the constituency executive of Fine Gael in Dublin South East, Garret FitzGerald's constituency. He had obviously become disillusioned with his leader and party by this stage.

Some of O'Malley's close supporters in Fianna Fáil were also thinking along the lines of a new political party. The two leading lights were the Dáil deputies Mary Harney and Seamus Brennan. They commissioned a poll from Irish Marketing Surveys, which showed around forty per cent support for the formation of a new party led by O'Malley. The sections of society most in favour were the middle class and the bigger farmers. Despite this positive feedback, the momentum for setting up the proposed new party flagged somewhat. Brennan withdrew from involvement and decided to stay put. O'Malley himself didn't seem so keen on the idea either and contemplated a future as an Independent Fianna Fáil deputy. Mary Harney, however, remained enthusiastic about a new party and, by that time, Charlie Mc-Creevy had rowed in behind her and was strongly supportive of her proposals. Charlie McCreevy wasn't prepared to hang about and he called for the immediate setting up of the new organisation. When this didn't happen, he, like Brennan, withdrew from the process.

While there were various meetings held over those months to discuss the setting up of the new party, I had no involvement in any of them. I suppose that, in reality, I was a loner in this as in many things. I felt that I did not need anyone to help me make up my mind and preferred to do it by myself.

But for the Anglo-Irish Agreement, which Garret FitzGerald signed with Mrs Thatcher in mid-November 1985, the new party might never have come into existence. The Fianna Fáil leadership resolved to oppose the agreement strongly in the Dáil and, indeed, Haughey decided to send Brian Lenihan to the US to lobby leading Irish-American politicians against it. This was, in my view, a serious mistake. His reception in the US was frosty but, Brian being Brian, it didn't seem to take too much out of him. I sensed there were some in the parliamentary party who believed that it would be wrong to oppose the agreement, that there was much of merit within it and that therefore it should not be simply dismissed. Indeed, there were a few of us who felt the government should be supported on this issue. I spoke strongly to this effect at a parliamentary party meeting, but I can't say that my view was shared by too many members, if the support I received on that occasion was a yardstick.

I saw in the Anglo-Irish Agreement a genuine effort at reconciliation and an effort to bring about a permanent peace led by the Irish and British Governments. The bonus was to be a permanent peace on the island of Ireland which happily has now become a reality. The Anglo-Irish Agreement was one of the elements to bring that about. My belief is that it was opposed purely on the basis of political opportunism.

Des O'Malley welcomed the agreement and, in the Dáil debate on the issue, Mary Harney spoke out in favour of it. In fact, they both went through the government lobby when the vote came. The upshot of this for Harney was that she, too, was expelled from Fianna Fáil and joined O'Malley on the Independent benches. Once again, I didn't have an opportunity to speak on the issue in the House and, because the whip was also rigidly imposed, had to traipse through the 'no' lobby in opposition to the government motion seeking approval for the agreement. It may well be that my action in supporting the party on this – and indeed on other – issues will be seen as unprincipled. All I can offer by way of explanation was that I was motivated by a mixture of party loyalty and a deep conviction that the culture of fear over which Haughey was, at that time, presiding, could not go on forever and that the party was bigger that him and certainly bigger than me.

Harney had now joined O'Malley in the political wilderness and, as a result of what he saw as Fianna Fáil's destructive attitude towards the Anglo-Irish Agreement, he became more receptive to her urgings to set up a new party. The decision to do so was finally taken sometime in late November, and a few days before Christmas the Progressive Democrats (PD) party was launched. Within a few weeks, up to five thousand people had enrolled as members and at the first public meeting in early January 1986, which was held in the Marine Hotel in Sutton, something like a thousand people were in attendance. Quite a number of activists, some of them key people, from my party organisation in Dún Laoghaire, left to join the new party. It was fairly widely expected, both in Fianna Fáil and in the PDs, that I would be leaving to join the new political organisation. This expectation was not without substance.

Not that long after the PDs were launched, I went to see Des O'Malley at his house in Dublin. I told him I was considering joining his new party but that I would need some time to think it out. At the time I found the idea of a new organisation, away from the misery of Haughey's reign, very attractive, but I decided to take some space to reflect deeply about the move. I realised what a momentous thing it would be for me to leave Fianna Fáil, the party I had served for twenty years and that had been such a part of my life from a very young age. It was around the time of an Irish-French rugby match in Paris, so, although I had never been one for going on these rugby weekends, I decided to take the opportunity to go to Paris to contemplate my political future and take in the match as well. But I didn't make it to the match. For that weekend, I must have walked many, many miles around Paris, thinking about my future and the decision I had to make. I did manage to see the game on television but didn't – and don't – regret all the walking because it helped me to make my mind up.

Annette came to meet me at Dublin Airport on my return and she knew as soon as she saw me, from my body language, what decision I had reached. She could tell that I had made up my mind to stay in Fianna Fáil. It was then my task to tell Des O'Malley that I would not be leaving to join his new party. He had probably been satisfied in his own mind that I would be joining. It is very likely that I had given him that impression when I called to his house. He was non-committal in his reaction to my decision, though I think he was both surprised and disappointed; but I hope we have retained mutual respect for each other.

Given all the misery, my decision to stay put was taken because I had been brought up in Fianna Fáil; because of my father's and my mother's long association with it; because it would have been too much of a leap, too much of a break with the past. Fianna Fáil had always been in my heart and soul – I'm not suggesting that it was a religion or a substitute for religion for me, not at all. But it was a political organisation to which I was completely loyal and in which I believed deeply. I would have had to desert a lot of very old friends and co-workers, a lot of very decent people, who had worked so hard for me over the years, and that I could not bring myself to do. I knew above all that Fianna Fáil would outlive Haughey.

My father had died just a few months before, in October 1985. He could see what was happening to the party he loved, but he didn't try to influence me one way or another. In truth, if I had made up my mind to go, it wouldn't have really have worried me what he thought. He was, as I have already said, very pro-Haughey, and was always asking me in his own old-Dublin way: 'What are ya doin' to that poor man?' As in the case of my brother Niall, my father and I had, from the first, agreed that we would never fall out over the Haughey issue and I am glad to say it didn't affect our relationship in any way.

Pearse Wyse from Cork was the next Fianna Fáil TD to join the new party. His move didn't occasion that much surprise, but when Bobby Molloy went, this was a real surprise and made people within Fianna Fáil feel pretty edgy. It was a very difficult time for them and people were inclined to throw up their hands and ask, 'Who'll be next?' or 'How many more are going to leave?' The party had taken a terrible battering since 1979 and the turmoil seemed to be getting worse. But, as it turned out, Molloy was the last to go and after that things began to settle down and return to relative normality.

DIVORCE – NOT YET

Two attempts were made to modify the constitutional ban on divorce in 1986. The first was a Labour Party Private Member's Divorce Referendum Bill, which was introduced into the Dáil early in the year. Divorce was one of those issues of private conscience that tended to arouse heated emotions both in the House and among the electorate. In my longest Dáil contribution on this particular Bill, I called for reasoned debate and said no name-calling should be indulged in during the exchange of views. I also referred to 'hysterical and aggressive' lobby groups who, I said, had no right to put deputies under personal pressure. I considered the Bill defective in its wording, although I understood and had sympathy with its intent. I pointed out that Fianna Fáil supported a referendum on the issue of removing the constitutional ban on divorce and that I personally supported the removal of that ban, so that when a referendum was put before the people, I would be voting to have the ban removed. I also gave my constituents my solemn word that I would be totally silent during the run-up to the referendum once I had had my say in the Dáil. My view was, 'let the people decide'. I felt the political parties should air their views in the Dáil but, once the referendum campaign proper began, the parties should stand back. I did not want to see a repeat of what happened during the so-called 'pro-life' referendum of 1983. I also expressed deep reservation about the lack of provision for protection of children in the Bill.

The Bill was quite easily defeated in the House, but the Fine Gael–Labour coalition introduced a government Bill a few months later proposing a referendum on the same issue. Fianna Fáil were ostensibly neutral, but it is true to say that the party's organisation was the backbone of the anti-divorce campaign in many parts of the country. In the Dáil, Haughey spent most of his time questioning the wording of the Bill, but in public he claimed to be approaching the issue from the point of view of the family and said he saw the measure as a threat to that fundamental social institution.

In the Dáil, I made it clear that I was in favour of the proposal. It was my hope that the debate on divorce would help to further separate church and state. The issues were personal and in some cases heartbreaking for the individuals concerned and individual moral conscience should be the final arbiter.

I urged the government to proceed to remove the distinction between legitimacy and illegitimacy and said that we would have to come to terms with the concept of an extended family in which the spouses of a new family would have to accept a moral, social and financial relationship and commitment to the spouses and members of the first family. If proper provision were to be made for dependent spouses and children, the concept of the extended family might be the most compassionate and psychologically sensible way of approaching the problem. The principle of irretrievable marriage breakdown had already been accepted in Ireland, I said, because we had decrees of separation and nullity and barring and maintenance orders, so why not the final step of divorce and the right to remarry? It was cruel to consign people to the single state of legal and moral limbo for the rest of their lives if they wished to remarry and I expressed the belief that a loving and compassionate God would not stand over such cruelty. People formed new homes after marriage breakdowns and started new families with new partners. Were they to be condemned to a life of illegal cohabitation and their children to the concept of illegitimacy? I pointed out that divorce had existed in Northern Ireland for some years and yet there had been no 'rampant abandonment of moral principles or corruption of standards within the family'. Traditional family life was strong in Ireland and it would not be any less so for the introduction of divorce. During the debate on contraception the previous year, similar dire warnings were heard about the great moral decline that would follow and it hadn't happened.

The following passage from the report of the *New Ireland Forum Report*, which I had signed, had a particular relevance in this regard: 'Civil and religious liberties and rights must be guaranteed and there can be no discrimination or preference, in laws or administrative practices, on grounds of religious belief or affiliation; government and administration must be sensitive to minority beliefs and attitudes and seek consensus.' I believed that that was what we were trying to do in that debate: seek a consensus. I also referred to both the *Report of the Joint Committee on Marriage Breakdown* and the 1967 *Report of the Committee on the Constitution*, in both of which I found support for my views. I finished my contribution to the debate in the following terms: 'I will give the benefit of my silence to the Irish people. When the debate is concluded in this House and in the Seanad, I will wait for referendum day, go to my local polling booth in Blackrock and vote for the constitutional amendment.'

On polling day, the electorate rejected the proposal to amend the Constitution by sixty-three per cent to thirty-seven per cent. Dún Laoghaire had the biggest margin in the country in favour of the proposal. That was as I had expected.

The popular rejection of the proposed constitutional amendment did not mean that, within the Dún Laoghaire Fianna Fáil constituency organisation, people were universally happy with my stance on the issue. There were some quite conservative elements in the organisation, whom my opposition to Haughey and my stance on social issues displeased. That could prove relatively stressful for me on occasion but, after a while, I could see that it was basically the same people who held these views and, however much I believed them to be wrong, they were absolutely entitled to their opinions.

The result of the referendum solved nothing, of course. The serious social problem of marriage breakdown remained and the Dáil would have to revisit it on another occasion.

CUTBACKS, EXTRADITION AND THE WHIFF OF SCANDAL

By the autumn of 1986, it was becoming clear that the Fine Gael–Labour coalition would not last much longer. Labour ministers were growing more disenchanted with the fiscal austerity measures favoured by their Fine Gael colleagues and it was clear that they wouldn't be able to agree a budget for the following year. It was over this issue that the government collapsed and the general election was called for 17 February 1987.

The election took place against a backdrop of the fiscal and economic issues of public spending, borrowing, high interest rates and high unemployment rates. Both Fine Gael and Labour exploited Haughey's role in the Anglo-Irish Agreement. That role certainly did not go down very well, as I was told in no uncertain terms on many of the doorsteps of Dún Laoghaire. Indeed, Fianna Fáil's unspecific national campaign was of no help in this mainly middle-class constituency. My own first-preference vote, at eight thousand five hundred, was up around eight hundred votes on my performance in November 1982. It wasn't a spectacular recovery, but it was certainly going in the right direction.

One of my running mates on this occasion was Edward McDonald, a councillor and a fine, able and honourable man from Shankill. Edward was a particular friend of mine and he and his family were always good supporters over the years. His campaign manager was a serious pessimist, always tending to see the bottle half empty rather than half full. He was Edward's constant companion and was repeatedly telling him how badly he was doing. Ed had a moustache, which seemed to droop more and more as the campaign went on and he got more and more downhearted under this individual's influence. It's hard enough being a candidate and convincing yourself that voters are going to look through the list of candidates on polling day and put you number one without having someone undermining your confidence. A certain amount of self-belief is needed to survive an election campaign. People might find it hard to swallow the notion that politicians lack self-belief, but I have known many politicians, and few of them are ever comfortable at election time.

The other party candidate was Richard Conroy, a medical doctor and also an entrepreneur in mineral exploration. I had no difficulty with him as a candidate but he wasn't popular with the constituency organisation. One reason for this was that he was seen as an interloper, having stood before in Dublin South West and lost. He was accused of extravagance and he certainly spent a lot of money on the campaign – to no effect, unfortunately. There was definite resentment about the amount he was spending – it was felt that it wasn't in the best tradition of Fianna Fáil in the constituency.

One thing I should mention about this campaign was that a rumour was put around the constituency about me, that my reason for remaining in Fianna Fáil was that I would use the party as a vehicle to get elected and then jump ship to join the PDs. There was, of course, absolutely no truth in this. The streak of vanity that exists in all of us, myself included, would dictate to me that I would have been elected anyway, regardless of what party I represented. Brave talk at this remove.

Both Edward and Richard got a respectable first-preference vote, Edward a couple of hundred votes over three thousand and Richard just about a hundred votes short of three thousand. Unfortunately, such respectable polling wasn't enough to get either man elected.

This was the first election contested by the new PD party. They pursued the curious strategy of running three candidates in Dún Laoghaire. Helen Keogh and Larry Lohan had been selected by the local organisation, but their headquarters decided to parachute in the journalist, now editor of *The Irish Times*, Geraldine Kennedy. Keogh was particularly resentful of this, all the more so when Kennedy took the only seat the party won in the constituency. When it was announced at the count centre that Kennedy had won a seat, there was a pop and out came the champagne, and some people thought: 'How PD!' Not for them the drinks of the commoners. It probably wasn't the most diplomatic thing in the world to have done. It certainly sent out a message. In my case, champagne was for home consumption.

Nationally, the PD performance was pretty impressive: they succeeded in winning fourteen seats on their first outing. This was to prove a high-water mark for the party in terms of election performances. Overall, Fianna Fáil won eighty-one seats, three short of an overall majority. This was the fourth time Mr Haughey failed to win an overall majority. He was, however, in by far the strongest position to form a government. He let it be known straight away that he wouldn't be doing any deals with anyone, unlike the unseemly bargaining for votes after the February 1982 election. When it came to his nomination as Taoiseach, he was supported by Neil Blaney and elected on the casting vote of the Ceann Comhairle, the former Labour but now Independent TD Seán Treacy, from Tipperary, whom he had been instrumental in appointing.

Haughey's new government surprised everyone by introducing swingeing cuts in public spending, which earned the Minister for Finance, Ray MacSharry, the nickname 'Mac the Knife'. The Minister for Health, Dr Rory O'Hanlon, became known as 'Dr Death' because of the cutbacks in his department, and a similar situation at Education drew down a lot of flak on Mary O'Rourke's head. There was no doubt that the country faced an enormous crisis at the time. In January 1987, the *Economist* magazine had an article on Ireland, 'How the government spent the people into a slump', which said that Irish bankers feared the International Monetary Fund (IMF) might have to step in and impose the tough conditions that Irish politicians themselves did not have the courage to introduce. The article also predicted that what it called Haughey's 'rural-based Fianna Fáil party' would soon be returned to power and would embark on unrestrained spending once again. As a result of this article, the myth that the IMF was ready and willing to seize control of the Irish economy gained a head of steam.

A few figures will give some idea of how disastrous the economic situation was at the time. The national debt stood at €32 billion: £1 in every £4 of current spending went on the interest to service this debt, which accounted for one-third of all tax revenue, and the interest bill was increasing by twenty per cent per annum. Many people felt the country was going down the tubes and this made the population in general more willing to accept draconian cutbacks in public spending.

Some Haughey admirers have, at least in retrospect, been inclined to credit him with applying the drastic medicine that our sick economy needed in order to make it better and turn things around. I don't share their view, and not because I was not an admirer of the man. If one person were to be singled out for credit, I believe that person would be Ray MacSharry. It was his courage at the time that rescued the situation. He was the one who did some straight talking to his leader and convinced him what ought to and had to be done. Haughey didn't like making unpopular decisions, but on this occasion, when persuaded, he went along with his Minister for Finance.

Alan Dukes, the new leader of Fine Gael, had been Minister for Finance for most of the 1982–87 period of the Fine Gael–Labour coalition, and had wanted to do exactly as MacSharry was now doing. His so-called 'Tallaght strategy' promised support for the budgetary policy now being implemented. This was unprecedented in Irish political history and he and his party deserve great credit for such principled politics. It was an act of patriotism and genuinely in the national interest, to use that much-abused phrase. The minority

Fianna Fáil government could not have survived without that support. Neither Dukes as leader nor his party reaped any reward for what they did.

Politics can be a cruel old game. It is my view that Fine Gael made a grave mistake when they dumped Dukes as their leader in 1990. It was an act that still puzzles me. They did both themselves and the country a disservice by their action and I believe Alan Dukes would have been a very good leader, the leader they were looking for, had they given him time and resisted the knee-jerk reaction to what many of his party viewed as collaboration with the enemy. A former party colleague of his, that distinguished academic lawyer and brilliant orator, John Kelly, often advocated a merger between Fianna Fáil and Fine Gael as a natural association of like-minded political ideologies, but he, like Alan, was unrewarded for such lateral thinking. Alan Dukes was a very fine parliamentarian and his particular strengths were Europe and agriculture. No, Alan Dukes never got the credit he deserves for his stance during those years, nor did he get much gratitude from Fianna Fáil, or indeed Fine Gael.

The Extradition Bill, which the government proposed to introduce in November 1987, provoked a lot of unrest on the Fianna Fáil back benches and at a parliamentary party meeting many TDs and senators – up to fifty, I recall – spoke out against extradition. The kidnapping of the Dublin dentist John O'Grady by the IRA and the hacking off of two of his fingers by his kidnappers, the horrific bombing of the Remembrance Day ceremony in Enniskillen, and the interception of an IRA arms shipment from Libya on board the Eksund, all produced a wave of revulsion and hardened public opinion considerably against terrorism. During my contribution to the Dáil debate on the Bill, I referred to the public horror caused by these atrocities, and I pointed out that against such a background it was difficult to plead for safeguards in the legislation and for civil liberties. Extradition, I said, was perceived as a weapon in the fight against terrorism, a purely legal means of fighting terrorism, and so it was hardly surprising that opinion polls revealed that a majority favoured its introduction. The question people were answering in the opinion polls was whether they favoured extradition. If they had been asked, however, whether they favoured handing Irish people over to the courts that convicted the Birmingham Six, it was unlikely that the response would be the same.

As a Taoiseach once said in the House, if you want the right answer, then you must ask the right question.

I felt that, while public opinion would inevitably and understandably oscillate in the light of the most recent atrocity or latest miscarriage of justice, the Dáil had the duty to consider the whole complex question logically and dispassionately. I defended the concept of extradition on the grounds that it was the means whereby civilised countries could prevent their territories from becoming havens for fugitive criminals from other jurisdictions. It was also a two-way process: we couldn't expect other countries to use their resources to capture and return persons wanted in our country if we weren't willing to reciprocate. Therefore, I felt that to suggest that there should be no extradition as an emotional reaction to some miscarriage of justice in a country with which we had no extradition agreement, was both missing the point and dangerous. To call for 'no extradition' was, in effect, to call for a withdrawal from the community of civilised nations. It was obvious to me that safeguards were needed and I pointed out the main new safeguards provided in the Bill, which were the need for prima facie evidence against the person whose extradition was requested, the individual vetting of each application by the Attorney General, the highest law officer in the land. If these were added to the existing safeguards, I felt the balance would be right. It was totally unfair to suggest that the safeguards were in some way a knee-jerk reaction to the views expressed at the Fianna Fáil parliamentary party meeting. It was to counter this attitude that I encouraged the principle that some form of accounting be made to the Dáil on an annual basis, so that we could see clearly how the Act was working and leave no doubt in the minds of people who had genuine fears about what the government was doing.

My contribution in the Dáil also gave me the opportunity to pay tribute to the Garda Síochána for their role in freeing Dr O'Grady and, indeed, for their success in rescuing the other kidnap victims, Dr Tiede Herrema, Ben Dunne Jr, Don Tidey and Jennifer Guinness. I condemned the Enniskillen massacre and paid particular tribute to Gordon Wilson, who lost his daughter in the atrocity. The faith that could bring him to forgive her killers humbled us all, and he deserved the highest praise possible.

It was wonderful that Gordon later became a member of the Seanad, when he was nominated by Albert Reynolds in 1993. Irish public life has been the better for his participation in our parliamentary process, and when one looks back on all the tragedy and terrible suffering, the horrors done in the name of some perverted philosophy or other, one can say without fear of contradiction that he was an example to us all and a brightly shining light, showing the way out of the awful darkness of those events and those times.

Meanwhile, the whiff of scandal was never far from Haughey. Suggestions emerged in early 1989 that he was abusing his position as a public representative to enrich himself. A Saudi prince on a visit to the country presented him with what is supposed to have been a jewel-encrusted dagger and Mrs Haughey was said to have received a valuable necklace. There was an ethical question to be answered about receiving such valuable gifts, and the gifts were said to contravene the Cabinet Procedure Instructions, which set down guidelines for cases like this. The incident led to something of a political storm and Haughey failed or refused to give much of an explanation to the Dáil about the gifts. To my knowledge, the gifts were never valued. If they had been, it may be that the whole furore could well have been dampened. There were all sorts of values placed on the dagger, some of which were, given the manner in which fact can be adjusted to suit the story, greatly exaggerated. Haughey did respond to a question on the issue put down in the Dáil. He pointed out that his predecessors had never been asked about gifts they received. If my memory serves me correctly, I think that de Valera had been quizzed by Oliver J. Flanagan, sometime in 1947, about a wristwatch he was supposed to have been given! He had said at that time that rumours about the value of the gifts were wildly exaggerated, that in any event they were personal gifts and that one didn't place a monetary value on such gifts.

I'm not sure that too many people begrudged the Haugheys keeping the gifts and I certainly did not and do not feel too strongly on the point. The so-called 'high moral ground' can be a lonely and insecure place and I never cared too much about trying to occupy it.

Another issue about which there was some controversy in 1989 concerned Ray Burke's performance as Minister for Energy and Communications. In that capacity he set up the Independent Radio and Television Commission, which was to oversee the establishment of commercial radio and television in Ireland. Concerns were expressed about the way licences were being allocated, especially the award of a national commercial radio licence to the Century consortium headed by Oliver Barry. I always considered Burke a good minister in whatever portfolio he had. He was a very able individual but, as events would subsequently show, he had weaknesses regarding money. In January 2000, it was revealed to the public that Barry had given Burke £35,000 during the 1989 election campaign. There may have been absolutely nothing wrong with the award of the licence to Century, but the risk is always that, unless these things are done – and seen to be done – with clean hands, the public are entitled to be suspicious: and if there is any suggestion of financial impropriety, there is and ought to be redress.

It always saddens me that the families of public representatives accused of wrongdoing were invariably dragged into the resulting mudpile and end up with a terrible stigma attached to them. To extort money or accept bribes in the course of public office is, of course, wrong, but it is not fair that the sins of the wrongdoer should be visited on the innocent family members and it can take generations for the implications of guilt by association to go away.

A NEW DEPARTURE FOR FF

It was a serious tactical mistake for Haughey to call the June 1989 general election. Fine Gael were still supporting the government's budgetary policy. Public spending had been brought under control. It's true that the government suffered some defeats on motions set during Private Members' time in the Dáil, but these weren't issues of such national moment as to justify collapsing the scrum and dragging everyone in the country through yet another election.

Haughey had just returned from a trip to Japan when he called in his ministers and told them that he would treat a defeat on a motion concerning payment of compensation to victims of defective blood products as appropriate grounds for calling an election. This shocked his ministers and dismayed TDs when they heard this most unwelcome news. Albert Reynolds, in particular, urged him not to precipitate an election, but Pádraig Flynn and Ray Burke were staunch in their support of the leader. Elections to the European Parliament were due on 15 June and, influenced by a strong Fianna Fáil showing in opinion polls, they argued that holding a general election on the same day would give the opportunity to gain an overall majority. The opinion polls also showed a collapse in support for the PD party and those in Fianna Fáil favouring an election considered an additional benefit would be to wipe out the upstarts that had left Fianna Fáil and had dared to start up another party. In victory, revenge and all that.

On four previous occasions, Haughey had failed to win an overall majority – he must have felt the time was now ripe to achieve that elusive goal. I have read that rumours circulated in Leinster House at the time that Haughey had gone to the country to raise money for himself in the guise of election expenses. I didn't hear any such rumours and if I had, I would have considered them fantastic, even given the capabilities that Haughey had. Subsequent tribunal evidence has shown that Haughey received £150,000 from Ben Dunne at this time (part of the £1.3 million he got from the same source in the period from 1987 to 1992). We also now know that Burke got £95,000 in donations at this time (£30,000 from Joseph Murphy Structural Engineers, £30,000 from Rennicks and £35,000 from Oliver Barry of Century). The property developer Tom Gilmartin says he gave Flynn a £50,000 donation during this campaign.

The opposition parties, especially Labour and the Workers' Party, attacked Fianna Fáil over the health cuts and this issue was to dominate the campaign. This was as true for my own constituency as it was for any other in the country. A slogan the party had used in the months before the 1987 election, 'Health cuts hurt the old, the poor and the handicapped', was resurrected and thrown at us in light of the severe cutbacks we had implemented while in government. In this way, the achievement of bringing public spending and borrowing under control was lost. A Fine Gael–PD pact was negotiated, which meant that those parties attacked the government rather than each other. Before the election was called, polls had shown Fianna Fáil at 52 per cent and some even had us as high as 54 per cent, but, after the election was called, that figure dropped to 47 per cent and, a week later, to 45 per cent. On polling day, the party took just under 44 per cent of the vote and lost four seats. It was one of the lowest turnouts in recent elections. The people clearly didn't think the election should have been called.

In Dún Laoghaire, my own first-preference vote was up by fifteen hundred on two years before and I was elected on the first count. How is my increased vote to be explained in the context of the national trend? Perhaps it was because some Fianna Fáil voters in the constituency finally realised that my opposition to Haughey wasn't based on personal whimsy and that I was genuinely concerned for the fate of the party. Perhaps it was down to my sustained hard work in the constituency. I find it hard to account for such a big increase given the national circumstances. The great thing about this improved vote for me was that my second preferences helped to get a running mate, Brian Hillery, elected. He was Professor of Industrial Relations at UCD and was a nephew of Paddy Hillery. He had been a senator since 1977 and had been Fianna Fáil spokesman on Labour in the Seanad since 1983.

My other running mate was Betty Coffey. In the end, by the time she was eliminated from the count she was only a handful of votes – around twenty-five – behind Brian Hillery. If one were to say which of the two candidates most deserved to be elected, it would have to be Betty Coffey. She was a wonderful councillor who had done a lot of hard work in the constituency. Brian Hillery is an outstanding academic, a very fine man with a delightful wife, but political longevity wasn't on his agenda. Another point worth making about Brian, who lost the seat at the next general election in 1992, was that he was a reluctant candidate for a Dáil election in the first place. He didn't really want to run and refused the invitation when first asked to do so. A lot of pressure was then brought to bear on him, to which he eventually succumbed. It is tough enough being a TD if you want the job, and the career just doesn't work if you don't. The hard graft and the monotony needed to survive won't be endured by a reluctant participant.

There was pretty intense rivalry between Betty and Brian once the campaign got going. Having reluctantly decided he would stand, Brian obviously resolved to give it his best. Their respective teams did things like putting up posters outside each other's houses. Betty had a jazz band in the middle of Dún Laoghaire on a Saturday afternoon and, when Brian got to hear of it, he did something novel to match it.

Headquarters were delighted with this, of course, because some in Fianna Fáil think that candidates cutting each other's throats is the way to win seats. I have never been convinced of the wisdom of that view.

Being a university lecturer, Brian was able to get out enthusiastic teams of youthful students to canvass for him. We had our own enthusiastic young team out for this election too. My son Barry, then a university student, rounded up some of his friends, so we weren't lacking in election workers. They stayed in the house and Annette recalls constantly feeding them – young men have healthy appetites. One of Barry's pals complained one evening when there was broccoli for dinner, remarking that we were always having broccoli in this house. Someone else then remarked that he was sure they weren't getting broccoli up in Brian Hillery's house. Eventually one of them decided to ring that house, pretending to be a newspaper reporter. He asked for Mrs Hillery and told her his paper was doing a series on election campaigns. One of his first questions to her was whether she had to feed the party workers. When she said yes, he said would she mind him asking her if she gave them a lot of broccoli. At that stage Miriam Hillery became suspicious and demanded to know who it was. He then told her the truth. Campaigns always have their funnier sides which serve to keep us all sane.

Up to that point, we had never used personal election literature during campaigns. In fact it was strictly forbidden in Fianna Fáil. Both my running mates got posters made with their own photographs on them and displayed them throughout the constituency. I decided not to do so and persisted with the party posters. Senator Don Lydon, who was working in Fianna Fáil, Mount Street Headquarters, called into our house one night during the campaign and said to me: 'David, people want to know if you are actually running in this election.' The reason for this strange comment was the predominance of posters of the other two candidates on poles all over the constituency and no sign of my face anywhere. When I pointed out that personal posters had never been the practice in the past, he said my behaviour was seen to reflect an over-confident attitude. He made the point that I was not doing everything possible to maximise my vote so that my transfers would get us the second seat. The result was that I had to get suitable photographs, posters and leaflets together at very short notice. Of course the printers could charge me more or less what they wanted to at that stage because, with time so short, I was at their mercy. We also had to think up a quick slogan to go with the personal posters and came up with the not so earth-shattering: 'You know him. You can trust him.' That election campaign set the precedent that had to be followed in subsequent contests.

Although Fianna Fáil was losing seats elsewhere, we had gained a seat in Dún Laoghaire. There was not, of course, to be any recognition of the achievement for me in the upper echelons of the party. The only recognition possible would have been for me to have been brought into Mr Haughey's Cabinet and that was a non-runner from the start. He was convinced of my lack of loyalty and I did nothing to disabuse him of this. It never bothered me – but I would have liked to have become a member of the Cabinet earlier than I did.

The PD vote slumped in the 1989 election and they dropped from fourteen to only six seats. A notable casualty was Geraldine Kennedy in my own constituency. She was overheard to remark, at the election count where she was losing her seat, that she could never understand how David Andrews got as many votes as he did in Dún Laoghaire. If I knew the secret, I was hardly going to share it with her anyway, so I doubt if her inquiry was genuine and suspect that it was flavoured by under-ripe grapes. It did give me reason for a small smile.

For a record fifth consecutive time, Haughey had failed to win an overall majority. Fianna Fáil was now in a weaker position, having dropped from eighty-one to seventy-seven seats. Interestingly, in a radio interview as the results came in, my former constituency colleague Barry Desmond, who was then an MEP, said the solution to forming a government was very simple: Fianna Fáil and the PDs had the numbers and they could form a government. Mary Harney, who knew from experience the price that Haughey had been willing to pay to get into government, saw that something could be salvaged from the wreckage of the election results for her own party. The day after the Desmond comment, she said that, however much they might dislike certain people or parties, the PDs had to play their part in giving the country a government for the foreseeable future. But Pearse Wyse of the PDs seemed to pooh-pooh the idea, saying said that in no circumstances could he bring himself to vote for Haughey as Taoiseach.

At a parliamentary party meeting after the election, but before the idea of going into coalition with the PDs was being contemplated or openly discussed, I recall that Jack Fitzsimons, a senator from Navan, and I stood up and said that we should at least consider going into coalition with O'Malley's party. Jack was an architect and author of a bestseller called *Bungalow Bliss*, a DIY manual on how to build your own small home. He and I were the first to advocate coalition. For the following few days we were utterly ostracised by our colleagues, accused of heresy of the worst order. When people saw me coming they deliberately avoided me and it is for this reason that I have such a clear memory of the event. It was all a bit silly really, but I suppose that people have to kiss many ugly toads before they meet the handsome prince and eventually the idea of coalition began to percolate through the party.

When the twenty-sixth Dáil met on 29 June, for the first time in the history of the State it failed to elect a Taoiseach. Haughey had held exploratory talks with other leaders but no arrangement had been reached. He had asked O'Malley for PD support for a minority Fianna Fáil administration, but O'Malley replied that the price of PD backing was coalition, to which Haughey responded that he couldn't sell the idea of coalition to his own party. It had been a long-standing policy of Fianna Fáil not to go into coalition; the National Executive voted unanimously against it at the time and on RTÉ Radio 1's *This Week* programme on 2 July, Haughey reiterated that coalition was completely ruled out.

At the parliamentary party meeting the following day, senior figures such as Reynolds, Flynn, Wilson, O'Hanlon and O'Kennedy spoke against coalition but, interestingly, Collins, Burke and Lenihan expressed the view that it was the only available option and that it could be sold to the party. Apparently, at a Cabinet meeting, Flynn had launched a scathing attack on Haughey, saying that his personal pursuit of power was the reason he contemplated coalition. On the following day, Flynn went on radio and said that the Cabinet had unanimously opposed coalition, that the National Executive, parliamentary party and grassroots had shown that this was a core value that had to be preserved. But Mr Haughey had other ideas. He met, again privately, with O'Malley and conceded the principle of coalition.

The negotiation of a joint programme for government was carried out by Albert Reynolds and Bertie Ahern for Fianna Fáil and Bobby Molloy and Pat Cox for the PDs. The parliamentary party agreed to the talks but not before Geoghegan-Quinn launched a bitter attack on Haughey – she had to suffer the added gall of having to accept that her former constituency colleague but now opponent, Molloy, was the chief PD negotiator and would likely get a Cabinet post.

Haughey and O'Malley met to iron out difficulties that arose between the negotiating teams. Haughey almost certainly took some decisions without reference to his two negotiators. This might seem strange and hard to believe but it has to be remembered that Haughey was monarchical and autocratic in style. And then, in Irish history, there is the precedent of the Truce negotiations in London in 1921. That debacle precipitated the Civil War. The story has gone abroad that someone asked Haughey at this time about opponents to coalition within Cabinet, and he replied, 'They're only a crowd of gobshites.' It may well be apocryphal, but that it was told at all reflects his leadership style.

The last stumbling block in the coalition negotiations was the number of PD Cabinet seats. They were stuck on two, but Fianna Fáil was willing to offer only one. Both Ahern and Reynolds went on radio to say the PD seat allocation would be one, but on the same day Haughey conceded two in his meeting with O'Malley. They also got one junior ministry and three of the Taoiseach's eleven Seanad appointments. The quip of one of my colleagues was appropriate: 'Never in the history of Irish politics has so much been given by so many to so few.' It was certainly an indication of the price Haughey was prepared to pay to remain in power.

Albert Reynolds was raging at the way Haughey went behind his back to make concessions. Bertie Ahern may also have been miffed – he wouldn't have been human if he wasn't – but he seemed to get over it and stayed in Cabinet to the end. The whole experience of going into coalition had certainly changed things at Cabinet level in the party. Former strong Haughey supporters such as Reynolds, Flynn and Geoghegan-Quinn had been alienated, and this was to have repercussions for him before too long.

THE 1990 PRESIDENTIAL ELECTION

The disaster for Fianna Fáil that was the 1990 presidential election could not have been foreseen. We nominated Brian Lenihan as our candidate and he was the favourite to win. John Wilson also sought a nomination but he didn't get the necessary support. I backed Brian, who was extremely bright and a very popular man. He was liked right across the political spectrum and had friends in every party. I have always had great regard for the Lenihan family. Brian's father, Paddy, entered the Dáil on the same day as I did and he was a deputy for Longford-Westmeath from 1965 until his death in 1970. He was a highly intelligent man and I got on very well with him, with Brian, and later with Brian's sons, Brian Jr and Conor. Ann, Brian's wife, is also a very likeable person. However, for some reason best known to herself, Brian's sister Mary O'Rourke took a dislike to me and never subsequently changed her mind. She doesn't hide her dislikes, which is a very refreshing thing in many ways. I neither liked her or disliked her. I had no reason to do one or the other, as our paths rarely crossed.

Unfortunately, Brian's presidential election campaign went badly wrong. In late October, on RTÉ 1's *Question and Answers* programme, he was asked if he had telephoned Áras an Uachtaráin in late January 1982 to urge President Hillery not to dissolve the Dáil after the minority Fine Gael–Labour coalition suddenly went over its budget. He vehemently denied doing so. As a matter of practice, based on convention, it would have been an act of foolishness to ring the president to ask him to behave in a political fashion. The president is above politics and wouldn't have taken the call anyway. Garrett FitzGerald, who was also on the programme, said he himself was at the Áras on the night in question and was told phone calls had been made. Brian had obviously forgotten that he had given an interview to a UCD research student in which he had admitted that he was one of the Fianna Fáil people who had phoned the Áras on that occasion. Worse, the student had taped the conversation in which Brian made this admission. The research student contacted *The Irish Times* to say he had the tape and from there the controversy grew and destroyed Brian's chances of becoming president.

It has to be said that Brian made a bit of a botch of the whole thing. He went on an evening news television programme the next day to repeat his denial of having phoned the Áras and created something of a sensation by gazing directly into the cameras instead of at his interviewer. Nobody who saw this will ever forget it. Poor Brian, staring into the camera, looking ill, as he was, and shifty, as he certainly was not. Apparently, staring into the camera is an absolute no-no when appearing on TV. When Alan Dukes referred in the Dáil to documentary evidence confirming the calls, an angry Haughey exacerbated the situation by declaring that FitzGerald had been completely exposed as telling lies. Shortly after that, *The Irish Times* released the text of part of the taped interview. I don't for one moment believe that Brian was deliberately telling lies. In his book, *For the Record*, which was published some months after the presidential election, he explained that he had been on heavy medication for his liver transplant when he gave the research student the interview back in May 1990, that the medication caused confusion and that he had no recollection of having given the interview. I feel this to be both plausible and reasonable and put his initial denials down to that memory lapse. He deserves the benefit of the doubt on the question.

Alan Dukes now decided to put down a motion of no confidence in the government, which was obviously aimed at testing the cohesion of the coalition. O'Malley left Haughey in little doubt that Lenihan would have to resign from the Cabinet. Brian refused to stand down, although Haughey asked him to do so at a private meeting in Kinsealy and, although the pressure mounted on him to resign, he steadfastly refused to take that course. At a subsequent parliamentary party meeting, Mary O'Rourke understandably defended her brother. I also spoke very strongly in his favour, contending that he should not have been asked to step down. The general mood of the party was pretty sour. Some of the younger deputies, such as Noel Dempsey, Seán Power and M. J. Nolan, spoke out strongly against forcing Lenihan to resign. But all to no avail. Brian persisted in refusing to resign, and Haughey used his constitutional prerogative to fire him. I was very saddened by his sacking. I considered it to be the beginning of the end of his political career. Brian was always sent into the heart of things to bat for the party, often in the face of appalling problems and difficulties. He never turned down requests to go out and do that; he never shirked situations from which many others would have run a mile; he was always prepared to man the 'bearna baol' on behalf of Fianna Fáil. He would bluster and obfuscate, 'turn logic on its head' as Dick Walsh remarked one time. There was never any challenge that Brian wasn't willing to face – he had a lot of courage. His cheerfulness and ebullience and refusal to concede, even when the odds seemed so stacked against him, often caused some of the sourpusses to accuse him of bluff and verbosity. The late John Kelly, in a witty moment of exasperation, was heard to say that there ought to have been an annual award for oratory in Leinster House and that it should always go to Brian – a statue with a wooden head and a brass neck! When Brian heard this, he laughed heartily and enjoyed the joke as much as anyone.

People were very sympathetic to him after his sacking and I think it inspired the organisation to go out and campaign more passionately on his behalf. He might just have turned things around but for Pádraig Flynn's massive own goal on the RTÉ Radio 1 programme, *Saturday View*. Referring to how Labour and the Workers' Party had reconstructed Mary Robinson's image, emphasising her role as a wife and mother, he said, 'But none of us, you know, none of us who knew Mary Robinson in a previous incarnation ever heard her claiming to be a great wife and mother.' Michael McDowell, a panellist on the programme, became very angry and called Flynn a disgrace. Flynn's insulting remarks got huge coverage in the last few days of the campaign and played into Robinson's hands. She had been appealing to 'mná na hÉireann' anyway and this was grist to that particular mill.

Despite all that had happened, Brian Lenihan polled extremely well in the election itself: he secured forty-four per cent first preferences and the highest number of votes that any candidate ever received in an Irish presidential election. Robinson received thirty-nine per cent of the vote and Austin Currie, the Fine Gael candidate, seventeen per cent. Most of Currie's transfers went to Robinson and she was elected. She proved to be an active and respected president. It was the first time Fianna Fáil had lost a presidential election and the first time Ireland had a woman in the Áras.

The inquest into the election was held at the parliamentary party meeting near the end of November 1990. Between 30 and 40 people spoke, myself among them. I said that the party was in a very serious mess and that I felt it wasn't being well led. What I said hardly came as a surprise to anyone present, and I'm sure the Haughey people were muttering to themselves: 'Here goes that ultimate troublemaker again.' Liam Lawlor was the only TD present who had the guts to tell Haughey openly that he should resign. Others may have hinted at it obliquely, but either he missed the hints because they were so oblique, or he chose to ignore them.

EXIT OTHELLO – NO TEARS

On the day of the presidential election count, Albert Reynolds, speaking in Cork, said that his hat would be in the ring for the party's leadership when a vacancy arose. This sent a clear signal to Haughey that he should think about leaving. By the end of 1990, ministers like Flynn, Michael Smith, Geoghegan-Quinn and Noel Treacy had gravitated towards Reynolds as leader-in-waiting. They had been derogatorily dubbed 'the Country and Western wing', by whom I'm not sure, but it was certainly not meant to flatter them. Of the other Cabinet members, Burke, Collins, O'Rourke and Ahern still supported Haughey. Like most of the parliamentary party, I was aware of these factions, the more so the nearer the demise of Haughey came. I wasn't a member of the pro-Reynolds faction. I had had enough of leadership contests.

The next threat to the coalition arose from the controversy in the Dáil over alleged malpractices in the Goodman meat plants. Haughey faced a possible PD revolt on the issue and the outcome was the government agreement to set up a judicial tribunal to inquire into the allegations. Haughey had his own way to some extent in that he insisted the tribunal examine the Irish beef industry as a whole and not just the Goodman plants. A series of controversies involving a number of business companies in late 1991 greatly damaged Haughey's position, beginning with the Greencore scandal, although I don't believe he had much connection with that particular one. The Telecom affair followed soon afterwards, which involved his close associate Dermot Desmond. The scandal also embroiled one of the country's most prominent businessmen, Michael Smurfit, chairman of Telecom. In a radio interview, Haughey said that Smurfit should step aside from that position. He hadn't consulted him before going on radio. I feel Smurfit was very badly treated on this occasion. In this same interview, Haughey created further problems for himself by repeating his intention to lead Fianna Fáil into the next election. Indeed, he joked that some Chinese leaders went on until they were eighty or ninety. If the implication was (and many a true word is spoken in jest) that he intended to stay on as leader for a long time yet, it went down very badly with some of his own TDs.

Around this time four backbench FF TDs – Dempsey, Power, Nolan and Liam Fitzgerald – publicly questioned Haughey's leadership. This was a very brave thing to do, particularly in the light of what had gone on in the past. Up to fifty people spoke at the subsequent parliamentary party meeting on 2 October. It was probably one of the last times I had my usual say about the damage being done to the party because of the leader it persisted in having. I was beginning to feel worse than John the Baptist as the voice of one crying – ineffectually – in the wilderness. Dempsey and Power openly challenged Haughey about the scandals and his links with people at the centre of them.

The next scandal to erupt concerned the public money given to UCD to buy Carysfort College, which had happened at the end of 1990. A businessman close to Haughey, 'Pino' Harris, who was a very wealthy man, had made a profit of £1.5 million on the land in just six months, it was revealed. There was also controversy in the Dáil about Haughey's association with Bernie Cahill, chairman of Greencore. Tired of the seemingly unending series of scandals, on 6 November the backbencher Seán Power put down a motion of no confidence in the leadership. Seán was a son of the former TD and minister Paddy Power, and one of a number of TDs who often pressed me to run for the presidency. Reynolds was probably not expecting this to happen so soon but had little choice but to declare public support for the motion. He refused to resign from the Cabinet and Haughey sacked him. Flynn supported Reynolds and was also sacked, and Geoghegan-Quinn, Smith and Treacy followed suit. In an emotional interview on television, Gerry Collins pleaded with Reynolds not to 'burst up' the party.

By the morning of the 9 November meeting to debate the motion of no confidence in Haughey, the Reynolds camp knew they didn't have the numbers. Some TDs, whose support they needed, including some who had encouraged Reynolds to make his move a couple of weeks before that, made it clear that they would be voting for Haughey. The meeting itself was another marathon fourteen- or fifteen-hour affair. Reynolds's fate was sealed when Haughey won a motion for an open vote by forty-four to thirty-three. Reynolds spoke of his Longford home being under surveillance from a white Hiace van and Dempsey and John Ellis alleged that their phones were being tapped. A number of TDs who had denounced Haughey behind his back now praised him heartily. 'How can you speak like that when you can't say a good word about him in the Dáil bar?' asked someone at one stage, as a TD declared passionate support for Haughey. Of all the speakers at the meeting, Pádraig Flynn was one of the most impressive. He made a first-class speech about the party and what it meant to him, and how he would be untrue to himself if he didn't vote against Haughey's leadership. I don't think I myself spoke at that particular meeting. I had a strong sense of déjà vu about the whole thing. I just felt that we were going through a ritual and that Houdini would escape once again. As things turned out, this meeting was a real turning point. It really was the beginning of the end for Haughey. At least some of those who expressed opposition to him were determined to see their opposition through.

Haughey himself gave a rather subdued – for him – speech at the end of the meeting, in which he said he would not be around forever, but that he wanted to deal with important EU business that was coming up. He defeated the motion of no confidence by fifty-five to twenty-two, and the only real surprise was the number of TDs who had been expected to support Albert Reynolds who changed their votes, whatever about their minds. The number who voted against Haughey was exactly the same as nine years before, but only three of the original 'Gang of 22' were the same: Charlie McCreevy, Willie O'Dea and myself.

Instead of promoting junior ministers to the senior positions now vacant in Cabinet, as he might have been expected to do, Haughey chose to promote two backbench TDs, Noel Davern to Education and Jim McDaid to Defence. A big controversy blew up over McDaid because of his association with an IRA man's extradition case a year before. He had been photographed with the man, a constituent, and other anti-extradition campaigners outside the Supreme Court after a request for the man's extradition had been defeated. O'Malley requested a meeting with Haughey, and a government crisis loomed, but it was defused when the unfortunate and accident-prone McDaid withdrew on the very day that he was to be appointed. The photograph wasn't politically correct, so poor old Jim had to bite the dust. I thought it was very unfair. I thought Haughey again showed weakness on this occasion, because McDaid had done nothing wrong. Madeleine Taylor Quinn's attack on him in the Dáil was totally over the top and on this occasion, had he chosen to face her down, I would have supported him out of conviction, if not out of party loyalty.

There was considerable grief and anger in the Fianna Fáil party at the way Jim McDaid was sacrificed. A lot of this anger was directed at the PD intervention – they had come looking for another head on a plate and they had got it. But it should be recalled that, in reality, the person who decided that Jim was dispensable was none other than the person who had just offered him the post.

To digress a little, I would like to relate one very odd incident that occurred in late December 1986. For years I had suffered with back trouble – the result of an old rugby injury, exacerbated by my height. All through that year I had had a lot of pain and my back consultant had been advising surgery. I decided to go ahead with it and timed it for as late as possible in December, so that I could recover during the Christmas vacation, missing as little as possible of the Dáil sittings. The date of my operation was set for 18 December and I duly notified the Whip's Office. I was told that I would be paired with Oliver J. Flanagan of Fine Gael, who was very ill and was at that time in the same hospital as me – St Vincent's private hospital. (For the uninitiated, a pair is when there is an agreement that a member of the government and a member of the opposition absent themselves at the same time from a Dáil vote. This is an arrangement to facilitate the continued operation of parliament when government ministers or deputies are unavailable due to state business, often abroad.)

I had my operation. I'm never too good on medical details, but as far as I remember a disc was removed and another two were fused and all apparently went well. Of course there were a good number of stitches and I would take a while to recover. Next morning I got a call from the Fianna Fáil Whip's Office. It was the last day of the Dáil before the Christmas vacation and there was a vote at about seven o'clock that evening. The call was to inform me that Oliver J. had decided to come in to vote that evening so I no longer had a pair. I was incredulous, and explained about my major surgery the day before, but my protest fell on deaf ears. Shortly afterwards the door of my room opened, and slowly and painfully, walking with the aid of a walking frame, in came Oliver J. He was a very sick man. He had cancer and in fact was dying. It seems that, in the circumstances, his family had prevailed on him to come into the Dáil to vote for one last time. He was very concerned for me and I assured him that I would work something out. We chatted for a while, like lifelong friends, and then he left.

Shortly afterwards Tadhg O'Donoghue arrived to see me. Tadhg is a very good friend and at that time was probably the most senior person in Fianna Fáil in Dún Laoghaire. He is someone to whom I would often turn for advice. I was glad to see him and told him of my dilemma. Tadhg was immediately suspicious: 'They are trying to set you up.' The vote that evening was not a vital one, although if the government lost it would make headlines and I would be blamed. 'You're going to have to go in,' he said. He left me then and said he would be back later. I think he planned to go into Leinster House to find out what was happening. My surgeon then came in to see me on his routine visit. I told him about my difficult position. He objected and said that under no circumstances would he give his approval for my going into Leinster House. Of course he couldn't stop me, but if I did go in, I would have to use an ambulance to get there and would have to go into the Dáil chamber in a wheelchair. Tadhg arrived back in the early afternoon and said that, having talked to a few people, he was convinced that I must go in and vote.

Just then Annette arrived. By sheer coincidence, it was the day of our twenty-second wedding anniversary. When I told her my story she was appalled. In fact, she just didn't believe me. She put a call through to the Whip's Office herself and talked to the Chief Whip, Vincent Brady. She explained who she was and asked him what the position was about the vote that evening. 'The position is that Deputy Andrews does not have a pair,' was the terse reply. She protested, explaining again about my surgery. He just repeated, 'The position is that Deputy Andrews does not have a pair.' I have never seen her so furious and she was very much against my going in. At that stage my son David joined us. Having been told of the position he was inclined to side with Tadhg. I eventually made the decision to vote, and they set about making the arrangements for the ambulance. Annette came to Leinster House in the ambulance with me. One of the conditions of coming in was that I was given no painkillers. It was considered that the pain would act to protect me from making any movement that could cause damage. I wasn't feeling great. When we arrived in the car park of Leinster House, having notified them in advanced of my arrival by ambulance, Dr Donny Ormonde, a TD, very kindly came out and accompanied me in. We had timed it so that I had to do very little hanging about. Of course, my colleagues were amazed to see me. I duly voted and almost immediately was wheeled back out to the ambulance where, before we left, the Taoiseach arrived out to see me, expressing concern for my welfare. When I got back to the hospital I was in a lot of pain and my wound was seeping, but I felt somehow that I had won! I suffered no ill effects, but of course the whole thing was ridiculous. Sometime later I met Sean Barrett, the then Fine Gael Chief Whip; and he told me that he was shocked at what happened. No one had approached him for a pair and he would have had no hesitation in giving me one if asked.

The morning after the vote, there was a photo of me in the wheelchair on the front of *The Irish Times* and a graphic account of me arriving in a wheelchair, pale and obviously in pain, on one side of the voting lobby and Oliver J. gaunt and halting arriving on the other side with his walking frame. It was all a total farce and I will never know what Vincent Brady, who was a devoted supporter of Haughey, was trying to achieve. It does, however, underline my unpopularity with some of the party hierarchy of the time.

To return to 1991, it had seemed for a long time that the party was destined to lurch from crisis to crisis under a leader who would never be shifted, when on to the stage walked Seán Doherty to administer the coup de grâce. Why he did it and at that particular time has been much debated. One suggestion is that he felt he had taken all the blame for the phone-tapping scandal in 1982. He felt that he had been promised reinstatement but it had never happened, unlike Ray MacSharry, who became an MEP and leader of the Fianna Fáil group in the European Parliament. Doherty lost his Dáil seat in 1989 and failed to get elected to the European Parliament in the simultaneous elections of that year. He did make it to the Seanad and became Cathaoirleach. This argument has it that his frustration and disappointment reached breaking point when Ray Burke, as Minister for Justice, published the Phone Tapping Bill at the end of 1991. Doherty asked him to withdraw or at least stall it so that he wouldn't have the embarrassment of having to handle it in the Seanad. Burke refused and this forced Doherty to take the course he did.

Another theory is that he was acting on behalf of the so-called Country and Western faction in the party and that Reynolds, Flynn and others realised that Doherty was the man who could bring down Haughey and project them into the leadership. They orchestrated the whole thing behind the scenes, according to this explanation of Doherty's action. Reynolds has always denied that this was the case. On the contrary, he has stated that he tried to discourage Doherty from taking the course of action that he did. Doherty himself also said that he was acting alone and not at anyone else's behest. I think both men deserve to be believed on this.

I remember very clearly Sean's appearance on the RTÉ Network 2 *Nighthawks* programme in mid-January 1992. I was staying in a holiday home I had just built in Baile na hAbhann in County Galway. When asked about the phone-tapping affair, he said he felt let down that people who knew what he was doing pretended not to. He went further a few days later at a press conference in the Montrose Hotel by saying that Haughey knew fully about the phone tapping in 1982 because he (Doherty) took transcripts of the phone taps to him. It would be interesting to know the ins and outs of that event.

My own understanding of what happened to Doherty – and I think it was genuine – is that he saw the light, so to speak. He had become very religious, a born-again Christian. In the Oireachtas, he was sending out circulars inviting people to come to prayer meetings. It may well be that what had happened in 1982 was on his conscience and it was like going to Confession; he felt he had to make a public confession to clear the air for his own peace of mind. They say the Lord works in mysterious ways his wonders to perform and, if so, Doherty was a living example.

Haughey tried to brazen it out at first, saying that Doherty was lying, that he was part of the 'Country and Western alliance' plot, and that he himself had no time frame in mind for retiring as leader. But his coalition partners were not convinced and issued a statement saying they didn't wish to interfere in an internal Fianna Fáil matter, but they wanted a speedy resolution. There was a striking parallel with what had happened to Brian Lenihan a little over a year before. Mary Harney and Bobby Molloy met Bertie Ahern and told him what would have to be done. Ahern passed on the message and Haughey decided to go. He announced his departure at the parliamentary party meeting a week later. Over eighty TDs and senators expressed their praise for his leadership over the years but, and this will occasion no surprise, I wasn't among them. My silence spoke for itself. It was hard for some of us there on that occasion – perhaps for most of us – to believe the Haughey era was finally over. But it wasn't completely over, of course, as he was to return to haunt Fianna Fáil for many years to come via the various tribunals inquiring into his activities.

BACK ON THE INSIDE

CABINET

Looking back at how the French Revolution appeared to its enthusiasts at the beginning, the poet William Wordsworth wrote: 'Bliss was it in that dawn to be alive/ but to be young was very heaven.' I was no longer young, of course, when the bright new era dawned in Fianna Fáil with the departure of Charles Haughey, but it was certainly bliss to have seen that day come at last. The saying goes that a week is a long time in politics and the thirteen long years of Haughey's ascendancy in Fianna Fáil seemed like an eternity to me. Ach, mar a théann an seanfhocal: 'Dá fhad lá, tagann oíche.' He was now gone and the business of choosing his successor went ahead.

Albert Reynolds was the leading contender and there was a very strong flow of support from the main body of the party for him. Having resigned his portfolio, his hand was strengthened even further. It was John Wilson and I who were the first, I believe, to suggest at the time that the 'dream team' to lead the party would be Reynolds as leader and Bertie Ahern as his deputy, the implication being that the latter would succeed to the leadership with Reynolds's retirement in the normal course of events.

I was very strongly pro-Albert. It wasn't that I had anything against Bertie. I felt that his time had not yet come. I also felt that he was more closely associated with Haughey than Albert had been. My belief was that Albert's time had come and that he deserved his chance. My record on backing leadership contenders was not great. I had backed George Colley when the party chose Jack Lynch in 1966, and got it wrong in the many leadership votes subsequently, when Haughey won every time. So my recommendation was hardly the one to put your money on, if experience was anything to go by.

The leadership race petered out as a contest. There was a vote, in that Mary O'Rourke and Michael Woods stayed in the ring, but neither could be said to have been a real contender. With Bertie Ahern not in the race, there was never any doubt about the outcome. The extraordinary thing about his participation was that Bertie never actually declared that he was in the race. He could never be described as a parliamentary groupie. He didn't hang around the Dáil or frequent the Dáil bar; he preferred the company of his Drumcondra friends and it was with them that he socialised. He had been an integral part of the Haughey group and I have no doubt that they – people like Brian Lenihan, Ray Burke, Gerry Collins and Rory O'Hanlon – wanted him to contest the leadership. But he took a very cautious approach, obviously not wanting to make an enemy of Reynolds. I would say that he surveyed the scene within the party, realised that he didn't have the numbers and decided to bide his time. One of the things that gave impetus to Reynolds's campaign was the frustration felt by younger TDs at the lack of any chance of promotion under Haughey. They calculated that there would be major changes at the top if Reynolds won but, because of Ahern's association with Haughey, that there would be only minor changes if Ahern won.

There were references in the national Sundays and dailies in late January 1992 about Ahern's personal life. Michael Smith was quoted in his local paper as referring to doubts about his suitability as Taoiseach because of his marital breakdown, and Reynolds was supposed to have remarked that people liked to know where the Taoiseach of the day was living. Perhaps this sort of thing might have featured more prominently had Ahern ever actually declared his candidacy. But I really don't think his personal life mattered to the vast majority of Fianna Fáil TDs. It certainly wasn't an issue a couple of years later when the leadership was open to contest again.

The leadership vote was held on 6 February and Reynolds was a clear winner with sixty-one votes to Michael Woods's ten and Mary O'Rourke's six. In the press conference after his victory, Reynolds said that what he wished to achieve most of all during his tenure of office was peace in Northern Ireland. This came as a surprise, as he had never been known to talk much about the North during his political career before then. But then he wasn't one to comment much on matters outside his portfolios. Peace in the North clearly meant a lot to him and he soon showed that he meant what he had said at that first press conference as leader.

I had the feeling that when Albert Reynolds made it to the leadership I had a very good chance of being made a full minister. I had been out of Cabinet and on the back benches for nearly fourteen years. My experience was limited and my age was against me as well. I often wish that I had had the chance to be a full minister when I was younger, but that was not to be. And, in the final analysis, you have to play the hand you are dealt.

There was an impromptu party in the restaurant of Leinster House the evening that Albert was elected leader. It was a joyous occasion, full of Longford men and women who were in celebratory form. For us it was a very strange experience to be 'on the inside' and at this sort of gathering after the very many years on the outer reaches of the party. A man who was very close to Albert remarked to Annette that there was some talk about my being made Attorney General. When I heard this, I was absolutely adamant that I wanted to be a senior minister and that, if offered the AG position, I would decline it. I went to the Law Library as usual the following day and was subjected to a lot of speculation and indeed general ragging about the Cabinet-elect and whether or not I would be in it. There was much speculation in the papers about who would be in the new Cabinet and I was mentioned quite a lot as a possibility. During the course of the day I went to see Albert and told him that I would like to be on his new team. Albert expressed some surprise and said that he had always believed I was more interested in my law practice than in being in government. So it was just as well that I had clarified my position with him.

I particularly remember the tension of the following few days. I had hopes of being appointed, but one really never knew. So I waited.

It was over a weekend and Annette and I were so tense that on the Saturday night we went out to a pub and had a few drinks, just to relax. By Monday, I was saying to Annette: 'Look, I would have heard by now if I was getting anything.' Annette wasn't for giving up and she went into Leinster House and met my secretary, Deborah Healy. She asked her if she had heard anything, knowing that Debbie would know all the other secretaries very well and hear every piece of gossip going, but she said she hadn't heard a thing, nor did she think anybody else knew either. Annette felt heartened by this. She was convinced that if Albert had started to hire or fire some news of it would have begun to leak out. Leinster House is a hotbed of rumour and gossip and word usually seeps around the corridors. So she felt it was still all to play for.

I went to the Law Library as usual that morning, feeling quite pessimistic, but determined to carry on as normal. I was certainly not going to be seen loitering hopefully around the corridors of Leinster House. That evening I had a meeting in the PMPA office at five o'clock and then called to see Eoin Ryan Sr, who had always been a great mentor to me. At six o'clock, Annette got a phone call at home from Albert himself asking to speak to me. She told him I wasn't there but that she would make contact with me and he said to tell me to phone him as soon as possible. She tried desperately to get me in the PMPA offices without any success, but eventually got me in Ryan's. I rang Albert and was asked would I serve, and in 'FA'. Of course I accepted. I then immediately rang Annette. When I told her Albert had said 'FA', she said to me: 'Are you sure he didn't mean "f**k all"?' I could understand her disbelief because I was feeling it myself. Foreign Affairs was the position I wanted above any other and I could scarcely believe it had come my way. Having been so long on the outside, it's not easy to take it in when your fortunes suddenly change. Naturally I was very anxious to be with Annette so that we could talk things over. I was warned by Albert to keep the news of my appointment to myself until he announced his new Cabinet in the Dáil the following day. Annette came over to the Ryans' house, where I was, but as they had a visitor, we could not talk, so we left shortly after she arrived. At that point we were desperate to tell someone and opted for our friends Joe and Fran Deane, whom we knew we could trust with a secret forever. So we called to see them and the four of us decided to go out for a meal. We thought it better not to go home because we knew people would be phoning and calling to the house to see if there was any news. Also, we obviously felt like a little quiet celebration.

We had a very enjoyable, fun-filled evening. Fran asked me would I continue to bring Annette breakfast in bed or would I have got too important? I replied that of course I couldn't think of continuing such a habit as Minister for Foreign Affairs but that I would get the driver of my new state car to do it. With other such fantasies we entertained ourselves for the evening. At one stage, we got to wondering what ministry Gerry Collins was going to get. We knew he really liked Foreign Affairs and hoped he would be happy with whatever position he got. I wondered if it could be Agriculture. Gerry and his wife Hillary were good friends of ours and I would have felt uncomfortable with the thought of Gerry not getting a reasonably good move. When we got home, we found that poor Sinéad, our daughter, had had a rough night answering the phone and having to lie all evening that there was no news and that she didn't know where we were. She said she found it particularly hard to lie to our good friend Tadhg O'Donoghue, partly because she suspected he didn't believe her.

Next morning, I went into the Law Library and, as secrecy was still the order of the day, I had to appear to continue as normal. Then I made my way to Leinster House. Annette remembers being in the Dáil gallery that day and seeing a lot of the old Haughey Cabinet on the floor of the House. She could see Gerry Collins chatting away. She knew that his former post had gone to me but she realised from his body language that he wasn't aware of that as yet. We had also learned that morning that he would no longer be a minister at all and felt pretty dreadful for him. It wasn't nice for Annette to know about his situation before he did and it put a bit of a blight on the joy we were feeling ourselves. When Albert returned from receiving his seal of office in the Áras, Annette was again in the gallery to watch him lead in his new cabinet, including me as the new Minister for Foreign Affairs. She said afterwards that she wished my father had still been alive to witness the occasion. I wished both my parents had been there. After the formalities, the House was adjourned while the new ministers went to Áras an Uachtaráin for their seals of office. As Annette came down from the gallery, she walked straight into Michael

O'Kennedy, who had just been dropped from the Cabinet. She felt embarrassed but Michael could not have been more gracious. He said something like: 'We had our day. Now David will have his and I wish him all the luck in the world.' It was very generous of him.

Next day, Hillary Collins phoned Annette in a very magnanimous gesture indeed. She was naturally very shocked and dreadfully upset for Gerry but she said that she knew that Annette would find it difficult to phone her in the circumstances and so she had taken the initiative. She said that if Gerry couldn't have the job of Foreign Minister that she was delighted that I was the one to be given the position. Annette and I hugely appreciated that phone call.

Reynolds's new Cabinet created quite a stir. No fewer than eight ministers of the Haughey Cabinet were sacked, including such senior figures as Burke, Collins and O'Rourke. Of Haughey's ministers, only Bertie Ahern retained his portfolio of Finance. Concerning Ray Burke, Reynolds later said that what influenced his decision were the rumours of planning corruption that were reaching Leinster House in various ways at the time. I recall those rumours and I have no doubt that they did influence the new Taoiseach in his decision not to reappoint Burke.

Probably the biggest surprise of the new Cabinet was the appointment of John O'Connell to Health. He had been in Labour and then joined Fianna Fáil after some years as an Independent TD. He had also been quite close to Haughey. Many – myself among them – felt that his day had gone and, I suppose, to some extent it had. His period as a minister was short and he resigned from the Cabinet and the Dáil in 1993 because of ill health. The new leader went on to sack nine of the twelve existing junior ministers, among whom were some staunch Haughey loyalists. The whole experience was Ireland's equivalent of the Great Purge or the Night of the Long Knives – a bloodletting the likes of which had never been seen before in Irish politics. It engendered great bitterness against Reynolds, some of which has still not dissipated. Why did he do it? I believe he wanted an almost completely new team around him. I can't say a new young team, although he did promote young TDs like Brian Cowen and Noel Dempsey, because he elevated me and I hardly fitted into that category. But what he was looking for was a new image for the party and he clearly felt that those who had served Mr Haughey had been around for long enough and that it was some others' turn now to be given a chance to show their mettle.

The strange thing about becoming a minister, having been a back-bencher, is that you are suddenly a 'minister' and you have no preparation whatsoever for the change. There is no such thing as a trainee minister. Gerry Collins met with me and gave me some key tips and was very helpful in filling me in to some extent about what was going on at the time in the department. But the following morning I was in there, Minister for Foreign Affairs, and I don't mind admitting that I felt nervous. If I was nervous, my personal secretary Deborah Healy was ten times worse. She was very young, of course, only in her early twenties. I returned home from my first day in the office having been overwhelmed with documents and reports and all sorts of reading material. Annette asked had Deborah been there and I replied that I thought she'd be joining me in Iveagh House the next day. Annette rang my old Dáil office next morning at eleven o'clock to find Debbie still there. She knew from the way Debbie responded that she was on the verge of tears. All the office equipment had been taken over to her new office, but the idea of walking into Iveagh House on her own was just too intimidating for her. Annette rang me and told me the situation and I said to tell Debbie to come over at exactly twelve and that I would come down to the door to meet her, which I did. In no time at all, she had settled into her new role.

Later that day I contacted Carmel Brennan and asked her to become my constituency secretary. Carmel was a good friend whose marriage had recently broken up and she was trying to get back on her feet. She was a daughter of the former minister Joe Brennan from Donegal, and had a great sense of politics. I knew she would be invaluable and I regard this as one of my best decisions. Carmel and Debbie were a marvellous combination and as I was to spend so much time away from the constituency, they were invaluable in keeping me in touch and looking after all the problems as they arose.

One of the odd things about becoming a minister is that you acquire a state car, complete with driver. Of course I had had one already as Parliamentary Secretary and Junior Minister. Over the years I had quite a few different drivers and most of them were extraordinarily obliging and decent men. I probably shouldn't single out anyone, but I can't but mention one – Jim O'Leary – because he became a great friend to both me and my family. He drove for me almost every time I was in government. He was the most obliging man I ever knew and was a very professional driver. He always knew where I was going before I knew myself! He also had a wonderful bass singing voice. His rendition of 'Old Man River' was really special. On more than one occasion late in the evening when I wanted to leave a Fianna Fáil dinner, I would have to wait as there would be a request for Jim to sing. One bizarre and funny incident happened to Jim while I was Foreign Minister. I was due to go to a Cabinet meeting at 3 p.m. (during the summer) and Jim parked outside and went up to the office. At that time there was some tension with the local police about parking in St Stephen's Green and it seems that some Sergeant had issued an edict that all vehicles parked there were to be towed away. On that day Jim came down from the office to find his state car being raised up on to the tow truck. Jim was incandescent. He told them it was my car and that I was about to go to a Cabinet meeting, but the officer in charge wasn't impressed. Jim looked after that car like a baby and he was furious, although I have to say that I nearly broke my heart laughing. A few calls were made to the Department of Justice and they eventually got on to Jim and offered to bring back the car. Jim told them not to touch it and he would collect it himself. I think he made the most out of the situation.

One of the first people I met in Iveagh House was the Secretary General of the Department of Foreign Affairs, Noel Dorr. I got on well with Noel, though I can't say we became close friends; but he was the complete professional and we had a good working relationship. He could be a bit Jesuitical at times. He certainly snowed me under with paperwork from the outset. I remember he almost invariably started any piece of advice with, 'Well, Minister, I'm not a lawyer but ...' He was a very clever and able man and I found him enormously helpful. His delightfully informal wife Cáitriona was a great asset to him and indeed to the department.

The first private secretary I was given was a young man called Dermot O'Mahony. I was told that he had been five or six years in the civil service but what I wasn't told was that most of that time had not been in Foreign Affairs – in fact, he had been only three months in the department. About a month and a half later, with the help of some advice from Declan Kelly, my private secretary when I was a Junior Minister, I acquired a new private secretary. Conor O'Riordan was an extremely clever and astute man with a lot of experience in Foreign Affairs and I had no hesitation in appointing him. He was to prove invaluable to me. However, I was concerned about Dermot and enquired what had happened to him. I was told he had been sent on promotion to Helsinki. Half way through Conor's first day with me, I believe he was asked how things were going. He replied: 'Very well. No mention of Helsinki so far!'

To complete my team I appointed a barrister colleague, Rory Mac-Cabe, as my special adviser. He had been a civil servant before becoming a barrister and knew how things worked. He was and remains a very bright and energetic individual and has a wicked tongue. Himself and his wife Mary Murphy have been immensely helpful to me over the years and we remain good friends. I am pleased that Rory has recently been appointed judge of the Circuit Court.

One person who was very kind to me at the Cabinet table – and he is a person about whom many unflattering things have been said and written – was Pádraig Flynn. He became Minister for Justice in the new government. He was a very experienced and practised minister by this time and he could see that, like all new ministers, I was struggling to find my feet. He was sensitive to my difficulties, and there were a number of issues on which he gave me very sound advice.

One thing that people may not realise about Cabinet conduct is that one has to fight one's corner. The officials in your department expect you to do your utmost for the department and when you go into Cabinet you have a queue of civil servants waiting outside to see how you got on. There were some quite strong arguments at the Cabinet table. For example, when it was proposed to open or re-open an embassy, I faced huge opposition, especially from the Minister for Finance. The same problem doesn't exist for a minister today because there are far greater financial resources available than there were in 1992. Our embassy in Kenya was closed down for lack of resources – which I believed was an act of foolishness – and I cannot understand why it still hasn't been reopened.

TRIPS

One of my first trips as minister was to Iran; this was a trip aimed at improving and developing trade ties between our two countries. A fairly large group of businessmen (no women came) accompanied me, and my role was to set up contacts and to accompany them to various meetings with senior Iranian politicians and officials, with a view to increasing their trade with Iran. The Iranian Foreign Minister at the time was Ali Akbar Velayati, whom I had met before when I went to Iran to try to bring about the release of Brian Keenan. I had established a good rapport with Mr Velayati at that time and he gave me a warm welcome on this occasion. The businessmen seemed happy with the level of contacts made.

Annette rather untypically didn't want to come on this trip – she felt it wasn't a country that was very welcoming to women – but Hillary Collins had already accepted the invitation from the Iranians. A programme had been set up for her, and it was felt in Iveagh House that it wouldn't look well if she refused. Of course, she would have to wear a coat down to her ankles and a scarf completely covering her hair at all times, and that didn't go down too well. She was also given instructions that she must never shake hands with a man. However, her main problem was a personal commitment she had to play a short piano recital in the home of John O'Conor just four days after our return.

Annette is an accomplished amateur pianist, and from her mid-thirties John O'Conor had taken her on as a mature student. He was hugely encouraging to her and decided that she should learn to perform, and this was the very first such occasion. For Annette to be away from a piano for a week at this time was unthinkable. When I explained this rather odd difficulty to the people in Iveagh House they assured me that they would arrange for her to have access to a piano while she was there. Frank Cogan was our ambassador at the time in Tehran and it was of course his dear wife Pauline who was given the job of tracking down a piano.

When we arrived in Tehran we found that a programme had indeed been set up for 'the wife', and a girl called Nina arrived every day from Iranian protocol to accompany her. Like all Iranian women

Nina wore a full chador – you could only see her eyes. However, part of every day was a visit to the home of an Australian diplomat whose wife, Ruth Cleary, had a piano and was very welcoming to them. Nina always waited outside, but on the last day Annette invited her in to be an 'audience' as practice for her performance. Nina obliged, but when she finished Annette was horrified to find her in tears. Then it all came out. She had been a career diplomat in the time of the Shah and had had a great love of classical music. She said that she had forgotten how much it meant to her. All western music, including classical music, is forbidden in Iran. Nina then opened up and told Annette how much she hated wearing the chador. She was happily married with two sons and the sad thing was that she said she was greatly relieved that she didn't have a daughter as she couldn't bear to put a chador on her. I'm afraid Annette didn't really like Iran.

On St Patrick's Day, I made the usual shamrock delivery trip to the White House and met President George Bush Sr and his Secretary of State James Baker. One thing I recall about James Baker was his keenness to talk to me about rugby, for which he had a great enthusiasm. At this time President Bush was dealing with some financial scandals in Congress and was somewhat preoccupied. However, he was very courteous and his wife Barbara was a charming lady who regaled us with stories of her grandchildren. We sat and chatted with them in the Oval Office for a short time. The talk was mainly and predictably about American-Irish relations. We then went out to the famous Rose Garden for the standard photo opportunity – me presenting President Bush with a bowl of shamrock. There was a large gathering of the press corps waiting for us. I'm afraid they had little interest in St Patrick's Day or shamrocks and were more concerned by the financial scandals bedevilling Congress. A small aside – the shamrock is always presented in a crystal glass bowl, usually Waterford. On this occasion I decided it might be a good idea to use a bowl made by one of the Northern Ireland glass companies. Maybe a good idea, but the result was quite a bit of flak from the Southern companies on my return. You can't win!

Over the next few days I attended many functions run by Irish societies. Annette remarked to me about our American trip – half jokingly, half in earnest – that I had almost as many stag meetings and meals there as I had had in Iran. Even the St Patrick's night celebration was a men-only occasion. Strangely, the culture of men-only functions as practised in the past in the US has extended into modern times in Irish-American circles – something I found less than appealing, as I always enjoy the company of women.

In early April there was a trip to London, where I met the heads of various Irish voluntary organisations at a lunch at our embassy, given by our excellent ambassador, Joe Small, and his wife Mary. This happened to be a day or two after the scandal concerning Bishop Eamon Casey had broken. One of the people we met there was Fr Bobby Gilmour, who had worked with Bishop Casey in London. He commented on the extraordinary amount of good Eamon Casey had done in London working with immigrants. We got the impression that Fr Gilmour was not altogether surprised by the situation in which the bishop now found himself. He described Casey as a huge risk-taker. He told how he would sometimes put a deposit on a house that he considered to be a good buy for use by Irish immigrants, without having the slightest notion where he was going to get the rest of the money, although of course he invariably did get it.

A pleasant non-official side to another London visit was attending the FA Cup Final at Wembley between Liverpool and Sunderland. Fergus O'Brien and the late John Boland of Fine Gael were sitting next to us at the match: I had managed to organise the tickets for them, knowing that they were soccer enthusiasts like myself. We had dinner with them later. They were both good company and John Boland liked to be a bit of an *enfant terrible*.

Two foreign trips in April 1992 were to Oman and Kuwait. I was particularly impressed by Oman. My first impression of its capital, Muscat, was of incredible order and cleanliness. The roads were superb. Healthcare and education are free for everyone in Oman. Much of the credit must go to Sultan Qaboos, who became leader in 1970 and still rules. Women are expected to dress modestly, but don't have to cover up, and there is a great tolerance of Western customs. In recent years, Oman has taken some steps towards democracy. Free and fair parliamentary elections, in which women have voted and stood as candidates, have been held and the Sultan has promised greater openness and participation in government.

Kuwait was a different story. Security there was intense – hardly surprising considering the First Gulf War was not long over. There were gun-toting soldiers everywhere and they looked very menacing. Annette told me she had her bag searched three times, always aggressively, while strolling around our hotel, even though she was wearing her identity tag all the time. We were all given a bottle containing sand from the desert and a few shell casings removed from the roof of the hotel after the invasion. Fortunately, we spent only one day in Kuwait.

That Easter, I was able to spend a few days with some of the family in our beloved Connemara. We visited Pádraig Flynn and his family for lunch in Castlebar. They gave us a great welcome. The Flynn family were very warm and friendly and enjoyed poking fun at 'Pee'. They were delighted to show us a cartoon of the 'Flynnstones' (the characters created by Dermot Morgan in the radio satire *Scrap Saturday*), which they had hanging up in the kitchen. Pádraig was able to take the fun being poked at him in his stride.

One of the things that is difficult to get used to as Foreign Minister is the whole business of protocol and security when we were abroad. While I can understand the need for it to an extent, it does become a bit absurd at times. I remember visiting Santiago in Chile in May as part of the meetings involving the EC (as it then was) and the Rio Group. I had a bit of free time on one of the days and was driven out into the country to the foot of the Andes. Protocol dictated that we had to have a motorcycle escort in front and a car with three detectives behind, which was a bit daft. Annette and I had a good walk in the snow, which we really enjoyed, but I must say I felt sorry for the accompanying detectives who were not great walkers and were anyway wearing light shoes with pointy toes! On our way back we stopped in a little village for a drink at an inn. It was straight out of the fifties: lace curtains, mirrors, Formica tops and a rickety old piano. Our motorbike outrider had been left outside, but I insisted that he be invited in, which seemed to miff the detectives for some reason – some sort of a hierarchy among the police, perhaps. He was freezing and his poor hands were like blocks of ice. Annette gave them a good rub to get the circulation going and then he had a mug of steaming coffee.

In early August, Javier Solano, then Spanish Foreign Minister, had invited me to Spain for bilateral talks in Madrid. We managed to coincide these talks with a visit to the Olympics being held in Barcelona. There Spanish protocol assigned us a young man called Salvador to be our guide for the three days. There were so many visiting VIPs that they were running out of protocol people and I gather Salvador was plucked from Diplomatic School for the duration. He was a cross between Basil Fawlty and Jacques Tati, tall and gangly, in his mid- to late twenties, slightly balding and with glasses. He wore narrow white trousers, a navy blazer and Olympic tie – all slightly grubby – and the trousers stopped somewhere between shin and ankle. He talked all the time, was very obliging and got most things just a little bit wrong.

One evening we were due to meet our Honorary Consul, Enrique Corcoraya, and his wife Anna for dinner. We were attending an Olympic event and told Salvador that we would come out from it at exactly 8.15, which we did. Salvador was there but there was no car. Three-quarters of an hour followed in which Salvador ran up and down clutching his briefcase, which he never left out of his hand. When he tried to make a phone call, he had no coins. When he tried to take down a phone number, he had no pen and no paper. (What was in the briefcase?) At one stage, as we were standing there beginning to fume slightly, he remarked cheerfully: 'Ees not so bad – ees not ryning.' We offered to walk to the nearest taxi rank. That was no good because Salvador didn't know the name of the restaurant to which he was to take us. Only the driver knew that. The car arrived eventually out of nowhere and we got in gratefully. However, by that time a lot of streets were blocked off and the driver had to take a circuitous route to get us to the restaurant. All the while, great arguing went on between Salvador and the driver, presumably about who was at fault. One had the feeling that finally they laid the blame on us.

A significant aspect of my first term at Foreign Affairs involved two state visits with President Robinson, one to Paris and the other to Australia. Both were pretty tough going, because she really packed her schedules and tried to fit in as much as possible, aided and abetted by her formidable personal adviser, Brid Rosney. Brid would, as a wag put it, eat a bite out of a shark. The Paris trip was fascinating, but all extremely formal. I recall the Australian trip in particular because my back was giving me a lot of trouble – I've had four major back operations – but I'm afraid the President just didn't want to know about my back. There were so many receptions to attend. I sought to be excused from some of them, but my pleas fell on deaf ears. I really couldn't see the necessity of my being at all of them, because the fact was that the people were coming to see President Robinson and not me. If we were in any way late for any of the receptions, there would be repercussions. Nothing would be said directly to me but my secretary, Conor O'Riordan, would be summoned to Brid Rosney's room at midnight and given a talking to about my being late or not wearing the right suit or whatever.

Brid was, of course, a huge support to President Robinson and first class at her job. Subsequently, we got to know one another better and relaxed a bit more in each other's company, but when something had to be done on her employer's behalf, she was extremely professional, often in an unforgiving fashion. There may also have been a notion of having to establish herself and be taken seriously, because she was a woman, advising a woman, in a milieu largely inhabited by men.

What was my impression of President Mary Robinson herself? I think she was basically a shy person. She managed to perfect 'the presidential persona' and did it very well – spoke very well, wrote her own speeches and presented them in a very accomplished manner. But I think she found it very hard to relax with people. She was as formal with Annette and me as she was when meeting foreign dignitaries, even though I knew her previously from both the Oireachtas when she was a senator and from the Law Library. There was a stiffness and reserve about her, which was reflected in her body language. I recall an occasion on that same visit to Australia when there was a trip on a boat in Sydney Harbour and afterwards there was lunch on the boat. It was a buffet – the food was laid out in a cabin below and there were tables set out up on the deck. The President was asked to serve herself first and did so. There were quite a few people before Annette and me in the queue. When eventually Annette arrived up on the deck with her plate of food, she noticed that there were many people sitting at tables but that President Robinson was sitting on her own. Her husband Nick hadn't come on this particular trip because he doesn't like boats. Nobody had offered to join her at the table because she was, in a way, unapproachable. It wasn't that they didn't wish to join her but that they weren't sure how she would react, whether she would want them to sit beside her, or if it were the right thing to do according to protocol. Annette instinctively felt the president hardly wanted to be sitting on her own, so she went over and asked if she might join her. She was struck by the look of relief on her face.

She and her team certainly did a fantastic job for the country. She brought great prestige to the office and to Ireland and won enormous respect for both herself and the country wherever she went.

A major experience during my first short stay in Foreign Affairs involved Somalia. I decided to go there after watching a television programme one night. It was one of the first to reveal to the world the dreadful conditions in Somalia, particularly in Baidoa, a city in the south central part of the country, northwest of Mogadishu, where between a thousand and fifteen hundred people were dying every day. The following day, on the plane on our way to Spain for our official visit, I spoke to my officials about the television programme. I felt that, as a Foreign Minister of an EU country, there must be something I could do. But the officials were generally sceptical: they argued that we had already contributed money and there was nothing further we could do. Conor O'Riordan was the only one who supported me. As soon as we got back from Spain, I asked to see representatives from all the NGOs and asked them if it would be any help if I went to Somalia. They all strongly supported the idea, but warned me of the chaos that existed there: no police force, no security of any kind, no hotels, no telephones or communications, nothing. Their reaction confirmed my resolve to go to Somalia, despite the strong advice to the contrary from my department officials. The NGO Concern facilitated my first trip, and accommodated us quite comfortably in one of their small houses. I remember we had to bring our own food rations in sealed plastic bags. I also remember asking that I never be photographed with sick or dying people. They had enough to endure without that.

I spent three days on that first trip. What I witnessed was a horror story of the first order: people dead and dying on the sides of the streets in the various towns to which I went, famine and chaos everywhere. I vividly remember one particular sight outside a Baidoa feeding station. There was an area as big as a football field with rows and rows of bundles of rags, which were in fact starving people. The feeding station could take in only a few people each day. What struck me most – in addition to the smell – was the silence. With that number of people there should have been children running round, laughter, and indeed crying, and lots of noise; instead there was only the awful silence as so many waited to die.

On my return to Dublin there was a lot of press coverage of my trip and President Robinson decided that she, too, would go to Somalia. I think this was a very fine and courageous decision on her part. Again, there was opposition to her going – particularly because of the security implications – but go she did and her husband Nick went with her. I accompanied them. The President was deeply affected by what she saw. We went from Somalia to Nairobi in Kenya, where the she made a very impassioned speech. She then announced that she would go to the UN, which we did straight from Nairobi. In New York she met with the Secretary General of the United Nations, Boutros Boutros-Ghali, and reported to him what she had seen in strong and graphic terms. Immediatcly aftcrwards she gave a press conference and made a very deep impression. I believe it was her contribution there that persuaded the Americans to get involved in Somalia. I returned to report my findings both at home and at a European Council meeting in Brussels.

The next important trip was to New York for the annual address to the UN. I had been given a speech by the department, which covered a whole range of subjects. I felt it was the sort of speech that any Foreign Minister could make and decided to change it completely and spoke only on the topics of Somalia, the Third World and human rights. My speech was very well received, especially by delegates from the African countries, who were very anxious to come and shake my hand. I also met again with the Secretary General, Boutros Boutros-Ghali, who seemed pleased by my forceful attitude on Somalia.

ABORTION AND OTHER REFERENDUMS

Albert Reynolds had the most unfortunate of starts as Taoiseach because the news of the X case broke on his very first day in office. The Attorney General, Harry Whelehan, feeling constitutionally bound to do so, had taken a case to the High Court to prevent a fourteen-year-old rape victim travelling to England for an abortion. The court upheld his right to prevent the girl from travelling. The public became totally absorbed in the case and it generated a lot of controversy. Ultimately, the Supreme Court ruled that the girl had the right to travel for an abortion, as her threat to commit suicide was a threat to her life.

As Minister for Foreign Affairs, I was dragged into the whole imbroglio because of the abortion protocol that the Irish government had had attached to the Maastricht Treaty in 1991. There was to be a referendum on the treaty in the summer of 1992. Gerry Collins had been leading the charge on the referendum and now that duty had passed to me. With the work involved in trying to read my way into a new brief, I really could have done without all the controversy stirred up by the X case.

In my work to ensure that Maastricht was carried, I was grateful for the help of a very capable civil servant, Noel Fahey, who afterwards became our ambassador to the US. His advice and the guidance he gave me through the various obstacles proved of enormous value.

I knew Harry Whelehan from the Bar. He is one of the most pleasant, most courteous and gentlest people one could ever have the pleasure of meeting. And his brothers are, yes, Tom and Dick. I'm afraid he didn't seem to have a political bone in his body. Perhaps he felt it his duty, as guardian of the Constitution, to do what he did. There is absolutely no doubt that he acted in good faith, but his actions belied a lack of awareness of the political implications of his position.

The whole issue of abortion has been an unmitigated disaster in Irish public life and none of us – politicians or political parties – has dealt in any way well with it. Commentators have said that it put a strain on the Fianna Fáil–PD coalition in the run-up to the Maastricht referendum, but this wasn't the case. There may have been deep differences between sections of each party's supporters on the issue, but those were not reflected in government. Pressure groups did try to make abortion an issue in the referendum but the government, with the support of Fine Gael and Labour, succeeded in winning the referendum, in June 1992, by some seventy per cent to thirty per cent.

The issues arising from the X case judgment then had to be put before the people in a further referendum in November. Three separate questions were asked: one concerned the right to information on abortion; the second the right to travel; and the third proposed to make abortion illegal except where the life of the mother was in danger (the so-called 'substantive issue'). The right to travel was carried by sixty-two per cent to thirty-eight; the right to information by the slightly lesser figure of sixty to forty, but the substantive issue was defeated by sixty-five to thirty-five. Again, as in the past where this issue was concerned, the whole debate on the problems to which the third question gave rise generated angst and unedifying grandstanding.

There are always some tensions between politics and the media generally. Albert Reynolds's relations with the media, which had been so good up to the time he became Taoiseach, turned sour very rapidly. His agreement to give a weekly, on-the-record briefing was unprecedented, but he soon came to regret it. Because of the events of the times, he was grilled weekly on the subject of abortion, with which he was clearly uncomfortable (who wouldn't be?), and he found himself making unwanted headlines.

Another cause of the worsening in his relationship with the media was that he disliked some of the things that were written about him and took legal action against papers he believed had libelled him. This came as a shock to journalists, who had grown used to Haughey's policy of never suing. But the journalists missed an important point about Albert: he didn't resort to personal abuse either inside or outside the Dáil, nor did he ever use rumour or character assassination to attack opponents. He could accept attacks on his competence but not on his personal integrity, and this explains why he was litigious when he felt that he was being attacked unfairly. He often remarked that his word was his bond and that he said it like it was, and if it was suggested that he was lying, he took that as a personal affront and a slight on his honesty.

Some of his colleagues felt he was spending too much time litigating against the media and were getting a bit fed up with his attitude towards them. I could understand where he was coming from and had a certain sympathy for him in this regard.

NORTHERN IRELAND PHASE 1

Albert succeeded in building up a very close rapport with the British Prime Minister, John Major. They had met while they were both Finance ministers, had hit it off straight away and had begun to discuss Northern Ireland from that time. When Albert became Taoiseach, relations between Dublin and London really improved, and in time this was to bear fruit. The Northern Secretary at the time was Sir Patrick Mayhew, a former Attorney General. His antecedents came from Castletownbere, County Cork, and Pádraig Flynn used to joke with him and tease him a lot. Sir Patrick took it all in good spirits and his invariable response in his magnificent, patronising tones was: 'Ah, yes, I always like the Irish!' He was larger than life in many ways and the longest-serving Secretary of State for Northern Ireland. I'm not saying that he was pro-Irish, for he could hold the line with the best of them, but he was an easy man to get on with. He had a junior with him called Jeremy Hanley, who had been MP for Richmond and Barnes since 1979, and it was something of a dog-and-pony show between the two men. They specialised in telling very blue jokes at times. As I understand it, Jeremy's parents were stars of the music hall. He had a fairly short stint as a junior minister and was then chairman of the Conservative Party for a while. But he was a genuinely funny man and, indeed, his participation makes me wonder how seriously the British took that first series of talks in which we were all involved.

Jeremy was one of the best mimics of Ian Paisley I have ever heard. He told me a story once about how Paisley came into his office one day in Stormont when the television was on. They happened to be reporting on the Pope and that he had had a tumour removed which was declared to be benign. 'It may well be benign,' roared Paisley, 'but the rest of him is malignant.'

Mayhew strongly maintained that without Paisley's party there could be no solution, but at that stage the Democratic Unionist Party (DUP) were very much on the margin. The main Unionist party was the Ulster Unionist Party (UUP), led by James Molyneux. I didn't find him a very appealing individual from a personal point of view, and he was extremely cautious in his approach. He had henchmen whom he used to send out regularly, the UUP Security spokesman Ken Magennis being the person the party was happiest with. I don't believe they held Magennis in very much regard themselves but they were happy to have him go out and bat for them in all sorts of situations. He was their version of the late Brian Lenihan. We got on well with him – he was a decent sort of man who used to attend all the home rugby internationals in Lansdowne Road. He may have been a major in the Ulster Defence Regiment, but I found him a friendly man who was willing to talk. The DUP representatives, on the other hand, would not talk to us socially and would not listen to us officially.

John Hume, in the face of dreadful criticism from some sections of the Southern media, bravely continued his talks with Gerry Adams and during 1992 the British government also had contacts with Sinn Féin behind the scenes. Sadly, the catalogue of atrocities continued, despite these positive developments. Indeed, in the perverse way of Northern politics, the constructive developments contributed to the strife, in that loyalist terrorists, fearing too many concessions to republicans, stepped up their sectarian murder campaign against innocent Catholics. They were now matching the IRA in the grisly game of sectarian murder. The worst tit-for-tat killings of that year were the Teebane massacre of innocent Protestant workmen by the IRA in January, followed by the UDA/UFF slaughter of five Catholics in a betting shop on the Lower Ormeau Road in early February.

Those early Northern talks of 1992 in which I was involved lasted some six months. Our ministerial team consisted of Pádraig Flynn, John Wilson and myself, with Desmond O'Malley interchanging from time to time with Bobby Molloy. These talks were the necessary precursors to the Good Friday Agreement, which came later, but, like all talks on the North, the pace was snail-like. They pursued such a roundabout route that they were a bit like a dog chasing its own tail. We seemed to end up with the same arguments again and again. A sort of Lanigan's Ball process. Someone reminded me recently that I referred to going to the North at that time as going into the 'heart of darkness', alluding to Joseph Conrad's great novel of that name, and the weekly trip to Stormont did become a wearing and frustrating routine.

There was, however, so much at stake that we simply had to persist and not give up. I can recall one particular incident, which both gave me hope and brought home to me how important the talks were. We would typically fly up from Dublin and go into Aldergrove or the City Airport in Belfast and either be driven across from the airport in bulletproof cars or be flown over by helicopter, dressed in helmets and flak jackets. When we arrived, there would be large numbers of senior police officers present. On one occasion, as I was going in, a very senior RUC officer, who almost had tears in his eyes, shook my hand and said something like: 'Make sure these talks don't fail.' I found it very encouraging to see a reaction like that at such a senior level of the RUC at that time. That certainly wasn't the kind of reaction we were getting from the Northern Ireland Office (NIO), who gave the impression that they were generally hostile to what we were trying to do. They were, in the finest tradition of that, willing to give every assistance short of actual help.

There were some amusing asides. Ian Paisley's daughter, Rhonda, who was quite a good artist, had an exhibition of her paintings during the course of the talks. Pádraig Flynn, himself no mean artist, wanted to buy one of her paintings. He was building himself up to ask her to sell one of her paintings and remarked, casually, within earshot of her father, 'Ah, I'll go along to the exhibition.' Big Ian's response was: 'If you go to the exhibition, we'll close it down.' The result was that Pádraig never got his painting from Rhonda. Flynn himself is quite a good artist. His speciality is landscape painting. I was in his house recently and I reminded him of Rhonda and Ian Paisley and how his hope of having a Paisley hanging in his house was frustrated. I then asked him if I could buy one of his paintings – he had around a hundred upstairs in his house – but I'm afraid he turned me down. So neither of us had much success in our aspiration of adding to our small art collections.

I recall another occasion when we were over at the Foreign and Commonwealth Office in Lancaster House in central London. We were quite shocked when our Foreign Affairs people informed us that every room in the building was tapped. I presume it was true. Anyway, we had to be very careful about what we said in private while inside. At one stage during the same visit, Seamus Mallon of the

SDLP, who had a great interest in the horses, gave us a tip for a nag called Aughfad which was running somewhere or other. We dispatched a few people to the bookies and everyone on all the teams, except the DUP of course, was on this particular horse. It strolled in at 8 to 1 and we did very well out of it. There was a real sense of multilateral co-operation at that stage, but I can recall no more betting coups in the course of the talks.

Much of my first, regrettably short, time as Foreign Minister was devoted to those Northern Ireland talks. In retrospect, I think those first talks were quite challenging, in the sense that one was up against absolute intransigence and we all knew there was nothing anyone could do or say that would convince Dr Paisley and his colleagues that we were anything but sup from the devil's milk. We were well aware of that reality and were not fazed by it. The talks were more about shadow than substance, but the fact that they took place at all was justification enough for all the hardship that all our team was required to suffer.

During those talks, Dr Paisley and his cohorts spent more time walking out than walking in. The Methodist minister Dennis Cooke analysed Paisley's religious writings and sermons in detail in his book *Persecuting Zeal*. In that book, he told how Paisley had been ordained a minister in 1946 at the age of twenty. After his ordination, a prominent evangelist is supposed to have said: 'I have one prayer for this young man, that God will give him a tongue like an old cow. Young man, go into a butcher's shop and try and run your hand along a cow's tongue; it's as sharp as a file. Please God this man will have a tongue that shall be as sharp as a file in the heart of the enemies of the king.' Was ever a prayer answered as fully as that one?

Paisley attended those first talks very much in a professional sneering capacity; he made it clear from the outset that he was there unwillingly and prepared to walk out at the drop of a hat – which he frequently did. The tendency of his DUP representatives was to sit on the other side of the table, listen, make speeches and then withdraw. They were prepared to shake their fists, but not our hands. I recall one of the occasions when Paisley had yet again walked out from the talks and Paddy Mayhew was trying to encourage him back in. They were in a room down a corridor at Stormont and we were just standing around waiting to see what would happen. There was nothing unusual in that particular scenario – it was very much a stop-go process. In any event, I was standing in the corridor with Pádraig Flynn and Rory MacCabe, when a door suddenly opened and out came Paddy Mayhew. He plodded along the corridor and, as he approached us, looking haggard and browbeaten, he said, of Paisley, 'The man is mad – he's mad! He's like a baby on the high-chair who throws his dinner on the floor and wants you, or I, or anybody else to pick it up for him!' It was a wonderful analogy and stuck firmly in my mind through the years.

In the face of all this, it might seem that we were wasting our time. In my judgement we weren't, and on occasion the diehards might let their guard drop and their attitude might almost become friendly. In the course of one of our three-day sessions, I noticed that an international soccer match was scheduled for Windsor Park that evening, with Northern Ireland playing Spain. Windsor Park was the home ground of the 'Blues' – Linfield Football Club, Belfast's equivalent of Glasgow Rangers. It is located in the heartland of loyalist east Belfast. I had the idea that we, the Irish delegation, would attend, in the interest of fostering better cross-border relations, of course. The officials in Foreign Affairs were a little chary at first, expressing concerns as to security, but eventually arrangements were made and off we went. We were swept into Windsor Park under heavy armed escort and ushered into the Linfield boardroom. We were made hugely welcome and given the red-carpet treatment by the Irish Football Association (the Northern Irish soccer governing body) in the grounds. There may have been some people there who were doing the Protestant equivalent of blessing themselves, because this was serious pollution of the atmosphere as far as they were concerned, but all in all we enjoyed the experience and I suspect that none of the local supporters and officials was any the worse off. I think the crowd were aware that we were there but there was no sign of any hostile reaction. We were held back after the game for security reasons to allow the crowd depart. I always felt that any interaction like this had to be worthwhile. Oh, and by the way, the game ended in a draw.

One of the inconveniences of life in Stormont was the massive protection we were under all the time. It was like going into an armed encampment. We were put into Stormont House every night under huge security, and we travelled around in very sophisticated armoured vehicles. We were told that the weakest point of the vehicle was the roof and that if a bomb was thrown at the roof, there was no hope! The only way to save ourselves, we were told, was to get out when we saw the bomb being thrown at the roof, and between that and the bomb exploding, we were meant to save ourselves! We could dine in Stormont House at night if we wished but it was something akin to a boarding school and the staff there were like staff in a boarding school – they exhibited studied politeness to Taigs but there was a reserve about the atmosphere. So we went out to eat as often as we could. When we did, we were always booked into restaurants under the titles of 'Mr Appleyard' and 'Mr Baird'. I remember John Wilson used to always insist on ordering Châteauneuf du Pape as our wine, in the hope that it might offend some Unionist sensibilities! He was not only a clever man, he also had a great sense of humour.

Whenever we went to a restaurant, there were always two tables, one for us, the Irish delegation, and the other for the security people. I hope they enjoyed the fare, because we certainly did. One Friday evening, as we were coming out of a particular restaurant, we noticed a Presbyterian hall beside us. There had been some sort of function, or perhaps service, in the hall and the people were coming out. We looked around for Flynn, who seemed to have disappeared and, sure enough, there he was in the middle of the Presbyterians, shaking hands with anyone who would shake hands with him. I don't believe, to this day, that they had the remotest idea who he was. But Pee Flynn, being Pee Flynn, expected them to know who he was. The people were very polite to him, although they might have washed their hands when they went home. In any event, the security people got hold of him and pushed him into the car as fast as possible.

Anglo-Irish relations were certainly good during my first period as Foreign Minister. I've already remarked on the rapport between Albert Reynolds and John Major. I sat beside John Major on a number of occasions and had very friendly conversations, and always found him an extremely honourable and decent man. I used to go occasionally to the England–Australia cricket matches at Lord's in London and would meet him at the invitation lunches. He was always very welcoming and pleasant, and his courtesy to everyone was unfailing.

EUROPE

Apart from the North, which took up the giant's portion of my time as minister, there was EU business to be looked after, and one of the central parts of my job was attending the meetings of the Council of Ministers every Monday in Brussels. So the first Sunday after my appointment I flew out from Baldonnel accompanied by my officials, all of who knew much more than I did about what was ahead of me for the next day. We travelled on the government jet, which though comfortable enough was a bit cramped for me. I could never stand up straight. However, it is a great advantage if only for the time saved. Even on the flight itself the work started. As soon as the 'Fasten Seat Belts' sign was turned off officials came and sat with me one by one with their files, briefing me for the day ahead. In Brussels airport we were met on the tarmac by our ambassador and whisked off to our hotel. There we had further briefings and I finally went to bed with an appointment for more consultations at seven the next morning. I thought at that time that it was the presence of a fledgling minister that made the officials nervous and precipitated all these briefings, but in time I discovered that this was the norm. Within a few weeks too I realised the quality of the officials in the Department of Foreign Affairs and their extraordinary dedication to the best interests of the country.

I attended my first Council meeting with a certain amount of apprehension – an apprehension that was well justified. The foreign ministers are a quite tightly knit club and it is difficult enough to break into that club as a new minister. Many of them had been in the job for a long time. For example, Hans-Dieter Genscher of Germany was in his seventeenth year and Uffe Elleman Jensen of Denmark had been there for eleven years. The place was swarming with civil servants – I couldn't believe how many – all very determined to push the interests of their particular country. In that sense the European ideal only exists up to a point. Each country clearly fights for its own country first and the common European good comes a poor second. At the meetings we sat in semi-circular fashion with the president of the day at the top, and each minister was accompanied by a group of civil servants watching everything closely. The presidency changes every six months as each country takes over the running of the EU. The meetings were very political and were conducted in a fairly informal fashion. Every minister had an opportunity to make a contribution. The subjects would be diverse, ranging from an earthquake in Greece to a conflict in Ethiopia, and obviously some subjects were of greater interest to Ireland than others. However, it was important to take an interest in each country's point of view as they might be seeking your support, and you might in turn need their support in the future. And then much of the real business happened in corridors and in one-to-one meetings with other foreign ministers.

I became aware at an early stage of just where Ireland ranked in the pecking order and it was fairly low down. Germany, France and Britain were the big boys – we came in somewhere before Luxembourg. Genscher was very much the kingpin and I'm afraid I thought him too full of a sense of his own self-importance. His overblown ego would not have been easy to puncture. Of course at that time Germany had been for so long the paymasters of the community. As a minister representing a small country, I found I had to push myself to make a mark so as to get a fair hearing for Ireland's interests and points of view. I found that it was vital to establish a personal relationship with as many of the ministers as possible. If you had established some sort of friendship, they would be more likely to support you round the table. These men and women were invariably surrounded by their officials and in the beginning I had to 'barge in' – and that is what it amounted to – and introduce myself to each minister. Imposing myself on people in that way is not in my nature, but I managed – and in the end became a member of the 'club' and made quite a few friends among them.

CHANGING GOVERNMENT PARTNERS

Albert Reynolds came to believe that the PDs were out to get him and intended to use the Beef Tribunal as the vehicle. He was very conscious of the tribunal and how important it was for his reputation, which meant everything to him, especially his principle of keeping his word and doing the right thing. In June, in his oral evidence to the tribunal, Des O'Malley reiterated the claim he had made in his earlier written evidence that the export credit insurance scheme was abused to the benefit of the Goodman companies. He had also stated in his written evidence that Reynolds, in the manner in which he had operated the scheme while Minister for Industry and Commerce in 1987–8, had favoured Goodman. Now, in his oral evidence, he referred to some of Reynolds's decisions as 'wrong ... grossly unwise, reckless and foolish'. Such language was less than helpful in the context of good relations between the partners in the coalition, having regard to the type of character he was dealing with in Reynolds. He must have known that Albert would be highly sensitive to such strong language and the implications it contained. As well as O'Malley, senior Fianna Fáil people like Haughey, Burke, MacSharry, O'Kennedy and Brennan had appeared before the Beef Tribunal and some of them did little to lessen the suggestion of culpability on Reynolds's part. So Albert was determined to gainsay both O'Malley and any implications from some of these people.

O'Malley's counsel pressed Reynolds on the operation of the export credit insurance scheme while he was minister, and he was provoked into calling O'Malley's evidence 'reckless, irresponsible and dishonest'. O'Malley's counsel gave Reynolds the chance to retract this, suggesting he amend 'dishonest' to 'incorrect', but unfortunately Albert stuck to 'dishonest'. I don't know if he realised it but he was, in effect, accusing O'Malley of perjury. I'm afraid Reynolds did not distinguish himself before the tribunal and, finding himself in difficulty, charged straight on, refusing the lifelines that were offered to him.

During his oral evidence, Albert said that, both in politics and business, he had never needed long, detailed files and reports; a single sheet was enough and if he needed more, he knew where to get it. As a result, some sections of the media sneered at him as a 'one-page man'. In reality, such sections of the media had sneered at him from the beginning, certainly from the time that he became Taoiseach. And I'm not so sure that they knew what they were talking about. One page can contain an awful lot of information, particularly if it is a well-prepared and concise résumé. Albert certainly wasn't a man for large files. The 'one-page man' fuss was nothing more than a cheap shot from people who had nothing more constructive to offer.

O'Malley, of course, wouldn't live with being labelled 'dishonest' and pulled his party out of government. This left us in Fianna Fáil facing an election in November 1992 in pretty grim circumstances. The first opinion poll showed a huge plunge in personal support for Reynolds, indicating that the people blamed him, rather than O'Malley, for the collapse of the government. This was a bit unfair because O'Malley contributed his share to the whole unfortunate mess as well. Albert asked me to be director of elections for the campaign, but I had to demur, on the grounds that I would be abroad too much pursuing my ministerial duties. I felt in any event that there were others better suited to this type of job.

Subsequently, there was an almost 'every man for himself' attitude about our campaign in November 1992. Many prominent TDs, some well-known Reynolds supporters among them, refused to go on television to defend the government. I appeared on television a number of times during the campaign myself and, to his credit, Brian Cowen was to the forefront in carrying the government's message to the people on radio, television and wherever else it was required. He was Albert's staunchest supporter. As the opinion polls got worse and worse, some in the party came to believe it was the end for Albert and sought to dissociate themselves from him. I'm happy to say that I wasn't one of them. I may not have been prepared to shoulder the responsibility of the director of elections job, but I wasn't about to desert the man who had given me my big break after so many years spent in the political wilderness.

The economy was probably the main issue of the election, but the opinion polls seemed to absorb people's attention most of all. These contained news of freefall for Fianna Fáil, stagnation if not decline for Fine Gael and the prospect of a major breakthrough for Labour. Dick Spring's personal rating went up and up over the three-week campaign and a significant section of the electorate seemed to be turning to Labour to solve all their problems. The polls were pretty accurate, as it turned out.

In Dún Laoghaire, I got my highest ever vote in an election, polling just short of 13,500 votes. I wasn't in the constituency that much during the campaign, because I was abroad on government duty quite a bit. It seemed that a lot of people were happy at my elevation to the

Cabinet and their support was by way of congratulating me, perhaps. Modesty prevents me from suggesting that my vote reflected a vote of confidence in my performance. During the course of this election, strange as it might seem, I became worried that my vote would be too high, and that we wouldn't get the second seat as a result. I spoke to Tadgh O'Donoghue, our director of elections, about this. However, the wisdom at that time was that vote management wouldn't work in Dublin, and the hope was that my transfers would elect the second candidate. Tadgh O Donoghue had great political judgement and I went to him for advice on many occasions. He was a pragmatist and a good negotiator and many a time he put out the bush fires that occur in any constituency from time to time, sometimes just by the simple act of delaying a meeting for a week or two. He always seemed to have some simple but effective solution to the occasional storms that would blow up. Tadgh was a Kerry man – from Valentia to be exact. I used to tease him by calling him Machiavelli – not a total misnomer! He was also a great fundraiser for the party and for many years organised a very successful St Patrick's Day lunch. He and his wife Eilish and indeed their family became very good friends of ours, although we see them less now as they have 'emigrated' to Athlone. He is presently Chairman of the ESB, having previously run a very successful accountancy practice for many years.

Concerning my electoral performance, Mr Haughey was heard to remark that maybe I should take a lesson from my high vote and recognise that the longer and the more I was out of the constituency (on Foreign Affairs business), the higher my vote would be! It is clear, he quipped in typical Haugheyesque fashion, that Andrews does better when the people don't see him. Although he was gone in disgrace, he couldn't resist a parting shot, I suppose.

My running mates were again Betty Coffey and Brian Hillery. Unfortunately, their first-preference votes were very much lower than at the previous election (Betty's was just over two thousand and Brian's a little short of three thousand), so that even my surplus of three thousand five hundred couldn't bring either of them in. Brian did hold on till the final count but he was about seventeen hundred votes behind the last candidate to be declared elected. Both he and Betty suffered from the national backlash against the party. The overall national result was a disaster for us: our percentage of the vote slumped to under forty, the lowest since 1927, and we lost nine seats. It was also something of a catastrophe for Fine Gael because they lost ten. Labour were the big winners: they gained eighteen seats, which brought them up to thirty-three in the Dáil. The PDs won four extra seats, bringing their total up to ten. The so-called 'Spring tide' was an extraordinary achievement for Labour, and they could have had more seats if they had run more candidates.

It was fairly widely expected that the new government would be a 'rainbow' coalition. John Bruton had introduced the term during the election campaign when he spoke of a combination of his own party, Labour and the PDs forming the next government. Albert Reynolds had been contemplating the possibility of coalition with Labour, even before polling day, but senior figures like Flynn, MacSharry and Brennan were in favour of reorganising in opposition. On the other hand, Brian Lenihan favored an alliance with Labour. I had mixed feelings on the matter. For long I had felt that the Civil War parties should get back together again. In many ways they are the most natural allies in Irish politics. I already referred to John Kelly's frequent comments in this regard when he was alive. However, we had a lot in common with the Labour party. Indeed, from the beginning, we got more of the so-called working-class vote than Labour did, and that continues to be the case.

Things looked bad for Albert Reynolds in the days after the election. It was generally believed, among politicians and in the media, that Fine Gael, Labour and some other party would form the next government. Vincent Brady, a former Fianna Fáil Chief Whip, was the only one to call openly for a change of leader in the party, but there was no doubt that well-known anti-Reynolds TDs, like Burke, Collins and others, wanted this as well. There was an attempt made to put my name forward as a possible successor. Late-night phone calls did not result in my taking such a step. Perhaps I would have made quite a good leader, but I never seriously entertained that ambition. Some of the younger TDs, like Seán Power and Noel Dempsey, were keen enough to support me, but there was no campaign on my behalf. In any event, I quickly scotched the suggestion, out of loyalty to Albert as well as reluctance to countenance the suggestion.

Some people were prepared to hang Albert out to dry at the time, which I felt was grossly unfair. He had placed trust in me as Foreign Minister and now I was being asked to desert him when he was at one of his weakest moments. This was why I referred to the suggestion of my candidacy at the time as 'unprincipled and obscene'. There was a move to get rid of Reynolds all right, but I had no intention of allowing myself to be used as the instrument.

Meanwhile, Fine Gael and Labour were unable to reach a deal. They didn't have the numbers on their own and would need either PD or Democratic Left involvement. We now know that Brian Lenihan, long an advocate of Fianna Fáil coalition with Labour, had met with Ruairi Quinn, so there were tentative contacts from our side with Labour as well. At Cabinet level, Joe Walsh thought a deal could be done and he urged that we prepare a policy document to be ready for talks at any stage. Some ministers (Flynn and McCreevy, for example) didn't want to have anything to do with Labour. I have seen my own name mentioned in this regard, but, while I saw virtue in the suggestion that Fianna Fáil could do with time in opposition to regroup, it is not true that I was one of this anti-Labour group.

Some people certainly had doubts about Spring himself and the view was expressed that he had a strong character, and that he would look for more than he was entitled to in any proposed coalition arrangement. Labour had at that time floated the notion of a rotating Taoiseach. In spite of all this, Albert was all for a deal with Labour and there was concern that, in his anxiety to remain on as Taoiseach, he might come to an arrangement that mightn't be acceptable, in a general sense, to Fianna Fáil. But, in fairness to him, I always found Reynolds a very straight person and, if it hadn't worked, I believe he would have walked away and taken his medicine on the opposition benches.

He got his adviser, Martin Mansergh, to prepare a policy document. Labour finally sent Fianna Fáil a copy of the joint Labour–Democratic Left policy programme for government and they had the Mansergh document in reply within an hour. They must have been pretty surprised by the speed of the reply and probably even more so by how compatible it was with their own policy document. At this time I accompanied Albert Reynolds and Bertie Ahern to Edinburgh for a very important EU summit, because there was the possibility of a very large amount of money becoming available to Ireland from the Structural Fund. Reynolds had declared he would secure £6 billion over five years, double what we had been receiving, but he went further and got a commitment for £8 billion in Structural and Cohesion Funds over seven years. It was certainly a negotiating triumph for him and he was now optimistic about putting a deal together with Labour.

The social side of the summit was interesting as well. The summit dinner for ministers was given on the royal yacht Britannia, now gone for ever. Most of the British royal family were in attendance: Queen Elizabeth, Prince Philip, Prince Charles and Princess Diana, Princess Anne and Princess Margaret. There was turmoil in the royal family at the time because the Prince Charles–Princess Diana marriage had become rather shaky. Having stood near and spoken to Diana, I could not for the world understand why Charles would not continue his marriage to this strikingly beautiful woman – who was a very pleasant person as well, as I found when I exchanged a few words with her. But I suppose one never knows. Princess Margaret was a small woman who was smoking cigarettes to beat the band, but it was with her niece, Princess Anne, that I had an interesting conversation. She complained, and meant it genuinely, that she couldn't come to Ireland because of the security situation. She was also unhappy with the established Church in England. She was getting married for the second time the following day, but had to do so in Scotland, where the church is disestablished. I found her a very interesting and open person.

At the end of the evening, before we all left, there was a line up of (I thought) both prime ministers and foreign ministers to receive a presentation from the Queen – a piece of silver or some small memento of the occasion. It would not be a very valuable thing but of historical and sentimental value to the individual of course. I took my place in the queue and was moving near the queen to accept my gift when I was tipped on the shoulder and told: 'Sorry, Minister, this queue is for prime ministers only.' I was momentarily embarrassed.

The Edinburgh summit was the last big engagement of my first short period as Minister for Foreign Affairs. Formal Fianna Fáil–Labour talks began in mid-December: Ahern, Cowen and Dempsey were our negotiators and Quinn, Brendan Howlin and Mervyn Taylor represented Labour. The discussions went rather smoothly, but lasted for some weeks against a backdrop of a currency crisis and increasing interest rates, which must have put some pressure on the participants to reach an agreement. I'm not sure how one would describe the mood in the parliamentary party as the talks went on: relief, perhaps, that we were likely to be going back into government, when things had looked so bleak. There were some, I know, who would have preferred us to go into opposition and regroup and reorganise and there was certainly a discontented Haugheyite rump who saw their chances of dumping Albert fading fast.

The two parties' negotiators concluded an agreement, *Programme for a Partnership Government 1993–1997*, which was put to specially convened parliamentary-party meetings of the prospective partners. The agreement was widely welcomed at both gatherings. Really what it showed was that the philosophies of the two parties weren't very far apart. In the new Cabinet, Labour got six of the fifteen full ministries, their biggest share of power in their history. More importantly for me, Dick Spring wanted Foreign Affairs. He had been apprised of the major developments that were taking place in Northern Ireland and he wanted in on them. When Albert Reynolds phoned me to let me know the situation, I had no intention of making matters in any way difficult for him. I was happy to serve in whatever way the Taoiseach wished. I was, however, genuinely disappointed and upset on a personal level. By that time I had been getting on very well and had begun to make my mark in Foreign Affairs, so I felt very much that it was a ministry interrupted. It had been a difficult year because of Maastricht and the Northern talks and would have been coming into an easier patch, which I could have enjoyed. But I suppose that's politics, and nobody ever said that one was meant to enjoy it.

I must also confess to feeling a bit let down by Reynolds. I felt I had given him a huge amount of support, particularly after the results of the election and when things looked pretty grim for him. While his popularity was going down (even to as low as eleven per cent in the polls), my own was soaring and I was being talked about in many quarters as a possible leader. But, as I already mentioned, I scotched such talk in no uncertain terms. I felt let down by Albert, because he didn't seem inclined to fight my corner when it came to the Foreign Affairs position. He told me that he would have re-appointed me there, had Labour not insisted that they wanted that portfolio, and that seemed to bc that. It was interesting to note the number of phone calls that came into the RTÉ Radio 1 chat shows (Gay Byrne, Pat Kenny and especially Marian Finucane) objecting to my removal from Foreign Affairs. It seems it was quite extraordinary and most unusual. It was all very gratifying of course, but it changed nothing. My new ministry was Defence and the Marine and I suppose I should have been happy to be still in Cabinet.

DEFENCE, MARINE AND ENDGAME

DEFENCE

As Minister for Defence, I had a fine office on Mobhi Road in Glasnevin and my private secretary was Gerry Gervin. The Secretary General of the department was Sean Brosnan – a man of enormous wisdom and patriotism. We had a close and fruitful relationship. The Department of Defence has often been seen as a down-the-line department but I was always very happy there. I felt there was a lot to be done, especially with the defence forces: the army, the navy and the air corps. I'm glad to say that I did some significant things for the army in particular.

I founded the United Nations Training School Ireland (UNTSI) in 1993 as a school of the Military College. It main aim was to ensure that the defence forces' training would be of the highest standards in all aspects of today's complex peacekeeping operations. The school is also a centre, which draws on the exceptional range of experience gained by Irish soldiers on many missions worldwide.

The school studies developments in peacekeeping in all its forms; it seeks to develop teaching, to conduct training courses and seminars and to ensure high standards of performance by defence forces' personnel missions abroad. In addition, UNTSI staff participate in instructor exchange programmes with a number of similar institutions in other countries. UNTSI has been very successful, and Ireland has built up a well-deserved reputation for peacekeeping throughout the world. It was also one of my ambitions to get the Army Equitation School new premises but, alas, I wasn't minister long enough to achieve that ambition.

A perhaps painful part of my record in Defence was the White Paper I launched on the Defence Forces, which recommended a reduction in their size. They didn't thank me for that, I need hardly remark. On a more positive note, I also sought to introduce some sort of strategy for the assimilation of persons with differing sexual orientations. At an early stage after my appointment to Defence, a reporter asked me whether gay people should be allowed into the army. I responded that no one was asked about his or her sexual proclivities on induction and that there should be no such discrimination. I also said that it might be necessary to introduce a code of conduct for both heterosexuals and gays to ensure against bullying and such like. My attitude was that what people did in their private lives after army hours was entirely a matter for them. Some senior army personnel didn't see it that way and didn't want to have anything to do with recognising sexual differences, so the matter was not progressed any further during my time.

I had great regard for the Air Corps and took the initiative of giving that body their distinctive blue uniforms, at the request of Brigadier-General Patrick Cranfield. They used to have a green military uniform just like the army and I decided, much to the annoyance of the Chief of Staff of the Defence Forces and a number of his aides, that it was a good idea to give the air corps a distinctive appearance. I was also responsible for bringing an air of reality to Casement Aerodrome at Baldonnel and for setting out a decent infrastructure there. It was my successor in office who got to open what I had begun – but that's the way of politics. I regret to say that I didn't get round to doing much for the navy. I did try to update some of their infrastructure in Haulbowline and at least give a kick-start to a training school there. I don't think the navy were very impressed by my sojourn in Defence but one thing I can plead on my behalf is that my time in the department was very short. One of my major initiatives, in conjunction with the Minister for Foreign Affairs, was to send two contingents of Irish troops on UN peacekeeping duties to Somalia

(UNOSOM) for two rotations of six months. Apprehension was expressed in some quarters about Ireland responding to the UN request to send troops to Somalia. It was asked if this was more than the traditional peacekeeping role our troops normally played on such UN missions, especially because of the presence in the UN force of a large and heavily armed US element. I said in the Dáil that I saw the sending of Irish troops as reflecting the will of the Irish people arising from their generosity to the people of Somalia. I also said that we Irish were born missionaries, whether in army uniform or clerical garb, and that as a small island on the periphery of Europe we had a moral role to play within the UN.

My principal concern throughout this time was that all our soldiers would come home safely. Our troops were not embroiled in the fighting, nor were they ever tainted by accusations of brutality, which had been made against several other contingents. They ran a transport company and did an excellent job with vehicles (MAN diesel trucks) most of whom were more than ten years old, but which had been refitted and repainted to look new. Most of our troops were stationed in Baidoa and their principal responsibility was moving badly needed supplies between Baidoa and Mogadishu. The Irish government had leased the transports to the UN and, when the mission was over, they were returned to be used at home. So we had discovered a niche role to allow us to continue to take part in UN operations: engaging small numbers of troops with little extra expenditure and acquiring welcome monetary compensation.

I have always felt that Ireland had a special role in Somalia. The Irish soldiers did a great job and adjusted extremely well to the cultural differences. They established a very good relationship with the local people in Baidoa and, much to my relief, they all emerged unscathed from what was sometimes a very chaotic operation in Somalia.

During this time I made a number of visits to Somalia and met the warlords – Ali Mahdi Mohamed and Mohamed Farah Aideed – and I established a good rapport with each of them. They had both been educated by Irish missionaries! I met both men subsequently in Nairobi. This was the first time they had met for a year, so historically it was a very important time. They were very welcoming to me, and Aideed, in particular, acknowledged my role in opening up Somalia to world attention. The impression I got was that both were committed to peace and I was hopeful that they might agree to establish some sort of interior government in Somalia. I told them that we were prepared to broker peace between them and any other party that might be involved in the conflict. But then, most unfortunately, the Americans came in and took a decision – and it turned out to be a wrong decision – to become involved with taking out Aideed. The film, *Black Hawk Down*, which tells the story of one of the battles in Mogadishu where the American Rangers fought Aideed's men, portrays quite accurately this botched American attempt to destroy the warlord. Had the Americans behaved differently, it is my belief that Ireland might have played a significant role in settling the Somali situation, as we did, for example, in East Timor. We might have brokered a peace in what is now a non-country and prevented so much further suffering and bloodshed. We had played a significant role in Somalia. President Robinson had visited the country and from there had gone to the UN and alerted the world to the tragic state of that country.

I know the Americans went to Somalia with the best of intentions – to bring peace. They were welcomed at first, but the situation turned sour on them and they started taking wrong options. Ultimately, instead of bringing peace to this unhappy land, they brought yet another sword, which was the last thing needed. Because of the disastrous things that happened to them, they just pulled out, and I believe that their bad experience in Somalia has affected their peace-keeping role in the world ever since.

One of my trips to Somalia was to visit our troops there around St Patrick's Day in 1994. On our way back, Annette and I took a few days' private holiday in Kenya. During that break, we spent a very interesting day in Kwangami with a Jesuit priest, Fr John O'Grady. Kwangami is a vast slum area of indescribable poverty just outside Nairobi. Most people in Nairobi will tell you that everyone in Kwangami is a thief and people won't go there after six in the evening. John brought us on a tour of the area, during which we came across the hut of a very old lady. It hardly deserved to be called a hut, more a lean-to made of bits of packaging and a small piece of corrugated iron. This was where the lady kept her few bits of possessions – a couple of black saucepans, a cracked cup, and a few dirty blankets. She was very welcoming and good-humoured as she showed us the terrible ulcers on her legs. It seemed that she had wonderful faith and survived on a pittance that her children scraped together for her from time to time. She was an inspiring example of the ability of the human spirit to survive even the most atrocious of conditions.

John then brought us on a tour of all the places he had built: a school, a hospital, a church and a carpentry shop. We also visited the craft centre where the women made all sorts of beautiful artefacts, which were then brought into special sales in Nairobi. There was a doll factory where all the dolls were made by women in the style of whatever country they came from – most of these women were refugees. Being built at that time was a facility for making artificial limbs and a training centre for people who needed them. As many of the people there were refugees from various countries where there were wars raging, such as Somalia, Ethiopia and Sudan, they often had limbs missing and no hope of getting any help from their own governments, which was why John O'Grady was setting up that facility. Not only were all the buildings there constructed by the residents of Kwangami, but all the building materials were made there too, by hand, which was of course very time-consuming. The quality was so good that people were beginning to come out from Nairobi to buy roofing tiles, window frames and building blocks.

The whole enterprise was quite a success story because the local people were getting more and more involved in their own survival and were beginning to have some pride in themselves and their achievements. Some of them may have been thieves, and indeed murderers, but there were definitely signs of hope in the area. A dedicated and gifted man like John O'Grady can do so much and he had a very good team. All sorts of people helped him out, including an Irish architect called Tony Gleeson, who practised in Nairobi. Fr O'Grady was in the best tradition of the Irish missionary. He was a man of great energy and compassion – unbeatable qualities. He was an ideas man and would have been a multi-millionaire in commercial life. These poor people of Kwangami were at least lucky to have a man like him. He was also great company and didn't take himself too seriously!

MARINE

I enjoyed my time in Defence but I cannot say the same for the Department of the Marine (at the time I had joint responsibility for both ministries). In many ways it was a neglected department, hidden away in Leeson Lane. Nobody knew where it was and I sometimes wondered whether the government of the day knew where it was. It was very underrated, understaffed and under-resourced. I always felt that it was an afterthought in many ways. It used to be attached to Agriculture in the old Department of Agriculture and Fisheries but was never properly recognised and certainly never given the status of Agriculture.

It was difficult to come to grips with all the various factions of fisherfolk, of whom there were so many countrywide. Fresh-water fishermen were seeking to prevent the fish farms because they said they were killing the sea trout. There was something in that, but if you put your head above the parapet to support that demand, you were knocked down immediately by other vested interests.

It was a case of constant battle with the salt-water fishermen, especially the Killybegs Fishermen's Organisation. Each Christmas the fishing quotas were set at EU level for the pelagic and non-pelagic fish. Invariably one got it in the neck around that time from the various fishing organisations because the quotas were not set in their favour.

It has to be admitted that the whole Irish fishing industry was very badly treated when we were negotiating membership of the Common Market, as it was then known. The industry was almost traded off for advantages in other sectors, especially agriculture. I don't think the fishermen had recovered from that bad beginning and they probably still haven't.

Joey Murrin, of the Killybegs Fishermen's Organisation, was probably, from the point of view of the Killybegs fishermen, the best thing ever, because not a fish would move around the coast of Ireland but Joey would know about it. One night, after being told that I would have to roll over for Spring, and having learnt what my new ministry would be, I made the throwaway remark, in the visitors' bar in Dáil

Éireann, that they were putting me into 'the Department of Fish and Ships'. There were a number of journalists in the bar and, of course, my quip appeared in some of the papers the following day. A meeting was demanded by Joey Murrin to know what I meant. He saw my remark as diminishing the whole fishing industry and as a clear reflection of my unhappiness at having to leave Foreign Affairs for the Marine. In any event, the meeting was held. Joey banged the table angrily and gave out to me. He told me I was letting down the fishermen and wanted to know what I was going to do about it. I replied that I was going to do nothing about it, that it was simply a humorous remark and that if he missed the humour in it that there was nothing I could do about it. The remark was intended to be light-hearted and not at all to reflect on the fishing community or anything like that. At the time my humour passed over his head, but in time we developed a relatively warm relationship

When news emerged in August 1994 that I would be going to Rwanda in my capacity as Minister for Defence, a heading in an *Irish Times* article ran: 'Andrews told to stay at home and concern himself with the tuna war'. The man telling me to stay at home was the bold Joey. He said that I thought that I was still Minister for Foreign Affairs and that I couldn't be 'three ministers – Marine, Defence and Foreign Affairs'. He simply couldn't understand my role as Minister for Defence. He probably wouldn't have minded if I paraded up and down in front of a few soldiers from time to time, but anything more infuriated him. In fairness to him, until my time he had been used to a Minister for the Marine pure and simple, and a Minister for the Marine with other responsibilities was an unwelcome development as far as he was concerned.

I'm afraid I didn't help my cause with Joey or the fishermen subsequently when I was interviewed as Minister for the Marine and asked what my favourite dish was. I replied that my wife made a very good beef stew and that that dish would be my choice if I were allowed a last meal. The headline that appeared in the *Marine Times* was: 'Minister in the stew'. This led to further reprimands from Joey and his colleagues. Obviously fish was expected to be my dish of choice. I'm afraid I was rather inclined to put my foot in it at times in the Department of the Marine.

As an island nation, we had a poor track record on the fisheries front. This had nothing at all to do with the fishermen and certainly was not their fault. There is one small thing that I did do for them. It was customary for their organisations to attend in Brussels each year when the fishing quotas were being set. On my watch, the Department of the Marine recognised for the first time that the organisations' representatives deserved better treatment when attending these talks, and we sought to set up better facilities for them in Brussels, in relation to their accommodation and such like. I feel that I wasn't long enough in that department to get any sort of real handle on any significant aspect of the fishing industry, although I did ask that great public servant, T. K. Whitaker, to chair a committee on the future of salmon fishing. As already mentioned, there was quite an amount of flak being fired between the farmed salmon and wild salmon concerns. I was inclined to believe that the wild salmon side was not being fairly treated.

There was much argument, for instance, about the sea lice on farmed salmon, and I thought there was something in that criticism. Subsequent events didn't prove me wrong, when there were revelations about the way farmed salmon were fed, which were pretty horrific. Scientifically it is generally accepted that the fish farms were largely responsible for the serious decrease in numbers of wild salmon. This is because of the packed nature of sea farming, which attracts a lot of sea lice. Escaping farmed salmon (and this is quite common) in turn pass the sea lice on to the wild salmon.

So there was a strong case to be made there, and there was also a strong case to be made for abandoning the netting of salmon at sea. The only effective thing that could have been done about that was to buy out the people with the licences once and for all. But it was deadly difficult to make any sort of headway against the vested interests involved at that time. Now the buy out has become a reality.

One interesting trip that I took in my time in the Department of the Marine was in early January 1994 to Taiwan. Its capital, Taipei, is one of the most densely populated cities in the world. Michael Garvey was the IDA man there, an interesting man who did an incredible job: apart from his IDA brief, he also acted as Honorary Consul and was generally Mr Ireland there. He had been four years on Taiwan by the time of my visit and had spent four years in Japan before that, and had a great love of the Orient. I had a series of meetings in Taiwan with the Fishery Council members with the aim of extending trade between our two countries. I met with Taiwan's Foreign Minister, Frederick Chien, whom I had met when I first visited the country in 1978, when we were both Junior Foreign Ministers. Political attitudes had changed hugely since that first visit. At that time, the Taiwanese government believed it was the legitimate government of all China and its aim was to return to Peking (as it was then called) and take over. Of course, even at that time no one really believed that was going to happen, but serious lip service was paid to the notion, and one had to be very careful not to say the wrong thing. For example, Taiwan had to be referred to at all times as the Republic of China on Taiwan. At that time, too, there were no opposition parties and the newspapers were organs of government.

By 1994 all that had changed. Frederick Chien now talked about how they would like to be accommodated within China as a whole, as long as their standards could be maintained. But they were still nervous of Communist China. They were looking to the UN to find a way to acknowledge the existence of divided countries such as theirs. He made the valid point that they had a population of twenty-one million and were a democracy and should no longer be ignored by the world. Frederick was a suave, urbane man and very good company. He was also well versed in the marine area. He talked about research that had been successfully completed into how to get prawns to mate in captivity. It seems that researchers had discovered that if the prawns were blinded they would mate, but the difficulty was that then they couldn't see to find food or anything else. I remember him speaking in deadly earnest on this subject during a lunch he hosted for twenty or more people. While the Chinese present shared their Foreign Minister's earnestness, I could see that some of the Irish present found it hard to keep straight faces at the thought of blind prawns mating.

Sadly, in early August 1994, the death occurred of Gerry O'Sullivan, who was my Minister of State at the Department of the Marine, and Labour TD for Cork North Central. A relatively young man, he had been diagnosed with cancer the previous October and had been battling the disease bravely ever since. Gerry was a man of much ability, which was now, alas, lost forever.

THE NORTH AGAIN

Behind-the-scenes progress was being made on the North for some time before the Fianna Fáil–Labour government took office. John Hume had been holding talks with Gerry Adams for two years. Charles Haughey had proposed to John Major the idea of a joint declaration between the Irish and British governments, which would set out the principles for an eventual agreement that would get the men of violence to confine their activities to peaceful political means. Albert Reynolds sought to build on these moves and in particular to get republicans involved in a realistic way in supporting the peace process. He kept Major well informed on the efforts he was making.

In early 1993, Reynolds pushed the process further by going all out to persuade republicans that the constitutional route was a far better way of pursuing their political goals than violence. But he had to disabuse them of the notion that they could get British agreement to a timetable for Irish unification. If they accepted the principle of consent, they would win the broad backing of constitutional nationalism on the island, he argued. What was new about Reynolds's attitude was his insistence on the principle of consent, but it had to be accompanied by a new expression of self-determination by all the Irish people, which was equally vital to republicans. Reynolds's approach was to concentrate all efforts on achieving peace first in the expectation that a political solution would follow. The timing was right because both the republicans and the British realised neither side could win the so-called war.

I won't go into the intricacies, clashes and compromises that produced the Joint Declaration signed by Reynolds and Major in Downing Street on 15 December 1993. The lead-up to it involved risks and some plain, tough talking by Reynolds with all involved, but it worked. The occasion has rightly been described as 'historic' and subsequently cleared the way for the IRA ceasefire and the Good Friday Agreement. It may well be the case that no one else could have done it but Albert and that it would not have happened but for his special relationship with John Major, who later wrote in his autobiography that the great thing about it was that they both liked each other and could have a row without giving up on the process. Albert was a superb negotiator and, what was more, he was willing to take risks. He always said he would never have got anywhere in business or in politics without taking risks. He could be a tough talker at times and wasn't prepared to settle for any half-measures. All sides in the talks came to respect his open, no-nonsense approach. He really put it up to the republicans and they put their faith in him and took the plunge.

Progress following the Joint Declaration was painfully slow – as it ever is in Northern Ireland – but Reynolds remained upbeat when many others despaired. As Minister for Defence, I wasn't very much involved in the process. I stood in from time to time for Justice or Foreign Affairs in the talks but that was the extent of my contribution at that stage. An Irish-American delegation of people who had influence with Sinn Féin arrived in Dublin in late August and met Reynolds and Spring. Reynolds was adamant that there had to be a permanent – not temporary – ceasefire and wanted any Sinn Féin statement written clearly and unambiguously. He was also adamant that the IRA would have to give up their weapons, on the basis that they were either at war or involved in peaceful politics. This attitude was typical of Reynolds; it was all or nothing and he was determined to go for broke. His approach worked. The IRA finally announced their ceasefire on 31 August.

Historically speaking, only a Fianna Fáil Taoiseach could have secured this agreement from the IRA. What I mean is that, if the IRA were to trust anybody – and I have no regard whatever for the IRA – they would be much more likely to trust a Fianna Fáil leader, rather than any of the other leaders. I would see it as a question of historical resonance, in that the Provisional IRA would have recognised where we were born and bred and would therefore have been more inclined to trust us, or at least interface with us as a prelude to trust. Of all the political leaders involved in bringing about this ceasefire, from Garret FitzGerald's Anglo-Irish Agreement onwards, most credit for the Joint Declaration and the subsequent end of the campaign of violence must go to Albert Reynolds. His energy, drive and single-minded commitment, and, indeed, willingness to gamble all, pushed things forward in a way nobody else could have done. Whatever else may have happened in his political life – and it was far from a story of continued triumph, particularly towards the end – what he achieved in Northern Ireland will be his lasting monument. I think that between them, Albert Reynolds and John Hume brought an end to the dreadful and bloody conflict that cost so many precious lives.

TENSIONS

Despite the great achievements in Northern Ireland, relations within the government itself were not so smooth. When the Reynolds–Spring government was formed, the talk went round that Fianna Fáil and Labour would govern together far into the future: as our party's eternal optimist Brian Lenihan put it, the 'Fianna Fáil–Labour production would run and run'. All Albert Reynolds had to do was to keep the ship of state on an even keel. But government advisers were a source of tension from the outset. The Programme for a Partnership Government had introduced a new system whereby each minister had a programme manager to ensure that the coalition programme was fulfilled. All the Labour managers were party activists, and additional special advisers were also brought in. The Fianna Fáil programme managers were mainly civil servants. I was in favour of the idea of programme managers and I have no doubt that it is here to stay. My previous Special Adviser, Rory MacCabe, had returned to the Law Library when I left Foreign Affairs. My new programme manager was not a civil servant but a former journalist, Liam Cahill. Liam was first-class and a great support to me all through my time in these departments. He had been recommended to me and I decided to go with him. I have the height of respect for civil servants but I decided that I didn't want one as my programme manager – I wanted someone from outside the department with independent views. I never regretted my decision. Ironically, for a time afterwards Liam became Communications Director for the Labour Party.

Some resentment came to be felt in our party about the programme managers' role because of leaks to the media that favoured Labour's position on issues of conflict. The Taoiseach took a dislike to Fergus Finlay, believing he was behind much negative press comment about himself. Finlay was extraordinarily loyal to Dick Spring and served him well. He is a very able and astute man. From a Fianna Fáil point of view, he was seen as something of a hate figure, but

I would find it difficult to make that judgement myself. It has been suggested that Spring and his close associates, Finlay and Greg Sparks, were suspicious of Fianna Fáil from the outset. I would say that there is truth in this contention. The ongoing Beef Tribunal was certainly a worry to them and they feared it could cause problems for them in time. But I very much believe that the rest of Labour, both ministers and TDs, got on well with their Fianna Fáil counterparts.

Michael D. Higgins (who had been appointed Minister for Arts, Culture and the Gaeltacht) and I were pals, and had been long before his party and mine coalesced. We had been active together on the human rights front, and had travelled abroad together on a number of occasions and knew each other very well. Michael D., as well as having a brilliant mind, is terrific company and has given me many a good laugh over the years. Shortly after he was appointed Minister for Arts, Culture and the Gaeltacht, he rang me and said he wanted to come and see me. He was finding it a bit difficult to adjust to the smaller details of being a minister. What added to his difficulties was that he was starting up a new department for the arts and also coping with the Department of the Gaeltacht, which really hadn't had a minister for a while. Remembering my own difficulties as a new minister I was delighted to help him out in any way.

His new department was based in the old Department of the Gaeltacht and some of the officials there were not taking too well to the addition of the arts to their brief. They considered Gaeltacht affairs – with which, of course, they were far more familiar – to be more important and many of them were not at all as interested in the arts. Referring to some Gaeltacht-related events that he had to go to, he sighed at one stage: 'Why do *I* have to inhale all the must of the national wardrobe?' He certainly had a way with words.

The Irish-language station Telefís na Gaeilge, which first came on air at Hallowe'en in 1996, was planned for during that Fianna Fáil–Labour government. Along with Michael D. and Máire Geoghegan-Quinn (Minister for Justice), I pushed very hard for the setting up of the service. I was keen not only that the station should be supported but also that it should be located in a particular part of the Galway West constituency with which I have always had a close association – Baile na hAbhann. This is one of the strongest Irish-speaking areas. Geoghegan-Quinn favoured another part of the constituency, in her own power base, for its location. Michael D. and I succeeded in having it located in Baile na hAbhann. The local publican, Gerry Walsh, who happens to be a Fine Gaeler, but a pal of mine none the less, sold a bit of land where the station was set up. I'm glad to say that the channel has gone from strength to strength since its establishment and it has been of enormous benefit to the development of the Irish language.

Niamh Bhreathnach, of Labour, was elected for the first time in November 1992 in my own constituency and was straight away appointed to the Cabinet as Minister for Education. It wasn't necessarily to her advantage because, busy as she was with ministerial duties, she never got very involved in the constituency as a TD and subsequently lost her seat.

Some commentators have put the tensions in the Reynolds–Spring government down to a personality clash between the two leaders themselves. Both men were touchy, demanded respect and never felt they got enough, this argument goes. I think it is true to say that they were touchy gentlemen and very strong-willed individuals as well. Spring was an extremely strong personality but tended to see hurt where it didn't exist and felt unduly sensitive when he needn't have. You had to be careful how you walked around him because of this strain of touchiness. Sean Duignan, in his book *One More Turn on the Merry-go-Round*, described Spring as tetchy and when he was not around, Finlay was being tetchy for him. Reynolds too could be touchy. Any perceived slight on his personal integrity would certainly provoke his wrath. And, like Spring, he was extremely strong willed, even to the point of stubbornness. His word was his bond and, if he felt he had given his word, he was most reluctant to be persuaded to follow an alternative course. This could and, ultimately and fatally for this government, did lead to serious trouble.

There were a number of issues which caused disagreement between the government partners. The most significant one in 1993 was probably the tax amnesty. Reynolds was all in favour of it but Spring and Labour felt extremely uneasy about allowing people who hadn't been paying their proper share of tax to get off with paying only a small percentage of what they owed. The purpose of the amnesty was to bring in much-needed money – a figure of £200 million was mentioned – to the exchequer. I have to confess to not having expressed a strong view one way or another at the time; I allowed it to happen, as it were. By any reckoning, the tax amnesty must be considered a public relations disaster as far as the government was concerned. It was dubbed a 'cheats' charter' and the public didn't like it at all.

There was another serious row, this time over residency for tax exiles. Labour let it be known that they would pull out of government if it went ahead and, having got the tax amnesty through the year before, Reynolds backed down on that one. In fact, residency was incorporated to some extent in the Finance Bill, in that tax exiles were allowed to spend six months in Ireland while keeping their non-resident status. What's often forgotten about these people – like J. P. McManus, for instance – is that some of them are enormous benefactors of various causes. If one were to set the amount of their benefaction against any possible tax liability, perhaps the difference might not be that great or might even be in their favour. In the case of J. P. I have personal experience of his extraordinary generosity to the Irish Red Cross, of which I am, at present, Chairman. He has given millions – not thousands, but millions – to the Irish Red Cross. I would add John Magnier of Coolmore Stud to that category.

The so-called 'passports for sale scheme' caused a major controversy when it emerged, in June 1994, that the Reynolds family pet food business had benefited from a £1 million investment from a Saudi family who had been given Irish citizenship. Spring requested and inspected the file on the matter in the Department of Justice and said everything was above board. But a torrent of media criticism followed. The sale of passports is something for which I have very little time. To me, the passport is an authentic national document and should be prized as such. You cannot put a price on citizenship. The passport-in-return-for-investment approach was accepted practice at the time in the interest of Irish jobs and the Reynolds family business was a significant employer in the Longford area. Had everyone been up front and open about it immediately, it would probably have died a death. Instead there was a lot of dodging and evasiveness and it all looked as if there was something to hide, which gave the Opposition a field day. Michael Smith was handling the issue for Fianna Fáil and did not exactly cover himself in glory.

With Des O'Malley, John Wilson and Padraig Flynn, at my first Northern Ireland talks. Note the 'No Entry' sign just behind us!

David Junior and myself with Ted Kennedy in March 1993.

With President Robinson and Nick Robinson in Somalia in 1992.

Niall and myself with Kofi Annan in Dublin.

With President Bush and Barbara Bush in the Oval Office of the White House on St Patrick's Day, 1992.

Top: At the first North/South Council meeting with David Trimble in foreground.
Bottom: As Minister for Defence in Somalia with Jimmy Scally, then working with the UN.

Unlikely looking golfers – Taoiseach Bertie Ahern and myself at a golf fundraiser.

With my father. This photo was used for the Kindred series in the *Sunday Tribune*.

Annette and I with our five children: Sinead, Barry, Claire, David and Mary.

With my five grandsons: Hugh, Daniel, baby Conn, Jack and Jake.

The European elections were due in June 1994 and the same Michael Smith had come to see me at home the previous 17 January to investigate the possibility of a member of my family running in the elections. As the conversation developed, it transpired that he wanted me to run and he asked me to consider the proposition. He was obviously an emissary from the Taoiseach. I did give the proposal some thought, but I considered that there were a number of factors against my running. Apart from feeling that it would be a backward step to go from being a government minister to an MEP, I also thought the lifestyle would not suit either Annette or myself. In addition, our daughter Claire was fifteen at the time – not a good age for her to move into a different education system. Furthermore, it was being suggested that I run in the Leinster rather than the Dublin constituency. Jim Fitzsimons, a friend of mine who was also close to my brother Niall, was one of the two sitting Fianna Fáil MEPs in the Leinster constituency at the time. The official view seemed to have been that he was unsure of winning back his seat, but I am certain that he wouldn't have been at all pleased to have me landed in on top of him. I soon learned that Michael Woods had also been approached with a proposal that he should run for Europe and that he had turned it down. For that election, the Leinster constituency had been changed from a three- to a four-seater, and the sitting MEP Paddy Lalor was retiring. Following a meeting with the Taoiseach and Michael Smith, I agreed, against my better judgement, to run. I know Annette was unhappy with the prospect but I told her that I must be loyal to the party and that I felt obliged, because the Taoiseach had asked me. I did, however, say to Michael Smith that my portfolio should still be available in the event of my not being elected. The reassurances I got were somewhat vague and I wasn't so sure about Smith, who fancied himself as something of a wheeler-dealer. His demeanour earned him the title of 'the Cardinal' in Leinster House.

There was speculation that the Westmeath man, Senator Donie Cassidy, would be on the Leinster ticket and I realised this would pose a lot of difficulty for me, because he had already been working towards the election for the previous six months and, as a county councillor of long standing, had a particularly good rapport with the county councillors who were so important in rural areas. Donie was also seen as Albert Reynolds's confidant and, if the Taoiseach really wanted me to run, he had to make it clear that he was supporting me totally. No one really knew what he was saying to Donie, who was one of his greatest supporters.

I also decided that there was no need for me to resign my ministry during the election campaign for Europe and that in fact I would refuse to resign, if asked to do so. I felt that to do so would be most foolish. There was no precedent for a minister running for this election, but there was a similar precedent when Brian Lenihan ran for the presidency. He was Minister for Defence at the time and no one expected him to resign during his campaign. So I let it be known that I would be willing to run but only under certain conditions. My intention was still a secret. I then decided to have a word with my son Barry about it. His reaction was that I was crazy and that if I was elected to Europe I would very quickly be bored to death. He also said that he found it very difficult to understand that, having spent a lifetime trying to get into Cabinet, I should not allow myself to be pushed out so easily. Annette was of the same view. To my family's opposition to my running was added that of close constituency workers, who had campaigned many years for me in Dáil elections. I was eventually persuaded that my political future should not follow the MEP route. When I went to see the Taoiseach to tell him of my decision, he was very disappointed and indeed quite angry. He felt that I was letting him down. This hostile reception was probably inevitable. Some pressure was put on me to change my mind, the argument being that without me the party would not retain the second seat in Leinster. This eventually eased off but I found it gruelling while it lasted.

In fact, in the June 1994 Euro elections, Fianna Fáil did well. The second seat in Leinster was comfortably retained, with Liam Hyland joining Jim Fitzsimons. I have to admit that I felt a certain amount of relief at the result. I was particularly pleased for Jim Fitzsimons. The Labour Party did badly. There were two by-elections on the same day as the European elections, Fine Gael winning one and Democratic Left the other. This meant the 'rainbow' now had the numbers to form an alternative government if the Reynolds–Spring coalition were to break up. No doubt Spring was aware of this, but so were we. We were professional politicians and were equally alert to the implications of the new figures. We did not, as was suggested, rejoice in Labour's poor performance in the European elections, believing that this tied them even more tightly into their arrangement with us and assessing that it would make them more reluctant to have to face the electorate. It's simply not true that this was the way Reynolds read the situation and that he determined that he would have his own way more in government decisions because Labour would have to simply grin and bear it given their new-found terror of the electorate. The Fianna Fáil–Labour government was a very good government and it was unfortunate that there were tensions between Reynolds and Spring. They were cut from the same cloth in many ways. This resulted in clashes that didn't augur well for the future. I believe that Spring was looking for a way out and that that scenario was made easier following those two by-election results of June 1994.

ENDGAME

By the summer of 1994, Mr Justice Liam Hamilton was ready to present his Beef Tribunal report and there was some nervous anticipation in political circles as a result. Jim Mitchell of Fine Gael caused something of a furore in the Dáil when he referred to a potential conflict of interest for Judge Hamilton, who was President of the High Court and the second most senior judge in the land. Mitchell said that judges who depended on government for promotion might not be as independent as they should be when asked to assess the behaviour of existing government ministers. He said that Judge Hamilton, as President of the High Court, was next in line to the Chief Justice, and to be promoted to that position he would have to be nominated by current ministers who had a vested interest in what he would have to say about them in his report. Liam Hamilton had something of a political background but he leant much more towards Labour than to either Fianna Fáil or Fine Gael. I thought it was an unworthy remark by Jim Mitchell, one that clearly impugned Judge Hamilton's integrity and cast aspersions on the independence of the judiciary as a whole. I believe Judge Hamilton to have been an honest man. He went out and about and was informal in his style and this tended to irritate the traditionalists at the Bar. There was certainly criticism of his Beef

Tribunal report. It was said by some that it was a lazy enough production, but that's really all it could be accused of. I don't think he did anyone any favours in it. I thought the remark of the late Jim Mitchell was not at all characteristic of the man, because he was a good person in so many ways. As the publication of the report became imminent there was much media speculation, some of it suggesting that Spring would leave government if the report found Reynolds culpable. This naturally angered Reynolds. I'm not sure who was behind the speculation, but Reynolds believed the source was Fergus Finlay. I am inclined to believe – though this is purely speculation, of course – that the advice he was giving Spring was not altogether conducive to persuading him to stay on in government with us.

Spring and Finlay were on holidays when the nine hundred-page report was delivered to Government Buildings on a Friday evening at the end of July. A copy of the report was delivered to my house by courier that evening. A team of barristers, advisers and civil servants quickly analysed the report for Reynolds. They concluded that although some of his actions were criticised, his integrity wasn't called into question. He now ordered his press secretary, Seán Duignan, to tell the political correspondents that he had been vindicated in the report. Labour claimed that this was contrary to an agreement made earlier that week that there would be no comments until both parties had studied the report. Tense exchanges followed between the two government partners as a result.

The Labour claim was justified, but in fairness to Albert Reynolds, he had been given a bad time in relation to the whole beef business. I can understand how anxious he was to indicate as soon as possible that the report exonerated him from any culpability. There had been a lot of adverse publicity in relation to his role in the events that caused the tribunal to be set up, and he took that badly. There is one thing that can be said with certainty about him and that is that he is an honest man, and he always wanted that honesty vindicated. Unfortunately, he jumped the gun on this occasion. His action was probably a mistake, because it meant that the media focused on his premature 'I'm vindicated' leak, rather than on the report itself. Had he waited, it would have become clear that the report didn't fault him unduly and little or no damage would have been done to him, but his premature reaction made the public suspicious that he had something to hide.

Things eventually calmed down in government, but the event was really the beginning of the end for that coalition – this was when the breakdown of trust began to move towards complete collapse. I'm not sure that Spring and his advisers trusted Fianna Fáil at any time. I think they took a poor view of us as a corporate group and considered that we were only one step away from being put behind bars.

In the meantime, the terrible Rwandan genocide had occurred in the second quarter of 1994 and there was a proposal that Irish troops be sent there as peacekeepers. I was greatly concerned both about what was happening in Rwanda and also what the exact role of our troops would be if they were sent there. I was determined to go to Rwanda and had got my vaccination shots in preparation. John O'Shea of GOAL, and various other NGOs, were keen that I go. But there was not much support in government circles for the idea. However, I felt very strongly that a government minister should go. I would have been genuinely satisfied if Dick Spring, the Minister of Foreign Affairs, had gone, but that was unlikely: he was too busy keeping an eye on Albert. I was speaking to Noel Dempsey at that time about Rwanda and my wish to go there. He in turn mentioned it to the Taoiseach and afterwards rang me to say that the Taoiseach's reaction to the idea was 'very negative'. This annoyed me no end and I went straight away and unannounced to the Taoiseach's office. Michael Smith and Brian Cowen were with Albert and they were all listening to the radio to news about – what else? – the Beef Tribunal. When Albert saw me, he said: 'If it's about Rwanda, the answer is no.' I replied that I would not take no for an answer and this made him angry. 'Are you trying to bring down the government?' he asked. He said this because Dick Spring had often in the previous two years been annoyed with me for what he saw as my treading on his Foreign Affairs toes. Obviously, the Taoiseach felt that there was enough tension between the coalition partners without my adding to it. So I asked him if he would mind if I had a word with Spring. 'Do that if you want to,' he said, 'and then come back to me.'

I went down to the ministers' dining room and there by chance was Spring. I asked him for a quick word. He was reluctant at first, probably thinking it was about the Beef Tribunal, but when I assured him that it was only for a minute, he came out with me. I explained the problem to him and he was totally supportive of my going to

Rwanda. He said he had hoped to go himself but could not because of the tribunal. I then went back to Albert's office and, when he heard that I had got the go-ahead from Spring, he said in amazement: 'But how did you get to see him?' This brought home to me the major coolness that had developed between the Taoiseach and the Tánaiste over the leaking of some of the report's findings.

I did go to Rwanda, as Minister for Defence, with a number of officials. The visit only confirmed the horror of the genocide that had been committed there. The international community and the UN in particular had utterly failed the Rwandan people. The purpose of my visit was to compile a report on the up-to-date position in that country, with a view to the possible involvement of an Irish peacekeeping contingent there.

I think Michael Smith felt that I didn't get involved enough at Fianna Fáil party political level (which was probably true) and that I didn't like to get my hands dirty. I remember having a private talk with him around this time (I think it was at Gerry O'Sullivan's funeral), the subject of which was of course the Beef Tribunal. Dessie O'Malley had just come back from France at the time and had launched a major attack on the Taoiseach. Smith wanted me to attack O'Malley in turn, which I refused to do, and a poor view was taken of my attitude. I believe Smith was thinking: 'With all the problems we're having with the tribunal, he can only think of Rwanda.' At the same time, I was thinking: 'There are thousands dying every day in Rwanda and all he can think of is the effing Beef Tribunal.' In my contribution to the Dáil debate on the Beef Tribunal report, I said that the nub of the issue was whether the Taoiseach had acted improperly and that the report was emphatic that he had not, so he emerged from the report with his political and personal integrity intact. Spring said that the way the publication of the report had been handled had damaged trust between the government partners, but that he and Reynolds were prepared to work to restore it. But I felt myself that the damage had been done; and this is not a retrospective but a contemporary judgement.

When the position of Chief Justice became vacant, Reynolds wished to appoint Liam Hamilton, whereas Spring wanted Donal Barrington to be brought back from the European Court to fill the position. Because of a legal difficulty, the latter option wasn't possible.

The Attorney General, Harry Whelehan, let Spring know that he would be interested in the vacant Presidency of the High Court if Hamilton were promoted. There was nothing unusual in this: the serving Attorney General traditionally has first option on senior judicial positions when they become vacant. Harry Whelehan was too conservative in his views for Labour tastes. Their nominee for the position was Ms Justice Susan Denham and they decided they would oppose Whelehan's nomination. They were willing to accept Hamilton's appointment as Chief Justice but wanted the filling of the High Court position to be postponed until Spring (who was then in the Far East) and Reynolds could sort things out. They warned that they would pull out of government if Reynolds tried to force through Whelehan's appointment.

The Sunday papers got wind of the disagreement and were full of it, but most government TDs and, indeed, the general public weren't too taken up by it. They didn't realise that the issue had become a serious head-to-head between Reynolds and Spring and that neither was willing to give way on it: it had become a breaking point between them. Harry Whelehan, instead of going for the Presidency of the High Court, should have accepted appointment as an ordinary judge of that court. I cannot speak highly enough of his character – one could not ask to meet finer – but his political nous was limited. It is amazing that a highly intelligent man could not see that his appointment was likely to bring down a government. Clearly he should have stood back and settled for the lesser position. Had he done so, he would have been a prime candidate for the Presidency of the High Court when the position next became vacant.

Somewhat surprisingly, the papers swung behind Reynolds and chided Spring for making such a fuss over a judicial appointment. But a *Sunday Press* article said that Spring would leave the government if the Whelehan appointment went ahead. The article cited Labour sources to the effect that Reynolds was a bully who would always seek to get his own way. This greatly annoyed Reynolds, so much so that some of us, his Fianna Fáil ministers, were worried that he was taking unnecessary risks. 'Why would you bring a government down over a judicial appointment?' was one of the questions being asked. Another question was that, while Harry Whelehan was a good Attorney General, what did we owe him collectively as a government? He should have waited his turn – his time would have come.

Labour backbenchers made their presence felt at this stage. They began to panic because opinion polls showed support for their party evaporating and many of them went on air to say a compromise would have to be found. This weakened Spring's position and he and Reynolds reached an agreement to overhaul the whole system of judicial appointments. Implicit in the deal was that the Whelehan appointment would go ahead.

Things seemed to have been patched up when, to my horror, the issue of the paedophile priest Fr Brendan Smyth blew up. He was in jail in Northern Ireland but the story emerged in the media that RUC warrants requesting his extradition had lain in the Attorney General's office for seven months without being acted upon. Spring now believed he had the means of blocking Whelehan's appointment, but Reynolds was adamant that they had a deal. At a Cabinet meeting, Whelehan explained the extradition delay, but Spring was unimpressed. Is it unfair to blame Harry Whelehan for the delay? Can it be excused on the grounds of archaic procedures and inefficiencies in the Attorney General's office? If those existed, and they seemed to, was it not the responsibility of those at the top, i.e. the Attorney General himself, to reform them? I don't really have the answers to those questions, I'm afraid, but the issues involved were certainly disturbing enough to give one pause in proceeding with Whelehan's appointment as President of the High Court. Albert appears not to have had any such reservations. He felt that he had given Whelehan his word and decided to press ahead with the appointment. The Fianna Fáil ministers present approved the appointment and none raised an objection. Spring led his ministers in a walkout from the Cabinet room in protest. Why did not one of our party's ministers raise an objection? We did not do so out of loyalty to Albert Reynolds. We were all there as a result of his confidence in us. But, more importantly, we could also see that he was adamant about having his way on this one, come what may, and any attempt to dissuade him would have been futile.

Another thing that has to be mentioned is the confusion that reigned at that time and in the days that followed. There were long meetings and everybody was stressed and tired and hassled. People were coming and going, and to-ing and fro-ing, and there was no cohesion or continuity at all. We should all – all the Fianna Fáil ministers

– have been there together for a sustained period so that things could have been ironed out properly once and for all. But ministers had their duties to attend to and people were constantly being called away and it was all very confused. That was our fault, jointly and collectively, and no one person should be asked to bear the blame for it.

The media now turned on Reynolds and criticised him for the rift in the coalition. Spring addressed an emergency Labour parliamentary party meeting and said that someone had to take responsibility for allowing a paedophile to be free longer than he should. Garbled versions of this reached the media and caused us in Fianna Fáil to feel we were being unfairly blamed for covering up for a child abuser. Labour TDs, who before this had been running scared, were happy to put this gloss on the issue in media interviews. While many thought an election inevitable, some leading Labour figures let it be known that if Fianna Fáil jettisoned Reynolds and replaced him with Bertie Ahern, the coalition could be reassembled.

I was very much aware of this at the time and felt very sorry for Albert Reynolds. At the same time, the transfer of power to Ahern, if it had happened then, would have been orderly in the circumstances. Politics is about power and Fianna Fáil, as by far the largest party, is about being in government. The individual – even the leader – would have to give way to the greater good of the party if the circumstances so dictated. But there were still some throws of the dice to go yet.

The new Attorney General, Eoghan Fitzsimons, was pitched straight into the centre of the political crisis engulfing our government. He had been utterly anti-Haughey and was an extremely able lawyer, but there was a stiffness and a reserve about him. I was surprised that he accepted the offer of the position of Attorney General. I always felt that he would have made a brilliant Supreme Court judge, as his credentials as a lawyer were impeccable. He was completely honourable, decent and honest, but he wasn't for bending. When he considered the Smyth case, it was black and white and there was no in between, as far as he was concerned. I don't believe the case should have brought down a government and I think that Fitzsimons could have handled it differently. He was, however, only hours in the job, the events occurred very quickly and the issues were complicated. There were plenty of headless chickens around the Cabinet table and there was no proper direction. Albert, who was inclined to stay up late drinking tea – sometimes not going to bed until four or five in the morning – was, I felt, very tired around that particular time. As a result his mind, which is normally very sharp, may not have been as clear and precise as it needed to be. One of the problems at that time was lack of leadership.

Another thing that struck me about Reynolds at that time was that he was terribly touchy. People were almost afraid to be critical of him in any way. The tetchiness was probably due to a combination of the tiredness and the strain that he was under. I suppose we were all responsible to some extent. There were a few twenty-four- or even forty-eight-hour sessions and that really was the worst thing we could have done in the circumstances. Inevitably, people were tired and cranky and fearful for the future and that was definitely part of the problem – that we didn't take time out to take stock of the situation. We argued endlessly and asked each other what would *we* do and, at the same time, we didn't want to hurt Albert, who was too tired anyway. All in all it was a mess and no one emerged from it untarnished. The Minister for Justice, Geoghegan-Quinn, asked Fitzsimons to examine Whelehan's handling of the Smyth case. Whelehan had reported to the Cabinet that the Smyth case was the first under the Extradition Act in which a lapse of time had to be taken into account. But Fitzsimons now informed the Fianna Fáil ministers that the earlier Duggan case (another priest/paedophile case) also involved a time factor. This information was imparted on Monday morning, 14 November. I was in Cavan on official Defence business when that Cabinet meeting was held, but I doubt very much whether the ministers present understood the full implications of what they were being told.

Fitzsimons was asked to request Whelehan to postpone his formal swearing in for a few days, but Whelehan refused. At that stage, he should really have been told, rather than asked, either to withdraw or at least to wait for a few days to see how things would work out. That this wasn't done was again down to Reynolds's mantra about his word being his bond. It's an admirable trait in a person, of course, but when you are losing your government, I'm not sure how practical it is.

I was present when some ministers, as well as Martin Mansergh and Tom Savage, who was Albert's brilliant media adviser, worked late into that Monday night on the draft of the speech Reynolds would make to the Dáil the following day. It was clear to me that, possibly because of exhaustion, we had all lost sight of our objective, which should have been to keep the government in power. In his speech, Albert would use the word 'regret' rather than 'apologise', as the Labour go-betweens had requested, but he would incorporate the other points they demanded. Whelehan was formally sworn in as President of the High Court on the Tuesday morning by a terse Mary Robinson, and the tired Fianna Fáil ministers returned for the Dáil session in the afternoon. It was unclear whether the Labour ministers would accept Reynolds's proposed speech as enough to save the government. Fitzsimons arrived after the Taoiseach had gone into the House and handed in documents with his definitive advice about the Duggan case. These documents eventually ended up with Ahern, who was sitting beside Reynolds. He didn't pass them on to Reynolds. It has been suggested in some quarters that there was something sinister in his failure to pass the documents to Reynolds. But I don't believe that for one moment. I'm not sure to what extent he glanced at the documents, but he could hardly have been expected to recognise their significance. I simply could not accept that he looked at them and then said to himself: 'If I don't pass these on to Albert, that will see the end of him and it will be my turn to take over as leader and Taoiseach.'

In the circumstances, considering the immense pressure he was under, Reynolds managed to deliver his speech very well. He expressed 'deep regret' for the delay in the Smyth case and promised an immediate overhaul of the Attorney General's office to ensure that the like never happened again. He explained the disagreement between Spring and himself over the Whelehan appointment, but defended his own role and said that it would be a pity if so many positive achievements, and especially the biggest advance in Northern Ireland in 25 years, should be endangered because of a misunderstanding over a single judicial appointment. He paid Spring a warm tribute for his contribution on Northern Ireland and promised to do his utmost to restore trust and partnership to the government.

Though it was delivered well, I didn't believe at the time that the Taoiseach's speech would be enough to get Labour back on board. From the very beginning, I felt the government was finished after the

Whelehan fiasco. That night the situation grew even more frenzied. Reynolds was furious that the Fitzsimons documents had not been passed on to him, felt betrayed by Whelehan and sent Fitzsimons once again to ask him to step aside but, again, to no avail. Fitzsimons was hardly the right person to be sending on this mission. He and Whelehan were close and 'brothers' in the legal profession. Perhaps somebody like Brian Cowen should have been sent. He would have approached the problem more directly.

That night we once again went into one of those long, tedious meetings in which we just seemed to go around in circles. Brendan Howlin of Labour was in contact, relaying certain of his party's demands that Reynolds was to speak about in the Dáil the following day. When Noel Dempsey told him those demands were acceptable and asked him could he guarantee that Spring would be satisfied, Howlin used the phrase that has since gone into political folklore when he said that 'his arse was out the window on this one'.

Early next morning, Howlin was shown Reynolds's draft speech, including the points Labour wanted included, in which he regretted his decision to appoint Whelehan and promised that the breach of trust would not happen again. Howlin said this would be enough for Labour, but Fianna Fáil ministers wanted written confirmation that Spring would be happy. It was Dempsey, I think, who drafted a note, which Spring duly signed. It seemed that Reynolds had saved the government and his own position.

However, all was not as it seemed. Spring learned that Reynolds had been given the advice about the Duggan case on Monday, before making his Dáil statement on Tuesday, in which he made no reference to that case. Spring contacted Fitzsimons, who confirmed that he had told Reynolds about Duggan on Monday. Spring, Quinn and Howlin then went to see Reynolds (there were some Fianna Fáil ministers present, but I wasn't). Labour wanted Whelehan to resign but Reynolds told them he had already tried and failed to get him to do so on a number of occasions. They then said that the government should call for his resignation in the Dáil or else try to have him impeached, but Reynolds responded that neither course was feasible. Salomé-like, Quinn then passed a remark that has also since become part of the political currency: 'We've come for a head, Harry's or yours – it doesn't look like we are getting Harry's.' The game was up for Reynolds.

I don't think that his position or the government could have been saved anyway, once the Whelehan appointment was made. I believe that, at that stage, Spring had decided to walk. He had come to the conclusion that it had been a mistake to go into government with Fianna Fáil and the appointment of Whelehan had given him his exit route. The emergence of the Duggan case was really the icing on the cake, as far as Spring was concerned. Reynolds's resignation the following morning was devoid of self-pity. He said he had set himself two political goals on becoming Taoiseach, peace in Northern Ireland and an economic turnaround, and was fortunate to have achieved both in such a short time. He was the last to leave the chamber when all the speeches were over and the TDs gone. On his way out, he made a remark to the press gallery, which is oh so true: one got over the big hurdles but that it was the little ones that tripped one up. I believe the country owes him an enormous debt and that he has never got enough credit for what he achieved in relation to Northern Ireland.

Like the honourable man that he is, Albert, having resigned as Taoiseach, also immediately resigned as Fianna Fáil leader. Ironically, Harry Whelehan then resigned as President of the High Court – had he resigned twenty-four hours earlier, Reynolds might have been saved. But Whelehan wasn't a politician and simply didn't seem to understand the enormity of what was happening. He would have been a very worthy High Court judge or, indeed, President of the High Court, but in different circumstances.

Looking back at those early-winter events from the vantage point of well over ten years, I'm still hard put to explain them in any sort of sensible or logical way. It is hard to believe that the government collapsed as it did, but the events that caused the collapse were really only the final act in a drama that had been going wrong for some time anyway. Trust had broken down and suspicion ruled. As I've said a number of times in the course of this narrative, Spring and his close advisers had come to conclude that their marriage to Fianna Fáil had been a mistake and they were seeking to dissolve it to the best possible advantage to themselves.

OPPOSITION AND RETURN TO DEFENCE

A NEW LEADER

Brian Cowen, in particular, was heartbroken when Albert Reynolds decided to step down as leader of Fianna Fáil. He, Máire Geoghegan-Quinn, Charlie McCreevy and Noel Dempsey probably tried to persuade him to change his mind. If Reynolds had thought of changing his mind – and knowing him as I did, I think that highly unlikely – there were elements in the party who would make sure that there was no going back. Those who had been disposed of on the 'Night of the Long Knives' would certainly not welcome any change of mind on his part.

Albert would have liked to see Geoghegan-Quinn succeed him as leader. I thought her a fine, competent, able minister. At Justice she had done some important things, including decriminalising homosexuality. She phoned me to ask for my support, but I had already decided that I would be supporting Bertie Ahern and I told her so. I did not make any attempt to mislead or prevaricate, because I had too much respect for her. As a result of her canvass of the parliamentary party, she decided to withdraw from the leadership contest. Following her withdrawal, Bertie Ahern was unanimously chosen as leader.

At forty-three, Bertie was the youngest ever leader of the party. After his election, he spoke of the need to heal divisions and end factionalism within Fianna Fáil. Many biographical sketches and analyses of his psyche appeared at the time of his election and, indeed, since then. He was described as an 'enigma', unknown to most of his fellow TDs. Opposite sides of his character were divined: his popularity with the public and a smiling, easy personality; but a ruthlessness and steely resolve behind the scenes. He was considered an unpolished public speaker, but acknowledged as a consummate politician. He was separated from his wife Miriam and was in another relationship, yet he was a traditional Catholic in many other respects.

There were a number of things about him that I always appreciated. When he was Chief Whip under Haughey, I always found him very fair and unfailingly courteous. He was a superb negotiator and he certainly proved this beyond any doubt during the Northern Ireland peace process. His private life is totally his own business and, for all the efforts made by the media, it never became an issue at any time with the Irish people. We're a very tolerant people, although we may not always have had such a reputation. Our problem is that we can't mind our own business; after that we let people get on with their own business – as long as we know what it is!

The notorious description that Haughey bequeathed him – 'the most cunning, the most devious of them all' – has dogged him. He is certainly very clever, very able and terribly hard working, but I could never see him as in any way devious. He never set out to be a Daniel O'Connell-style orator and I doubt that he spent much time in the Bunny Carr School for the Potentially Sincere, but I think most people find that lack of oratorial ability an endearing quality in him. His thought process often seems to overtake his pace of delivery. At the end, I don't think listeners are ever left in doubt as to what he means, which is surely vindication of him as a communicator.

One of his main assets is his ability and willingness to listen. He is not, as a former colleague of mine described his mother, 'wired for transmission only'. He is also legendary in one-to-one situations. Often politicians are regarded for their ability to 'work the room', but nobody does it better than Bertie. And it isn't contrived. A lot of politicians, when they are shaking hands with people, are looking over the person's shoulder. When Bertie shakes hands, he looks you straight in the eye and, as he is going away – as he is being dragged away to meet the next person – he is still looking at you. He gives the person the impression that he would like to stay and talk and I have no doubt that, at least in some cases, he means it. Everybody he meets is left with the feeling that he was really glad to see them. These are some of the explanations for his popularity everywhere he goes. As to his Catholicism, I consider his devotion genuine. We have had plenty of hypocrisy in this country on that score, but I don't see any element of that on his part. It is obvious that he gets great comfort, succour and support from the practice of his religion. In relation to his private life, the Irish media have generally stood back and let him get on with it.

During the period immediately after he became leader, when there was so much focus on his private life, we invited him, with his partner, Celia Larkin, and a few good friends to dinner in our house. We had a very pleasant evening and they were very relaxed. I think he appreciated that gesture. There was certainly a great welcome for Bertie Ahern in the Fianna Fáil organisation. He was seen as the person to calm things down after the turbulence of the Haughey and Reynolds years and with him came a terrific drive for unity in the party, something that had been missing in Fianna Fáil since as far back as the disaster of the arms crisis in 1970.

Something else that should be mentioned to his credit, and to the credit of Albert Reynolds as well, is that they managed to wipe out the huge party debt that was one of Haughey's legacies. Fianna Fáil was somewhere in the region of £3 million in debt at the end of the Haughey era. It has occurred to me many times since that not one of us in the parliamentary party stood up to ask how this enormous sum of money was being spent or how we got to be so deeply in debt. Hindsight is a wonderful thing, of course, but that was a sad failing on the part of the parliamentary party during those years, and I take my share of blame.

It was widely believed within the parliamentary party that our new leader would do a deal with Spring and that the Fianna Fáil–Labour coalition would resume. Talks with Labour were quickly instigated and it appeared certain that a deal was done. Bertie Ahern certainly believed he would be the next Taoiseach. But at the last minute, Spring pulled out of the arrangement. It has never been satisfactorily explained why he did so, though various reasons have been suggested. One possibility is John Bruton's criticism of him on the radio, for his willingness to get into bed with someone he alleged had caused the Reynolds government to fall. Another suggestion was an *Irish Times* editorial attack on Spring, which was as strong an indicator as they needed that the paper would remain antagonistic to Labour, and to Spring personally, if they took up with Fianna Fáil again. Geraldine Kennedy wrote an article in *The Irish Times* on 5 December, saying that all the Fianna Fáil ministers, including Ahern, were fully aware of the Duggan case on 14 November, and not just Reynolds. There was nothing new about this, but the story gave Labour pause for thought, so this argument goes; if they found themselves unable to stay in government with Reynolds, because he had supposedly failed to let the Dáil know of his awareness of the Duggan case, how could they now go into government with Ahern, against whom the same accusation could be validly levelled?

These are all plausible reasons to some extent, but I suspect that Spring's advisers, Sparks and Finlay, gave him the sort of advice that he wanted to hear. I have no evidence to support this suspicion, but I'm pretty certain that they were very disinclined to go back into government with us and that they pushed him in the direction of Fine Gael and Democratic Left. So Bertie found himself leader of the Opposition rather than leader of the country.

This was a bitter pill for Bertie to swallow but, to his credit, he swallowed it and carried on with great determination. It was, needless to say, a disappointment to us all in Fianna Fáil, and especially to those of us who might have expected to be in Cabinet, but it had to have hit Bertie harder than the rest of us, and it must have taken the shine off his new role as leader of the party. His front bench appointments certainly went a long way towards healing the divisions in our party. He brought Ray Burke back to shadow on Foreign Affairs, which was a big disappointment to me. I don't deny Burke's ability, but I would hardly be human if I hadn't felt disappointed. To compound my disappointment, I was given a brief that wasn't exactly challenging – Tourism. It was really only a way to keep me on the front bench. I went back to the Bar and re-started practice, so in a way it suited me because Foreign Affairs would certainly have been much more challenging and would have absorbed far more of my time.

I was a Senior Counsel by this time. In 1992, shortly after becoming Foreign Minister, the Bar Council had honoured me by inviting me to become a Senior Counsel. We had a little celebration at home to mark the double elevation. One of those who attended was Liam Hamilton, a long-standing good friend. For a long time he had been telling me that (a) I should take silk and (b) I should be a minister. So, at our little party, Annette said to him: 'Well, are you satisfied now with David? He's a Senior Counsel and he's in the Cabinet.' Quick as a flash, Liam replied: 'No, I want him to be Taoiseach.' Liam was determined to keep driving me on!

Commentators have said that Ahern and his new front bench managed to inflict little damage on the government at first and that Mary Harney of the PDs was the much more impressive leader on the Opposition side of the Dáil. This might be true to some extent initially: Harney is a very good extempore speaker, with a strong background in university debating in Trinity, and Ahern, in my view, placed no great store in how he sounded in front of a microphone. He was and is a very good organisation man and what he had to do, while Harney was being impressive in the Dáil, was to reorganise the Fianna Fáil party from top to bottom. He carried out a thorough overhaul of the organisation countrywide and the party emerged from that process fitter and leaner.

That done, Bertie was able to concentrate more on the Dáil itself. He and Mary Harney got on extremely well and worked very effectively together in opposition, which in turn paved the way for their long partnership in government. In March 1995, the government introduced their Abortion Information Bill. It has been remarked of Bertie Ahern that this was his first real leadership test, but that he abdicated responsibility and let his backbenchers decide their attitude to the measure. The strategy, so this argument goes, was successful in that it kept the party united, but no one knew where he personally stood on the issue. It is true that he did not seek to dictate to people how they should vote on an issue of personal conscience: he took the view that we were all adults and capable of making up our own minds on the question. So I think it is very harsh to say that this was an abdication of responsibility on his part. And I agreed with him, of course, so he must have been right!

I made my own attitude clear in my speech in the Dáil at the time and what I said was consistent with my stance on this and other issues of conscience such as divorce. I told the Dáil that I regarded the export of our social problems as a national disgrace. I accepted that our society was deeply divided about the way in which we legislators should reflect in law its views on issues such as abortion and I regretted our dismal reluctance to take responsibility for our problems and our preference for dumping them on the doorsteps of other countries. Sad and solitary boat trips to unfamiliar cities and conveyor-belt abortion services were hardly reasons for celebrating our seventy-three years of independence from Britain.

For many years thousands of Irish girls and women, often frightened, ignorant, alone and confused and always in emotional and physical turmoil and distress, had gone to England and other countries for abortions because they felt unable to see their pregnancies through to birth. I had hoped that the Bill would provide for proper counselling services for women in advance of an abortion and the provision of funding for organisations that provided those services.

By referendum, the electorate had determined that there was a right to obtain or make available information about abortion services outside the State. The Bill sought to specify the conditions under which that information might be made available and its measures were, I thought, the very least the Dáil could take to comply with the limited expression of the people on the subject. It was a very small step in acknowledging the seriousness of the problem with which we had to deal. It wouldn't solve the problem – I didn't know if there was a solution in the conventional sense – but it would offer some degree of comfort to pregnant women who might wish to terminate their pregnancies. I accepted that abortion was illegal in Ireland and would remain so until the electorate decided otherwise, but that was not to argue that legislators had the duty to marshal the forces of law against what was often referred to as 'the evil of abortion'. I said I was glad that the Catholic Church had expressed its opinion on the Bill – I did not agree with that opinion but defended its right to express it. As a Catholic, I found myself in a very difficult position and did not know if God would forgive me but it was a chance I would just have to take.

I saw no reason why a doctor or counsellor should not be able to advise a pregnant woman on the options available to her. To take that contention one step further, I saw no reason why a woman who, having been advised on all the options open to her, and having decided to have an abortion, could not expect her doctor to write a letter of referral, setting out such pertinent facts as might be necessary from a medical point of view, which she could give to the abortion clinic she attended. Surely this was the least a caring society should have to offer its people.

I told the House that I looked forward to the day when as a nation our self-sufficiency extended to all areas of social and economic life. The only surprise I expressed about the Bill, and this was something other members of my party made much of, was that it had been introduced in advance of the outcome of the various court decisions on the matter, and perhaps it should have been deferred.

Bertie Ahern was utterly unequivocal with regard to the referendum on the issue of divorce in November 1995. Michael J. Noonan, a Fianna Fáil TD from Limerick West, was expelled from the parliamentary party for abstaining in the Dáil vote on the referendum. As in 1986, I supported the principle behind the referendum. I had no difficulties then, and still have no difficulty, with the provision for divorce in our Constitution. When two people have irreconcilable differences and separate, I believe they should have an entitlement to a second chance at marriage, if they so desire.

On 1 November 1995, our good friend and colleague Brian Lenihan passed away. There was a feeling of great sadness right across the Dáil – and indeed I would say the whole country – about his passing. We really believed he would live longer because he had been looking so much better since his liver transplant. Alas, it wasn't to be. Brian had that quality that I liked in a politician – a friendly, open, outgoing disposition that meant he made no enemies. He had an amazing capacity to stand before an audience and speak. At many ardfheiseanna, he did the warm-up before the leader's address, and he did it very successfully. He was a much-underrated person and always understated himself. I often felt upset about that because Brian was extremely well read and as bright as they come. One could not ask for a better colleague and I felt a great sense of sadness at his passing.

REVELATIONS 1996, AND BACK IN POWER

In late 1996, Michael Lowry, the Minister for Transport, Energy and Communications in the Bruton–Spring government, resigned following revelations that the business tycoon Ben Dunne, had paid to have work done on Lowry's house. But information soon began to seep out that Dunne had financed another politician far more generously – none other than Charles J. Haughey, who for so long had kept the source of the wealth that funded his lavish lifestyle well hidden from the public and the revenue commissioners alike. The upshot was that the Dáil set up the McCracken Tribunal to inquire into payments to both Lowry and Haughey, which began to hear formal evidence in April 1997.

It came as a deep shock to the majority of the Fianna Fáil party – and especially to his dedicated supporters, who felt desperately let down – that Haughey had been financed by Ben Dunne (among others, as it subsequently emerged). Many years after Haughey's departure, I recall discussing his financial carry-on with a senior civil servant who had worked in his Department of the Taoiseach. He expressed himself as being astonished when it was revealed that Haughey was in such hock to friends and others. It was his view – and the common view, I feel – that Haughey had made money through land deals and, perhaps, what I might describe as 'ordinary graft'. By this I mean the type of insider knowledge he may have acquired in the course of his political career. Nobody ever dreamt that he was a serial bankrupt, relying on handouts – admittedly large ones – to survive.

I feel that Lowry got off more lightly than Fianna Fáil delinquents like Haughey, Burke and Lawlor. I have to confess to having little sympathy for Lowry. He was a didactic and hectoring individual, who tended to adopt the high moral ground when, as events were to reveal, he had little grounds for doing so. He had spoken of cleaning up 'cosy cartels' and smashing 'golden circles' in the semi-state sector – not very appropriate for one who knew the deals he was doing himself. He had launched a particularly savage attack on the chairman of CIE at the time, Dermot O'Leary, falsely accusing him of staying in the Waldorf Astoria Hotel in New York and being driven around in a limousine at the company's expense. Apart from his failure to tell the truth, the sheer hypocrisy of the man is staggering, when one considers the skeletons that were rattling about in his own cupboard.

Ben Dunne's evidence to the tribunal, that he had given Haughey more than £1 million between 1987 and 1991, did Fianna Fáil untold harm and continues to do so. The damage is not only to Fianna Fáil but also to Irish politics in general. That the chief executive of Ireland Inc. was on the take seriously undermined good people's faith in politicians and the practice of politics. It was very hurtful for many, indeed I would venture to say for most of us in politics, to hear the unflattering comment, 'Sure, they're all the same.' We did not like to be tarred with the one brush of wrongdoing.

At the time, of course, the Dunne revelations had the potential to inflict huge harm on the new leader and his party. At the ardfheis just before the tribunal opened, Ahern sought to put as much clear blue water as he could between himself and his former mentor and leader. He also sought to focus on his party's future rather than its past, promising to write new ethical standards and independent enforcement into the country's legal code. Referring to the past, he said: 'Certainly there would be no place in our party today for that kind of behaviour, no matter how eminent the person involved or the extent of their prior services to the country ... We would not condone the practice of senior politicians seeking or receiving from a single donor large sums of money or services in kind.' The speech went down well with the media, as it signalled a clear break with the past.

However, when Ahern then proceeded to appoint P. J. Mara as Fianna Fáil director of elections for the upcoming general election, he seemed to reforge the link with the Haughey era very strongly, because Mara was so closely associated with Haughey. I must confess to finding that decision strange. Mara was an extremely effective, able and astute man and I liked him personally. He got on well with all sides in the parliamentary party and that may have been considered an extra point in his favour. It turned out that he was a very successful director of elections, in fairness to him, but his presence was certainly a very vivid reminder of the regime of his 'duce'.

The June 1997 election was the last one I fought. Five years before I had received a massive vote, nearly 13,500 – my biggest ever. My running mate in 1997 was Mary Hanafin, daughter of Des Hanafin, a former Fianna Fáil senator. She had previously contested a Dáil election unsuccessfully for the Dublin South-East constituency. We were to run a third candidate in the constituency. Larry Butler, a local councillor, had been chosen by the selection convention, but headquarters decided they wanted only two candidates to run this time, so Larry stood down and Mary Hanafin was added by headquarters. An extremely hard worker, Larry had been the heart and soul of the party in the local government constituency for some time, and that is still very much the case. He also had been my director of elections on several occasions and was always a source of great energy and encouragement during the various campaigns. He showed great courage and commitment to the party in agreeing to stand down and in my opinion never received recognition for doing so – at least until July of this year when to my great delight he was elected to Seanad Éireann.

I was under a lot of pressure, as a member of the front bench, to bring in a second TD in Dún Laoghaire. It was generally felt that the only way we could do that was to engage in vote management, as Hanafin was showing poorly in the polls. It was decided to divide the constituency in half and that letters should go out, signed by me, asking supporters in one half of the constituency to give their number ones to Mary Hanafin.

It was a high-risk strategy, but I did it because Bertie Ahern asked me to do it and it turned out to be a success. My first-preference vote was down on 1992 by some four thousand five hundred, coming in at just under nine thousand. Hanafin got just over five thousand first preferences and secured enough transfers, especially from Helen Keogh of the PDs, to get elected. During the campaign in the constituency, there was a lot of flak about the Haughey revelations. They certainly generated an amount of bad feeling. The combined vote of the two Fianna Fáil candidates was not so great, indeed not much better than my own first-preference performance in 1992. We were down some five thousand first preferences this time, so it was a pretty good achievement to secure two seats on twenty-five per cent of the vote. Once more, and it was something I never took for granted, I had a great team of people to run my campaign. Tadgh O'Donoghue's wife Eilis took over as manager and my long-time friend Maureen Brennan ran the office in Cornelscourt every day during the three weeks of the camgaign.

I would like to be able to say that my last election was a pleasant experience, but that would not be truthful. The Haughey revelations were one element of the unpleasantness, and also there were tensions between my election team and the Hanafin team, something I had not experienced before. An example of this, not without an element of humour, involved an incident that occurred one Saturday during the campaign. By then, it was commonplace to find that the posters your supporters had erected were defaced, removed or replaced with those of other candidates from other parties. Not a serious matter, perhaps, but irritating nevertheless. As I drove past the Blackrock Shopping Centre on that day, I noticed a man up a ladder and he seemed to be tampering with one of my posters. I pulled up a distance up the road and observed for a while. He seemed vaguely familiar to me. I then noticed that he was replacing my poster with another and, lo and behold, the new poster displayed the face of my running mate. Was he surprised when I walked up and wished him good morning! Had he fallen off the ladder, the farce would have been complete.

There was no real disagreement between the various political parties over the main issues of the election: the economy, which had been doing well; and Northern Ireland, where the peace process had come to a halt and the IRA ceasefire had broken down. Bertie Ahern travelled the country meeting people and had a superb campaign. He very obviously enjoyed being among the people and the party was able to use these images of him very effectively, so that it was a clear public relations victory for Fianna Fáil. He was certainly the party's greatest vote-getting asset.

On polling day, the *Irish Independent* ran a large front-page headline – 'Payback time' – clearly endorsing the Fianna Fáil–PD alternative and especially our emphasis on big cuts in taxation. Some people found the *Independent* position strange and indeed questionable. But if you were on our side, you wouldn't complain about a headline like that. Its propaganda value was enormous, given that the paper is the biggest-circulation daily in the country. There is no doubt that it was to the disadvantage of the outgoing coalition.

There was no increase on 1992 in the Fianna Fáil percentage of the vote, but transfers from the PDs and Independents and a rub of the green gained us nine extra seats. On the other hand, the PDs had a disastrous campaign. They had become a bit accident-prone with policy statements on single mothers and on cutbacks in the public service. This enabled the Rainbow parties to dub them 'Thatcherites' who would slash the social welfare system and make people in the public sector unemployed if they got into government. They did very badly on polling day and held on to only four seats, having won ten in 1992.

Labour also had a disastrous election and dropped from their thirty-three-seat total of 1992 to just seventeen in 1997. The final figures made it pretty clear that the Rainbow wouldn't have the numbers to go back into government and that Bertie Ahern would be Taoiseach for the first time, but he needed the support of three Independents: Jackie Healy-Rae from Kerry, Mildred Fox from Wicklow and Harry Blaney from Donegal. These three were referred to as being from the Fianna Fáil 'gene pool'.

The negotiation of support for Ahern went relatively smoothly and rapidly. The three Independents had a series of demands for their own constituencies, of course, and these had to be met to a lesser or greater degree. In fairness to them, their support for the government, once it was formed, was steadfast, and they did not seek to rock the boat. A lot of the credit for the skilful management of their support must go to Seamus Brennan, who acted as government Chief Whip for the duration of the twenty-seventh Dáil, the last one in which I was to serve.

The first call I received from Bertie Ahern about my appointment was that I was going to be Minister for Foreign Affairs and that Ray Burke was going to have responsibility for Northern Ireland. I was of course delighted with this, but my delight was short-lived. It seems that Burke objected strenuously to being given the limited responsibility of just Northern Ireland. An hour later Bertie rang me back to say that he had had to change his mind and that I was going to be Minister for Defence and European Affairs, with Burke holding on to the rest of the Foreign Affairs brief, including Northern Ireland. This is what he duly announced when he listed his new Cabinet in the Dáil next day.

However, this turned out to be much more complicated than it had seemed at first and the introduction of special legislation would have been needed to carry the appointment through. If I were to occupy this new position in some sort of junior capacity at Foreign Affairs, the department that had traditionally had responsibility for European affairs, this would introduce a constitutional difficulty. As a full senior minister at Defence, I could not at the same time be subordinate in Cabinet to another minister, i.e. the Minister for Foreign Affairs. Constitutionally, one could not be a senior and a junior minister at the same time. That evening I tried, without any success, to get some clarification on my position.

I think it was the Taoiseach's intention to hive off European affairs from the Department of Foreign Affairs when he announced my appointment as Minister for Defence and European Affairs. This got the mandarins in Foreign Affairs up in arms, because they didn't want to lose any of their domain's powers, and I understand that Ray Burke backed them strongly in this stance. I'm not sure that the Taoiseach had thought through all the implications of his proposed action and I certainly doubt that he had anticipated all the complications.

It seems that the Taoiseach's special adviser, Martin Mansergh, was very involved in this whole project and, indeed, it may well have originated with him. If I understand the whole messy situation correctly, Bertie originally wanted to appoint me to Foreign Affairs, but came under intense pressure from Burke to give him that post. Burke was very ambitious and I heard afterwards that he literally haunted Ahern's office looking for the job. My attitude to appointment to Cabinet had always been to stay away and hope for the best. Because of the pressure from Burke, Bertie looked for some way in which he could appoint the two of us at the same time to Foreign Affairs.

The following evening Annette and I went out to dinner with some friends. When we got home our daughter Sinéad, who happened to be looking at teletext for something, could tell us that she had seen my title had been changed and I was now simply Minister for Defence. That is how I found out, via teletext rather than by personal communication, what the change in my status was.

The appointment of Ray Burke in the new government was controversial because of all the rumours that had been circulating about him. Bertie Ahern had sent his namesake from Louth, Dermot Ahern, to London to ask Joseph Murphy Jr of Joseph Murphy Structural Engineers (JMSE) whether there was any truth in these rumours. It has been pointed out that Bertie had already spoken to Michael Bailey about the whole story. Bailey was the man who had been named by James Gogarty as being with him when they, on behalf of JMSE, paid Burke money in 1989. Curiously, Bertie does not seem to have alerted Dermot to this fact before sending him to London.

I wasn't privy to any of this, and I'm not sure of the reason for sending Dermot Ahern to London. It seemed a strange way of investigating what was, after all, a very serious set of allegations against Ray Burke. Nevertheless the latter's appointment had not come as a great surprise to me. I thought he had performed very well as Opposition spokesman on Foreign Affairs. Indeed, he had performed well in any of the ministries he had occupied or shadowed. He was a very capable individual, which made his later political demise all the sadder. I felt particular sympathy for his family.

Considering they had only four TDs, the PDs did well out of the formation of the government. Mary Harney became Tánaiste and Minister for Enterprise, Trade and Employment; Bobby Molloy was Minister of State to the government and was described as a kind of 'super junior minister' because of the number of roles he had; Liz O'Donnell was appointed Minister of State at Foreign Affairs, and they were given four of the Taoiseach's eleven Seanad nominees. As Mary O'Rourke was being photographed with her nephews Brian and Conor Lenihan, who were both TDs, she joked that if the Lenihans had one more TD, they too could be given ministries, junior ministries and senate nominations.

Inevitably, there was some bad feeling in the Fianna Fáil parliamentary party about how much the PDs had been given. There is always some ill feeling after a government is formed, because one has the appointed and the disappointed, and the latter are, hardly surprisingly, upset. Since the formation of the PDs, there had been an ambivalence towards them in Fianna Fáil. There was, in particular, the feeling that they had parked themselves on the moral high ground and that they were looking down on Fianna Fáil from that vantage point, while at the same time taking anything they could get their hands on by way of power.

Our party's backbenchers, especially, were uncomfortable about the association with the PDs. I had no problem with that association because the political realities dictated that we had to have the PDs if we wished to be in government. Effectively, the PDs were Fianna Fáilers by another name, albeit right-wing Fianna Fáilers, particularly in terms of economic policy. While they might say that they kept us on the straight and narrow – a comment that some of us took grave offence to – we, in our turn, could say that we dragged them closer to our centrist political philosophy and introduced a dose of reality into their cosy and comfortable world.

There had been some talk during the general election campaign of a secret arrangement between representatives of our party and the IRA about the timing of the restoration of the IRA ceasefire. I knew nothing about such an arrangement. I am inclined to think that it was highly unlikely, although rumours about it wouldn't have done Fianna Fáil prospects any harm in the election. I say that because people were crying out for a ceasefire and for the wretched IRA to lay down their arms. The ceasefire was restored in July, which was a great boost for the government in its early days, and the way was now cleared for seeking a political solution in Northern Ireland.

Meanwhile, the rumours about Ray Burke intensified. He was named publicly for the first time and details and amounts of money he had received began to emerge. In a radio interview, he himself confirmed receiving £30,000 from JMSE via Gogarty and Bailey. There was certainly some serious concern in Cabinet after that interview and there was a strong feeling that more revelations would follow.

Personally, I have no problem about politicians receiving reasonable amounts of money towards their election expenses as long as they declare it openly; once there is openness and everyone knows the position, then there is no place for misinterpretation or rumour-mongering. I am not in favour of public funding of political parties because I don't think the taxpayers should face this additional burden. Once the politicians declare what they get and pay their taxes and whatever else is owing, I don't see that there is a problem as long as the amounts are sensible. Politicians are well paid now and have good expenses and the public simply should not be made liable for their election costs.

In relation to payments to politicians, the McCracken Tribunal, which had been set up to investigate the Dunne payments to Haughey and Lowry, reported in late August 1997. Judge McCracken didn't pull his punches in his comments on Haughey, saying that he found some of his evidence to be 'quite unbelievable'. He pointed out how money had been funnelled to Haughey from Dunne via Ansbacher accounts in the Cayman Islands. The tribunal found it totally unacceptable that any member of the Oireachtas should receive personal gifts of this nature because 'the potential for bribery and corruption would be enormous' if such gifts were permissible.

Haughey's appearances before the tribunal, the ongoing revelations about Burke, and now the McCracken report, apart from being fascinating street theatre, were contributing to a ripple effect that wasn't making for smooth sailing for the new government. Some people said at the time, and continue to say, that Haughey did nothing wrong for all that money that he received, and that he got it as series of gifts with no strings attached. An obvious response to that argument is to point out that he never declared the money and therefore broke the country's tax laws. It was a terrible blow to Fianna Fáil, and what Judge McCracken said left a great sense of unease in the party and, indeed, in the political system as a whole.

I didn't speak in the subsequent Dáil debate on the report. I seldom made any contribution in the Dáil on the subject of Haughey, because I felt I was prejudiced and would have been unlikely to give a balanced account.

ANOTHER PRESIDENTIAL ELECTION AND ANOTHER RESIGNATION

The 1997 presidential election, or more particularly what went on in Fianna Fáil beforehand, has been the subject of some controversy, especially regarding what happened to Albert Reynolds. A meeting is supposed to have taken place in January 1997 in the Berkeley Court Hotel in Dublin at which Bertie Ahern persuaded Reynolds to contest another general election. He wanted him to do so in the hope that Fianna Fáil could gain an extra seat in Reynolds's Longford-Roscommon constituency. The inducement for Reynolds, so this story goes, was Ahern's support for his nomination as Fianna Fáil candidate for the presidential election, and, on that basis, Reynolds agreed to contest the June 1997 general election.

I understand that Albert intended to leave politics at the general election following his resignation as Taoiseach and leader of the party.

I also understand that the only carrot that would keep him in active politics was the possibility of becoming a presidential candidate. I wasn't of course aware of what took place between himself and Bertie, but can well believe that there may have been some sort of offer made. Of course, the Fianna Fáil candidacy for the presidential election would not have been in the gift of Ahern. All he could have done was to say to Reynolds that he should run and to express his own support for that action. Others would be sure to put themselves forward to contest the nomination as well.

Albert retained his own seat in the general election, but the party didn't gain another seat in his constituency, as had been hoped. After the election, Ahern stated publicly that he believed Reynolds would be a very good president, and Reynolds began to organise his campaign. But it should be remembered that there was a strong anti-Reynolds faction in the party and their slogan was 'ABA' (Anybody But Albert). Mary McAleese had been working since March to win the party's presidential nomination and had built up support among this anti-Reynolds faction. In July, she went public on her ambition. John Hume's name was then floated as a possible candidate but I don't think he ever seriously considered running.

I know it has been said that Bertie Ahern refused to allow me to put my name forward as a candidate for the party nomination because of the risk of not winning the by-election that would ensue in Dún Laoghaire if I were to be elected. Some people did ring up and say that I should run for the presidency and we talked with a few TDs and friends about it. It was suggested that I would have a better chance of winning than Albert, but I was never terribly pushed about the prospect and I certainly didn't canvass support.

It has been said about me that I publicly backed John Hume when the Taoiseach made it clear to me that I wouldn't be allowed to run. If I never stated that I wanted to run, why then would the Taoiseach have to tell me that I couldn't? As to supporting John Hume, I did state that if he were interested in the position, he should put his hat in the ring. That is the full extent to which I backed him.

In August, Michael O'Kennedy entered the race, encouraged to put his name forward, it is said, by Ahern. In fact, it is a mystery to me why O'Kennedy allowed his name to go forward. I don't think he would have had much chance of winning the nomination. When

Hume announced that he wasn't interested in the position, the Reynolds–O'Kennedy rivalry intensified. McAleese was still in the frame, of course, but my mind was always made up to back Reynolds in the event of a parliamentary party vote to select our candidate. It has been suggested that the ABA faction felt McAleese wouldn't be strong enough to beat Reynolds and that they tried to draft Ray Mac-Sharry in, but that he declined. This story then goes that there was a new approach from the Taoiseach's office to persuade me to run. Apart from a general indication that there would be no objection to my running, it wasn't the case that either the Taoiseach or his office contacted me and requested me to run.

Anyway, by that stage it was far too late for me. I was away at that time representing the government at Mother Teresa's funeral in Calcutta. On my way home, I rang Bertie from London to say that I wouldn't be running, because I simply didn't have nearly enough time to canvass support or prepare for the parliamentary party meeting that was to choose our candidate. We were within a day or two of the meeting at that stage. I also went on the *Morning Ireland* programme on RTÉ Radio 1 from Heathrow that morning to say that I wasn't a runner, that the whole thing had come far too late for me and that the others had too great a head start on me.

Even now, the Reynolds camp was still confident that their man would win. Perhaps it was ominous for him that, of the members of Cabinet at the time, only Brian Cowen, Charlie McCreevy and I publicly said that we would be voting for him. Neither he nor O'Kennedy had any speech ready for the actual meeting and it appears they thought that the candidates wouldn't be required to make speeches at the meeting. But McAleese had a good speech ready and delivered it very confidently and well. I thought that Reynolds did not speak well, but then he had nothing prepared and it is not easy to make an impromptu speech on an occasion like that. He couldn't be described as a great public speaker at the best of times, but he was obviously taken aback by the course events took at the meeting.

Up to the last, he had believed he would win the vote, but it was McAleese who emerged victorious. I was terribly upset for him; it was a deep humiliation, possibly the worst he had suffered in his life, especially because it was so unexpected. He deserved better. I don't understand why Ahern opted for McAleese instead of Reynolds.

After all, the transition from the latter's to his own leadership had been smooth and I would have thought there was a certain political indebtedness there. Perhaps, at bottom, it was an example of realpolitik at work. It was feared that Reynolds wouldn't get elected president because he wasn't perceived as popular enough. Politics can be a very cruel business at times and this was one of those times when it was particularly cruel to Albert Reynolds.

In early September 1997, the government agreed to the establishment of the Moriarty Tribunal to inquire further into payments to politicians, as the terms of reference of the McCracken tribunal were limited. I recall the discussion at Cabinet about the establishment of this tribunal. Judge Michael Moriarty's name had been proposed and when I was asked about his qualities, I said that he was extremely bright, a man of the very highest integrity and that I had no hesitation in recommending him for the job. I am not certain that he would thank me, in view of what has happened since, given that he is still presiding over that tribunal ten years later.

As further stories surfaced in the media about Ray Burke, on 7 October, the day of his brother's funeral, he resigned, not only from the Cabinet, but also from the Dáil. It certainly came as a shock at the time that he decided to leave politics altogether, and in such an abrupt fashion. Looking back, however, one can understand why he did. Had he stayed on, he would have been the subject of the most extraordinary ongoing scrutiny as he went about the Dáil, and he clearly realised that. In addition, his brother's tragic death that same week may well have made up his mind that he had had enough.

I will always recall an incident towards the end of his short time in Foreign Affairs. My office was beside his on the ministerial corridor in Leinster House. It was either just before or after he had made his 'line in the sand' speech in the Dáil and I remember going in to see him and asking him if I could do anything for him. His response was: 'No, there is nothing on God's earth that you can do for me.'

I caused a bit of a scene in the Dáil on the day the Taoiseach announced Burke's resignation. When John Bruton rose to speak, following Ahern's announcement, I angrily demanded: 'Do we have to put up with this humbug and hypocrisy?' and went on to say that Bruton should have 'the decency not to make a speech'. I said that I was going to leave the House in protest, that it was 'an outrage' and that

Bruton 'did not have the decency to keep his mouth shut when he knew Mr Burke's brother had died that day'. And I then left the House. My colleague from the Clare constituency, Síle de Valera, remarked once that she never knew anyone who could 'do outrage' as well as I could. But I was genuinely upset for Ray Burke on that particular day. It was difficult enough for him that he was burying his brother, but his long – twenty-four-year – political career was coming to an abrupt and ignominious end. Better, on that particular day anyway, the charity of silence than the language of condemnation.

The presidential election campaign got into full swing in October. One of the surprise candidates in that election was Dana Rosemary Scanlan; she had already amazed everyone by being elected an MEP in the Connacht/Ulster constituency in the previous European election. On this occasion she made history by securing her nomination through a few county councils, for which there is provision in the Constitution. She made quite an impact – I think it was partly the novelty factor, although that had worn out a little since her first election. One of the things that boosted her chances was a harrowing interview she did with Vincent Browne. He gave her a terrible time, and a lot of sympathy went her way as a result.

Dick Spring, in an effort to repeat his Mary Robinson success, persuaded Adi Roche of Cork to run. She is an admirable lady who does an extraordinary amount of work for the unfortunate children of Chernobyl, but was hardly of the same substance as Robinson, and she had a rather dismal election. Another candidate was Derek Nally, an ex-garda who was at the time involved with a victims of crime organisation. Fine Gael's candidate was Mary Banotti, who had been an MEP for some time.

Meanwhile, our candidate, Mary McAleese, was the target of stories about documents leaked from Foreign Affairs that intended to show that she was close to Sinn Féin. The leaks caused quite an amount of controversy but did not damage her campaign, as it was clearly intended to do. What actually happened was that the controversy united the Fianna Fáil organisation behind McAleese and enabled the party to declare its nationalist and republican credentials. It also enabled it to attack John Bruton of Fine Gael as being unsound on the national question.

I don't think this was fair to Bruton. He is a decent and good man and a good Irishman. However, when it came to Unionism, he tended to bend over backwards to placate those of that tradition. This naturally made nationalists, and especially republicans, wary in their attitude to him. On the other hand, in my experience Unionists didn't want that sort of approach either. They mostly expected nothing more than to know where you stood on an issue.

Mary McAleese campaigned very well and won the election. She is very much a people's person and her personality was probably her biggest asset during the campaign. She is blessed with a natural, friendly and open disposition, the ideal one, really, for public life. Her husband, Martin was a big plus, a very able man who gave his wife total support. Her presidential terms have been acknowledged as being enormously successful.

FOREIGN AFFAIRS MARK TWO

NOTHERN IRELAND TALKS

Following Ray Burke's resignation, the Taoiseach appointed me to the Department of Foreign Affairs for a second time. I was glad to get back to Iveagh House. This time the Secretary of the Department of Foreign Affairs, or Secretary General as they were now known, was Padraic McKernan. I had known him when he was ambassador to the EU and he was a very bright and able man with whom I had got on well. I was once more assigned a young private secretary. I was then surprised and pleased to get a phone call from Conor O'Riordan, my previous private secretary. I had presumed that he wouldn't be interested in taking up the post for a second time. He told me, however, that he felt mired in a very boring job in statistics and was very anxious to come back on board. I was delighted, as he had been such an excellent private secretary during my previous term in the department. I passed on my request to the Secretary General and ran into immediate and surprising opposition. The Secretary General didn't approve of this appointment. He said it would be a bad move for Conor's career. However, I was satisfied that Conor was wise and experienced enough to know what he was doing and was very keen to make the move, and I was anxious to have him, so I decided to press the matter. It was hard to see what the difficulty was. It was of course my call, but it took a few weeks before I succeeded, and this disagreement initiated a deterioration in the relationship between myself and the Secretary General that was to endure for the remainder of my time as minister.

I asked Gerry Gervin to be my programme manager. He had been my private secretary in the Department of Defence and, although he had no experience of Foreign Affairs, he was a bright and canny man, whom I could trust totally. I felt that it was useful to have someone who was independent of the department and, when my tenure in Foreign Affairs ended, he would return 'safely' to the Department of Defence. I also asked Rory MacCabe to be my special adviser again and he agreed, this time on the condition that he was not required to travel, given that he had a young family. I was very happy to have him on that basis. I was also delighted to find that Mary Cusack, who had worked in the office during my previous time there, applied to return and work again with me. She had always been extremely efficient and I had enormous regard for her. She also had an innate kindness and got on well with everyone. Of course I still had my secretary Debbie, but unfortunately Carmel Brennan had moved on and was now very happy in a job at *The Irish Times*. She had to look to the greater security she enjoyed in that position, which I accepted, though I was disappointed not to have her back. However, happily, Ann Duke then came on board to continue her work.

The Northern Ireland talks that I had been involved in back in 1992, and which had run into the sand at that stage, had moved on quite a bit. One major development was that Senator George Mitchell, a former US senator, had become deeply involved in the process and had been chairing the talks since mid-1996. When he took up the appointment, he thought the process would take a matter of a few months, but fifteen months later he was still there, and the going was very tough.

From the beginning, he saw how difficult was the task he faced, as he explained in his excellent book on his experience as chairman, *Making the Peace*. In the book, he said that presiding over talks involving two governments and ten political parties was a complicated enough task. But two of the parties, the DUP and Robert McCartney's UKUP, were so opposed to his being chairman that they stormed out in protest, while another party, Sinn Féin, was trying to get in but couldn't because the IRA hadn't declared a ceasefire at that stage. As he wrote: 'Not for the last time, I wondered how I could ever get them to agree on anything of substance when they couldn't even agree to sit together in the same room.' On a personal level, Senator Mitchell had gone through a very tough time. In July, his brother, to whom he was very close, had died, and in September his wife had lost their baby.

The talks became so bogged down in procedural matters that, nine months on, they had got nowhere. At that stage, he seriously thought there was nothing more he could offer and was strongly tempted to walk away. He talked the matter over with close and trusted friends and especially with his wife Heather, who fortunately was pregnant again. That he decided to stay on shows the innate nobility of the man. This is what he wrote about what really made up his mind for him: 'But what really mattered were the people of Northern Ireland. The brutal murders ... the bombings and the beatings, the savagery of sectarian strife and the hatred and fear it spawned: no one should have to live like that. I was in a position to help. I didn't seek or expect it, but it was a reality. How could I turn away from it now? I had been taught that each human being has an obligation to help those in need; I had preached the same thing to young Americans countless times. Did I really believe what I said? And if I did leave, and the war resumed, how could I reconcile myself to the deaths that would result, deaths that might have been prevented if I had stuck with it? Finally, and most powerfully, what would I tell the child Heather was now carrying when, by God's grace, he or she was old enough to understand, and inevitably asked me about Northern Ireland?'

His son Andrew was born on 16 October and he dedicated his book to Heather and their son, and their son's 'sixty-one friends in Northern Ireland'. One night shortly after the birth, he had sat late into the night watching Andrew sleeping. He began to imagine what the boy's life would be like and how different it would be had he been born in Northern Ireland. He wondered how many babies had been born in the North on 16 October and got one of his staff to find out for him: the number was sixty-one.

Heather and he had such high hopes and dreams for their son and surely, he reasoned, the parents of those sixty-one babies had the same hopes and dreams. The aspirations of parents for their children are the same the world over. But could those aspirations be fulfilled if Northern Ireland reverted to sectarian strife? This thought made him more determined than ever that the negotiations would end in agreement. He wrote: 'For the sake of those sixty-one children, and thousands of others like them, we had to succeed.' Hence the dedication of his book.

George Mitchell's special assistant was Martha Pope and she was enormously impressive; she knew every crack in the paintwork of the place. Ms Pope was the senator's eyes and ears and her presence, work and advice were invaluable. She was very much inclined towards the nationalist tradition. Paisley, in particular, had no time for her. Her surname didn't help because his mantra, of course, was 'No Pope here'. He was very comfortable saying that.

Another change since the 1992 talks was that the DUP had excluded themselves. They were basically outside chanting and having their little prayer meetings down at the bottom statue on the big roadway up to Stormont, chaining themselves to the gates on a regular basis, and indulging in suchlike futilities.

An important change was the involvement of President Clinton and Prime Minister Tony Blair. There was a big push on to achieve something solid this time. Sinn Féin had also become involved in the talks now, in contrast to 1992.

The British Secretary of State at this time was the late, great Mo Mowlam. She absolutely outraged the Unionists, in whom there exists, it seems to me, a deep-seated misogyny. Her informality was studied and once she got the sense that they hated her, I think she saw that as a weapon that she could use. I suppose by diplomatic standards, she *was* outrageous. She used to come into a room, take her wig off and drop it on the table (she had been on chemotherapy for a brain tumour), or she would take her cup of tea and eat your biscuit while putting her leg up on the table, and you would have to look up at the ceiling or anywhere to avoid embarrassment. Mo was well aware of the effect she had on people.

I got on very well with her and we had many chats over a cup of tea or a glass of whiskey, to which she was partial. Whenever I visited her in London, I always brought her a bottle of the best Irish whiskey. She was such fun and great company and also a tireless and consummate politician. Whenever I was in trouble with the Unionists, she would always come to my rescue, and I tried to do the same for her whenever she aroused nationalist, or indeed Unionist, wrath. I liked her very much – there was a fundamental decency about her. She was a generous-hearted person and she died too young after a brave battle against cancer.

She played a crucial role on many an occasion to keep the talks going. One example of this was in January 1998. The shooting dead of Billy Wright in the Maze prison caused the PUP to pull out of the talks. The Irish government's release of political prisoners for Christmas also aggrieved the loyalists. Courageously, Mo went into the Maze to talk to loyalist prisoners – mainly members of the UDA – to persuade them to support the talks. Although she got praise from some quarters, the UUP and Alliance parties and the conservative press condemned her. Some of the press was pretty nasty and, knowing what it was like to be on the receiving end of such invective, I rang her to lend her my moral support. I needn't have worried – her comments on her detractors are unprintable! But her gamble paid off and the UDA decided to support the talks.

The talks took place from Monday to Wednesday each week. I would spend most of Sunday at home preparing for the next day, with all the relevant files. Then I would fly to Belfast the following morning with our team, and the talks or the talks about the talks would commence. The patience required to put up with the intransigence of some of the participants was immense and I have to admit that patience isn't my strong suit. However, I gritted my teeth and got on with it. I was usually back in Dublin by lunchtime on Wednesday to attend the Dáil, only to start over again the following Sunday. It was very frustrating, at times very boring, but we all knew that it had to be done and that the potential for peace was there. On a few occasions Brussels required my presence on the Monday, but mostly I had to stick with the talks in Belfast.

I got off to a rocky start in the talks myself. I stated that Articles 2 and 3 of the Irish Constitution were sacrosanct and not up for negotiation – which, of course, proved to be absolutely untrue. My reason for taking this stand was that it was our initial bargaining position, from which we knew perfectly well we would have to move. This brought me straight into conflict with the Unionists, who promptly walked out of the talks. That was on a Thursday. I didn't realise that what the Unionists were doing was merely throwing shapes. It was only later in the talks I realised that one could say almost anything one liked to them and they would walk out of and into the negotiations on a regular basis. The following Monday, the Unionists walked back into the talks without a murmur.

Around the end of November, I got into hot water when I responded to a question during a BBC Northern Ireland interview about the proposed North-South bodies by saying they should have powers 'not unlike a government'. It was a seven-minute interview, which was generally very conciliatory in tone, but this one phrase was extracted and used as a promo all morning on BBC radio. That set off the alarm bells among the Unionists because their great fear was that those bodies would be the precursors of a united Ireland. They criticised me bitterly and I had no option but to backtrack.

What was interesting was that not only were the Unionists hard on me – which was to be expected – but sections of our own media in Dublin lambasted me in even harsher terms, questioning my capacity to carry on as Minister for Foreign Affairs. There was, and is, a very strong anti-nationalist strain in some sections of the Irish media. John Hume suffered their ire in his time, especially for his talks with Gerry Adams.

The Unionists blew up my passing remark out of all proportion and walked out of the talks, along with the Alliance and David Ervine's PUP. It's worth pointing out that David Trimble's initial reaction (he said my remark was 'silly' and that he would have to give me a piece of his mind when next we met) was comparatively mild, but after media reaction he decided he had to crank up his indignation a number of notches. There were calls all day from the Unionists for me to be replaced. Trimble said Bertie Ahern should send someone 'sensible' to the talks instead of me and Ervine said that I was either 'not up to the job or mischievous'. The Alliance also called on me to step down. The SDLP and Sinn Féin were very supportive but of course that didn't interest the media very much.

I had a torrid meeting the following day when I found myself alone, ranged against the combined forces of fourteen Unionists of all shades. They didn't spare me. I did my best to assuage their anger but, for the moment, they weren't having any of it. As I sat there eating humble pie, I looked around at some of my accusers, thinking of the irony of the situation that at least a few of these people were men of violence. I remember phoning Annette that afternoon and saying that I must resign because I couldn't afford to be the cause of the collapse of the talks. I also felt – wrongly as it turned out – that that was also the general view of the civil servants involved.

However, on the six o'clock news programme on RTÉ television that evening, the issue was only the fifth item and was described more as a row than a crisis. In an interview on the programme, I said that if I could 'unsay' the expression 'not unlike a government', I most certainly would. I then soon discovered that our officials felt very strongly that there should be no question of my resignation. Their view was that it would send out a terribly depressing message to nationalists if Unionists could have an Irish Foreign Minister removed for expressing such a view.

Although I was to have stayed in Belfast that night, in the circumstances I felt I should return to Dublin to confer with the Taoiseach. He was most encouraging and reassuring and wouldn't hear of my resigning. My worst fear was that the Unionists would refuse to go back into the talks until I resigned – which was the position they had adopted. The bad press continued for me the next day with condemnation all round. However, my opposite number in Fine Gael, Gay Mitchell, said: 'David Andrews is noted for being outspoken – one of his endearing qualities. On this occasion, he should have saved his breath to cool his porridge. I will not be asking him to consider his position.'

Next morning, the Unionists walked back into the talks without a word. As far as they were concerned, they had made their point about the North-South bodies and the matter was finished. I found the whole experience pretty shattering and it took my dented confidence a few weeks to recover. I also found it very disillusioning in that I had thought that I had set up a good rapport with David Trimble but I had clearly been wrong about that.

As a result of this episode, the papers of the following Sunday carried a number of profiles of me. One was a pretty dreadful piece rubbishing everything I had ever done throughout my political life – everything from the Birmingham Six to Somalia. There was no serious political comment in this article – it was unfair, cynical and designed to hurt, which it did. But some other articles were much fairer and Chris Glennon's in particular was supportive.

The most hilarious piece was by Eoghan Harris, who said that it had all to do with erotic envy – the Dublin male journalists resenting me because of my attractiveness to women! Eoghan said that one day he saw me canvassing a chemist's shop full of women and that it was like Johnny Cash visiting a women's prison! Annette and my family found this immensely funny – as I did myself, of course.

The following Tuesday, I went on a scheduled trip to Algiers and a really stupid newspaper article the same day suggested that I went or had been sent there to get away from my problems in Belfast. Apart from being patently untrue, it was an example of lazy journalism. It would have been so easy for the journalist to find out when the trip had been planned (about three weeks before) and it didn't take a lot of brains to work out that with the sort of security problems that existed in Algeria, one couldn't just decide overnight on a ministerial trip there. I also found it extraordinary that people seemed to be so concerned over the appalling amount of killing of innocent people in that country, and yet when I, in my capacity as an EU Foreign Minister, wanted to go to investigate, such a cynical view could be taken.

Despite this unfortunate initial experience, Senator George Mitchell writes very well of the performance of our team at these vital talks. As well as praising my own role and that of Liz O'Donnell, who was Minister of State at Foreign Affairs, he describes the contribution of Dermot Gallagher, at the time Second Secretary of the department in charge of the Anglo-Irish Division, as 'outstanding', which indeed it was. Dermot developed very good personal relations with many of the Unionist representatives, which were to prove invaluable in the difficult final stages of the talks. He deserves the highest praise for being such an utterly devoted and dedicated civil servant.

Two others on our team who made a vital contribution were Martin Mansergh and David Donoghue. Mansergh, long-time special adviser to Fianna Fáil Taoisigh, had many close contacts in and an extensive knowledge of the republican movement. He gave Bertie Ahern much essential advice. Donoghue was the Irish head of the Joint British-Irish Secretariat in the North. He had so many contacts and was so very knowledgeable of the Northern Irish and British political scene that he made a telling contribution to the talks. Two other names that come to mind as having made a great impact are Tim Dalton, Secretary-General of the Department of Justice, and Paddy Teahon of the Taoiseach's Department.

The people that I found I could communicate with best were David Ervine, Martin McGuinness and Ken Magennis. The late David Ervine of the PUP was a working-class politician with a directness and honesty in his approach, which was very refreshing. I had a good working relationship with him. I found it difficult to get close to Gerry Adams, but was always comfortable with Martin McGuinness. I would say that he was one of the top negotiators in the process and had a good sense of humour. I found that I could safely discuss sensitive issues with him in the knowledge that they would remain confidential. Ken Magennis, a staunch Unionist, was a rugby fan and had often travelled to Lansdowne Road for international rugby matches. He was of a friendly disposition and I found him easy to talk to, reasonable and more prepared to listen than any of the UUP team. Of all the participants in the talks, the Dublin civil servants were the best group in terms of preparedness and performance. I believe that was recognised by the other participants.

One of the really outstanding figures at the talks was Seamus Mallon, the deputy leader of the SDLP. I could see that George Mitchell developed an enormous regard for the Armagh man as well. Seamus had been a strong opponent of IRA violence for many years and a staunch holder of the middle ground, that most precarious of places to occupy in the politics of Northern Ireland. Along with Bertie Ahern and Martin McGuinness of Sinn Féin, they were the three best negotiators.

The main UUP negotiating team comprised their leader, David Trimble, Sir Reg Empey, Ken Magennis and Jeffrey Donaldson. I can recall some extraordinary situations with that team round the table. One would be sitting there with one's papers and Trimble would reach over and grab those papers and look at them. He could be a very rude man and the information that was available to us at the time was that he had severe anger management problems. He certainly wasn't a man who was nice to deal with and is not what might be called a people-person. Empey was mainly an adviser – a lawyer and an intellectual, but a gentleman and pleasant to deal with.

Donaldson is a bright, sharp individual but I know he had a very low opinion of us, and of me in particular. However, I think he had a low opinion of a lot of people, a lot of those on his own side of the house included. He appeared to have scant respect for Trimble, who he obviously considered a liability to his brand of Unionism.

The UUP were really inclined to do their negotiating at the table in front of us. They didn't seem to have made many preparations beforehand and I often wondered if they had worked out their policies, let alone their strategy, at all. They had such a long tradition of negativity, of saying 'no' to everything – 'No surrender' and 'Ulster says no' – that they seemed distinctly uncomfortable engaging in constructive dialogue that might result in their having to say 'yes' to something for a change.

David Ervine and his colleague Billy Hutchinson were pragmatic people and I could relate to them for that reason. The Taoiseach, in particular, got on extremely well with both these men. Unfortunately, the PUP and the other small loyalist party, the Ulster Democratic Party (UDP), had very little support in the broader Unionist community – certainly nothing like the support Sinn Féin, their nationalist equivalent, had. It was such a shame that these two men did not get the political support that their ambitions and abilities deserved – because they were very able people. A man who had undoubtedly had a 'dangerous' past was Gusty Spence, but strangely I established a relationship of a sort with him. He was gregarious and very proud and unrepentant about his extreme loyalist views and involvements, but unusually he seemed to have no difficulty mixing with a 'taig', unlike most of the DUP. In fact on the famous Good Friday when it was all over he gave me a present of his identity card as a souvenir!

No matter how you may feel about them, Gerry Adams and Martin McGuinness of Sinn Féin have to be described as 'class acts'. Tim Dalton remarked to my special adviser Rory MacCabe, a barrister: 'By God, if those two were in the Law Library in Dublin, they'd be making pots of money.' They were truly skilled performers; they would take a position, argue it calmly, never get tired or bored or irate and, try as you might, you would not get them to change their position. I used to describe their performances as 'the single transferable speech' because there seemed to be some uncanny telepathy between them – and that applied to all the Sinn Féin representatives.

Another important element in the talks was the Women's Coalition – a courageous group of women, but disparagingly referred to by some as the WC. It was indicative of the attitude of Unionism to women, particularly those participating in politics. However, the Women's Coalition, led by Monica McWilliams, did make a significant contribution to the talks and I had a lot of admiration for them.

What the British tried to do regularly, through the process, was to send out people to mix with Foreign Affairs and the Irish political structure at every level – politicians, advisers and staff. They would all be asking the same questions to see if they could get a different answer. They certainly would never get a different answer from anybody in Sinn Féin because that party's representatives would all be on-message, all well trained and briefed, very energetic and very committed.

I don't think Sinn Féin could be classed as great 'negotiators' because they didn't have fallback positions; they made their statements and they stuck with them. The UUP, I believe, were more inclined to do business but they were very wary of the DUP sniping at their flanks. They were terrified that the backwoods boys would abandon them – and that was what ultimately happened.

There was a perception that what would happen to the DUP would be that the religious fundamentalists would go off to their tin chapels and that the secular side – the Peter Robinson side of the party – would cosy up to the UUP, while Paisley and Willie McCrea would fulminate unavailingly from their pulpits. But that didn't happen, or hasn't happened, because events overtook the possibility. Instead, the UUP managed to implode.

It is hard to believe that it took from June 1996 until October 1997 for substantive talks to begin. The amount of wrangling that went on before that over procedural matters was quite extraordinary and it is to George Mitchell's eternal credit that he persisted so patiently and doggedly in keeping the talks going until they reached the point when at last the participants might focus on achieving something worthwhile.

The talks were conducted in three strands. Strand One was concerned with political arrangements within Northern Ireland and was chaired by the British government representative, Paul Murphy. Strand Two had to do with North-South relations. This strand was widely expected to be the most difficult and in the end that was how it turned out. Strand Three, between Dublin and London, was carried on directly between the two governments, keeping the other participants informed of our discussions. This was probably the least difficult of the three strands. Relations between Ahern and Blair and, indeed, between the other representatives of the governments were good. As well as Mo Mowlam, I was lucky enough to have a good relationship with her junior, Paul Murphy. The two governments had worked hard together over the years to get the process off the ground and there was no doubt about our determination to work together to reach the desired result.

When writing earlier about the 1992 talks in which I was engaged, I referred to the hostility I sensed from within the Northern Ireland Office (NIO) to the presence of representatives from the government of the Republic of Ireland in their sphere of influence, and to that office's general hostility to the peace process itself. It is interesting that another outsider, Senator George Mitchell, should also have had reason to comment negatively on the role of the NIO.

He referred to the long series of leaks to the press from within the British government going right back to the very beginning of the talks. He accepted that leaks were to be expected but said those from the NIO were different, having the apparent intent of undermining the peace process, even though the British government was one of the architects of that process. He also felt that the leaks were intended to embarrass Mo Mowlam, because the timing of several of them appeared to be aimed at causing her as much difficulty as possible.

In January 1998, the two governments published their new settlement proposals and in late February, to put pressure on everybody, they fixed Easter of that year as the target for final agreement. Senator Mitchell fixed 9 April (Holy Thursday) as the deadline.

In relation to the British-Irish strand, the conjunction of Reynolds and Major in the first instance, and then of Ahern and Blair, was simply a stroke of luck. To Blair's lasting credit, he put his heart and soul into bringing about a structure in the North that wasn't seen as direct rule from London. In recent times he has seen his ambitions fulfilled with the closure of the Good Friday Agreement and the establishment of the Northern Ireland Executive. For Bertie Ahern, back then, this was an extraordinarily difficult period, as his mother died that Holy Week. Although he was very close to his mother, he did not absent himself but travelled to and from Dublin and kept in the closest contact with the talks.

It was Strand Two, dealing with the powers of the North-South bodies that almost caused the talks to collapse early in Holy Week. The lists of the areas to be covered by these bodies (known as the annexes) had been negotiated by the officials of the two governments on the Monday. These annexes proved too detailed for the Unionists' liking; they refused to accept them and insisted that they be renegotiated. This insistence was conveyed to George Mitchell in no uncertain terms. The senator contacted Blair and expressed his view that there would be no agreement if they weren't renegotiated. Blair asked him to contact Bertie.

His aides had to disturb the Taoiseach at his mother's removal service and brief him on what was happening. They said to him that Dublin had negotiated in good faith with London, that the two prime ministers had reached an agreement, and they recommended standing firm and rejecting the Unionist demand. He agreed with them, but after the service he went for a walk to think the whole thing over. He eventually came to the conclusion that perhaps renegotiation should be considered and then decided to go to Stormont the following morning to meet Blair. About this decision, George Mitchell wrote: 'It was a big decision by a big man. It made possible everything that followed.'

What he did the following day shows his huge energy and commitment. He flew to Belfast at sunrise for a breakfast meeting with Blair, then on to Stormont for a number of meetings, before returning to Dublin for his mother's funeral at noon. By late afternoon he was back in Belfast for another series of meetings lasting well into the early morning hours. Senator Mitchell records being with him at two o'clock in the morning and says he had never seen anyone so totally exhausted but also so determined. Although his face was grey with exhaustion, his eyes burned like coals, as he said to the senator: 'George, we've got to get this done.' I was also very concerned about the Taoiseach's state of exhaustion given the death of his mother and all that entailed, as well as the fierce pressure of the talks. I kept a very close eye on him throughout this period.

One person who also showed great concern for the Taoiseach was John Taylor of the UUP. He stopped the talks during the night a few times to ask him if he was all right and to see if he wanted a break. This shows the common humanity that can exist between politicians on opposite sides of the fence, even at the most stressful of times. It certainly reflects very well on John Taylor. He was a man I always found I could communicate with. I always admired his bravery in continuing in politics in the light of previously having survived a murder attempt for his beliefs.

Had Bertie insisted on the Strand Two arrangements that he had worked out with Tony Blair there would have been no Good Friday Agreement. From the breakfast meeting between the two men on Spy Wednesday morning until around five o'clock on Good Friday afternoon – nearly two and a half days and nights in total – there was little let-up in the talks. Blair took over a suite of offices on the top floor of the building in which the negotiations were held, and Ahern set up our offices on the floor below, and back and forth we went, from meeting to meeting, in a ritualistic dance on which so much depended, and from which there was little respite.

I have some vivid memories of the last tense hours before the signing of the agreement. I can recall people sleeping on chairs and indeed falling off chairs in their sleep, worn out by pure fatigue and anxiety. Others were looking for places to lie down to sleep at two or three in the morning, talks all the time proceeding in one way or another, as people looked for other people to consult or talk with. I remember Tony Blair looking for Mo Mowlan and calling me over – this at three in the morning – to see if I knew where she was. When I responded in the negative, he asked in exasperation: 'And why don't you know where she is?' It's funny the things exhaustion does to people.

In that very fraught Holy Thursday/Good Friday period, when there was a meeting from one a.m. to about five-thirty a.m. between the Taoiseach, Tim Dalton and Dermot Gallagher on the one side, and Sinn Féin representatives on the other, I am convinced that the Unionists did not believe that Sinn Féin was going to come on board. So they had largely not actually addressed their minds to reading, line by line, the document that was there because they did not believe they needed to consider it seriously. Instead, they were trying to figure out the logistics of how they were going to load the maximum blame for the collapse of the process onto Sinn Féin, and they thought they themselves would come out of it all smelling of roses. To their complete astonishment, and largely due to the patience, persistence and determination of the Taoiseach, news went round Castle buildings that Sinn Féin had agreed to sign up.

All of a sudden, there was a huge problem for the UUP because now they had to take a position on the document. So they all vanished back to their Glengall Street headquarters to consider the situation, and what apparently transpired there was that they had what was effectively a snap leadership vote and Trimble survived by one. As a result, they all, except Donaldson, came back to Castle buildings. One may glean from all this that Donaldson was the only one of them to have read the document line by line. He had serious reservations about what he had read and foresaw the problems for the UUP if they were to sign up.

Decommissioning and the release of prisoners had been the two main issues in the last, fraught days of negotiation. When the final text was given to the UUP on Good Friday morning, they discussed it in detail and then returned to Blair to express unease about Sinn Féin participation in the new executive without prior IRA weapons decommissioning, and about the early release of prisoners. Blair wrote them a reassuring letter on these two issues.

Unfortunately for them, decisions had to be taken very quickly. Senator Mitchell had obviously informed the White House that there was a good chance of agreement because Sinn Féin had come on board, so the spotlight was now on Trimble. The senator, Tony Blair and President Clinton (by phone) worked on him until he agreed to sign. But it wasn't clear until the last minute that he was going to say 'yes'.

It didn't come as a shock to me that Donaldson walked away at the last minute. He has since shown that he is good at walking away from things and suiting himself. He is hugely popular, of course, in his own heartland, and there is no doubt that he is a person of substantial ability, but his role in the whole peace process was a very negative one. In the meantime Donaldson has left the UUP and and transferred his affections successfully, from an electoral point of view, to Dr Paisley of the DUP.

On the other hand, on a personal level, Trimble deserves a lot of credit for taking the risks that he did. On one side he had Paisley breathing down his neck and on the other he had people from within his own party sniping at him. He displayed a lot of courage on that Good Friday in 1998. He was eventually to pay a great political price for his courage but while he may have lost personally, his beloved Northern Ireland has gained greatly from his brave decision at the time.

One of the most significant things that was said during that period, and it was said by Martin McGuinness of Sinn Féin – and I'm not sure that this has been registered anywhere else – was that Sinn Féin accepted that there were some elements of the republican movement that were 'ungovernable'. One interpretation of this very significant statement would be that it gave both governments a licence to deal with those people with an implicit assurance that Sinn Féin would not make an issue of it. Up to that time, the expression 'the republican family' had been in use, despite the many splits that had occurred.

When all the negotiating parties signed up to the agreement, there was such a sense of relief and elation, despite the exhaustion we were all feeling, having been up for two successive nights. The word 'historic' is often bandied about too much in relation to various events and achievements and agreements, but if ever there was anything that occurred in the history of Ireland and Anglo-Irish relations that deserves the epithet, the Good Friday Agreement surely does.

The central issue of the Good Friday Agreement – and I don't think this has ever been given enough prominence – is the principle of consent. Everything is posited on consent and nothing can be done without it. I really wished the Unionists could have gotten this basic fact into their heads: the country cannot be united until they consent to its being united. (There was a suggestion during the talks that a referendum be held every five to seven years to see what the mind of the people of Northern Ireland was on the question.) That was the great strength of the Good Friday Agreement and it should remain so forever, and anyone who makes an attempt to interfere or tamper with it would be making a very serious error of judgement.

One provision of the agreement was that referendums were to be held on both parts of the island. On our part, the issue to be put to the people was to replace Articles 2 and 3 of the Irish Constitution, which claim jurisdiction over Northern Ireland, by an aspiration to unity. There was some substantial difficulty in persuading the Fianna Fáil parliamentary party and the party's National Executive to accept the abolition of these two pivotal articles of de Valera's Constitution – Fianna Fáil people always saw it as 'our' Constitution. To me fell a leading role in persuading my colleagues and the party members, and indeed the electorate in general, to accept the change in the Constitution. There were some heated debates in the parliamentary party, with strong reservations being expressed, particularly by some deputies from the southern part of the country, such as strong-minded people like Batt O'Keeffe and Ned O'Keeffe.

The party grassroots were quite suspicious about the changes. But I believe there is a fundamental republican streak in Fianna Fáil, one not inclined towards any sort of violent action, and marked most of all by decency. This explains to me why so many of these republicans were willing to give up the claim on the North in the interest of the greater good of the island as a whole. They came to accept the change as one of emphasis with the aspiration to unity still always there. Anybody who wanted to claim Irish citizenship in Northern Ireland could continue to do so but, in the interests of better neighbourliness, we were willing to replace a claim – albeit a virtually unenforceable one – with the less threatening aspiration.

The vote in favour of change among the electorate as a whole was overwhelming: ninety per cent of those who voted in the referendum in the Republic agreed to replace Articles 2 and 3. To me this displayed the generosity the Irish people are capable of when it comes to what they perceive to be the greater national interest. The referendum was carried in the North with about seventy per cent in favour. There was a great feeling of achievement about the agreement and the referendum that followed. It was the first time since 1918 that an all-Ireland vote was held, with people on both sides of the border voting on the same day. Those with a sense of history must have been glad that they were alive to see such an event unfold.

The progress of the talks that followed the agreement was very slow. This was hardly any cause for surprise: centuries of conflict, and particularly the most recent thirty bloody years and the loss of more than three thousand precious lives, weren't going to be settled and made good in a few short years.

Then came the terrible Omagh bombing, on 15 August 1998, the worst single atrocity in the North of those thirty terrible years. It would be a severe test for the agreement.

That dreadful day stands out vividly in my memory. My immediate reaction was that I would go to Omagh the following day to sympathise with the tragic victims and pay my respects to the people of the town. However, my departmental officials advised me not to go. I took their advice but to this day I regret that I didn't go with my first instinct. George Mitchell has said that his most fervent prayer is that history will record that the Troubles ended in Omagh on that sunny Saturday afternoon in August.

Following the bombing, I visited Buncrana in Donegal to call on the families of two of the schoolchildren murdered in Omagh. The people of the town were devastated by what had happened.

The resilience of the agreement is shown by the fact that the process survived the atrocity. Indeed, it could be said to have been a defining moment because all the parties to the agreement united in condemning the awful deed, and this included Sinn Féin. The talks were not derailed by the outrage but continued with renewed vigour. It took a long time, of course, as it always seems to in Northern Ireland but, finally, in late 1999, a power-sharing executive was set up.

For the first time in the almost eighty-year history of Northern Ireland, Unionists were willing to sit in government with republicans – it was indeed an extraordinary leap forward. The development filled the island with hope. Here at last might be the solution to a problem that had bedevilled the country for centuries.

What was perhaps even more extraordinary was that the ministers from the various groups seemed to get on quite well, or at least they were able to work well together. It was revealing how competent some of these complete newcomers to office were as administrators. The Sinn Féin ministers, Martin McGuinness (Education) and Bairbre de Brún (Health, Social Services and Public Safety), impressed many people by their ability and dedication. From the other side of the divide, the DUP ministers Peter Robinson (Regional Development) and Nigel Dodds (Social Development) impressed for the same reasons. The experience of having ministerial power and being able to do tangible and concrete things for the communities they represented brought out a welcome streak of pragmatism in them.

Sadly, it wasn't to last. The executive was suspended in mid-2000 because of the continuing row over IRA decommissioning. Although it was restored again in 2001, it collapsed the following year when the Assembly itself collapsed. Contacts and meetings continued over the years and hope was never abandoned. Tony Blair and Bertie Ahern remained fully engaged.

It could be 'third time lucky'. Eventually, in early 2007, after protracted talks, the Assembly was elected and the Executive is now up and running as if it had been in existence for years. Normalcy is the order of the day at last. Back in 1998 I would never have believed that the two front runners in the Assembly election would be the DUP and Sinn Féin, but that is how it was. Who then would have thought that they would see the smiling photographs of Dr Ian Paisley and Martin McGuinness together as First and Second Ministers respectively?

OTHER FOREIGN AFFAIRS ACTIVITIES

For some time I had felt strongly that the Minister for Foreign Affairs should be Minister for Foreign Affairs only and that there should be either a Minister of State or a full, senior minister for Northern Irish affairs. I think that it would be constructive to have a full-time minister from the government of Ireland devoted to our relationship with the North. This would make our system on a par with the British system, where they have a Secretary of State for Northern Ireland, who deals exclusively with the government's affairs there. Then they also have a Foreign Secretary, who looks after their foreign affairs. For the Irish Foreign Minister, trying to do these two jobs at the same time is quite difficult and onerous. In fact, I was the subject of criticism from time to time for neglecting my duties in Brussels. The problem was that I should have been in Brussels every Monday, and Monday was also the first day of the Northern talks each week. I had every faith in my officials and junior ministers to fly the flag safely in Brussels in my absence, but of course it was not an ideal situation. However, at least this time I was going in with some experience behind me. Many of the Foreign Ministers I had known had moved on and I set about getting to know the new members of the 'club'. Hans-Dieter Genscher had long since retired and Joschka Fischer was the new German minister. I have to say he was much more approachable. I also developed a good relationship with Giorgios Papandreou (and later Theo Pangalos) of Greece and Jaime Gama of Portugal; and Robin Cook became a good ally. Of course there were new faces every so often, but I no longer felt in any way intimidated by them.

Liz O'Donnell was my junior minister during my second time in Foreign Affairs and I always felt very free to allow her to engage in the Northern talks to the fullest extent, or indeed to do 'Brussels' duty. She was very impressive in everything she did. I was confident enough in her ability to give her a free hand. My approach was, and always had been, to let people get on with the job without interference from me. It was a question of all shoulders to the wheel as far as I was concerned.

In relation to the EU, the Amsterdam Treaty was one of the issues that had a central place during this period in Foreign Affairs. It had been formally signed on 2 October 1997 and after two referendums and decisions by the member parliaments, it would come into force on 1 May 1999. The result of two years of negotiations, it placed greater emphasis on citizenship and individual rights and gave more democracy through increased powers for the European Parliament. It also gave new employment rights, and laid greater stress on freedom, security and justice within the EU. Under the treaty, the tentative beginnings of a common foreign and security policy were also initiated – and it provided for the reform of EU institutions in preparation for enlargement.

We held a referendum on the treaty in May 1998. I again had the prime responsibility in government for ensuring that the electorate would support the 'yes' side. Those who wanted a 'no' vote ran a stout campaign, focusing especially on the treaty's implications for our neutrality, sensing that this was its Achilles heel. Fortunately, the electorate accepted my main contention that the treaty was good for both Ireland and Europe. The result of the referendum was sixty-two per cent yes and thirty-eight per cent no. This was the fourth time a majority of the people had given positive voice to our role in Europe.

In welcoming the result of the referendum, I said that the treaty contained many provisions of direct relevance to the needs of the Irish voters, and that it underlined the EU's commitment to human rights and fundamental freedoms. Although the treaty was a complex document, I said, it was about down-to-earth issues: jobs, freedom and security, a clean environment and accountability to the voter. I expressed the belief that the treaty equipped us to face the challenges ahead, including those thrown up by further enlargement.

I mentioned that the treaty provided for reform of EU institutions. One of the important things it did was to strengthen the hand of the European Parliament, making the European Commission more accountable to it. Subsequently there was something of a cause célèbre when, after investigation into allegations of corruption concerning individual commissioners, the entire Santer Commission (in office since 1995) resigned in March 1999. The commissioner most criticised was Édith Cresson from France, and the criticism focused on her appointment of her dentist as a special adviser! I had met Madame Cresson on quite a few occasions. She was a glamorous but quite haughty individual.

Because she refused to resign, alleging that all commissioners were involved in the same kind of activity, the commission had to resign en masse. Romano Prodi reappointed most of the commissioners when he became president of the next commission, but not Pádraig Flynn: he had destroyed his prospects by his extraordinary performance on the *Late Late Show* in January 1999. David Byrne became our new commissioner. He was outstanding in this role.

Irish neutrality featured as a major issue during the referendum campaign for the Amsterdam Treaty. Non-participation in military alliances (specifically NATO) had evolved into part of our very definition of our neutrality. But in the post-Cold War world, NATO was developing into something of a collective security organisation, a role in which it co-operated with both the Organisation for Security and Co-operation in Europe (OSCE) and the United Nations. In this guise, it was offering itself as a means for multilateral peacekeeping missions. In 1994, it had launched its 'Partnership for Peace' initiative, to which the Irish government had responded somewhat coolly, saying it was NATO by another name. But in 1996, a government White Paper asked whether or not we should participate in this co-operative initiative, which most OSCE member states had joined, and which had already assumed an important role in European security co-operation, especially in areas such as training for peacekeeping and humanitarian undertakings.

Criticism of any moves in the direction of joining the Partnership for Peace centred on it being merely a back-door way of joining NATO. However, Irish troops served in the NATO-led Stabilisation Force in Bosnia-Herzegovina (SFOR), a move that was given the go-ahead by the Fine Gael–Labour–Democratic Left coalition in 1996. In February 1997, Minister for Foreign Affairs Dick Spring indicated in the Dáil his own personal support for the Partnership and said the question of Irish membership was being kept under constant review.

When I became Minister for Foreign Affairs, I said in the Dáil, in February 1998, that I looked forward to 'an open and well-informed debate on Partnership for Peace in the House in due course'. A vigorous debate ensued, not only about joining the Partnership but also about whether such a decision would require a referendum. The issue was debated in the Dáil in late January 1999; in May of that year the government issued an explanatory guide, and in November, by a resolution in the Dáil supported by Fianna Fáil, Fine Gael and the PDs, Ireland agreed to take part in the Partnership for Peace and the associated Euro-Atlantic Partnership Council.

FOREIGN TRIPS – INFORMAL AND FORMAL

The job of a Minister for Foreign Affairs is in many ways quite unlike any other ministry. It entails a lot of travelling and also a lot of entertaining. I have to admit that I found the latter difficult as I'm not really very gregarious by nature. There were regular lunches and occasional dinners in Iveagh House (or sometimes Dublin Castle) which Annette and I hosted. These would be either for visiting politicians and statesmen – anyone from Kofi Annan to unknown foreign ministers from countries aspiring to the EU – or perhaps in support of some major international event that might be taking place. There was also a lunch 'to say farewell' to every ambassador who was leaving for another post. Sometimes I would be saying farewell to someone I was meeting for the first time!

With the constant pressure of work, in the North especially, I often had to arrive at these events a bit behind time, which didn't please protocol very much although I must say that they were an extraordinarily professional group. Two people whom I found very helpful and indeed understanding of the situation were Brian Nason and Joe Brennan, both of them senior protocol figures. Joe, among his many talents, played the piano very well, to the delight of some of our foreign guests.

At these lunches there were of course the usual speeches when I would go on about the strong links between Ireland and whatever the visiting country was, and their representative would duly respond in kind. I'm afraid it had all the hallmarks of the single transferable speech. However, everything was very well organised; the reception rooms in Iveagh House are elegant and striking and, of course, Dublin Castle is spectacular. Our guests were always impressed and I think left with a good feeling for the hospitality offered.

Another unusual aspect of the job was what was known as the 'informal weekends' – which were anything but informal. These weekends were a gathering of all the EU foreign ministers and their wives. They would be held in whichever one of the EU countries had the presidency, and countries would vie with each other to impress. There was always a very high attendance. Ireland's presidency never came round during my tenure, but Annette and I attended many informal weekends in different countries. They are referred to as informal because the ministers meet together without any civil servants present. I suspect that this makes the latter very nervous indeed.

The foreign minister of the host country chaired these meetings. We would all sit around a table in no particular order of seniority. One of the strange aspects of these meetings was that there was no agenda, but very quickly the issues of the day would be raised. The idea was that in this atmosphere ministers could express their points of view freely and indeed there would be a lot of back-and-forth discussion and argument in a fairly relaxed way. Of course, the bigger countries dominated.

The first informal weekend we attended was in Portugal. It was shortly after my initial appointment to Foreign Affairs in 1992 and the first time we had the experience of our car being accompanied by police outriders. For some reason, we travelled at a terrifyingly high speed, with the outriders weaving in and out of the traffic daredevil fashion. On one short journey alone, two of our outriders came down, and we heard afterwards that one of them had broken a leg! We stayed in a lovely old *pousada* and at the first reception met a number of well-known faces – people like Genscher, Elleman-Jensen, Hurd of the UK, Poos of Luxembourg and de Angelis of Italy (who came to grief over some scandal later), and of course the Head of the Commission at the time, Jacques Delors. Our host was the Portuguese Foreign Minister Jao Pineiro, who was subsequently to become an EU Commissioner.

Both Annette and I found it all a bit daunting at first, but they were a reasonably friendly bunch, although pomposity was a common enough trait. Hurd was a civil man and his wife Judy was very kind to Annette, who was a bit nervous on this first outing. That evening there was music after dinner, and Jao joined in with the musicians, singing a number of lugubrious *fados*, the Portuguese equivalent of a come-all-ye. This was the last of these weekends for Hans-Dieter Genscher of Germany. He was inclined to throw his weight around a bit, as also did the French (for example Hubert Védrine, who went on endlessly about his views on agriculture).

However, the smaller countries did get to express their views too. One of my earlier contributions was on the subject of Somalia. I had just returned from my first visit and was able to describe in graphic detail the horror of everything that I had seen. The Council Troika (a committee made up of the foreign ministers of the previous year's, the present year's and the following year's presidency) had visited a few weeks earlier, but just for a few hours. In fairness, they listened carefully to what I had to say, although it was the UN that I would rely on most for effective action. After that meeting, I remember Uffe Elleman-Jensen of Denmark coming over to me and saying: 'Come on, David. You didn't really stay three days in Somalia. For heaven's sake, there isn't a single hotel there.' I was of course indignant and explained to him how well I had been looked after by Concern. He believed me, but I think he thought it might have been a dangerous or at least a foolhardy mission.

During another of these weekends, Ireland and Denmark happened to be playing a soccer match. Uffe teased me endlessly and wore a Danish scarf throughout the weekend (including the meetings). Unfortunately, I didn't have an Irish one with me.

We had two separate informal weekends in the UK, the first in a beautiful stately home called Hatfield House, not far from London. Douglas Hurd was the host and our room was called the Prince of

Wales Suite. When our meetings on the first day finished it was still early afternoon and we were informed that there were some activities available. We had a choice. There was tennis, croquet, fishing, archery, or walking. I opted to go fishing and Connor valiantly joined me. There seems to be no limit to what a private secretary has to endure to support his minister! I know that the two of us looked ridiculous getting into a little punt on the lake, still in our business suits and shiny leather shoes. Need I say we didn't catch anything? Annette decided on croquet, although she had never played the game before. Douglas and Judy Hurd also played croquet and, as they seemed to know how, showed everyone what to do. Some of the civil servants tried archery. The joke going around was that they were pinning photos of their ministers to the board.

That evening dinner was black tie, and just before we were to go down I discovered I had no cufflinks. Annette offered to go and find Connor, on the principle that he always seemed to have a solution to problems. However, as she rushed out of the door, she ran straight into David Owen and his American wife. David Owen was attending the weekend as an observer. They enquired where she was rushing. When she explained, David said that he had a spare pair and went back into his room for them. Later on in the evening when I was returning them, he told me that he had been very tempted during the course of the dinner to point out to everyone present that I was wearing cuff links with the engraving 'ER II'. I had never noticed. He thought it was a great joke. The following day we had a fairly informal lunch with everyone sitting as they pleased. There was a beautifully superior butler called Allen serving us. The first course was smoked salmon and I asked him if it was Irish. He hesitated only slightly and said in a fruity voice: 'I'm bound to say yes, sir'!

We also had informal weekends in Luxembourg and Austria. Luxembourg, perhaps because they are so long in the EU, didn't break the bank with entertainment. On this occasion there was a pianist tinkling in the background during dinner. The Greek Foreign Minister, Theo Pangalos, was sitting next to Annette and towards the end of the meal, when the pianist had packed up, he said to Annette: 'I believe you can play the piano. So now you will play for us.' Annette looked at me across the table in horror but before she could say anything, he stood up and in his loud booming voice announced that the wife of the Irish Foreign Minister was going to play the piano. Everyone started to applaud and she felt she had no choice but to play. She acquitted herself well with a Chopin waltz and got a great reception. Theo was really very mischievous because when she came back to her place he said, 'So you really can play!'

What I remember most about Austria was the cold in the wonderful old castle where we had dinner. Our host was Wolfgang Schüssel, later Chancellor of Austria.

Finland was another venue for one of these weekends and it was held in Lapland. Our hostess was Tarja Halonen, now President of Finland. She is a very friendly, no-nonsense sort of person and one of the foreign ministers with whom I forged a good relationship. The weekend was very enjoyable and good fun when we got through our meetings.

One of the last weekends we had was again in the UK, but this time in Edinburgh with the late Robin Cook as host. This was just after Robin had been 'outed' as having an affair with his secretary, Gaynor. The story goes that Tony Blair, or someone on his behalf, had phoned Robin at Heathrow airport just a few weeks earlier when he was about to go on holiday with his wife. It appears that he was told that his affair was about to hit the newspapers and that he would have to decide immediately between his wife and Gaynor. Quite a predicament! Anyway, he decided on Gaynor and she was with him in Edinburgh for the weekend. She looked quite scared, which was understandable. Some of the wives could be fairly formidable. However Annette, remembering how she had felt at the first informal weekend, befriended her and they became the best of mates after that. Cook was good company and very much enjoyed holding forth at the various dinners and lunches. He was a great raconteur and I was saddened to hear of his premature death.

Another duty of the Foreign Minister is to accompany the President whenever she travels abroad, although, because of the pressure of work in the North and Brussels, other ministers often had to take over this duty from me.

We were in Paris and Australia with President Robinson and, as I have already described, these were very busy and formal occasions. Her husband Nick always accompanied Mary, and they both really worked very hard at the job and made a great impression, although these tours were inclined to be a bit tense for those of us in the 'entourage'.

During my second spell in Foreign Affairs we went on two tours with President McAleese – one to Washington and one to Canada. She was just as impressive as President Robinson, but much more relaxed by nature. Her husband Martin is a real gentleman, very committed to doing the best for the country, and we became good friends with both of them. On one occasion when we were in Canada, we were on St Edward Island and were attending a concert organised by the Irish community. During a performance of Irish dancing, a little girl of about six somehow got her steps mixed up and to everyone's consternation dashed off the stage in tears. Before the next performers came on, President McAleese asked to see the little girl and she spent the rest of the concert sitting on the President's knee.

I found the presidential tours difficult because, while your presence as Foreign Minister is required, basically you are only there in case the President is confronted with any political issues that she is not empowered to answer. This doesn't happen too often and you really have very little to do; there is a lot of hanging about, which I didn't really enjoy. However, it was very interesting to see both presidents in action and to see what a great impression they both made.

In 1997, Mary Robinson was appointed UN High Commissioner for Human Rights. There was considerable lobbying for the position and it was an indication both of Mrs Robinson's own standing and of Ireland's strong position at the UN that she got the support of Secretary-General Kofi Annan and the backing of the General Assembly.

Ireland was also elected to the UN Commission on Human Rights for the 1997–9 period and, in 1999, Ireland was elected to chair the commission session in Geneva. I was very proud to announce our election to this position in the Seanad. I said that this was one of the most important events in the human rights calendar. Ambassador Ann Anderson, our permanent representative in Geneva and a fine diplomat, would be chairing the session. Her election was a recognition of the consistent and progressive policies on human rights adopted by successive Irish governments and a measure of Ms Anderson's standing at the United Nations in Geneva. This was one of my more pleasant duties as Minister for Foreign Affairs during that period. Ann Anderson is now Irish ambassador in Paris and continues to bring honour to her country.

Mentioning human rights brings me to one of the more memorable of the many foreign trips during my second time in Iveagh House, a visit to China in late February 1998. I was accompanied by a number of businessmen and the main purpose of the trip was to facilitate them, the aim being to develop Sino-Irish trading links. There was also a series of political meetings. We had a number of sessions with government ministers and representatives. The issue of human rights was discussed vigorously, as was the situation in Iraq. I left feeling that at least we had been given a hearing.

Apart from business and politics, the highlight of the trip was a visit to the Great Wall – deservedly one of the wonders of the world. Nothing prepares one for the sight of this extraordinary and enormous structure meandering right across the country as far as the eye can see, up hills and down valleys. Climbing to the top was well worth the effort.

One thing I found off-putting was the level of security that our Chinese hosts felt we needed. There was a bunch of plain-clothes security men ahead and behind us all the time. What I really found embarrassing was when they literally pushed members of the public aside to make way for us. The people seemed to accept it but it made me feel very uncomfortable.

Another unforgettable trip was to South Africa in June 1998 where I had the honour of meeting the great Nelson Mandela in his home in Pretoria. The first surprise for me was how tall he was – nearly as tall as myself. I found him very easy to talk to – we talked a lot about human rights and he also spoke about the importance of forgiveness, of which he is a shining example. We spoke for quite a while. He has such an engaging personality as well as genuine warmth for Ireland.

The issue of East Timor featured prominently during my second period in Foreign Affairs. It had been a Portuguese colony until 1975 when it was invaded and occupied by Indonesia, although it was seeking independence. The East Timorese guerrilla force, the Falintil, fought against the Indonesian occupying forces from 1975 until 1999. The civilian population suffered the most in this conflict because the Indonesians took their frustration out on them, torturing and killing them under the pretence that they believed that the local people were helping the guerrillas. The Australians originally supported Indonesia, but later switched, and are now of great assistance to the East Timorese. During the period of the occupation, up to 200,000 people (or a third of the entire population of East Timor) were killed in an extremely brutal Indonesian campaign, which featured some terrible massacres.

This anti-civilian brutality got little coverage in the Western press. The Americans did not want to embarrass their ally, President Suharto of Indonesia, and preferred to highlight instead the atrocities of the Khmer Rouge regime in Cambodia. This was when an Irish bus driver from Ballyfermot in Dublin entered the picture. Tom Hyland became involved when he happened to see a television documentary called *Cold Blood: the Massacre of East Timor*. So disturbed was he by what he saw that he set up the East Timor-Ireland Solidarity Campaign. He proved a natural at heading a campaign to win the attention of the public. He worked tirelessly to bring the horror of what was happening five thousand miles away to the awareness of the Irish people and eventually to the attention of the international community.

His determined lobbying of politicians such as Prime Minister Keating of Australia, and of senior Irish figures such as Dick Spring and myself, paid off. I was very impressed by his sincerity. While in opposition I met him regularly and after I became Foreign Minister I continued the contact. He persuaded me to visit East Timor, and I was the first Foreign Minister from the West to visit the island. During this first visit I began by visiting Xanana Gusmao, the captured guerrilla leader, in prison. He was being held in relatively open prison conditions. He was a very charismatic and gentle person – not at all one's image of a guerrilla leader. He gave me a first-class account of what was happening in East Timor and in turn I undertook to bring the matter to the attention of the EU. I then met with the President of Indonesia, who I felt was a rather weak man and completely under the control of the military.

We then went on to Dili, capital of East Timor. We went into a very unstable situation. There were no hotels there and I brought my own sheets and towels because I was staying with locals who had very little – basically down-market bed and breakfasts, but run by very decent and courageous people.

One of the people we visited there was the Governor of East Timor, who was really an agent for Indonesia. He was an aggressive individual and gave me the impression that he was a bully and indeed he turned out to be very brutal in his dealings with the local population. He wasn't interested in what I had to say. I felt he wasn't listening at all and I left him on very cold and unfriendly terms.

I also visited the very brave Bishop Belo. I sat in his house discussing his country's desperately serious situation. While we were chatting, and much to my horror, we heard shots, which we realised were very close by. A man dashed in to tell us that a young man had just been shot dead by the local militia. It turned out that the murdered man was the son of a local politician who was a supporter of Gusmao. That apparently was reason enough for him to be killed.

My visit had an important role in the events that followed. I reported what I had seen in detail to the EU Council of Ministers and they appointed me their delegate to East Timor. I made a return visit in that capacity and produced a number of detailed reports for the council. As a result of a UN-sponsored agreement, a referendum was held in East Timor at the end of August 1999. The UN supervised it and there was an enormous turnout of voters. Their courage and determination in coming out to vote in such numbers was inspiring. The result was an overwhelming vote in favour of independence.

But the Indonesians weren't about to let go easily. Their military, together with pro-Indonesian Timorese militias – thugs, really – instigated violent clashes in which many died. The Australians sent in a peacekeeping force to restore order and the militias withdrew across the West Timorese border but continued to launch sporadic raids. This is where I played an active role again in having established a UN peacekeeping force, which included an Irish contingent, and a Transitional Administration for East Timor. There was also significant Irish involvement in the elections, which were internationally supervised. East Timor became the first new country of the twenty-first century and also a member of the UN. The people there had reason to be grateful to Ireland and especially to Tom Hyland, who has continued his admirable involvement with the country.

There was for me one rather moving occasion while I was in East Timor. One member of the small Irish military presence there had been tragically killed earlier in a shooting accident. His name was

Peadar Ó Flatharta and he came from Connemara. I had the honour of unveiling a monument to his memory in Taroma, near West Timor. The local Timorese gave me a gift, which I was later able to present to his parents. I hope that it might have given them some small comfort that he wasn't forgotten in the country where he had so tragically lost his life.

One of the major features of my second period in Foreign Affairs – and the one that perhaps gave me the most satisfaction – was having Ireland elected onto the UN Security Council in 2000. The responsibility for doing so was mine for most of the campaign. Earlier, in fact within a few weeks of my appointment, I had gone to Madrid for the opening of Ireland House. Our ambassador there was a man I knew slightly, Richard Ryan. I was enormously impressed by what he had achieved in Madrid. He had persuaded all the Irish agencies (such as the IDA, Bord Fáilte, Bord Bia, and others) to base themselves in the same building, an arrangement which has enormous benefits for all concerned but which is not easily achieved, whether through the opposition of vested interests or sheer bloody-mindedness. At the lunch held to celebrate the event, Richard really had all the people of influence in Madrid as his guests. The new Ireland House was impressive, very well set up and was an extremely good advertisement for Ireland.

I had already been mulling over the Security Council and how to approach it and knew that I had to have someone special as our ambassador to the UN. I immediately decided on Richard. He was very bright, extraordinarily hard working and confident, even, dare I say it, pushy. I felt he was just the man we needed. Mind you, I ruffled some feathers in the department when I made this appointment. They had other plans, but I knew I was making the right decision and his subsequent performance justified my confidence in him. I set up a small committee in the department run by very bright people. Richard Ryan was to head our lobbying efforts at the UN itself, while Ambassador Mary Whelan led the efforts in Dublin. In addition, six of our ambassadors aided the campaign on a part-time basis as special envoys to areas such as Africa, South America and Oceania.

The other decision I made was to concentrate especially on the smaller countries. Every country has just one vote, which means that, for example, the vote of China has exactly the same value as the vote of the island of St Lucia in the West Indies.

The Security Council is the most powerful and prestigious body in the UN, consisting of five permanent members and ten others elected for two-year terms. It is a body unique in its capacity to initiate a whole range of actions, such as mediation and diplomatic pressure, economic sanctions, and military action if necessary. When the council decides on a course of action, that action tends to gain widespread international acceptance and legitimacy. Although any of the permanent five members has the power of veto, using it tends to give the impression that that country is isolated on a particular question. A resolution needs nine votes in its favour for it to pass, so even if the permanent five support it, they have to persuade at least four of the non-permanent ten to back the resolution as well.

Membership for us would mean a high profile and require us to take a position on a range of international issues. Our opponents for the two European places on the council were Italy and Norway. Turkey was seeking a place initially, but the Italians persuaded them to withdraw from the contest. At the outset, Ireland was not seen as having much of a chance of getting elected because we were not perceived as having the diplomatic or economic clout of our rivals.

In May 1998, having written to more than a hundred and eighty foreign ministers informing them of our candidacy and formally seeking their support, the campaign was stepped up a gear. Members of the government used every suitable opportunity to raise our candidacy with other governments, as did members of the Opposition. As Minister for Foreign Affairs, the campaign demanded and deserved a considerable proportion of my time and energy. I recall, for example, that in early 1999 I went to the Caribbean for ten days and visited no fewer than eight countries, lobbying for their support. It is hard enough work because you have to read up an extensive brief on each country before you visit it, so that you can discuss their affairs with them with some degree of knowledge. So, as we flew from one island to another, I would be immersed in the file of the next country. I returned fairly confident that we would get the fourteen votes of the Caribbean countries, but we could never actually gauge the extent of our progress with any degree of certainty.

The big push of our campaign took place in September 1999 during the UN General Assembly in New York. Of course I had to make the usual speech, but all the emphasis this time was on getting elected to the Security Council. Richard Ryan and his team had already been working all the hours of the day in pursuit of every possible vote, but he considered the face-to-face meetings between myself and other foreign ministers to be vital and had set up an enormous number of meetings for us. To give some idea about the extent of our canvassing, sometimes my officials and I met as many as twenty foreign ministers in a day. It was a massive undertaking and I am glad to say that I got on very well with most of the foreign ministers I met.

We got votes for all sorts of reasons. A young Panamanian was one of the eighty or so foreign ministers I met during that period in New York. We had no particular claim on this vote. However, to my surprise, we were greeted warmly and before I could even start making my pitch, this very charming minister informed us that he had at least one Cork ancestor. As a result, he had a great fondness for Ireland and the ensuing interview was all about developments in Ireland. Although we never got to talk about the Security Council, we left with Panama's vote securely in our pocket.

Cuba was another country that definitely gave us their vote. The Cuban Foreign Minister, Felipe Roque, was an impressive young man and we struck up quite a rapport. In fact, we have stayed in touch since then, exchanging the odd note and Christmas card. In recent times, his name has been mentioned as the possible future President of Cuba. I will be watching out for him with interest.

Another example of support was from Ethiopia, which I had visited on a number of occasions. There we found a deep appreciation of the continuity of Ireland's development aid programme over a difficult period in their history. The Ethiopian Prime Minister specifically singled out the role played by Minister of State Liz O'Donnell in ensuring the continuity of funding for bilateral aid projects. Another vote gained!

That is not to say that the whole idea to put us forward for elected membership of the Security Council was mine. We had last been elected to the council in 1961, so it was our turn to put ourselves forward again. While the Rainbow government's White Paper on Foreign Affairs in 1996 contained the suggestion that Ireland pursue membership of the Security Council, it was when the Fianna Fáil–PD government assumed office in the summer of 1997 that the decision was made to campaign actively to that end. However, as I have already said, we were not really expected to succeed. But we gave the lie to that misperception, achieving a massive 130 votes in the first round, with Norway taking second place and Italy losing out. I know that Ambassador Mary Whelan and her team and indeed the department in general felt a great sense of achievement with this result.

My departmental team and I and the strong campaign we ran can claim some but not all of the credit for our success. Our election was also certainly a major tribute to our country's standing in the General Assembly, which then had over a hundred and eighty members. Our good standing in the General Assembly was due to our strong and positive voting record over the preceding two decades. Especially worth noting was our voting record on the most important issues raised by the poorer southern part of the world. The concerns of the developing states there are reflected much more in the General Assembly than in the Security Council. Resolutions on Palestine and the Middle East in general, on apartheid (until it ended in 1994) and colonialism, and on human rights and disarmament represented some seventy per cent of all the resolutions. Our voting record on such resolutions showed that we were the EU state most likely to support them.

The issue of non-proliferation of nuclear weapons had been a central aspect of Irish policy since the early years of our membership of the UN. I had the opportunity to launch an international drive to rekindle efforts towards nuclear disarmament – *Towards a Nuclear-Free World: the Need for a New Agenda*. In a move co-sponsored by New Zealand, Sweden, South Africa, Brazil, Egypt, Mexico and Slovenia, we sought to strengthen the non-proliferation regime and give fresh impetus to nuclear disarmament. The aspirations contained in the document are as relevant today as they were then. Richard Townsend, a senior and dedicated official in the department, was the author of this document and merits most credit.

EVENTS

Not long after the referendum on Articles 2 and 3 in relation to the Good Friday Agreement, the current affairs magazine *Magill* published an article saying that Rennicks had paid Ray Burke £30,000 in June 1989, around the same time that JMSE had given him the same amount. I have read that there was trouble in government when it emerged that Bertie Ahern hadn't kept Mary Harney informed of the news when he first learned of it. There may have been some mild ripples of unease – not unusual in a coalition arrangement at the best of times – but I never felt that the cohesion of the government was threatened. The upshot was that the terms of reference of the Flood Tribunal were extended to permit it to investigate other payments to Burke and other politicians as well.

A number of reputations have been destroyed at this tribunal, particularly by Frank Dunlop. As government press secretary, he had been close to Jack Lynch and then to Charles Haughey. Afterwards, he became a public relations consultant and political lobbyist. I didn't know him very well but had always understood him to be an honest man and a man of reputation. His later revelations before the tribunal came as a great shock to me as I am sure they did to many others in public life.

One of the saddest examples, to my mind, of the reputations that he seriously damaged was that of young Liam Cosgrave, a former constituency colleague of mine who represented the Fine Gael party. His father Liam senior and his mother Vera were very kind to me when I came into the Dún Laoghaire constituency. I knew Liam junior well and I don't believe for one moment that he is corrupt. The sums involved were not substantial. The problem in the Cosgrave case was that he had not declared receiving the donations. I was very upset for Liam, his immediate family and the Cosgrave family in general. They deserved better and they certainly, to borrow a phrase, did the State some service.

A month or so later, news came that the £2 million tax assessment against Charles Haughey had been reduced to zero by a Revenue Appeals Commissioner, and there was uproar in the Dáil when it was revealed that the commissioner in question was Bertie Ahern's brother-in-law and that he had been appointed while Bertie was Minister for Finance in 1994. The thing provoked some controversy but it was subsequently proved that the commissioner, like Caesar's wife, was above suspicion. Nor did the Taoiseach have anything at all to do with the decision regarding Haughey's liability or non-liability for tax.

Neither Burke's nor Haughey's misfortunes gave me any *schadenfreude*, nor did Pádraig Flynn's extraordinary performance on the *Late*

Late Show in January 1999. I cannot figure out what possessed him to behave in the way he did that particular night on television. Anyone who knows him knows that that performance was a pure aberration, a bit like the night that Peter Brooke sang 'My Darling Clementine' on the same show: it was unthinking and unintended. Pádraig spoke, I believe in all innocence, about the burden of having three houses and three housekeepers. The ordinary 'man in the street' had no sympathy for him and the average viewer met his remarks with derision.

Pádraig also made the serious mistake of dismissing developer Tom Gilmartin's allegation that he had given Flynn £50,000 in 1989. In any event, his comment that the Gilmartins were ill so angered the Sligo-born builder that he changed his mind about appearing before the Flood tribunal.

This had implications for the Taoiseach because Gilmartin said he had met Ahern a number of times in relation to his development plans for Dublin. At first, Ahern had said that he had met Gilmartin only once, but he had to revise this. To be fair to Ahern, in one's memory of these things, it's very hard to go back ten years and recall all the people one met. How many people does the Taoiseach meet every day? Ministers do have diaries that are kept for them and in which their appointments are written, but these diaries do not give a minute-by-minute or hour-by-hour coverage of an average day in their lives. If they are waylaid in a corridor and brought into a meeting, in those circumstances an official would not note the meeting.

It is thus hardly a matter of great moment how many meetings one may have had with individuals. I do not think the Taoiseach's credibility was damaged by the uncertainty over how many meetings he had with Tom Gilmartin. It was suggested that this matter caused some strain in the coalition of the time, but I neither noticed nor experienced such strains.

Then there was the so-called 'Sheedy affair' in spring of 1999, which led to the resignations of the Supreme Court Judge, Hugh O'Flaherty, Judge Cyril Kelly and the Dublin County Registrar, Michael Quinlan. Philip Sheedy was an architect who had been convicted in 1997 of causing the death of a young woman in a car accident. He was released after serving only one year of a four-year prison sentence. There were victims in the whole affair, most tragic of all the victim of Sheedy's dangerous driving. I believe the action that had to be taken by the government was taken. If the judges and the county registrar had not resigned, there is no doubt that we could have had a constitutional crisis on our hands, and there would have been severe difficulties for the government. Also, the fact that Sheedy returned to prison to complete his sentence helped to calm things down.

I was very sorry for the awful tragedy experienced by the family of the victim. I also had a personal interest in the case of the two judges, and indeed I know Moya Quinlan, the mother of the county registrar. She has been a good friend and supporter of mine over the years. Altogether it was a sorry saga for all parties concerned, though I'm not in any way comparing the tragedy of the loss of a human life with the loss of position or remuneration.

Bertie Ahern had made representations for Sheedy's early release and had informed Mary Harney about this fact before news of it became public, but when he later appeared to dismiss her concerns and said she hadn't asked him to make a Dáil statement about the matter of his own involvement, she refused to attend a Cabinet meeting, and for twenty-four hours or so there was some unease within government circles. The Taoiseach quite rightly backtracked on his stance, apologised to her and thus succeeded in restoring good relations. It was simply a miscalculation on his part; for her part, I think she was making the point that she wasn't to be taken for granted. I don't believe there was ever any danger of the government falling over this issue: the relationship between the two leaders was too strong and solid to crumple over this – admittedly serious – issue.

Meanwhile, throughout the spring of 1999, the Moriarty Tribunal revealed how Mr Haughey had financed his lavish lifestyle. The contributors to that financing read like a *Who's Who* of Irish commercial life: names like Ben Dunne, the AIB, Michael Dargan, Joe Malone, P. V. Doyle, Seamus Purcell, Larry Goodman and Patrick Gallagher. I've remarked already that I have no problem with small political donations, but I do have a problem about the size of some contributions. Reasonable political donations are acceptable – as long, of course, as they are declared – but when you get to an accumulation of somewhere in the region of £10 million in political donations to the chief executive of the country, that is quite shocking.

No one dared speak up during the Haughey years about this palpable wrongdoing – myself included. People have asked me why I didn't challenge him if I felt so strongly about it, but they forget that we had very stringent defamation laws in this country. To accuse somebody of something, you had to be absolutely certain of your facts, and you had to have your evidence ready to hand, and that evidence had to be watertight. Nobody had that evidence at that stage. Yes, many asked themselves, 'How does this man maintain his lifestyle?', but the fact is that one had no evidence to show how he did it: that came out much later, purely by accident.

It also emerged from the tribunal that some of Haughey's party leader's allowance, which came from the public purse, ended up funding expenses such as dining out in expensive restaurants and purchasing Charvet shirts. There were two signatories of the cheques and Bertie Ahern was one of them. He appeared before the tribunal in July 1999 and explained that he pre-signed large batches of blank cheques for administrative convenience. Some have considered this a strange practice, especially for one with a training in accountancy. I don't find it so strange, because if one trusted one's co-signatory (in this case it was Ray MacSharry), there was no reason not to pre-sign large batches of cheques. It's a practice I wouldn't recommend, but I can understand the administrative convenience point of view.

All the while in the late nineties, the economy was doing enormously well. Minister for Finance Charlie McCreevy's tax-cutting budgets were popular although there were mutterings that they favoured the rich. He had had a spat in 1997 with the Irish League of Credit Unions that many Fianna Fáil backbenchers felt uneasy about. But his 1999 budget provoked the biggest row over the so-called 'tax individualisation', which favoured two-income families. The Independent TDs who supported the government, and Fianna Fáil backbenchers, their clinics flooded with complaints about discrimination against stay-at-home mothers, began to protest to McCreevy and the government. In my own constituency clinics, there was what I would call a trickle rather than a flood of complaints but the complaints were registered on a fairly consistent basis. I had reservations about the whole concept of what McCreevy was trying to do – although I could see that he was trying to encourage more people, especially women, into the workplace. He succeeded in deflating the issue in his Finance Bill where he improved allowances to single-income families.

In his political philosophy, and especially his economic philosophy, Charlie McCreevy could probably be described as right-wing, and he would be nearer to the PDs in that regard than to Fianna Fáil.

EXIT

During the first half of 1999 I made the decision to retire from my ministerial post, having also decided that it was time to draw the curtain on my career in Dáil Éireann at the following election. By the next general election (which was likely to be held in 2002 because the Taoiseach had again and again made it clear that he intended his government to run its full term) I would have been a TD for almost forty years. I was in the second half of my sixties then and past the standard retirement age.

I announced my retirement from the Dáil at a constituency dinner in Killiney around the middle of May. The response was very muted. I think the party faithful in the constituency would have preferred me to stay on but I believed myself that it was time to go. I also had hopes that my son Barry, already a local councillor, would succeed me in Dáil Éireann.

Another reason for my retirement was that I felt that a younger person and someone with a future in Fianna Fáil could better serve the country's interests at Foreign Affairs and enhance their own profile at the same time. Brian Cowen was then Minister for Health and Children and I had felt for some time that I would like to see him as my successor in office. This wasn't in my gift, of course, but I was optimistic that that was the way the wind was blowing. So I went to the Taoiseach and told him that I intended to retire and would like to give Brian a chance to have a decent run-in to the next election in his new portfolio. I am glad to say that that is how things turned out and that I was to be proved right in the confidence I reposed in Brian Cowan. My belief is that Brian Cowan may well be the next leader of Fianna Fáil, with challenges from Dermot Ahern, Mícheal Martin and Brian Lenihan.

My original intention was to go in early June, but the Taoiseach asked me to stay on until late September. He didn't want me to leave until the summer marching season in the North was over. The two weeks of lobbying for the Security Council in New York was also coming up in September. So I stayed on and we got through the summer safely. Then a date in early October was fixed for my departure, but that was also postponed. Brian Cowen, as Minister for Health, was deeply involved in dealing with a nurses' strike at that time and it would have been a bad time to move him to another department. It was November before the nurses' dispute was settled and I was then asked to wait until after Christmas as the signing of the North-South agreement was to take place with Peter Mandelson in Iveagh House in late December. Finally 26 January was settled on as the date for my departure.

By chance the signing coincided with an invitation that President McAleese had received to visit the British Queen for lunch in Buckingham Palace, and Annette and I were to accompany her. The signing of the Agreement had to take place at 9.30 in the morning and then we were whisked off to the airport to take the plane to London. On this particular occasion, knowing that it was near the end of my tenure in Iveagh House, I was very relaxed. However, to use an expression of our American neighbours, it was fairly awesome to walk through the impressive portals of Buckingham Palace. We were led down through a portrait-filled corridor into a small reception room where the Queen and her son, the Earl of Wessex (Prince Edward), greeted us. Prince Edward is the youngest son of Queen Elizabeth and he struck me on this occasion as an extremely uncomfortable young man. I don't know what my republican father would think but I was quite taken with the Queen's broad smile and was almost shocked to hear that unmistakeable voice. Having passed through the greetings ritual, we then proceeded to lunch. The Queen sat in the middle, President McAleese on her right and I to her left. On my left there was a most pleasant lady-in-waiting, the Honourable Mary Morrison. Annette sat opposite me, next to Prince Edward, who I gather she found tough going.

The Queen and I got on very well indeed. I told her that I had five children and we talked about the worries of bringing up children. She explained in some detail the fear the new millennium held for her, based on what she called her 'annus horribilis' during which so many things went wrong in the royal family – divorces, deaths, press leaks and many other problems. In fact she said that she didn't think that she would make it into the millennium. I replied, 'I don't know why you should feel that. You are a fine-looking woman, Ma'am.' At that she threw back her head and laughed heartily. In the ordinary way, my remarks could have been taken as irreverent, but Queen Elizabeth obviously has a good sense of humour and took them in good part. She is a decent woman and had all the worries and concerns for her children that the rest of humanity have. Whatever it was about that particular occasion, she wanted to talk family. She also told me about how keen she was to visit Ireland. She said that her father had always wanted to come, but never could, and that she really wanted to 'break that mould'. I said she would be welcome any time. It was obvious that the President also had a very good rapport with her. This visit was a very memorable occasion for all of us. It was an interesting finish to my ministerial career.

Although I didn't stay on for the actual UN Security Council vote, our election seemed to have been secured. It appeared to me that our campaign had gone extremely well – and as it turned out subsequently, it had. Now that our election had been assured, I felt there was little more I could contribute. The Northern talks were ongoing, of course, in their awful circularity, with little sign of the finishing post in sight.

In December, references began to appear in the papers about my possible retirement. I remember in particular a line from a *Sunday Business Post* piece that read, 'The Diva of Dún Laoghaire has a few swansongs in him yet'! There were some nasty suggestions in a few papers in January that I was being pushed rather than having chosen to go, so I issued a statement to scotch that particular rumour.

However, in early January the word was seeping out all over the place about my imminent retirement, so I decided I had better preempt it and so announced that I was stepping down from the department. There was some surprise and a lot of conjecture about the reason for my going – nearly all of it incorrect. It is fairly unusual for a Minister in full health to decide to step down of his own volition, and some people wanted to believe that I was pushed. I issued a statement giving my reasons. But for some journalists it is a question of why believe a statement from the horse's mouth when you can make up a more interesting story. The day I actually left there was a small farewell reception held in Iveagh House and my family came along. We then adjourned for lunch to the now defunct Commons restaurant and I must say I felt very at peace with myself.

No longer a minister, I was of course still a TD and I returned to an office in Leinster House. I really didn't miss the perks of office. After all, I still had my own secretary, the ever-faithful Debbie. We had a wonderful suite in the new Millennium Building of Leinster House – a far cry from the desk and occasional use of a typist I started out with. I resumed my practice at the Bar, although with the Dáil sitting in the daytime it was extremely difficult to develop a practice. I think I was a bit of a scourge to Chief Whip Seamus Brennan during this period, though he tried to be very accommodating.

When the General Election was called in June 2002 and my political career was finally at an end, I have to admit I felt a more than a twinge of sadness. Not for the work or the status – more for the friends, the camaraderie, the banter. I suppose this is what everyone feels when they retire, although it is said that Leinster House is one of the most exclusive clubs you can belong to.

By far the biggest hole in my life was that left by the loss of my secretary, Debbie Healy. Debbie had started out with me at the age of eighteen, about fourteen years earlier, raw out of secretarial school. Her father is Ritchie Healy of Meath, a deeply committed Fianna Fáil supporter and at one time treasurer of the party. He was a fervent Haughey supporter. When Debbie started with me I had to explain my attitude on Haughey to her and she undertook never to repeat at home anything she might hear, and vice versa. She remained faithful to that promise. Debbie developed into a wonderful secretary as the years went on – perceptive, efficient, intelligent and compassionate. She had a great sense of humour and I know she got to know me better than most. She also became a good friend to all my family.

When I retired she also opted to leave Leinster House. Perhaps influenced to an extent by the years we worked together on projects in developing countries, she took up a job in Bangladesh, where she still works, training people in the democratic process. We keep in close touch with her.

In the election that followed my son Barry was now a candidate in Dún Laoghaire. His running mate was Mary Hanafin, who had been appointed Chief Whip in the small reshuffle caused by my retirement. Barry fought a great campaign. He had a wonderful though inexperienced young team behind him. Of course all the family rowed in and I did quite a bit of canvassing with him.

He was well elected and it gave me an enormous amount of pleasure and satisfaction. I was and continue to be very proud of Barry.

Perhaps I might be allowed to say at this stage that Annette and I are very proud of all our five children. They have all done well in their different spheres and I suppose that is one of the things a parent hopes most for. We also take great joy from our five wonderful grandsons – Daniel, Jack, Jake, Hugh and Conn. Maybe one of them will one day walk into Leinster House as a new TD!

All through my political life I found myself very much drawn to humanitarian causes and as time went on, to the terrible difficulties experience by people in the developing world. When I retired I continued this interest. I was asked by the government to accept the post of Chairman of the Irish Red Cross. One of the first initiatives I took, as Chairman, was to set up an International Overseas Aid Division, and this operation is working very well. This of course is in addition to the great work being done by the Red Cross in towns and villages throughout Ireland where Irish Red Cross volunteers provide essential local services to people in their own communities.

The Overseas Aid Division has been involved in dealing with many international disasters of one kind or another, from earthquakes to famine, and one of my main roles has been fundraising. My friends tell me that they are fed up hearing me constantly appealing on radio for funds, but I have to say that many of these appeals have been very successful. I have also travelled to a number of countries to see first-hand what work is being done on the ground to help people who are suffering as a result of war, poverty and natural disasters and to ensure that money donated by Irish people to the Red Cross is being spent in the most effective way.

One of the first such trips I took was to re-visit the Middle East in 2002. I travelled there with a number of senior Red Cross officials. This was just after a period of intense violence in the area, including the siege of the Church in Bethlehem, attacks on the seat of Palestinian Authority and the offices of Yasser Arafat in Ramallah and also on the town of Jenin.

Early in the visit I met with President Arafat in Ramallah. He was virtually a prisoner in his compound and had extreme difficulty getting in or out. He seemed very stressed and we felt that at this stage he was just an old man who was merely a figurehead – no longer in control. In Ramallah we also met with many medical personnel and with officials of our sister organisation, the Red Crescent. As the visit progressed and I realised the problems these people were dealing with I grew to have immense admiration for their dedication and courage. They worked in very difficult and dangerous circumstances.

Getting from one place to the other was very difficult because there were so many hold-ups and roadblocks. On our way back from meeting with the Red Crescent our group had to leave our Red Cross vehicle and clamber across rubble to get from one side of a roadblock to another. Of course, this was what the local people had to do every day of the week.

When we visited Bethlehem (having been held up, at gunpoint, at a roadblock for quite a while) we were very shocked by what we saw. The evidence of destruction was everywhere – not a car to be seen that hadn't been overturned or burned out – and every house bore the scars of gunfire. Lamp posts were pushed over and used as see-saws by the ever-resilient children. Waste hadn't been collected for weeks. This particular visit was quite tense. The rules of travel for us (because of ongoing curfews) meant that the windows of the car had to be kept fully open at all times, the hazard lights flashing and the hands of all (non-driving) occupants of the front seats placed on the dashboard throughout the journey.

It was all very shocking, but our reason for being there was to assess the needs on the ground and, as I said at the time, 'to help prevent further innocent lives being lost, and to highlight the work of the

Red Cross to the Irish people and win their support for our appeal to help those who have already been injured'.

The single biggest sudden disaster since my involvement was the tsunami on St Stephen's Day 2004. This most horrendous event provoked huge sympathy from the Irish public and money simply poured in – €31 million to the Red Cross alone. This money was and continues to be put to very productive use. One example is a very successful project in Sri Lanka – a housing programme of sixty units, a school and a community hall in the suburbs of Colombo. The local authorities were very appreciative, as indeed were all the newly housed families. We continue to be involved in various ventures in Banda Aceh and parts of Indonesia.

In Malawi the Irish Red Cross has an outstanding and ongoing project sinking wells, bringing clean water to many thousands of people, which of course makes an enormous difference to their lives and general health. We are constantly in touch with our partner organisation in Malawi, monitoring the schemes.

All through the drama of the tsunami, the misery and horror of some African countries, and particularly Darfur, continued and continues. For some reason it is more difficult to raise funds for these disasters, although thousands of people are dying through no fault of their own. I suppose there is such a thing as donor fatigue, and the Irish people are so generous I can't blame them. However, I would love to see the eyes of the world turn to Darfur now to try to alleviate the misery that is daily life there. I am heartened to learn that the UN is now setting about establishing a multi-nation peace-keeping mission for Darfur. I look forward to seeing Ireland, with its strong peace-keeping record, becoming involved in this mission.

The most striking thing about the Irish Red Cross is the dedication of the people both at home and abroad. They are people of the very highest integrity and all the monies collected are spent in a culture of accountability, openness and compassion.

I was also appointed to an organisation now called Irish Aid, which is chaired by former TD Chris Flood, an excellent chairman. This is a government body which dispenses aid to various African countries and hopes to reach a figure, set by the UN, of 0.7% of GNP by 2012. The committee has an advisory capacity to the senior and junior ministers in the Department of Foreign Affairs. Apart from regular meetings, my function involves undertaking trips from time to time with some of my colleagues to oversee how the money is being spent and to examine new projects.

Another chairmanship I hold is that of the Remembrance Commission, which was given the remit to compensate the survivors and the dependants of the Dublin and Monaghan bombings. This process is ongoing, as some of the survivors continue to suffer the sometimes dreadful psychological and physical effects of those terrible events. I believe the commission works well, and I sometimes feel it is in a way a continuation of my work in Northern Ireland.

I like to think that my various involvements in humanitarian causes over the years has influenced my children to some extent. My eldest son, David, who is quite an unconventional character and a successful comedian, literally travelled the world in his twenties. At one stage, under the auspices of a priest he had met in Boston, he went to Peru where he worked on the construction of a community kitchen in a very remote village a couple of hours away from Lima. He would come in to Lima once a month, when we could phone him and find out how he was faring. He also tried to teach some local lads to play the guitar and put together a band so that they might make some money. However, he was a bit careless about the water he drank which resulted in an extreme case of dysentery. He had no choice but to leave after only a few months, as there was little medical care available there. However, his heart was in the right place.

My second son, Barry, now a TD, has shown a lot of interest in the developing world, particularly Africa, which he has visited five or six times. I am confident that he is serious about the increased commitment we need to make to those so much less fortunate than ourselves.

Number three is my daughter Mary. Her humanitarian interest was here in Ireland and her support for Women's Aid. She has been very involved in various fundraising events, including some exhausting-sounding sponsored cycles and a sponsored trip to the Middle East. She has shown herself a very successful fundraiser. She hasn't been able to do much in recent times due to a very lively son and a demanding job in fashion PR and event management.

Next is Sinead, and she is probably the one who has got the bug the strongest. She has worked for various NGOs – first with Concern, where she had responsibility for a refugee camp in Tanzania just after the Rwandan massacres. Then she went with GOAL to Calcutta, where she was looking after street children. Her next posting abroad was post-tsunami to Sri Lanka and from there she went on to Kenya, again with GOAL, where she was country director. She now works with the UN in New York.

Finally Claire, just qualified in medicine, spent two of her summers as a student working in hospitals in Africa. Two years ago she was particularly taken with a very remote and primitive hospital she worked in in Malawi She so admired both the people and a very dedicated English doctor who ran the hospital that on her return she decided to run the marathon to make money for the hospital. She collected just over €4,000.

I can't begin to claim all the credit, but my children certainly all grew up knowing that there is a lot of misery and suffering in the world. And I have to admit that my family are not at all unique. It is very striking how many young Irish people opt to give their time to work in areas of deprivation. Any young person who decides to do this (and it is important to say that it doesn't suit everyone) benefits enormously from it. I hope I won't be accused of chauvinism if I say that is a particularly Irish thing and something of which I am very proud.

What did I achieve in my almost forty years in public life? Really, that is up to others to assess because one cannot objectively measure one's own contribution. I *can* say what I involved myself in over my four decades as a TD but only others can judge whether my presence tended towards good or ill. I came through public life relatively unscathed and with my reputation intact.

I consider it an achievement that I passed the judgement of the people eleven times when I presented myself before them for election – and topped the poll in a third of those contests. That was certainly one of the highlights of my career and I am very grateful to the generations of good people in Dún Laoghaire-Rathdown for granting me the honour of being their representative and placing their faith in me. I took some vital decisions at vital times and I feel that my capacity to make decisions was a strength on my part. They may not in every single instance have been the absolutely right decisions but at least they were made and that was important.

From my first period as Foreign Minister, my work on Somalia stands out as the high point – the fact that I went there on my own and against departmental advice, acting on instinct. My action influenced the President, who in turn went to the UN, and then things really began to move. It was such a tragedy the way things turned out there in the end but I have no regret about trying to do something about an awful situation.

During my second term in Foreign Affairs, being associated with the Good Friday Agreement was a great honour and privilege. Seeing East Timor achieve independence was so satisfying, and securing Ireland a place on the UN Security Council left me with a sense of a job well done.

I would like to think that I served my constituents well and that I left them with a few decent benefits, not least in terms of the infrastructural development of Dún Laoghaire itself, most particularly the harbour area.

I expressed my own opinion within the party rules as I saw fit, and paid for that with banishment to the political wilderness for some fourteen years – a large slice out of my political career. I didn't get on with Charles Haughey but at the same time I never criticised him openly, as I felt it would be wrong to snipe publicly at the party leader while remaining on in the party. When he was Taoiseach he asked me to do things from time to time and I responded positively to those requests.

I hope I played a constructive role in combating miscarriages of justice and also in relation to human rights abuses.

It seems fashionable to quote Shakespeare on one's retirement. Mr Haughey quoted Othello to the effect that he had done the State some service – which indeed he had.

Another Shakespearean principle that I often thought of during my public life comes from a few lines in *The Merchant of Venice*: 'How far that little candle throws his beams! So shines a good deed in a naughty world.' I hope I performed at least some good deeds during my long political career.

INDEX

A

Abbey Theatre, 23
abortion, 97, 199–201, 250–2
Adams, Gerry, 203, 272, 275, 276
Africa, 313, 314. *see also* Rwanda; Somalia
Agriculture, Department of, 223
Ahern, Bertie, 49, 87, 101, 104, 171, 175, 182, 183–4, 188, 214, 215, 241, 243, 249, 252, 255, 256, 301, 304
    Gilmartin, and, 302
    Good Friday Agreement, 278–80, 285
    leader of Fianna Fáil, 246–7, 249, 250
    Northern talks (1997–98), 272, 273, 274, 275, 278
    personal characteristics, 247–8
    personal life, 184
    political donations, speech on, 254
    presidential elections 1997, 261, 262, 263–4
    Sheedy affair, 303
    Taoiseach (1997), 257
Ahern, Dermot, 144, 258, 259, 307
Ahern, Liam, 52
Ahern, Miriam, 247
Aideed, Mohamed Fareh, 220–1
Aiken, Frank, 20, 21, 47
Aiken, Maudie, 21
Air Corps, 219
Airfield Farm (Dundrum), 6
Algeria, 142
Algiers, 274
Alliance Party, 271, 272
Allied Irish Banks, 81, 303
American Rangers, 221
American University (Beirut), 137, 138
Amman (Jordan), 141
Amnesty International, 120, 124
Amsterdam Treaty, 286–7
An Evil Cradling (Keenan), 137
Anderson, Ann, 293, 294
Andrews, Annette (D.'s wife), 12, 16, 17, 21, 22, 25, 26–7, 36, 38, 39, 44, 53, 54, 66, 69, 71, 77, 78, 79, 87, 145, 155, 168, 179–80, 185, 186, 187, 188, 189, 197, 250, 258, 273, 274, 310
    electoral campaigning, 28, 29, 30, 31, 44, 67
    Foreign Affairs meetings, 288, 289–92
    trips abroad, 192–6, 197–8, 307–8
Andrews, Barry (D.'s son), 41, 42, 168, 234, 306, 310, 313
Andrews, Bernadette, 30
Andrews, C. S. 'Todd' (D.'s father), 1–2, 4, 7, 41–2, 60, 86
    autobiography, 19, 21
    Catholic Church, and, 1–2
    de Valera, and, 40
    political activities and interests, 19–23, 27, 66–7, 155
    republicanism, 22, 23
Andrews, Catherine, 1, 33
Andrews, Christopher, 1, 7
Andrews, Christopher (Niall's son), 30
Andrews, Claire (D.'s daughter), 71, 233, 314
Andrews, David
    childhood and early years: Dundrum, 1–6; summers in Carraroe, 6–8; early work, 16–18
    education, 8–10, 11, 15–16
    election campaigns, 18, 19–24, 28–34. *see also* Dún Laoghaire–Rathdown constituency
    Foreign Affairs ministry, 186–209, 216–17, 267–300. *see also* Foreign Affairs ministry
    friendships, 58, 71, 76–7
    Haughey, relationship with. *see under* Haughey, Charles
    humanitarian causes *see* Birmingham Six; East Timor;
        Guildford Four; humanitarian causes; Maguire Seven
    legal career. *see* legal practice
    marriage and family, 25–7, 38–9, 40, 41, 48, 52, 53, 54, 58–9, 71, 87, 88, 310, 313–14
    Northern Ireland talks. *see* peace process
    political career: Dáil deputy (1965), 32–6; Chief Whip, 48–55, 57; Parliamentary Secretary, 53; Opposition (1973–77), 57–67; Minister of State, 70–2; backbencher, 78, 80–4, 99–100; New Ireland Forum, 146–8; conflict within FF, 149–55; divorce referendum, 156–8; Foreign Affairs ministry, 186–209, 216–17; hospital confinement and Dáil vote (1986), 178–80; Defence and Marine ministry, 65, 217, 218–26, 258; Foreign Affairs ministry, 267–300; retirement from politics, 306–10, 315
    sports interests, 10–13
Andrews, David (D.'s son), 38–9, 58–9, 180, 313
Andrews, Hugh, 1, 7
Andrews, Mary (D.'s daughter), 48, 85, 87, 313
Andrews, Mary (D.'s mother), 2–3, 5, 6, 7, 36, 41
    political interests and activities, 19, 20, 22, 23, 27
Andrews, Niall (D.'s brother), 1, 3, 15, 30, 60, 67–8, 103, 120, 121, 123, 138, 155, 233
    election to Dáil, 66, 67
Andrews, Sinéad (D.'s daughter), 52, 53, 54, 187, 313–14
Anglo-Irish Agreement (1985), 117, 153–4, 159, 228
Anglo-Irish Division (Foreign Affairs), 46, 274
Anglo-Irish Inter-Parliamentary Union, 114
Anglo-Irish relations, 63, 97, 202, 207
Anglo-Irish summit (1980), 83
Anglo-Irish Treaty (1921), 19
Annan, Kofi, 288, 293
Anne, Princess, 215
Aontacht Éireann, 62
Arabian Nights, 143
Arabs, 143, 144
Arafat, Yasser, 311
Áras an Uachtaráin, 40, 60, 169, 187
arms crisis (1970), 38, 44–9, 56, 75
Armstrong, Patrick, 113, 120
army, 218, 219, 220, 288
Army Equitation School, 219
Arnold, Bruce, 100
Articles 2 and 3 (Irish Constitution), 271–2, 282–3, 300
Assen, David, 124
Australia, 196–7, 292, 295, 296
Austria, 292
Avon and Somerset Constabulary, 117

B

Baghdad (Iraq), 140, 141
Baidoa (Somalia), 198, 220
Baile na hAbhann, Co. Galway, 230, 231
Bailey, Michael, 258–9, 260
Baker, James, 193
Ballybrack, Co. Dublin, 65, 85
Ballybrack Housing Co-op, 61
Ballyjamesduff, Co. Cavan, 25–6
Banotti, Mary, 265
Bar, the, 18. *see also* Law Library
Bar Council, 250
Barcelona (Spain), 195
Barrett, Seán, 85, 180
Barrington, Donal, 238
Barry, Oliver, 165, 166

Barry, Peter, 106
    and Birmingham Six, 112, 113, 114, 117, 118, 127, 128,
        129
BBC, 15
BBC Northern Ireland, 272
beef industry, 175
Beef Tribunal, 209–10, 230, 235–6, 237, 238
Behan, Hettie, 51
Behan sisters (Monkstown), 39
Beirut (Lebanon), 137
Belfast, 45, 108, 109, 134, 206, 271
Belgrave Square, Dublin, 26
Belo, Bishop, 296
Benchers' Society, 18
Benn, Tony, 111
Berry, Peter, 47
Bethlehem, 311
Bhreathnach, Niamh, 231
Biden, Joseph, 124
Biggs-Davison, Sir John, 111, 136
Birmingham bombings (1974), 107–8, 110, 111
Birmingham Six, 100, 107–30, 162, 273
    campaign, 110–30
    compensation, 132–3
    Court of Appeal hearings, 113–14, 115, 118, 128–9, 132
    quashing of convictions, 129, 132
    re-categorisation (1989), 121, 122
    release of prisoners, 129, 131
    smear campaign, 131
    Washington hearings (1990), 124
Black Hawk Down, 221
black market, 5
Blackrock, Co. Dublin, 27, 61
Blair, Tony, 136–7, 292
    multi-party talks, and, 270, 278, 279, 280, 285
Blake, Bruce St John, 28
Blaney, Harry, 257
Blaney, Neil, 36, 37, 39, 40–1, 43, 44, 50, 73, 120, 160
    arms crisis, 45, 46, 47, 48, 49
Bloody Sunday (1920), 19
Boland, F.H. (Freddie), 23–4
Boland, Hazel, 85
Boland, John, 194
Boland, Kevin, 37, 39, 41, 61–2
    arms crisis, 45, 47, 48, 49
Boomtown Rats, 88
Booterstown, Co. Dublin, 30
Booth, Lionel, 29, 32, 33, 37, 43
Borill, Richard, 131
Bosnia-Herzegovina, 288
Boutros-Ghali, Boutros, 199
Bradford, Paul, 140, 142
Brady, Seán, 28, 29, 33
Brady, Vincent, 179, 180, 213
Brannigan, Dick, 9, 63
Brennan, Carmel, 189, 268
Brennan, Joe, 45, 189, 289
Brennan, Maureen, 255
Brennan, Seamus, 90, 101–2, 152, 153, 210, 213, 257, 309
Briscoe, Ben, 77, 101, 104, 105
British army, 134
British Government, 46, 203
    Birmingham Six case, 107, 111, 120, 125, 126, 129, 132,
        133, 137
    Guildford Four and Maguire Seven cases, 112, 113, 114,
        115, 116–17, 120, 136–7
    multi-party talks (1997–98), 277, 278
British intelligence, 97
British-Irish Parliamentary Body, 112, 128
British judicial system
    miscarriages of justice, 131–2, 133. see also Birmingham
        Six; Guildford Four; Maguire Seven

British Legion, 134
British royal family, 215
Brooke, Peter, 302
Brosnan, Sean, 218
Brown, Willie, 11
Browne, Aidan, 28
Browne, Vincent, 265
Brugha, Cathal, 19
Brussels, 70, 82, 199, 208, 225, 285
Bruton, John, 89, 213, 249, 253, 264–5, 265–6
Bryan, Tommy, 16
Buckingham Palace, visit to, 307–8
Buncrana, Co. Donegal, 284
Bungalow Bliss (Fitzsimmons), 170
Burke, Anne, 79
Burke, Ray, 79, 98, 164–5, 165, 166, 170, 175, 181, 184, 188,
        210, 213, 249, 253, 267, 300–1
    Foreign Affairs ministry, 257, 258, 259
    payments controversy, 258–9, 260, 261, 300–1
    resignation (1997), 264–5
Burke, Richard, 92
Bush, Barbara, 193
Bush, George Sr., 124, 193
Butler, Ada, 29
Butler, Larry, 255
Butler, Nóirín (Ní Scoláin), 62
Butler, Paul, 27
Butler, Seán, 27, 28, 62
Byrne, David, 287
Byrne, Gay, 217
Byrne, Mary, 28

C

Cahill, Bernie, 176
Cahill, Liam, 229
Cahirciveen, Co. Kerry, 63
Calcutta (India), 314
Callaghan, Hugh, 108, 109, 115, 121, 122, 123, 126, 127,
        128, 132
Callaghan, Leybourne ('Callaghan of India'), 13
Calleary, Sean, 11
Cambodia, 295
campaigning. see elections
Canada, 293
Caribbean, 298
Carlisle Pier, Dún Laoghaire, 65
Carr, Bunny, 247
Carraroe, Co. Galway, 6–8
Carty, Michael, 38
Carysfort College, 176
Casement Aerodrome (Baldonnel), 219
Casey, Bishop Eamon, 194
Cassidy, Donie, 233–4
Catholic Church, 1, 2, 14, 35, 251
Catholics, 16, 20, 44, 72
Cayman Islands, 261
censorship, 14
Central Remedial Clinic, Dublin, 99
Century, 165, 166
Charles, Prince, 215
Chief Justice, 238, 239
Chief Whip, 48–55, 57
Chien, Frederick, 226
Childers, Erskine, 20, 21–2, 25, 47, 58–60
Childers, Erskine, Jr, 60
Childers, Rita, 59–60
China, 12–13, 226, 294
Christian Brothers, 8, 9
Church of Ireland, 5
CIÉ, 2, 41, 253
cinema, 3

circus, 4
Cistercians, 9
Citizen Defence Committees (Northern Ireland), 44
Civil War (1922–23), 1, 19, 21, 22, 23, 36, 171
Clarke, David, 124
Clarke, Sr. Sarah, 133–4, 135
Clarke, Tom, 113, 115
Cleary, Ruth, 193
clerical abuse, 14
    Smyth and Duggan cases, 240–5, 249
clinics, 98–9
Clinton, Bill, 270, 281
Club of Twenty Two, 95, 177
Cluskey, Frank, 52, 113
coalition governments. see Fianna Fáil–Labour coalition
    (1992–94); Fianna Fáil–PD coalitions; Fine Gael–
    Labour Coalitions; rainbow coalition
Coffey, Betty, 167–8, 212
Cogan, Frank, 192
Cogan, Pauline, 192
Coláiste Mhuire, Parnell Square, 8–9
Cold Blood: the Massacre of East Timor (TV documentary), 295
Colley, George, 34, 39, 40, 41, 44, 69, 70, 73, 81, 89, 184
    characteristics, 74, 75, 149
    death (1983), 149
    leadership contest (1979), 74–7
Colley, Mary, 75, 77
Collingwood Cup, 11
Collins, Gerry, 71, 102, 125, 140, 143, 144, 170, 175, 176,
    184, 187, 188, 189, 213
Collins, Hillary, 143, 187, 188, 192
Collins, Michael, 19
Collins Barracks, Dublin, 53
commercial radio and television, 165
Commission on Security Co-operation in Europe (CSCE),
    125
Concern, 198, 290, 313
Condon, Colm, 80
Congressional Human Rights Caucus (Washington), 124
Conlon, Gerard, 113, 114, 120, 124, 127, 134
Conlon, Patrick 'Giuseppe,' 112, 113, 134, 135
Connacht League, 11
Connacht rugby team, 11
Connemara, Co. Galway, 6–8
Connolly, Paddy, 92–3
Conrad, Joseph, 203
Conroy, Richard, 159, 160
Conservatives (Britain), 111, 134, 202
constituency work, 33–4, 61, 65–6, 69, 98–9
Constitution of Ireland, 200
    abortion referenda (1992), 200–1
    Articles 2 and 3, 271–2, 282–3, 300
    divorce, 156–8, 252
Constitutional Committee, 34–5, 39, 158
contraception, 46, 59, 62, 72, 150
Cook, Robin, 286, 292
Cooke, Dennis, 205
Cooney, Garret, 16
Cooney, Paddy, 58
Corcoran, Tony, 11
Corcoraya, Enrique and Anna, 196
Corish, Brendan, 58
Cork Celtic, 10
Cork Hibs, 10
Cornelscourt, Co. Dublin, 85
Cosgrave, Liam, 31, 43, 55, 63, 64, 68, 85, 301
    coalition government (1973–77), 62–4, 68
Cosgrave, Liam Jr., 301
Cosgrave, Vera, 68, 301
Costello, Lt.-General Michael Joe, 22
Costello family, 18
Coughlan, Clem, 102

Council of Europe, 70–1
Council of Foreign Ministers. see European Community/Union
Court of Appeal (England), 136
    Birmingham Six case. see Birmingham Six
Cowen, Brian, 10, 188, 211, 215, 237, 244, 246, 263, 306–7
Cox, Pat, 171
Coyle, Donny, 15, 152
Coyle, Eithne, 2
Coyle, Mary (D.'s mother). see Andrews, Mary
Coyle, Nancy, 2
Coyle, Nora, 2
Coyle, Roisín, 15
Coyle, Rosemary, 2
Coyle family, 19
Cranfield, Brigadier-General Patrick, 219
Cresson, Édith, 287
cricket, 207
Criminal Justice Act 1967, 42
Crowley, Bishop (London), 128
Crown Prosecution Service, 127
Cruel Fate (Callaghan), 123
Cuba, 299
Culliton, Gerry, 9
Cumann na mBan, 19
currachs, 6
Currie, Austin, 174
Cusack, Fr. Aidan, 9
Cusack, Annette (D.'s wife). see Andrews, Annette
Cusack, Mary, 268
Cusack, Paddy, 25–6
Cusack, Paddy (Pete Briquette), 88
Cusack, Peggy, 25

D

Dagenham, Essex, 17
Dáil Éireann, 6, 18, 32–3, 34
Birmingham Six campaign, and, 112, 113, 114, 118
    elections to. see general elections
    pairing, 178–9
    salary, 33
    secretaries, 36
Dalton, Tim, 275, 280
Danagher, Gerry, 152
Darfur, 312
Dargan, Michael, 303
Davern, Noel, 177
de Brún, Bairbre, 284
de Courcy Ireland, John, 99
De La Salle football club, 12
de Valera, Eamon, 19, 21, 40, 51, 58, 148, 164
de Valera, Síle, 76, 265
de Valera, Sinead, 40
de Valera, Terry, 40
Deane, Joe and Fran, 186–7
decommissioning, 281, 285
Defence, Department of, 218, 268
Defence, Parliamentary Secretary for, 53
Defence and Marine ministry, 65, 217, 218–26, 237, 238
Defence Forces, 219
Delors, Jacques, 290
Democratic Left, 214, 234, 249, 288
Democratic Unionist Party. see DUP
Dempsey, Noel, 173, 176, 177, 188, 213, 215, 237, 244, 246
Denham, Susan, 239
Denmark, 290
Denning, Lord, 110
Derby Justice for All Campaign, 132
Derry, 45, 108, 109
Desmond, Barry, 38, 169
Desmond, Dermot, 175
Devlin, Lord, 136

Devon and Cornwall police inquiry, 115, 125, 126, 127, 128
Diana, Princess, 215
Dili (East Timor), 295
Dillon, James, 35–6
divorce, 35, 46, 156–8, 252
Dockrell, Percy, 31
Dodds, Nigel, 284
Doherty, Seán, 74, 93, 100, 104, 105, 149–50, 180–1
　Nighthawks interview (1992), 181
Dóilín, Carraroe, 7
dole, 8
Donaldson, Jeffrey, 275, 276, 281
Donegan, Mary, 63
Donegan, Paddy, 62–3
Donnelly, Brian, 124
Donoghue, David, 274
Dooley, Johnny, 11
Dorr, Noel, 112, 190
Dowling, Joe, 49
Downing Street Declaration (1993), 227–8
Dowra affair, 93
Doyle, P.V., 303
Drumcondra football club, 4
Dublin and Monaghan bombings, 313
Dublin bombings, 5, 55
Dublin Castle, 147, 288, 289
Dublin Made Me (C.S. Andrews), 19
Dublin Schoolboys' League, 4, 10
Dublin West by-election (1982), 92
Duffy, Joyce, 41
Duggan case, 242, 243, 244, 245, 249
Duignan, Seán, 231, 236
Duke, Ann, 268
Dukes, Alan, 161–2, 173
Dún Laoghaire–Rathdown constituency, 27, 40, 58, 60, 61,
　62, 65–6, 85, 314
　car ferry terminal, 65
　development, 65–6
　divorce referendum (1986), 158
　election campaigns, 28–34, 42–3, 67–8, 84–6, 89, 97, 98,
　　99, 159, 167–9, 211–12, 254–5
　Haughey, and, 60, 84–5, 89
　liberal views, 42, 97
　marina, 65
Dundon, Bernard (Bernie), 4
Dundrum, Co. Dublin, 1, 3–6, 10, 20
　Fianna Fáil cumann, 20, 24, 27
Dunlop, Frank, 301
Dunne, Ben Jr., 163, 166, 253, 254, 303
DUP (Democratic Unionist Party), 202, 205, 284, 285
　political talks (1996–98), 268, 270, 276, 277, 281
Durham jail (England), 135
Durkan, Bernard, 113

E

East Timor, 221, 294–7, 315
East Timor–Ireland Solidarity Campaign, 295
Easter Rising 1916, 52, 103
Economic Planning and Development, Department of, 69
Economist, 161
economy, 68, 69, 73, 83, 86, 87, 89, 92, 95, 97, 158–9,
　160–1, 165, 211, 216, 304
Edinburgh, 292
EU summit (1992), 214–15
Education, Department of, 160–1
Edward, Prince, 307, 308
Eksund, 162
elections. see also European elections; general elections;
　presidential elections
　campaigning, 28–32, 43–4, 56–7, 64, 67–8, 84–6, 88–9,
　　97–8, 99, 159–60, 167–9

'Haughey factor,' 84, 89
　personal literature, 168–9
electrification, 14
Elizabeth, Queen, 215, 307
Elleman-Jensen, Uffe, 208, 290
Ellis, John, 177
embassies, 191
Emergency period (1939–45), 5
emigration, 8, 13, 14
Empey, Sir Reg, 275
Enniskillen bomb (1987), 162, 163
Error of Judgment (C. Mullin), 112
Ervine, David, 272, 275, 276
ESB, 212
Ethiopia, 299
Euro-Atlantic Partnership Council, 288
European Assembly Elections Bill, 73
European Commission, 287
European Community/Union, 70, 71, 195, 208–9, 214–15,
　258, 285–8, 296
　Amsterdam Treaty, 286–7
　Council of Foreign Ministers, 125, 208; informal
　　weekends, 289–92
　Partnership for Peace initiative, 287–8
European Council, 199
European Court of Human Rights, 119, 120
European elections, 73, 166, 181, 233–5, 265
European Parliament, 73, 121, 286, 287. see also European
　elections
Evening Herald, 85
Evening Press, 52
Ewart Biggs, Christopher, 62
External Affairs, Department of, 46. see further Foreign
　Affairs, Department of
extradition, 115, 162–3

F

FA Cup Final, 194
Fahey, Jackie, 74
Fahey, Noel, 200
FAI, 12
Falintil, 294
Falklands War (1982), 92
family planning. see contraception
Farmers' Journal, 100
farmers' taxation, 73
Farr, Sir John, 111
Faul, Fr. Denis, 110
Faulkner, Pádraig, 45, 69, 90, 95
federal Ireland, 46
Federation of Irish Societies in Britain, 116
Fianna Fáil, 6, 19, 20, 24, 27, 28, 37, 113, 114, 288. see also
　Dún Laoghaire–Rathdown constituency
　'ABA' faction, 262, 263
　anti-Haughey camp, 82
　ardfheiseanna, 45, 61, 81–2
　arms crisis (1970), 44–9, 56
　Articles 2 and 3, 283
　business interests, and, 41
　coalition governments. see also Fianna Fáil–Labour
　　coalition (1992–94); Fianna Fáil–PD coalitions;
　　negotiations, 169–71, 214–16
　contraception, policy on, 62, 72, 150
　'Country and Western wing,' 175, 181
　election campaigns, 34, 42–3, 56–7, 68, 72, 89–90
　extradition, and, 162–3
　finances, 248; Taca fundraising, 40–1
　'gang of 22,' 95, 177
　general elections. see general elections
　Haughey era, 77, 78–82, 148, 149, 150–1, 154, 155, 183,
　　248, 254; departure of Haughey (1992), 181–2, 183

internal conflict, 151–2
leaders. see Ahern, Bertie; Haughey, Charles; Lynch, Jack; Reynolds, Albert
leadership contests, 39–40, 74–8, 90–1, 93–6, 101–6, 175, 176–7, 181–2, 183–5
New Ireland Forum, 146, 147, 148
Northern policy, 45, 46, 47, 70, 75, 97–8, 147, 148, 153
O'Malley's expulsion, 150–1
payments to politicians controversy. see payments to politicians
presidential elections. see presidential elections
unity, 44, 49, 248
Young Turks, 36
Fianna Fáil–Labour coalition (1992–94), 216, 227
breakdown of trust, 237–8
Labour withdrawal, 248–9
Reynolds' resignation, 245, 246
Smyth and Duggan cases, 240–5, 249
tensions, 229–35, 236–45
Fianna Fáil National Executive, 59, 170
Fianna Fáil–PD coalitions, 170–1, 173, 257, 259–60, 301
abortion issue, 199–201
Beef Tribunal, 209–11
controversies and scandals, 175–6, 209–11, 299–304
Finance, Department of, 82
financial matters, 33. see also economy; payments to politicians
Taca fundraising, 40–1
Fine Gael, 9, 16, 18, 20, 29, 31, 36, 40, 43, 49, 50, 51, 52, 55, 57, 73, 84, 85, 87, 88, 89, 90, 92, 97, 99, 106, 113, 114, 129, 140, 147, 152, 158, 162, 165, 174, 178, 180, 194, 200, 211, 213, 214, 231, 235, 249, 265, 273, 288, 301
coalition governments. see Fine Gael–Labour coalitions; rainbow coalition
general elections. see general elections
'Tallaght Strategy,' 161–2
Fine Gael–Labour coalitions, 56, 57, 62–4, 68, 86, 87, 88, 89, 90, 99–100, 169
(1982–87), 156, 158
Finland, 292
Finlay, Fergus, 229–30, 236, 249
Finucane, Marian, 217
First Tuesday (ITV), 114
Fischer, Joschka, 285–6
fishing, 16
fishing industry, 65, 223, 224, 225
Fitt, Lord, 136
FitzGerald, Garret, 49, 86–7, 89, 97, 99, 112, 148, 152, 153, 172, 173, 228
Fitzgerald, Gene, 82
FitzGerald, Joan, 87
Fitzgerald, Liam, 176
Fitzpatrick, Tom, 31
Fitzsimons, Eoghan, 241, 242, 243, 244
Fitzsimons, Jack, 170
Fitzsimons, Jim, 233, 234
Flanagan, Oliver J., 50, 164, 178, 179, 180
Flood, Chris, 312
Flood Tribunal, 301
Flynn, Errol, 3
Flynn, Pádraig, 74, 165, 166, 170, 171, 174, 175, 176, 177, 181, 191, 195, 202, 213, 214
Late Late Show appearance (1999), 287, 301–2
NI talks (1992), 203, 204, 206, 207
Flynn family (Castlebar), 195
food rationing, 5
football, 4, 10–13, 16, 17, 194, 206, 290
For the Record (Lenihan), 173
Foreign Affairs, Department of, 70, 71–2, 76, 82, 112, 114, 132, 190–1, 257, 258, 265–6, 274, 312. see also Foreign Affairs ministry

Anglo-Irish Division, 46, 274
Foreign Affairs Committee, 139
Foreign Affairs ministry, 186–99, 267–300, 315
Andrews' appointments: (1992), 186–91; (1997), 267–8
Burke's resignation (1997), 264–5
entertaining, 288–9
European affairs, 208–9, 214–15, 285–8
foreign trips, 192–9, 274, 288–300
high points, 315
informal weekends, 289–92
Northern Ireland talks, 202–7, 268–85
Presidential visits, 199, 292–3, 307–8
protocol and security, 195
UN Security Council, 297–300
Foreign and Commonwealth Office (London), 204
Forever Lost, Forever Gone (Hill), 133
Fox, Mildred, 257
Foxrock, Co. Dublin, 85
French, 287, 290
Full Sutton prison (England), 121
fundraising, 40–1

G

GAA, 11
Gadaffi, Colonel, 138, 144
Gaeltacht, Department of the, 230
Gaeltacht (Connemara), 6–8
Gallagher, Dermot, 274, 280
Gallagher, Pat the Cope, 113
Gallagher, Patrick, 303
Galway, 15, 64
Galwegians Rugby Club, 11
Gama, Jaime, 286
gang of five, 74
gang of twenty two, 95, 177
Garda Síochána, 14, 54, 163
Gartree prison (England), 121, 122, 125
Garvey, Michael, 225
general elections
1960s: 1965, 27–8; 1969, 42–3
1970s: 1973, 55, 56, 62; 1977, 67–8, 72
1980s: 1981, 84–7; 1982, 88–90, 97–9; 1987, 158–60; 1989, 165–9
1990s: 1992, 211–13; 1997, 254–7
2002, 309, 310
Geneva, 293
Genscher, Hans-Dieter, 208, 209, 285, 290
Geoghegan, Johnny, 6, 64
Geoghegan-Quinn, Máire, 6, 64, 171, 175, 176, 230–1, 242, 246
Germany, 209, 286
Gervin, Gerry, 218, 268
Gibbons, Jim, 38, 39, 47, 72, 78, 90, 96
Gibraltar killings, 120
Gifford, Lord, 124
Gildea, Eamon, 119
Gillespie sisters, 135
Gilmartin, Tom, 166, 302
Gilmore, Fr. Bobby, 194
Gilmore, Eamon, 99
Glasgow Rangers, 206
Gleeson, Carmel, 37, 43
Gleeson, Tony, 222
Glenart Avenue, Blackrock, 88
Glenmalure Park, Milltown, 10
Glennon, Chris, 274
GOAL, 237, 314
Gogan, Dickie, 52
Gogarty, James, 259, 260
Good and Murray, 80

Good Friday Agreement (1998), 203, 278–85, 300, 315
  multi-party talks (1997–98), 268–85
Goodman, Larry, 303
Goodman affair, 175, 210. *see also* Beef Tribunal
Gormanston Military Camp, Co. Meath, 45
Goulding, Lady Valerie, 99
Granada Television, 111, 113
Great Wall (China), 294
Greece, 286, 291
Greencore, 175, 176
Gregory, Tony, 91, 97, 120
Guardian, 110, 129
GUBU period, 91, 92, 93
Guerin, Brendan, 11
Guildford and Woolwich bombings (1974), 113, 117, 134
Guildford Four, 108, 113, 114, 115, 116–17, 118, 119, 121,
  124, 131, 136
  quashing of convictions (1989), 120
Guildford Four Relatives' Committee, 114, 116
Guinness, Jennifer, 163
Gulf War, 140, 194
Gusmao, Xanana, 295, 296

H

H-Block hunger strike, 84, 86
Hall's Pictorial Weekly (RTÉ television), 64
Halonen, Tarja, 292
Hamilton, Liam, 235–6, 238, 239, 250
Hammam Hotel, Dublin, 19
Hammond, Owen, 99
Hanafin, Des, 254–5
Hanafin, Mary, 254–5, 256, 310
Hand, Michael, 17
Hanley, Jeremy, 202
Harcourt Street line, 2, 40
Hardiman, Adrian, 152
Harkin, Henry, 28
Harney, Mary, 113, 152, 153, 154, 169, 182, 250, 259, 301,
  303
Harris, Eoghan, 274
Harris, 'Pino,' 176
Hartnett, Hugh, 152
Harvey, Mary, 86
Harvey, William (Bill), 85, 86, 99
Hatfield House (England), 290
Haughey, Charles, 36, 41, 43, 68–9, 99, 121, 141, 159, 173,
  177, 178, 188, 189, 210, 247, 248, 315
  Anglo-Irish summit (1980), 83
  ardfheiseanna, 81–2
  arms crisis, 45–8, 49
  challenges to leadership of, 90–1, 93–6, 101–6, 175,
    176–7, 181–2
  coalition negotiations with PDs (1989), 169–71
  contraception legislation, 72
  controversies and scandals, 100–1, 104–5, 164, 175–6,
    181–2, 253, 254, 260–1, 301, 303–4
  David Andrews, and, 60–1, 100, 106, 107, 146, 212, 315
  divorce bill, and, 156
  Dún Laoghaire, and, 60, 84, 85, 89
  economy, and, 87–8, 89, 160–1
  Falklands War, and, 92
  finances and lifestyle, 80–1, 164, 166, 253; payments
    controversy, 253, 254, 260–1, 301; Tribunal
    revelations, 303–4
  GUBU period, 91, 92, 93
  leadership of Fianna Fáil (1979–92), 38, 39, 74–8,
    80–4, 107, 148–9, 150–2, 154, 155, 175;
    departure (1992), 182, 183
  New Ireland Forum, 146, 147, 148
  Northern policy, 44, 45, 148, 153
  phone-tapping controversy, 100–1, 104–5, 181–2

presidential style of government, 82–3, 171
return to front bench (1975), 61
'Rise and Follow Charlie,' 81–2
supporters, 74, 75, 76–8, 84, 93, 102, 103, 105, 171, 175,
  177, 184
Taoiseach, 160–1
wilderness years, 18
Haughey era (1979–92), 77, 78–9, 248
Haughey factor, 84, 89, 103
Haulbowline (Cork), 219
Hayes, Mary, 22
health cuts, 160, 166
Healy, Brendan, 4
Healy, Deborah (Debbie), 186, 189, 268, 309–10
Healy, Sean, 11
Healy-Rae, Jackie, 257
Hearne, Maurice, 17
Hefferon, Colonel Michael, 47
Hennessy, Jim, 121
Hennessy, J.J., 120
Herrema, Dr. Tiede, 163
Hezbollah, 137, 138
Higgins, Michael D., 139, 140–1, 142, 144, 230, 231
High Court
  Whelehan appointment, 239, 240, 243, 244, 245
Hill, Patrick (Paddy), 108, 109, 120, 121, 122, 123, 125, 126,
  127, 128, 129, 132, 133, 134
Hill, Paul, 113, 114, 117, 120, 121
Hillery, Brian, 167–8, 212
Hillery, Miriam, 168
Hillery, Paddy, 167, 169
Hilliard, Michael, 36
Home Office (London), 119, 120
Houphouët-Boigny, President, 57
House of Commons, 113
House of Congress (Washington), 124, 193
House of Lords, 110, 118
Howe, Sir Geoffrey, 114
Howlin, Brendan, 215, 244
Hudson's Bay Fur Company, London, 16
human rights, 293, 294
humanitarian causes, 107–45, 310–13, 315
  developing world, 139–45
  East Timor, 294–7
  Keenan, Brian, 137–8
  miscarriages of justice. *see* Birmingham Six; Guildford
    Four; Maguire Seven
Hume, Basil, archbishop of Westminster, 129, 136
Hume, John, 126, 147, 148, 203, 229, 262, 263, 272
Hume–Adams talks, 203, 272
Hunter, Gerard (Gerry), 108, 109, 115, 116, 119, 121, 122,
  123, 125, 127, 128, 132
Hunter, Sandra, 132–3
Hurd, Douglas, 112, 113, 114, 116, 117, 118, 290–1
Hutchinson, Billy, 276
Hyland, Liam, 103, 234
Hyland, Tom, 295, 296

I

IDA, 225
Independent Radio and Television Commission, 164–5
Independents, 28, 51, 52, 73, 86, 88, 90, 91, 129, 188, 257
India, 13, 314
Indian community (Dublin), 144, 145
Indonesia, 294, 295, 296
industrial relations, 35, 83
Inter-Parliamentary Union, 57
International Monetary Fund (IMF), 161
International Overseas Aid Division, 310
IRA, 1, 19, 22, 44, 46, 55, 107, 108, 116, 120, 121, 162, 177,
  203, 256, 269, 275. *see also* Birmingham bombings

(1974); Provisional IRA
  ceasefire (1994), 227, 228
  decommissioning, 281, 285
  kidnappings, 162, 163
  Libyan connection, 144
  restoration of ceasefire (1997), 260
  violence, 124
Iran, 138, 192–3
Iraq, 140, 141
Ireland House (Madrid), 297
Irish Aid, 312–13
Irish aid, 139, 299
Irish-Americans, 153, 193–4, 228
Irish Football Association, 206
Irish in Britain Representation Group (IBRG), 111
Irish Independent, 90, 100, 256
Irish language, 230–1
Irish League of Credit Unions, 304
Irish Marketing Surveys, 152
Irish News, 121
Irish Press, 17, 63, 100–1, 110, 113, 114
Irish Red Cross, 232, 310–12
Irish Sugar Company, 22
Irish Times, 118, 131, 134, 160, 172, 173, 180, 224, 249, 268
Israelis, 138, 139
Italy, 298
ITGWU, 81
ITV, 114
Iveagh House, 189, 190, 192, 267, 288, 289, 309. *see also*
  Foreign Affairs, Department of
Ivory Coast, 57

J

Jenkins, Roy, 136
Jersey cattle, 4, 5
JMSE (Joseph Murphy Structural Engineers), 166, 258, 260,
  300–1
John Paul II, pope, 136
Joint British–Irish Secretariat, 274
Joint Declaration (1993), 227–8
Jordanian Foreign Affairs Committee, 141
judicial appointments
  Whelehan controversy, 239–40, 243, 244, 245
junior ministries, 70
Justice, Department of, 71

K

Keating, Justin, 98
Kee, Robert, 113
Keenan, Brian, 137–8, 192
Keery, Neville, 43, 56, 60
Kelly, Cyril, 302
Kelly, Declan, 72, 191
Kelly, Frances, 24
Kelly, Captain James, 47
Kelly, John, 47, 52, 162, 174, 213
Kemmy, Jim, 86, 88
Kennedy, Geraldine, 100, 114, 118, 160, 169, 249
Kennedy, Joe, 121, 124
Kennedy, John F., 33
Kennedy, Martin, 28
Kennedy family (USA), 121
Kenny, Pat, 217
Kenya, 191, 221–2
Keogh, Helen, 160, 255
Kerry, 62, 63
Khmer Rouge, 295
kidnapping, 162, 163
Killilea, Mark, 59, 74

Killybegs Fishermen's Organisation, 223, 224
Kilmainham Gaol, Dublin, 19
King, Tom, 114
King's Inns, Dublin, 16, 18
Kinlen, Dermot, 62, 63
Kitt, Tom, 128
Kuwait, 194–5
Kwangami (Kenya), 221–2

L

Labour Court, 35, 83
Labour Party, 29, 31, 42, 52, 55, 56, 58, 73, 89, 90, 113, 114,
  147, 156, 158, 166, 174, 200, 211, 213, 229, 231, 234,
  235, 239, 240, 257, 288
  coalition governments. *see* Fianna Fáil–Labour coalition
    (1992–94); Fine Gael–Labour Coalitions; rainbow
    coalition
  elections. *see* general elections
  negotiations for government (1992), 214–16
Labour Party (Britain), 111
Lalor, Paddy, 233
Lamb, Charles, 7
Lamb, Katherine, 7
Lamb family (Carraroe), 7
Lannigan, Michael, 144
Lansdowne Road, Dublin, 203, 275
Lantos, Tom, 124
Lapland, 292
Larkin, Celia, 248
Late Late Show (RTÉ), 287, 301–2
Law Library, 18, 33, 50, 58, 80, 93, 152, 185, 186, 187, 197,
  229, 276
Lawlor, Liam, 175, 253
League of Ireland, 10
Lebanon, 137, 138
Lee, Joe, 39
legal practice, 17, 18, 33, 51, 58, 80, 81, 95, 96, 185, 186,
  249, 309
  Senior Counsel, 150
Leinster House, 34–44, 48, 96, 309. *see also* Dáil Éireann
  'characters,' 52
  conditions in 1960s, 36–7
Lemass, Seán, 14, 20, 22, 27–8, 31, 34–5, 36, 44, 51
  Northern policy, 34, 45
  retirement as Taoiseach (1966), 39
Leneghan, Joe, 50, 51–2
Lenihan, Ann, 169
Lenihan, Brian, 36, 37, 41, 81, 82, 83, 87, 102, 103, 114,
  115, 118, 153, 170, 182, 184, 203, 213, 214, 229, 234
  death (1995), 252
  presidential election campaign (1990), 169–74
  For the Record, 173
Lenihan, Brian Jr., 169, 259, 307
Lenihan, Conor, 169, 259
Lenihan, Paddy, 169
Lenihan family, 169
Leonard, Biddy, 6
Leonard, Eric, 56
Leonard, Julia, 6
Leonard, Mr. ('The Bird'), 6, 7
Leonard family (Carraroe), 6
L'Estrange, Gerry, 57–8
Leverett and Fry's grocery, Dundrum, 4, 22
Libya, 138, 144, 162
Linden Convalescent Home, 40
Lindsay, Patrick, 18
Linfield Football Club, 206
Little, Brenda, 92
Loftus, Seán Dublin-Bay–Rockall, 86, 88
Lohan, Larry, 160
London, 16–17, 194, 204, 290

Long Lartin Prison (England), 114, 121, 122, 126
Longford, 232
Longford–Roscommon constituency, 261
Lord's (London), 207
Lord's Resistance Party (Uganda), 139
Lough Mask, 16
Loughnane, Billy, 76, 96
Lowry, Michael, 253–4, 260
loyalist bombs in Dublin, 55
loyalists, 203, 206, 271, 276
Luxembourg, 291
Luykx, Albert, 47
Lydon, Don, 168
Lynch, Jack, 39, 40, 41, 42, 43, 44, 47, 55, 57, 59, 64, 67, 69,
    72, 80, 81, 99, 184, 301
  arms crisis, and, 47, 48, 49
  characteristics, 61
  Northern policy, 45, 46
  reinstatement of Haughey (1975), 61
  retirement from leadership (1979), 73, 76

M

Maastricht Treaty, 200, 216
Mac Eoin, Seán, 16, 20
Mac Intyre, Tom, 47
McAleese, Martin, 266, 293
McAleese, Mary, 262, 263, 265, 266, 293, 307–8
McAndrew, Pat, 132
MacArthur, Malcolm, 92
McAteer, Bean, 8
MacCabe, Rory, 191, 206, 229, 268, 276
McCabe, Terry, 11
McCaffrey, Mary, 114–15
McCann's field, Dundrum, 4
McCartan, Pat, 114, 117, 118
McCartan, Patrick, 20
McCarthy, John, 138
McCartney, Robert, 268
McCracken Tribunal, 253, 254, 260–1, 264
McCrea, Willie, 277
McCreesh, Raymond, 86
McCreevy, Charlie, 74, 88, 152–3, 177, 246, 263, 304–5
  challenges to Haughey's leadership, 93, 94, 95, 96, 103
McDade, James, 108
McDaid, Jim, 177–8
McDermott, Mr. (teacher), 17
McDonald, Edward, 159, 160
McDowell, Michael, 152, 174
McEllistrim, Tom, 74, 76
MacEntee, Seán, 39, 47, 94
McGarry, Seamus, 116
McGuinness, Martin, 275, 276, 282, 284, 285
McIlkenny, Kate and Maggie, 126
McIlkenny, Richard (Dick), 108, 109, 112, 115, 119, 121,
    122, 125, 127, 128
McKay, Robert, 124
McKernan, Padraic, 267–8
McManus, P.J., 232
MacNeill, Eoin, 152
MacNeill, Róisín, 152
MCreevy, Charlie, 214
MacSharry, Ray, 74, 90, 92, 100, 104, 160, 161, 180, 210,
    213, 263, 304
McWilliams, Monica, 277
Madrid (Spain), 195, 297
Magennis, Ken, 203, 275
Magill, 300
Magnier, John, 232
Maguire, Anne-Marie, 134
Maguire, Annie, 111, 112, 113, 114, 115, 133, 134–6
Miscarriage of Justice (1994), 134, 135

Maguire, Paddy, 134
Maguire, Patrick, 111
Maguire, Patrick Jr., 134, 135, 136
Maguire, Vincent, 134, 135
Maguire, Vincent and Patrick, 112
Maguire Seven, 100, 108, 111–12, 113, 114, 115, 117–18,
    120, 132–7
  quashing of convictions (1992), 136
Major, John, 202, 207, 227–8
Making the Peace (Mitchell), 268
Malawi, 312
Mallon, Seamus, 124, 147, 204–5, 275
Malone, Joe, 303
Man of No Property (C.S. Andrews), 19, 21
Mandela, Nelson, 294
Mandelson, Peter, 307
Manning, Maurice, 129
Mansergh, Martin, 82, 214, 242, 258, 274–5
Mao Tse Tung, 13
Mara, P.J., 74, 148–9, 254
Margaret, Princess, 215
Marine, Department of, 223–6
Marine Times, 224
Martin, Gus, 9
Martin Micheál, 307
Masterson, Bernadette, 116
Mauritania, 142
May, Sir John, 120, 136
Mayfair Hotel, London, 17
Mayhew, Sir Patrick (Paddy), 202, 205, 206
Maze prison, 271
media, 201, 272, 273–4
Mellon, Eddie, 4
Mellor, David, 112, 115, 117
The Merchant of Venice (Shakespeare), 315
Merriman, Lizzie, 5
Middle East, 139, 311–12, 313
militant republicanism, 45, 46. see also IRA
Military College, 218
military parades, review of, 53
Milner, Sue, 126
Minister for Foreign Affairs. see Foreign Affairs ministry
ministers of state, 70
Miscarriage of Justice (Maguire), 134, 135
miscarriages of justice, 107, 131–2, 315. see also Birmingham
    Six; Guildford Four; Maguire Seven
Mitchell, Andrew, 269
Mitchell, Gay, 273
Mitchell, George, 268–70, 274, 275, 277, 278, 279, 281, 284
Mitchell, Heather, 269
Mitchell, Jim, 235, 236
Mogadishu (Somalia), 140, 198, 220, 221
Mohamed, Ali Mahdi, 220
Molloy, Bobby, 34, 37, 70, 78, 149, 155, 156, 171, 182, 203,
    259
Molyneux, James, 202–3
Montgomery, David, 16
Montgomery, Gertie, 16
Montrose Hotel, Dublin, 181
Mooney, Paschal, 118, 120, 128
Moore, Eamon, 77–8
Moore, Joe, 77, 94, 95
Moran, Fanny, 16
Morgan, Dermot, 64, 195
Moriarty Tribunal, 264, 303
Morning Ireland (RTÉ), 263
Morocco, 142, 143
Morrison, Mary, 308
motor tax, abolition of, 68
Mowlam, Mo, 270–1, 278, 280
Muhammad Ali, 52–3
Mullin, Chris, 111, 112, 119, 129
Mulvey, Mary, 20

Murphy, Joseph Jr., 258
Murphy, Mary, 191
Murphy, Paul, 277, 278
Murray, Paul, 125, 126, 127, 128
Murray, Fr. Raymond, 110
Murrin, Joey, 223–4
Muscat (Oman), 194

N

Nairobi (Kenya), 199, 220, 221, 222
Nally, Derek, 265
Nangle, garda, 93
Nason, Brian, 289
national debt, 83, 87
nationalists, 44, 203, 266, 270, 271, 273, 275, 276
NATO, 287, 288
navy, 219
neutrality, 287
New Ireland Forum (1983–84), 146–9
New Ireland Forum Report (1984), 147, 157
New York (USA), 199, 298, 299
Ní Dhálaigh, Máirín, 62, 63
Nighthawks (RTÉ), 181
Nolan, M.J., 173, 176
Noonan, Michael, 100
Noonan, Michael J., 252
North–South agreement (1999), 307
North–South bodies, 272, 273, 279
North–South relations, 63, 277
North Strand, Dublin, bombings (1941), 5
Northern Ireland, 23, 34, 44, 45, 63–4, 70, 82, 83, 97, 147,
150, 202–7, 216, 307, 313 *see also* Good Friday
Agreement; IRA; loyalists; nationalists; peace process;
unionists
    Anglo-Irish Agreement (1985), 117, 153–4
    Downing Street Declaration (1993), 227–8
    Fianna Fáil policy, 45, 46, 47, 70, 75, 97–8, 147, 148, 153
    Hume–Adams talks, 203
    hunger strikes, 84, 86
    IRA ceasefire (1994), 227, 228
    Omagh bombing (1998), 284
    political talks: 1992, 203–7, 216; 1996–98, 268–82
    restoration of IRA ceasefire (1997), 260
    sectarianism, 45, 269, 270
    violence, 44–5, 53, 62, 108, 124, 203, 269, 284
Northern Ireland Executive, 278, 284, 285
Northern Ireland Office (NIO), 204, 278
Norton, Willie, 10
Norway, 298
nuclear disarmament, 300
Nuremore Hotel, Carrickmacross, 79

O

Ó Dálaigh, Aengus, 63
Ó Dálaigh, Cearbhall, 60, 62–3
Ó Flatharta, Peadar, 297
Ó Méalóid, Claire, 89
Ó Méalóid, Pádraig, 89
Ó Móráin, Micheál, 42, 47
Oakley Grove, Blackrock, 33, 88
O'Brien, Conor Cruise, 91, 98
O'Brien, Fergus, 194
O'Byrne and Fitzgibbon, tailors (Dublin), 20
O'Casey, Seán, 23
O'Connell, John, 188
O'Connell St., Dublin, 19, 20
O'Connor, Eugene, 15, 22
O'Connor, Pat, 91
O'Conor, John, 192

O'Dea, Willie, 177
Odeon Cinema, Dundrum, 3
O'Donnell, Brendan, 74
O'Donnell, Liz, 259, 274, 286, 299
O'Donoghue, Eilis, 255
O'Donoghue, Martin, 67, 68, 69, 76, 78, 82, 85, 89, 90, 91,
93–4, 98, 100, 104, 105
O'Donoghue, Tadhg, 179, 180, 187, 212, 255
Offences Against the State (Amendment) Bill 1972, 55
O'Flaherty, Hugh, 17, 302
Ógra Fianna Fáil, 41
O'Grady, Dr .John, 162, 163
O'Grady, Fr. John, 221, 222
O'Halloran, Paddy, 9
O'Hanlon, Dr. Rory, 160–1, 170, 184
O'Hara, Patsy, 86
O'Higgins, Paul, 152
O'Higgins, Tom, 40, 58
O'Higgins family, 18
oil crises, 69, 73
O'Keeffe, Batt, 283
O'Keeffe, Ned, 283
O'Kelly, Seán T., 20
O'Kennedy, Michael, 34, 59, 70, 71, 76–7, 82, 95, 101, 170,
187–8, 210, 262–3
Old Bailey (London), 118
O'Leary, Dermot, 253–4
O'Leary, Jim, 190
O'Leary, Michael, 31
Olympics (Barcelona), 195, 196
Omagh bombing (1998), 284
O'Mahony, Dermot, 190–1
O'Mahony, Senator Flor, 112
O'Malley, Des, 38, 48, 49, 55, 69, 70, 74, 76, 89, 148, 153,
154, 155, 173, 203, 238
    Beef Tribunal evidence, 209–10, 211
    coalition negotiations with FF (1989), 170, 171
    expulsion from Fianna Fáil, 150–1
    FF leadership contests, 90, 91, 93–4, 101
O'Malley, Donogh, 36, 37, 39, 41
O'Malley, Pat, 38, 151
Oman, 194
One More Turn on the Merry-go-Round (Duignan), 231
O'Neill, Patrick, 112
O'Neill, Terence, 34
O'Neill, Dr. Tony, 12, 13
orchard-robbing, 3
O'Reilly, Breifne, 115
O'Reilly, James, 16
O'Riordan, Conor, 191, 197, 198, 267–8, 291
Ormeau Road killings (1992), 203
Ormond Cinema, Stillorgan, 28
Ormonde, Dr. Danny, 180
O'Rourke, Mary, 161, 169, 173, 175, 184, 185, 188, 259
Orr family (Dundrum), 5
OSCE (Organisation for Security and Co-operation in
Europe), 287
O'Shea, John, 257
O'Sullivan, Colin, 22
O'Sullivan, Gerry, 226, 238
O'Sullivan, Toddy, 22
O'Sullivan, Tony, 11
Overend, Letitia and Naomi, 5–6
Owen, David, 291

P

Paisley, Rev. Ian, 202, 204, 205–6, 270, 277, 281, 285
Paisley, Rhonda, 204
Palestine, 139
Palestinian Authority, 311
Palmerston Football Club, 11, 12

Palmerston Gardens, Rathmines, 77
Panama, 299
Pangalos, Theo, 286, 291
Papandreou, Giorgios, 286
Parc, 140, 141
Paris (France), 154, 196, 292
parliamentary secretaries, 53, 70
partition, 45, 46, 83, 146
Partnership for Peace, 287–8
passports for sale scheme, 232
Patten, John, 116, 117
Paul, Dr. David, 109
Paul, Tibor, 21
Pavilion Centre, Dún Laoghaire, 66
PAYE workers' protests, 73
payments to politicians, 41, 166, 253, 254, 258–9, 260–1,
    264, 300–1, 302
  Moriarty Tribunal revelations, 303–4
PDs (Progressive Democrats), 113, 114, 154–6, 160, 166,
    169, 182, 213, 250, 255, 256–7, 259–60, 305. see also
    Fianna Fáil–PD coalitions
  coalition negotiations with FF (1989), 169–71
peace process, 185, 227–9, 247, 256, 268–85
  ceasefires, 227, 228, 260
  Good Friday Agreement, 278–85, 315
  Hume–Adams talks, 203, 272
  political talks (1996–98), 268–82
peacekeeping, 218–19, 287, 288, 296
Peking (China), 226
Persecuting Zeal (Cooke), 205
phone-tapping scandal, 100–1, 104–5, 149, 150, 180, 181–2
Pierce, Gareth, 119, 123, 124, 129
Pineiro, Jao, 290
planning corruption, 188
The Plough and the Stars (O'Casey), 23
PMPA (Private Motorists Protection Association), 77, 94,
    95, 96, 186
Polisario, 142
political donations. see payments to politicians
political satire, 64
Pope, Martha, 270
Portugal, 66, 286, 289–90
poverty, 7–8
Power, Paddy, 103, 176
Power, Seán, 173, 176, 213
Power, William (Billy), 108, 109, 112, 115, 119, 121, 122,
    125–6, 127, 132
Presbyterians, 207
presidential elections, 20, 40, 58, 172–5, 261–6
Prevention of Terrorism Act (Britain), 107–8, 134, 135
Prodi, Romano, 287
Programme for a Partnership Government 1993–1997, 216, 229
Programme for Economic Recovery, 14
programme managers, 229
Prole family, 4
Protestants, 5, 20
Provisional IRA, 23, 228
Provisional Sinn Féin, 116
PUP (Progressive Unionist Party), 271, 272, 275, 276
Purcell, Seamus, 303

Q

Qaboos, Sultan (Oman), 194
Questions and Answers (RTÉ), 169
Quigley, Paddy, 10
Quinlan, Michael, 302
Quinlan, Moya, 303
Quinn, Pat, 45
Quinn, Ruairí, 114, 214, 215, 244
Quinnsworth, 45

R

radio, 64, 164–5
Radio Éireann, 48. see also RTÉ
railway line closure (Harcourt Street line), 2, 40
rainbow coalition, 213, 234, 253, 257, 288, 299
Ramallah (Palestine), 139, 311
rates, abolition of, 68
rationing, 5
Red Crescent, 311
Red Cross, 310–12
Red River Valley (film), 3
Redmond, Fay, 28, 29
Rees, Merlyn, 136
Reilly, Norbert, 26
Remembrance Commission, 313
Rennicks, 166, 300
Report of the Committee on the Constitution (1967), 158
Report of the Joint Committee on Marriage Breakdown, 158
republicanism, 23, 75, 109
republicans, 266, 283, 284
Reynolds, Albert, 74, 164, 165, 170, 171, 207, 213–14,
    216–17, 231, 234, 239, 248, 249. see also Fianna Fáil-
    Labour coalition (1992–94)
  'ABA' faction in Fianna Fáil, 262, 263
  abortion issue, 199–201
  Beef Tribunal, 209–11, 236
  Cabinet appointments, 185–9
  challenges to Haughey leadership, 175, 176–7, 181
  leader of FF (1992), 185
  media, relations with, 201
  negotiations with Labour (1992), 214–16
  passports for sale scheme, and, 232
  peace process, 227–9
  presidential elections 1997, 261–4
  resignation as Taoiseach, 245
  Smyth and Duggan cases, 240–5
Rice, Christopher, 136
Richardson, Carole, 113, 135
Rio group, 195
Robinson, Mary, 140, 174, 196–8, 221, 243, 265, 292–3, 293
Robinson, Nick, 140, 197, 199, 292–3
Robinson, Peter, 277, 284
Roche, Adi, 265
Roche, Dick, 120, 125, 126, 128
Roche, Dickie, 11
Rochford, John, 28
Rogers, Roy, 3
Roque, Felipe, 299
Roscrea College, Co. Tipperary, 9–10
Rosney, Brid, 196, 197
Ross, Shane, 129
Rotunda Hospital, Dublin, 71
Royal Irish Academy of Music, 21
Royal Irish Fusiliers, 109
RTÉ, 15, 64, 89, 102, 169, 170, 174, 181, 217, 263, 273, 287
RTÉ Authority, 21
RTÉ Symphony Orchestra, 21
RUC, 97, 204, 240
rugby, 11, 12, 203, 275
rural electrification scheme, 14
Rwanda, 224, 237, 238, 314
Ryan, Eoin, 138, 148, 186
Ryan, Richard (ambassador to Spain), 297, 299
Ryan, Richie, 64

S

Saddam Hussein, 140
Saharaoui people, 142–4
Said, Salim, 141
St Edward Island (Canada), 293

St Joseph's football club, Terenure, 10, 11
salmon fishing, 225
Salylnoggin, 65
Sandycove, Co. Dublin, 66
Santer Commission, 287
Santiago (Chile), 195
SAS, 120
Saturday View (RTÉ), 174
Savage, Tom, 242
Scanlan, Dana Rosemary, 265
Scarman, Lord, 136
Schüssel, Wolfgang, 292
Scoil Bríde, 8
Scrap Saturday (RTÉ radio), 64, 195
SDLP, 147, 205, 272, 275
Seanad Éireann, 129, 181
Second World War, 20
Secondary Modern School, Dagenham, 17
SFOR, 288
Shakespeare, William, 315
Shamrock Rovers, 10
Shankhill, Co. Dublin, 61, 85
Sheedy affair (1999), 302–3
Shelbourne football club, 10
Sheridan, Joe, 51
Sinn Féin, 19, 109, 116, 203, 228, 265, 285
    political talks (1997–98), 270, 272, 275, 276, 277, 280–1,
        282, 284
Skelly, Liam, 113
Skuse, Dr. Frank, 118–19, 127
Small, Joe and Mary, 194
Smalley, Errol, 114, 116
Smalley, Teresa, 114, 116
Smith, Michael, 175, 176, 184, 232, 233, 237, 238
Smith, Noel, 80
Smith, Paddy, 36
Smurfit, Michael, 175–6
Smyth, Fr. Brendan, 240, 241, 242, 243
Smyth, Seán, 112
Sneem, Co. Kerry, 62
soccer. *see* football
Solano, Javier, 195
Somalia, 140, 198–9, 219–21, 273, 290
South Africa, 294
South County Dublin, 67
Spain, 195–6, 198, 206
Spanish Sahara, 142
Sparks, Greg, 230, 249
Spence, Gusty, 276
The Spirit of the Nation (Mansergh), 82
Spring, Dick, 9–10, 99, 132, 148, 211, 214, 216, 228, 229,
    230, 231, 232, 248–9, 253, 265, 288, 295. *see also*
    Fianna Fáil–Labour coalition (1992–94); rainbow coalition
    tensions in coalition, 236–45
Sri Lanka, 312
Stafford, John, 121, 122
Stardust fire (1981), 84
Srillorgan, Co. Dublin, 85
Stormont, 202, 205, 206–7, 270, 279
Structural and Cohesion Funds, 215
Sturze, Vera, 22
Suharto, President, 295
Sunday Business Post, 308
Sunday Press, 100, 239
Sunday Tribune, 88, 100, 123
Sunningdale Agreement, 63–4
Sweetman's dairy farm, 4
Sydenham Road, Dundrum, 4

T

Taaffe, Fr., 126
Taaffe, Tony, 125, 128

Taca, 40–1
Taipei (Taiwan), 225
Taiwan, 225–6
Tallaght Strategy, 161–2
Taney Church of Ireland (Dundrum), 4, 5
Taney Road, Dundrum, 3, 4
Tanzania, 313
Taoiseach, Department of the, 46, 83
Taoiseach's Department, 275
Tariq Aziz, 141
Taroma (East Timor), 297
tax amnesty, 231–2
tax exiles, 232
taxation, 73, 88, 304
Taylor, John, 279–80
Taylor, Mervyn, 118, 215
Taylor-Quinn, Madeleine, 178
TB, 2
teachers' pay award, 83
teaching, 17
Teahon, Paddy, 275
Teebane massacre (1992), 203
Tehran (Iran), 192
Telecom affair, 175–6
Telefis Éireann, 15. *see also* RTÉ
Telefis na Gaeilge, 230–1
telephone tapping. *see* phone-tapping scandal
television, 14–15, 31, 42, 64, 111, 173
Teresa, Mother, 263
terrorism, 55, 107, 108, 144, 162, 203
Thatcher, Margaret, 83, 124
They Died with their Boots On (film), 3
This Week (RTÉ), 102
This Week (RTÉ Radio), 170
Thomas, Fr. (Roscrea College), 9
Thornley, David, 98
Through the Bridewell Gate (Mac Intyre), 47
Tidey, Don, 163
Tidy Towns competition, 25
The Times, 109
Timmins family (Dundrum), 4
Tolka Park, Dublin, 4
Towards a Nuclear-Free World: the Need for a New Agenda, 300
Townsend, Richard, 300
Treacy, Noel, 175, 176
Treacy, Seán, 160
Trial and Error (Kee), 113
tribunals, 166, 175, 209–10, 230, 235–6, 253, 254, 260–1,
    264, 301, 303
Trimble, David, 272, 273, 275, 276, 281–2
Trinity College, Dublin, 67
Trócaire, 140
tsunami (2004), 312
Tubridy, Dorothy (Dot), 121
Tully, Jim, 42
Tunney, Jim, 101, 102, 105
Tunney Committee, 101, 104, 105
Turf Development Board, 2
Turner, Tom, 22

U

UCD Soccer Club, 11, 12–13, 16
UDA (Ulster Defence Association), 203, 271
UDP (Ulster Democratic Party), 276
Uganda, 139
UKUP, 268
Ulster Defence Regiment (UDR), 203
Ulster Workers Council, 63–4
unemployment, 86
unionists, 45, 146, 202–3, 205, 207, 266. *see also* DUP; PUP;
    UUP
    political talks (1996–98), 270–3, 275–6, 277, 279–82, 284

united Ireland, 83, 147, 148, 282
United Nations, 23, 142, 199, 221, 226, 238, 287, 290, 293,
    296, 312, 314
  Commission on Human Rights, 293
  General Assembly, 298–300
  peacekeeping duties, 219–20
  Security Council, 297–300, 308, 315
United Nations Training School Ireland (UNTSI), 218–19
United States of America, 144, 153, 199, 200, 295
  visit to, 193–4
University College Dublin (UCD), 11, 12–13, 15–16, 36,
    167, 176
University College Galway (UCG), 11, 15
UNOSOM, 220
UTV, 15
UUP (Ulster Unionist Party), 202–3
  political talks (1996–98), 271, 275–6, 277, 279–80, 281–2

V

Védrine, Hubert, 290
Velayati, Ali Akbar, 38, 192
Virginia, Co. Cavan, 25

W

Walker, John, 108, 109, 122, 123, 126, 127, 128
Walsh, Dick, 44, 174
Walsh, Gerry, 231
Walsh, Joe, 90, 214
Walshe family (Dundrum), 3
War of Independence (1919–21), 1, 16, 19, 23, 52
Ward, Judith, 131, 135
The Way Forward, 92, 95, 97
Wembley, 194
West Midlands Serious Crimes Squad (WMSCS), 119–20,
    121, 125, 132
West Timor, 296
Western Sahara, 142–3
Wheeler, John, 136
Whelan, Mary, 297, 300
Whelehan, Harry, 199–200, 239, 240, 242, 243, 244, 245
Whip's Office, 51, 178, 179
Whitaker, T.K., 14, 225
White House, 193
Widgery, Lord, 109
Wilson, Gordon, 163–4
Wilson, John, 83, 102, 148, 170, 183, 203, 207
Windsor Park, 206
Winson Green Prison (England), 109
Women's Aid, 313
Women's Coalition, 277
Woods, Michael, 184, 185, 233
Wordsworth, William, 183
Workers' Party, 91, 97, 99, 114, 166, 174
World in Action (Granada TV), 111, 113
Wormwood Scrubs prison (London), 112–13, 115, 119,
    121, 122
Wright, Billy, 271
Wyse, Pearse, 100, 155, 169

X

X case, 199–200, 201

Y

Yeats, Michael, 32
Yeats, William Butler, 23
Young Turks, 36